Uri Bar-Joseph

Intelligence Intervention in the Politics of Democratic States

The United States, Israel, and Britain

The Pennsylvania State University Press
University Park, Pennsylvania

Library of Congress Cataloging-in-Publication Data

Bar-Joseph, Uri.
    Intelligence intervention in the politics of democratic states :
the United States, Israel, and Britain / Uri Bar-Joseph.

        p.   cm.
    Includes bibliographical references and index.
    ISBN 0-271-01331-1
    ISBN 0-271-01332-X (pbk.)
    1. Intelligence service—United States. 2. Intelligence service
—Great Britain. 3. United States—Foreign relations—Israel.
4. Great Britain—Foreign relations—Israel. 5. Israel—Foreign
relations—United States. 6. Israel—Foreign relations—Great
Britain.   I. Title.
JK468.I6B37   1995
327.12′09171′3—dc20   93-43352
                                                          CIP

Published by The Pennsylvania State University Press,
University Park, PA 16802-1003

It is the policy of The Pennsylvania State University Press to use acid-free paper for the
first printing of all clothbound books. Publications on uncoated stock satisfy the
minimum requirements of American National Standard for Information Sciences—
Permanence of Paper for Printed Library Materials, ANSI 239.48–1984.

For My Parents

Contents

PART III   CONCLUSIONS

Acknowledgments

This book originated as a Ph.D. dissertation for the Department of Political Science of Stanford University. For their generous financial aid, which permitted me to write it without having to worry about the economic aspect of life, I would like to thank Stanford University, the MacArthur Foundation, and Dr. Reuban Hecht. The Brookings Institution and George-town University helped me when I stayed in Washington, D.C., in 1989–90. The archivists of the Israeli State Archives in Jerusalem, the Public Record Office in London, and the National Archives in Washington were always helpful.

Veteran Israeli and American intelligence officers whom I interviewed cleared much of the fog that clouded certain historical aspects of this study, especially in connection with the Israeli "unfortunate business affair." Some of them preferred to remain anonymous and I respected this request. The names of the others appear at the end of the reference list of this study. For their academic and personal help I would also like to thank Richard Betts, Yu Bin, Benny Miller, Ben Mor, and Dan Avni Segre, as well as Rolie and Ziva, Arnon and Irit, Avi and Pnina, and many other friends who were always there when I needed them.

Investigating intelligence-politics relations in three different political cultures is a rather ambitious task. Being an Israeli, I comprehended this country's politics with relative ease, and spending five years in the United States enabled me to grasp better the nature of American politics. But relations between politicians and intelligence officers in Britain in the 1920s could have remained an enigma for me if it were not for the great help of John Ferris of the Department of History at Calgary University. John not only read and made excellent comments on earlier drafts of the British case studies (as well as other parts of this work) but also provided me with many important documents that made the reconstruction of these cases feasible.

As any Ph.D. student knows, the dissertation committee can determine much of his or her ability to complete the study successfully. I was highly fortunate in this respect. David Holloway of the Department of Political Science at Stanford University was always helpful and supportive. Michael Handel of the U.S. Army War College was my intellectual godfather since we first met at the Hebrew University in 1980. Always encouraging me to continue my studies, Michael was responsible more than anyone else for my decision to pursue studies in the United States. Serving on my dissertation committee, he was influential in selecting the subject of research and in shaping the final outcome through numerous useful and important comments on earlier drafts. Being a personal friend, moreover, Michael always made me feel as though his was my second home in the States, and for this hospitality I thank also his family. Alexander L. George became my intellectual mentor from the time I first met him at Stanford in 1985. For five years his "open door" policy, intellectual openness and sharpness, enormous knowledge and experience, and personal interest and readiness to help students were remarkable and made my educational experience under his tutelage a truly valuable one. As the chairman of my dissertation committee, Alex offered guidance and wise counsel that significantly improved the final product.

On the more personal side I would like to thank my parents, to whom I dedicate this book, and my brother and his family for always encouraging me to pursue my studies. Some of the ideas presented in this work were born during talks about politics in general and intelligence in particular that I held with my father in his study. His intellectual curiosity and personal integrity have always inspired my thinking, and I thank him for that.

For three years at Stanford, until her sudden death in Israel in the summer of 1989, Susan Avital Hurvitz filled my life with joy and satisfaction. Knowing how much she wanted me to complete this work successfully, I dedicate it also to her memory.

List of Tables

List of Abbreviations

BDCC	British Defence Coordination Committee (Britain)
CEF	Cuban Exile/Expeditionary Force (US)
CIA	Central Intelligence Agency (US)
CIGS	Chief of the Imperial General Staff (Britain)
CINCLANT	Commander in Chief, Atlantic (US)
CNO	Chief of Naval Operations (US)
COP	Chief of Operations (US)
CPGB	Communist party of Great Britain (Britain)
DCI	Director of Central Intelligence (US)
DDCI	Deputy Director of Central Intelligence (US)
DDP	Deputy Director for Plans (US)
DDRS	Declassified Documents Reference Service (US)
DIA	Defense Intelligence Agency (US)
DMI	Directorate of Military Intelligence (Israel)
DMI	Director of Military Intelligence (Israel and Britain)
DNI	Director of Naval Intelligence (Britain)
DOD	Department of Defense (US)
EW	Early Warning
FO	Foreign Office (Britain and Israel)
FRD	Frente Revolucionario Democrático (US)
GC&CS	Government Code and Cypher School (Britain)
GCHQ	Government Communications Head-Quarters (Britain)
GSO	General Staff Officer (Britain)
HO	Home Office (Britain)
IAF	Israeli Air Force (Israel)
IDF	Israeli Defense Force (Israel)
IKKI	Executive Committee, Third International (USSR)
INR	Bureau of Intelligence and Research (US)

IS	Intelligence Service (Israel)
ISA	Israel's State Archives (Israel)
IWM	Imperial War Museum (Britain)
JCS	Joint Chiefs of Staff (US)
JCSM	Joint Chiefs of Staff Memorandum (US)
KATAM	Katzin leTafkidim Meyuhadim (Special Duties Officer; Israel)
LAKAM	Lishka Lekishrei Mada (Scientific Liaison Bureau; Israel)
MAPAI	Mifleget Po'alei Eretz Yisrael (Israel Labor party; Israel)
MEDO	Middle East Defence Organization
MELF	Middle East Land Forces (Britain)
MID	Military Intelligence Department/Division (Britain)
MI5	Security Service (Britain)
MI6	Secret Intelligence Service (Britain)
NATO	North Atlantic Treaty Organization
NAW	National Archives, Washington (US)
NESA	Near East and South Asia (US)
NID	Naval Intelligence Department/Division (Britain)
NIE	National Intelligence Estimate (US)
NIO	National Intelligence Officer (US)
NSA	National Security Agency (US)
NSC	National Security Council (US)
OAS	Organization of American States
O/B	Order of Battle (US)
ONE	Office of National Estimates (US)
OSS	Office of Strategic Services (US)
OTP	One Time Pad
PALMACH	Plugut Machatz (Striking Companies; Israel)
PALYAM	Palmach Yami (Naval Palmach; Israel)
RAF	Royal Air Force (Britain)
SDI	Strategic Defense Initiative
SHABAK	Sherut HaBitahon HaKlali (General Security Service; Israel)
SHAI	Sherut Yediot (Information Service; Israel)
Shin. Mem.	Sherut Modi'in (Intelligence Service, or IS; Israel)
SIGINT	Signal Intelligence
SIS	Secret Intelligence Service (Britain)
SNIE	Special National Intelligence Estimate (US)

SOE	Special Operations Executive (Britain)
SOP	Standard Operational Procedure
T	Treasury (Britain)
WH/4	Western Hemisphere Division, Branch 4 (US)
WO	War Office (Britain)

Introduction

This book examines the interference by intelligence agencies and individuals with the politics of their own governments in the modern democratic state. It investigates only democracies since a fundamental norm of this type of regime is that intelligence organizations serve the national interest and should, therefore, be separate from politics. In contrast, in nondemocratic regimes the use of intelligence agencies by the government in power for its own parochial interests (for example, against political opposition) or the participation of intelligence organizations in the internal struggle for power are dominant norms that by definition, make the intelligence community part of domestic politics.

In theory, intelligence work, much like academia, should be objective, autonomous, and free of political influence. It should be limited to two main tasks: first, to supply policymakers with objective information, analysis, and advice designed to assist action; and, second, to implement policy in accordance with political direction, through covert action. In reality, however, intelligence work is seldom autonomous and free from political pressures. Moreover, in many cases intelligence work ceases to be objective. Political preferences and intra- and interbureaucratic interests, as well as personal ones, can influence the conduct of the intelligence work that should ideally be done solely on the basis of its "professional ethic."

This book attempts to explain the behavior of intelligence organizations and individuals in such situations by focusing on three questions: (1) Under what *conditions* will political considerations dominate intelligence work? (2) What *motivates* intelligence organizations to interfere with the political decisionmaking process? (3) In what *ways* and by what *means* do these organizations intervene in politics?

It is important to emphasize that this book is not a study of the general relationship between the intelligence makers and the governmental decisionmaking apparatus. Although a general framework of this relationship is constructed in the theoretical part of this work, it serves only as a context for the more focused discussion of intelligence interference in politics. This study does not address the subject of political intervention in professional intelligence work (which, according to intelligence officers, is no less important). Neither does it discuss the intelligence profession's abuse of power in relation to other components of the state system, such as the legislative or the judicial branches, or fundamental norms of public and moral behavior. Although these by themselves are important issues that have received academic and nonacademic attention in the past, I prefer to confine my research only to situations in which intelligence organizations and individuals abused their power in their relations with the highest level of the decisionmaking apparatus—the leader of the state.

Limited as this scope is, it nevertheless constitutes an integral part of the broader subject of the intelligence-state relationship. Hence Part I of this study discusses some of the theoretical aspects of the relations between intelligence and policymakers. This part begins with a review of the major studies on this subject and identifies some of their main weaknesses. It concludes that the essential condition for preventing the corruption of this relationship is maximal separation between intelligence and politics. It then suggests that intelligence-state relations should be analyzed in a theoretical framework similar to that of civil-military relations and compares these two types of relationships. On the basis of this comparison this study proposes that two variables—*professionalism* of the intelligence community at the bureaucratic level and the effectiveness of the *control system* at the state level—determine the success of the separation of intelligence from politics.

Part II is devoted to the examination of four case studies in which intelligence agencies and individuals abused their power in their relations with their own governments. This part begins with a definition of intelligence intervention in politics and presents three types of such action. It then proceeds to detailed descriptions of each of the cases. It begins with the American "Bay of Pigs" episode of 1961, in which central CIA officers overestimated the operation's likelihood of success in order to elicit presidential support for this venture. As will be shown, high-ranking officers in the CIA acted this way because they believed that the operation should be undertaken regardless of political and operational limitations set earlier by President Kennedy, hoping that once the operation was under way these limitations would be suspended.

The second case study, the 1954 Israeli "unfortunate business affair" (also known as the "Lavon affair"), represents an even more serious case of abuse of power, since here the intelligence operation was not only undertaken without proper political authorization but was also diametrically opposed to the foreign policy of Moshe Sharett, Israel's Prime Minister and Minister of Foreign Affairs at the time.

The last two case studies are taken from British history of the 1920s and represent the most serious form of intelligence interference with politics. The first, and the less well known of the two, is the "Henry Wilson affair," an episode in which military and intelligence officers conspired to wreck the Russian policy of Prime Minister Lloyd George; the second, and more familiar, is the "Zinoviev letter," an episode in which certain intelligence officers leaked a secret document to the press in the midst of a general election campaign in order to force the Labour government out of office.

The concluding chapter of the book summarizes the findings of the case studies and offers some suggestions as to how to limit the ability of the intelligence community to interfere with politics in the future.

Part I

Intelligence and Politics:
The Theory

Introduction

While academic and nonacademic interest in the relationship between intelligence producers and consumers has grown significantly in recent years, the theoretical aspects of this relationship have not received comparable attention. The goal of Part I of this book is to partially bridge some of the existing theoretical gaps by addressing certain principal aspects of intelligence intervention in politics and political interference with professional intelligence work.

The first section of Part I seeks to understand the problem in general. It begins with a review of some fundamental aspects of intelligence-politics relations and then turns to focus on the expanding body of theoretical literature on this subject. It traces the normative positions of three main groups of theorists—"realists," "professionals," and "realist professionals"—and calls into question the noncomparative and nonsystemic nature of these schools of thought.

In order to overcome the methodological weaknesses thus revealed, the second section compares intelligence-politics relations with the more theoretically advanced field of civil-military relations. This comparison yields two conclusions: first, although the two fields deal with similar problems, no single theory of civil-military relations can be completely adapted to the study of the relations between intelligence producers and consumers owing to certain unique features of the latter field; second, two variables—intelligence professionalism at the bureaucratic level and the type and quality of political control at the state level—determine the degree to which intelligence can be isolated from politics.

These conclusions of the theoretical discussion, when transformed into formal propositions, will be empirically tested through four case studies in the second part of the book.

1

The Problem

THE UNIVERSAL NATURE OF THE PROBLEM

If intelligence is, indeed, the "second oldest profession," then the problem of political biases and misuse of the intelligence product is just as old. The most famous intelligence mission of ancient times, that of the twelve spies sent by Moses "to spy out the land of Canaan" (Numbers 13:17), clearly illustrates this point.

As the Bible tells us, the dozen spies agreed, initially, that Canaan was a land that "floweth with milk and honey." They disagreed, however, on the ability of the Israelites to conquer it: ten of them believed that the enemy was too strong, and only two—Joshua and Kaleb—estimated that it was not. Although the debate began in legitimate professional terms, it quickly degenerated into a corruption of intelligence work. In an attempt to convince their consumers—Moses, Aaron, and the whole congregation of the children of Israel—that the occupation of Canaan was unfeasible, the ten "intelligence officers" changed their earlier estimate regarding the nature of the country and now claimed that it was not "the land of milk and honey" but "a land that eateth up the inhabitants thereof" (Numbers 13:32). Moses believed the minority's report, but when the mob threatened to stone Joshua and Kaleb, he yielded to popular pressure and despite his better judgment accepted the majority's rule.

A professional analysis of the episode reveals that three fundamental mistakes doomed it to failure from the start. First, being representatives of their tribes, the men chosen for the assignment were selected on their political rather than professional merits. Second, the question of whether

Canaan could be conquered was not a problem of intelligence but of national estimate. Third, the forum in which the spies presented their findings and evaluations could not be isolated from political pressures since the whole Israelite congregation—not only a small group of policymakers—participated in the decisionmaking process.

Such mistakes will always increase the likelihood of corrupting the intelligence process, and this behavior exacted a heavy price in ancient times. The Lord (who appears to have had a keen eye for this type of action) decided to punish the Israelites and their leader for altering intelligence reports for political reasons. Following the routine bargaining process with Moses regarding the severity of punishment, the Lord informed him that: "After the number of the days in which ye searched the land, even forty days, each day for a year, shall ye bear your iniquities, even forty years, and ye shall know my breach of promise" (Numbers 14:34). The punishment of the ten intelligence officers who betrayed their professional integrity was even more severe: they died "by the plague before the Lord." Joshua and Kaleb were rewarded for their integrity and were the only two of the desert generation to enter the Promised Land.[1]

Indeed, the Old Testament is an endless source for similar examples. The most common practice in ancient times was that of "intelligence to please," that is, prophets (biblical "analysts") who gave their forecasts according to what they believed the decisionmaker (usually the king who employed them) wanted to hear. A typical example is that of Ahab, the King of Israel who asked his "intelligence staff" of four hundred men whether or not he should initiate a war to conquer Ramoth in Gilead. All four hundred answered "go up" (1 Kings 22). Needless to say, such a high level of consensus reflected the need to please the king rather than to tell him the truth. In this case, Ahab was the one to pay the price. He took the advice and died in the war that followed.

---

1. This, of course, is my interpretation. R. V. Jones, who discussed this episode (but hardly its professionally unethical aspects), maintained that the punishment was the outcome of the Lord's anger with the majority's lack of faith in him. Moreover, while I believe that the ten spies simply yielded to popular pressure, Jones had a more sophisticated explanation for their conduct:

> Put yourself in the position of one of the spies. If you report that the Canaanites are vulnerable, the consequent operational decision will be to attack. If the attack is successful, then your intelligence contribution to it, although accurate, may well be overlooked; but if the attack is unsuccessful you will be held to blame. So you are in a "no-win" situation. But if you report that the Canaanites are invulnerable it hardly matters whether you are right or wrong because the operational decision will be not to attack, and the accuracy of your report will not be tested, and so you win both ways. (Jones 1990, pp. 289–90)

Not much has changed in this regard since biblical times. From the twelve spies to the Iran-contra scandal, relations between intelligence producers and consumers have usually been an ongoing obstacle race in which both sides express dissatisfaction with actions taken by the other. Basically this occurs because reality always places inevitable political pressures on the conduct of professional intelligence work, and in many instances professional intelligence work does not meet the needs of policymakers. This failure leads to temptation on the part of policymakers to interfere with the professional aspects of intelligence work and creates the conditions under which intelligence makers tend to use their product in order to gain political influence.

The complexity of intelligence-politics relations has attracted growing academic interest in recent years. At the locus of this discussion are three subjects. The first two involve analytical questions: what is the nature of the problem and what are its sources; and what are the factors that determine its severity? The third subject often discussed in the professional literature is of a more normative nature: how should intelligence producers behave within this complex relationship?

THE SOURCES OF THE PROBLEM

In theory, intelligence work should be objective, autonomous, and free from political influence. It should be limited to two main tasks: first, to supply policymakers with objective information, analysis, and, upon request, advice designed to assist action; and, second, to implement policy in accordance with political direction, through covert action. Ideally, it is expected that policymakers, who bear the responsibility for making proper use of the intelligence product available to them, will do so because they believe that this is an effective means to improve the quality of their policies.

In reality, however, this is rarely the case. For various reasons that will be discussed later, intelligence work is seldom autonomous and free from political pressure. Moreover, oftentimes intelligence work ceases to be objective. Political preferences and intra- and interbureaucratic interests, as well as personal ones, can influence the conduct of intelligence work that should ideally be done solely on the basis of its "professional ethic." The result, as one writer has put it, is that "intelligence is subject, object and instrument of power politics" (Ransom 1987, p. 25).

Principally, however, intelligence work is no different in this regard from that of other professional state bureaucracies. And yet there is a consensus among experts that conflict between the real and the ideal worlds of intelligence-politics relations is both deeper and more significant to state affairs than conflict the state has with any other agency. This is so mainly because of four characteristics of intelligence work that make it both desirable and feasible for political interference.

The first of these features is the nature of the intelligence product. Intelligence organizations produce information. Information is power or a means to obtain power, and striving for power is predominant in politics. Although intelligence agencies have no monopoly on information relevant to policymaking, they do have a high degree of monopoly on secret information. Given that the law of supply and demand works in the political market as it does everywhere else, it is clear why secret intelligence—a relatively rare commodity—is so valuable for the participants in a political struggle.

The second feature has to do with the role of intelligence in deciding the fate of debates on foreign policies. When such a debate occurs among policymakers, intelligence estimates may serve as an important—sometimes critical—factor in determining whether to prefer one foreign policy alternative to another. This is so because, unlike policymakers who are known to be committed to the policies they formulate, intelligence officers are considered to be objective and unbiased professionals. By providing objective estimates of the target's intentions, capabilities, and possible reactions to the suggested policy, they assess also, though indirectly and perhaps against their will, the merits of the debated policy. Needless to say, under such circumstances the involved policymakers will have strong incentives to influence the shape of the intelligence product so that it suits their political agenda.

The third feature involves the secretive environment in which intelligence functions. Secrecy is, certainly, a necessary condition for the proper functioning of intelligence, yet it also hampers external inspection, thus making political and intelligence misconduct more feasible. Here, indeed, arises the need to distinguish between two types of secrecy. One is *functional* (or professional) and involves all aspects of intelligence activities— operational techniques, sources of information, or estimates that derive from these sources—that need to be kept secret to ensure the successful operation of the intelligence organization. The second is *political* secrecy, concerning information that involves controversial activities and failures of the intelligence agency. Such information is kept secret not from external enemies but from other actors at home, since its exposure could embarrass the intelligence organization and damage its reputation.

In reality, however, the distinction between functional and political secrecy involves two principal problems. First, in many cases the line between political and functional secrets is too thin, and secrets that are perceived by some as professional are considered by others as political. Second, the exposure of political secrets will always be resisted by those politicians and intelligence officers who share a vital interest in concealing their professional misconduct. Thus these two factors yield an environment in which intelligence and politics interference with each other is highly feasible. No other state bureaucracy works in such an environment.

The value of the intelligence commodity in power politics and the ability of intelligence to decide political debates, coupled with secrecy, explains both the temptation of politicians to interfere with professional intelligence work and the feasibility of such conduct. This, it should be emphasized, does not imply any ethical judgment: the use of information obtained by state bureaucracies to gain personal power or to advance parochial interests cannot be justified ethically under any circumstances. It merely explains that in reality one can expect such behavior from politicians, given the nature of their occupation and their personal skills.

Theoretically, however, the desire for power does not explain similar behavior on the part of intelligence officers, since the nature of their work and the value of its product are fundamentally different from that of politics. Intelligence is not about making policy but about describing and analyzing reality—the context in which policy is formulated and conducted—as a *means* to improve the quality of the policymaking process. Unlike politics, where the quality of action is measured by the increase or decrease in the ability of an individual, a bureaucracy, or the state to influence the behavior of others, the quality of the intelligence product is rated by three measures: *timing*—whether it is submitted in time to be of optimal use to the consumers; *accuracy*—how well the intelligence product (always a picture and never a photograph) describes reality; and *relevance*—how important it is to the national interest. The intelligence product must be timely if it is to be taken into consideration in the policymaking process; it must be as accurate as possible and free of motivated biases in order to improve the quality of the decisionmaking process; and it must be relevant for the national interest since the defense of this interest is the raison d'être of the intelligence community. Hence, in theory at least, intelligence institutions and individuals are not required to get involved in politics in order to gain influence over the policymaking process.

In reality, however, intelligence makers do get involved in the political process, as a result of the fourth feature of the intelligence-politics relationship. Although intelligence professionals are usually the best experts on certain aspects of foreign policy, they nevertheless have to compete with other types of input to gain the attention of central policymakers as a means to influence their decisions. In the United States, for example, more than two hundred governmental agencies participate in this contest (Gates 1989, p. 36), on top of nongovernmental sources of information and advice, such as the media, academics, political contacts, friends, family, and sometimes even astrologers.

In addition, policymakers are rarely satisfied with the intelligence they get. Among the reasons often cited in the literature for this attitude are the following: the intelligence product increases rather than decreases the level of uncertainty; it is formulated in too vague a style, so that when compared to other inputs it is harder to exploit successfully; it exposes controversies within the administration; new intelligence estimates compel policymakers to reevaluate existing policies; policymakers are not familiar enough with intelligence work and its limitations; they do not know what type of intelligence they need and therefore fail to task the intelligence community properly; they prefer "hard facts" to complicated analysis and, though they usually understand the general problem, have difficulties in grasping the subtle aspects of intelligence interpretations; they are influenced by past intelligence failures; they dislike the growing direct relationship between the intelligence community and the legislative branch; and they believe that parochial bureaucratic interests prevent intelligence agencies from meeting their needs (Betts 1980, pp. 118–19; Gates 1989, pp. 38–39; Hughes, pp. 4–7; Hulnick 1986, pp. 215–16; Hulnick 1987, pp. 132–33; Laqueur, pp. 90–109).

The intense competition for the decisionmaker's ear, coupled with the inferior position in which intelligence usually finds itself in this contest, often poses something of a dilemma for intelligence officers: by the definition of their profession they must adhere to their professional norms, yet the need to successfully gain the decisionmakers' attention detaches them from this very ethic. This is so because there exists an inherent tension between accuracy and objectivity, as demanded by the intelligence ethic, and gaining power to influence policy, which is the imperative of political competition.

Under such stress intelligence producers often depart from their professional ethic.

The most common distortion of the intelligence product is the "intelligence-to-please" pattern of behavior, where intelligence officers modify their product in order to produce a new one, not as objective but far more attractive to the ultimate consumer. The alternative pattern—which is the main subject of this book—is just the opposite. It occurs in situations in which intelligence officers believe that they know better than their political masters what policy best serves the national interest. In such cases they sometimes alter—through manipulation of information, unauthorized action, or conspiracy—the latter's policies. In between these two there is a third pattern, in which intelligence chiefs consciously fail to properly submit their estimates to their consumers. They do so either because they believe that the concerned policymakers will ignore their product anyway or because they are under political pressure to keep silent.

Though partly of a contradictory nature, these three patterns of behavior stem from the same four characteristics of the intelligence-politics relationship already described. The intensity of their occurrence is the function of additional variables.

VARIABLES

Students of the relationship between intelligence producers and policymakers have focused mainly on variables that determine the likelihood of the occurrence of the "intelligence-to-please" pattern of behavior. Many of these factors, however, are also applicable to the other two patterns of intelligence misbehavior. Their presence, moreover, yields a similar result: a lack of sufficient separation between intelligence and politics, which creates an ideal environment for intelligence intervention in politics and political interference with professional intelligence work.

The following is a short discussion of the variables most often cited as producing such an environment.

IDEOLOGY. It is generally (and rightly) assumed that the more ideological politicians are, the higher is the likelihood for the politicization of the intelligence process (e.g., Handel 1987, p. 30; Harkabi, p. 126). But intelligence officers can also be ideologically motivated, and when they are, the likelihood of intelligence interference with politics becomes higher. When politicians and intelligence officers share the same ideology (as Director of Central Intelligence [DCI] William Casey did with President Ronald Reagan), "intelligence to please" will be the dominant pattern of behavior. When there are significant ideological differences between the two groups (as there were in Britain when the Labour party came to power in 1924, for example) intelligence intervention in politics against the government is more likely.

LEVEL OF CONSENSUS. Consensus regarding the ends and means of foreign policy can be divided into four subcategories: the nation as a whole; the policymaking milieu; the intelligence community; and the intelligence and the policymaking groups. Ransom (1987, p. 43) is clearly right when arguing that a high level of national consensus will favor a high level of separation between intelligence and politics. The same is true with regard to the other three categories. Lack of consensus will obviously yield the opposite results.

Of special interest is the fourth category. In situations where disagreements between central policymakers and their intelligence experts take place, four outcomes are possible: policymakers can either attempt to "tame" the intelligence or ignore it; and the intelligence officers can either press their estimates or keep silent. Two typical examples of such situations reveal a similar pattern of behavior on the part of policy and intelligence makers alike. In the spring of 1970 DCI Richard Helms avoided pressing an estimate of the CIA's Office of National Estimates (ONE) on a possible American invasion of Cambodia, even though he was aware that planning for such an operation was under way, because he knew that the paper contradicted the policymakers' stand regarding this venture. President Richard Nixon, who suspected that "the real problem was the CIA's bias against the war itself" (Powers, p. 247), declined to ask the agency's advice in this matter. Similarly, in 1981–82 Israel's Directorate of Military Intelligence (DMI) and its chief, Major General Yehoshua Saguy, estimated that the Lebanese Phalangists were neither a reliable nor a capable ally. Yet, under pressure from Defense Minister Ariel Sharon and Chief of Staff Rafael Eitan, Saguy preferred, as he himself put it, to "step aside" rather than import his organization's and his own estimates, which, ex post factum, proved to be correct (Naor, p. 54; Schiff and Ya'ari, pp. 205–6). In both cases the intelligence chiefs intervened *passively* in the policymaking process by not pressing their cases hard enough, and policymakers interfered with the intelligence process either passively (as in the case of Cambodia) or actively (as in the Lebanese case) by preventing their intelligence officers from expressing their views.[2]

PUBLIC DISCLOSURE. There is a consensus that the level of public disclosure of intelligence estimates influences the likelihood of intelligence and politics interfering with each other. Experts, however, disagree on the direction this influence takes. Hastedt maintains that, in order to prevent the politicization of intelligence estimates, "the primary need is to halt the trend toward the widespread publicizing of intelligence" (p. 48). Gates, on the other hand, argues that keeping intelligence too classified leads "to leaks; to White House suspicion of obstructionism, bureaucratic games, or pursuit of contrary policy agenda by intelligence professionals; and concerns on the part of intelligence officers over the appearance of politicization of intelligence by White House or other policymaker-directed declassification of information" (1989, p. 44).

Gates's arguments for a more liberal declassification policy indeed make sense, since such openness can remove, at least partially, the thick veil of secrecy under which political and intelligence misconduct can take place. From Gates's perspective, however, there is nothing wrong with selective intelligence disclosure "to gain support for national security decisions" (ibid.). Yet this is precisely the political rather than the professional standard for disclosure, and it can increase the intensity of intelligence and politics interference with each other rather than decrease it. Hence it seems that concealing intelligence products from the public is a better method than a selective disclosure, but objective disclosure is superior to both.

BUREAUCRATIC STATUS. Logically, it is expected that independent intelligence organizations will be less vulnerable to outside bureaucratic pressures than agencies that are part of larger bureaucracies. This assumption, indeed, was one of the main reasons for the establishment of the CIA as an

---

2. In both cases the chiefs of intelligence paid for their misbehavior. In an inner-circulated paper against Helms the CIA's analysts protested Helms's not sending their estimate to the White House. This was "an act of protest unprecedented in the Agency's history" (Powers, p. 249). As a result of one of the conclusions of the Kahan investigation commission, Saguy had to resign from his position as Chief of the DMI allegedly for not alerting civil and military policymakers to a possible massacre in the refugee camps of Sabra and Shatila but also for failing to press his organization's estimates under Sharon's pressure.

independent organization directly subordinate to the president. Reality, however, shows that this factor is of only minor relevance to our subject. Although the CIA's bureaucratic status has not changed since its establish‑ ment, the level of its involvement in politics has varied significantly over the years. At the same time, the Bureau of Intelligence and Research (INR) has remained, for the most part, politically neutral despite being an agency of the Department of State. The experience of other countries shows similar results. Some British intelligence agencies interfered significantly with politics in the 1920s (as will be described later), yet this pattern of behavior had nothing to do with the fact that they all belonged to larger bureaucracies. Similarly, although the Israeli DMI (which is charged with producing the national intelligence estimate) is an integral part of the Israeli Defense Force (IDF), there is hardly any evidence that this dependency has ever influenced its estimates.

Bureaucratic connections seem to be more significant when it comes to intraorganizational relationships. Here the closer the linkage between the operational and analytical units within a single agency, the higher the risk that operational needs will dictate the intelligence analysis. This happens when intelligence chiefs have both the tendency to rank operational needs higher than analytical ones and the ability to act accordingly. Such a situation was vividly evident in preparations for the "Bay of Pigs" operation under DCI Allen Dulles and Deputy Director for Plans (DDP) Richard Bissell. As a result of being so committed to launching this venture, both men successfully isolated the analytical sections of the CIA from the policymaking process, since the analysts regarded its likelihood of success as very low.

ANALYTICAL PLURALISM. Analytical pluralism is generally recognized as an important instrument in overcoming the problem of the dogmatic intelligence process. It can take place at three levels: between organizations (such as the analytical units of the Defense Intelligence Agency [DIA], CIA, and INR); within organizations (the National Intelligence Council and the Directorate of Intelligence within the CIA being one example); or on an individual basis within single analytical units as suggested by Betts (1980, p. 126).

Experience shows, however, that not only is analytical pluralism no panacea to the problem of the dogmatic intelligence process (Kam, pp. 225–28) but it can also generate new opportunities for policymakers' interference with intelligence work. When policymakers are confronted with different, even contradictory estimates, they are likely to select—consciously or not—the ones that best suit their own assessments or political needs and agenda, regardless of the estimates' professional quality. A typical example is the way policymakers acted at the outset of the Iran-contra affair. The intelligence rationale for the Iranian venture came from the reports of Graham Fuller, the National Intelligence Officer for the Near East and South Asia (NIO/NESA), prepared—partly in collaboration with National Security Council (NSC) officials—in May 1985. The reports estimated that there was a real threat of Soviet intervention in Iran and hence that the United States should try and gain some leverage in Teheran by strengthening the "moderate forces" of the Iranian leadership. These assessments contradicted the consensus among Soviet and Iranian analysts in the Directorate of Intelligence, as well as other intelligence agencies, who claimed that there was no such Soviet threat or such moderate Iranian leaders. Although Fuller's minority view was not supported by any high-quality intelligence, senior CIA and NSC officials preferred his assessments and ignored the majority's stand simply because it suited their political agenda. This political rather than professional selection was possible only because analytical pluralism existed in the CIA.[3]

NATURE OF THE INTELLIGENCE PRODUCT. Intelligence products can be divided into different categories according to several measures. Most relevant for our subject are two criteria: the nature of the problem (whether it involves questions of intentions or capabilities); and the function of the product (such as warning and alert, current intelligence, basic intelligence, or estimates).

It could be assumed that the more technical and quantitative the nature of the problem, the less it would be vulnerable to political influence. Hence problems of an adversary's capabilities could be expected to draw less

3. *Report of the Congressional Committees Investigating the Iran-Contra Affair with Supplement, Minority, and Additional Views,* 100th Cong., 1st sess. (Washington, D.C., 1987), pp. 164–65; *The Tower Commission Report: The Full Text of the President's Special Review Board* (New York: Times Books, 1987), p. 21; "Graham Fuller Memorandum, dated May 07, 1985, re: The US-Soviet Struggle for Influence in Tehran"; "Graham Fuller Memorandum, dated May 17, 1985, re: Toward a Policy in Iran"; "Douglas J. MacEachin Memorandum, dated January 28, 1987, re: The Record on Soviet-Iranian Issues"; "Thomas M. Barksdale Memorandum, dated Dec. 02, 1986, re: The Iranian Imbroglio: Implications for the Intelligence Process." See *Hearings before the Select Committee on Intelligence of the United States Senate,* "On the Nomination of Robert M. Gates to be Director of Central Intelligence, 16 September–18 October 1991," U.S. Senate, 102d Cong., 1st sess. (Washington, D.C.: 1992).

political attention than questions regarding his intentions. The rationale for this assumption is twofold: first, policymakers are expected to show more interest in rivals' intentions than capabilities; and, second, the methods employed to solve problems of capabilities are more scientific, thus less vulnerable to outside intervention.

Experience shows, however, that this is not the case. Technically and quantitatively oriented problems, such as the number of Soviet bombers or ICBMs during the 1950s, the order of battle of the Vietcong in the mid-1960s, or Soviet Strategic Defense Initiative (SDI) capabilities in the early 1980s, had all become a bone of political contention and all involved some political intervention in professional intelligence work and vice versa. Needless to say, intentionally oriented problems are vulnerable to such misbehavior just as well. The main reason is that in modern politics, in which the line between domestic and foreign policy is very thin, the adversary's capabilities are as relevant to the political agenda as his intentions. Thus Kennedy used the alleged "missile gap" to increase his electoral chances in his 1960 presidential campaign; domestic support for the continuation of the war in Vietnam was significantly dependent on public beliefs regarding the size of the Vietcong forces; and the fate of the American SDI could be decided not only by its technical feasibility but also by intelligence estimates regarding Soviet SDI capabilities, which had a major impact on public support for this project.

The function of the intelligence product bears more relevance to our subject. As the many studies of strategic surprise show, political interference with intelligence warnings and alerts is quite rare, and the causes for this type of intelligence failure are to be found elsewhere. This finding concurs with the logical assumption that the higher and more imminent the risk to national security, the lower will be the tendency of policymakers and intelligence officers to involve political considerations in professional intelligence work. Basic intelligence involves no major political gains and losses. For this reason it draws very little political attention. Current intelligence, on the other hand, may attract more political attention since it is far more relevant to current politics. Estimates, particularly Special National Intelligence Estimates (SNIEs), but also regular NIEs, are the products most vulnerable to political intervention, mainly because they are so valuable in deciding the fate of political debates over foreign policy.

PERSONALITY OF THE LEADER. Three features in the leaders' personalities seem to be most relevant to our subject. First is their ability to control and direct the decisionmaking apparatus, of which the intelligence system is one component. Second is the level of their openness to intelligence inputs that contradict their personal beliefs. Third is the attention they pay to intelligence work and its products.

Authoritative leaders are usually able to tame and control the national security apparatus, thus limiting the intensity of the bureaucratic competition that makes organizational and personal misbehavior within this machinery more likely. Weak leaders, on the other hand, leave too much freedom of action to their subordinates, thus setting the ground for an intensive, even uncontrolled, bureaucratic competition in which intelligence and politics interference with each other can become the rule rather than the exception.

Notwithstanding the importance of this variable, it should be noted that other factors involved might influence the ability and the will of leaders to control this competition. One, of course, is the level of the bureaucratic and political contest. The higher and the more institutionalized this competition is, the less it can be managed. Second is leaders' interest in controlling the competition. If they believe that divide-and-rule is the optimal way to gain hold of the system, then increasing rather than decreasing the bureaucratic competition will become their prime interest. Thus, for example, under an extremely authoritative leadership style such as Adolf Hitler's, an intensive bureaucratic and political competition took place. This was partly the result of the Nazi ruling system allowing other leaders to build private bureaucratic latifundia as personal power bases and partly the result of Hitler's divide-and-rule managerial style.

The tolerance of leaders for intelligence inputs that contradict their own beliefs and political agenda will determine, to a large extent, the quality of their interaction with the intelligence community. Handel (1987, pp. 27–33) identifies two extreme categories of leaders. At one end are the Hitler or Stalin types, whose tendency to reject such inputs is extremely high. At the other is the leader—Handel takes Israeli Premier Golda Meir as an example—"who accepts all intelligence as gospel" owing to lack of policy, or knowledge, or both of the subject at hand (ibid., p. 28). As Handel correctly points out, leaders' and their advisors' openness or closeness is largely a function of the political system and culture. Totalitarian regimes will produce closed-type leaders and sycophantic advisors. Democratic cultures will foster more openmindedness in leaders and a policymaking milieu in which personal integrity is more dominant.

By definition, closed-type leaders will show no genuine interest in objective intelligence, since it can contradict their beliefs. Hence they will either interfere with the intelligence process in order to ensure that its product suits their political beliefs and needs or else ignore it, thus undermining its value as an effective instrument of foreign policymaking. Even relatively openminded leaders, however, are likely to value the intelligence product not only by its professional standards (availability, relevance, and accuracy) but also according to its impact on their policies. As Hughes (pp. 25–26) maintains, from the leader's perspective the worst intelligence product is precisely the one that has all three professional qualities but that also casts doubts, even contradicts, the leader's preferred policy.

The final feature is leaders' personal interest in intelligence: the higher it is, the more active policy-intelligence interaction is likely to be. Winston Churchill is probably the best example of a leader with a strong, even enthusiastic interest, in intelligence, especially in its raw forms. Consequently he kept close ties with intelligence officers not only when serving in the government but also during his desert years in the opposition. At the other end of the pole are leaders who have little interest (or trust) in intelligence and who perceive it as rather irrelevant for their work. A typical example is British Prime Minister Harold Wilson, who noted once: "I saw so little of the heads of MI5 and MI6, that I used to confuse their names" (Andrew 1985, p. 502).

In summary, openminded consumers with keen interest in intelligence and the ability to control the policymaking apparatus are likely to develop a politically unbiased relationship with their intelligence community. Authoritarian, closeminded intelligence consumers who are interested only in supportive intelligence are likely to make the corruption of the intelligence process far more probable. These outcomes, however, are not the function of leaders' attitude toward intelligence alone. To a large extent they are also dependent on the attitude of their intelligence officers.

INTELLIGENCE PRODUCERS. In his brilliant monograph *The Fate of Facts in the World of Men*, Thomas Hughes divides intelligence officers into three types. The one who almost always wins the race to the policymaker's ear is the *butcher*, who cuts raw pieces of usually current intelligence, according to the consumers' taste, and supplies them without any estimations. The *baker*, in contrast, is the far more cautious and politically unbiased intelligence analyst, who carefully cooks information and estimates together to produce the perfect analytical dish. Consumers, however, dislike the baker's product. Being so vague and full of probabilities, conditions, and doubts, it becomes a nutritious but tasteless health food, which policymakers regard as useless. In between the butcher and the baker is the *intelligence maker*. Like a "psychiatrist alternating between the couches of intelligence and policy," this "market analyst and salesman, middleman and promoter" (p. 53) tries to bridge the widening gap between pure intelligence and current needs of daily policymaking in order to optimize the value of the intelligence product for consumers. Assuming, as Hughes (p. 22) does, that policy and intelligence making are, at most, "a marriage of inconvenience," the intelligence maker is, indeed, the optimal combination the intelligence community can offer policymakers.

Hughes's analysis employs two standards to measure the quality of intelligence officers: their usefulness to policymakers and their adherence to the professional intelligence ethic. From the perspective of our discussion, however, these two contradictory standards do not carry the same weight. By professional intelligence measures the bakers are superior to intelligence makers because their product reflects better the complex and uncertain realities with which policymakers have to wrestle. Intelligence makers, effective as they are, are more prone to mix intelligence and politics. Thus the likelihood of intelligence and politics interfering with each other is the highest when spineless butchers—who, by definition, are the eager suppliers of "intelligence to please"—provide the link between the two communities. Policymakers will find it harder to corrupt the intelligence process when intelligence makers are their counterparts and will meet the strongest resistance to such attempts when bakers serve in these capacities.

Within the tangled web where intelligence and policymakers interact, none of the factors discussed above seems to be either a necessary or a sufficient condition to determine the nature of this complex relationship. This, however, does not imply that all these factors carry the same weight or have the same impact. Indeed, five of them influence more the *interest* of intelligence and policymakers to interfere with each other's domain, whereas the other three have more to do with their *ability* to do so.

Interest is a function of ideology, level of consensus, type of intelligence product, personality of the policymaker, and the intelligence officer's level of professionalism. Closed-type leaders who are highly committed to their ideology (especially if it is of an extreme kind) are likely to interfere with intelligence work—especially with current intelligence—when the intelligence product contradicts their beliefs. However, when the product is a matter of warning or alert, they are less likely to do so. The less intelligence officers adhere to their professional ethic, the less interest they will have in resisting such political pressures and the more likely they will be to interfere in politics. By the same token, openminded leaders and highly professional intelligence officers, none of whom is too ideologically committed and all of whom share similar perceptions regarding national security goals and the means to obtain them, afford an optimal combination, especially when it comes to strategic warnings. This combination ensures that the politicians will be less interested in interfering with professional intelligence work and that intelligence officers will not intervene in politics.

The other three factors have more to do with the *ability* of intelligence officers and policymakers to interfere with each others' domain. Legislative, judicial, and public media supervision of the intelligence-politics relationship is the most significant obstacle to such behavior. Bureaucratic independence of intelligence organizations, especially when combined with an adherence to the professional ethic, is highly relevant as well. Analytical pluralism offers opportunities for political and intelligence misconduct, but again much depends on the personal integrity of the analysts.

Altogether, then, the interests and the abilities of the participants in intelligence-policymaking interaction will set the environment in which this interaction takes place. In ideal circumstances intelligence and politics will be kept totally separated, but for the reasons already put forward, such an environment is utopian. Thus the question is: To what extent should intelligence be kept separate from politics in practice? This question has often been discussed in academic literature. In the last decade it also gained a practical dimension, especially in connection with the CIA's relationship with its political superiors. The theoretical and the practical dimensions of this debate are the subject of the next sections.

THE THEORETICAL DEBATE

Most students of the relationship between intelligence producers and consumers agree that a tension exists between the "ideal" and the "real" worlds. They all agree that ideally intelligence and politics should be kept separate, that intelligence work should be free from political pressures, and that policymakers should get the best intelligence product and make the best use of it when planning and conducting their foreign policy. Furthermore, most agree that in reality such separation and behavior cannot completely be achieved. Hence the focus of the debate here is about the optimal mix of the two worlds: How far should intelligence and politics be kept apart? Should intelligence objectivity and integrity be preserved at the cost of losing its influence on the policymaking process? How far should objectivity and integrity be sacrificed in order to gain such influence?

Three approaches can be identified in this debate. On the one hand are the so-called *realists* or *activists* (or *radicals*), who regard intelligence involvement in politics as not only a necessary but also a legitimate means to increase the impact of intelligence on the policymaking process. The opposite approach is expressed by the *professional* or *traditional* school, which maintains that such involvement is professionally unethical and practically counterproductive. In between are what I term *professional realists* or *traditional activists,* who mostly attempt to burn the candle at both ends by emphasizing the need to increase the impact of intelligence on the policymaking process while preserving professional integrity.

The rationale of the realist argument is based purely on practical considerations. Experience shows that, without some degree of involvement in politics, intelligence may be timely and accurate but will ultimately lack influence on the policymaking process. Such influence—that is, the net contribution for changing a policy or supporting it against pressure to change—is the justification for the existence of intelligence. Intelligence must therefore get involved in politics. As Richard Betts puts it, "when intelligence products are successfully kept out of this maelstrom, remaining untainted by the hurly-burly of policy debate, they may preserve purity at the price of irrelevance" (1980, p. 119).

Perhaps the most enthusiastic proponent of this approach is ex-DCI Robert Gates, whose stand in this debate has been expressed in recent years not only in words but also in deeds. The main concerns of Gates, though a professional intelligence officer himself, are the policymakers' needs. The contribution of intelligence necessary to fulfill these needs, especially for presidential policymaking, he argues, is too small and rather dissatisfying (1989, p. 35). Indeed, according to Gates, the CIA has three responsibilities: collection, analysis, and distribution of intelligence information; covert action; and gaining influence with policymakers. Despite being quite problematic, this last task is the most significant of all three:

> It is in the dynamics of this relationship [between intelligence and policymakers] that the influence and role of the CIA are determined. The Agency's effectiveness depends on whether its assess-

ments are heeded, whether its information is considered relevant
and timely enough to be useful, and whether the CIA's relationship
with policymakers, from issue to issue and problem to problem, is
supportive or adversarial. (1987/1988, p. 216)

Two key officials determine, to a large extent, the quality of this
interaction: "Disinterest or reluctance on the part of the DCI (or national
security advisor) to take an activist, even aggressive role in this respect is a
severe—even irreparable—handicap to ensuring that intelligence information and assessments reach the president" (Gates 1989, p. 38). The
principal solution to this problem is, then, to tighten the cooperation
between the intelligence and the policymaking communities:

> The DCI with his senior managers and the president with his staff
> must both promote and maintain close personal ties at all levels.
> Both must aggressively seek new ways to inform the intelligence
> officers about policy initiatives under consideration or under way in
> order to determine how intelligence can make a contribution and
> how best to put intelligence information and assessments before the
> president. (Ibid., p. 43)

Measuring the quality of intelligence-policymaking relations almost solely
according to this standard, Gates concludes that the CIA reached its highest
level of effectiveness under the Reagan administration. President Johnson,
for example, compared his intelligence advisors to his cow Bessie, who used
to swing "her shit-smeared tail" through the bucket of freshly squeezed milk,
and President Nixon asked, rather bitterly, "What the hell do those clowns
do out there in Langley?" (ibid., pp. 42, 35). In contrast, during the 1980s
the CIA "had unprecedented access to the Reagan Administration, from
the president on down," an access that led to "a dynamic, healthy relationship" (Gates 1987/1988, pp. 225–26).

Another proponent of the activist school, Arthur Hulnick, asserts, just
as does Gates, that intelligence-policymaking relations of the past were futile
owing to bureaucratic, operational, philosophical, and stylistic differences
between the two communities. The situation, however, started to change in
1982 with the reorganization of the CIA's Directorate of Intelligence, which
placed *activism* as the established policy of the agency. Hulnick, a veteran
of more than thirty years in American intelligence, enthusiastically supports
this new approach that emphasizes the need for close, even "networking"

interactions between intelligence producers and consumers, and he argues that the new environment yields intelligence "products that are timely and relevant" (1987, p. 133). Moreover, according to Hulnick, the initiative to develop this tighter relationship must come from the intelligence side (1991, p. 86). And since, as Hulnick maintains, "there is not just one link between intelligence and policy, but rather many intersections between the two systems" (1986, p. 230),

> the necessary liaison falls to [intelligence] managers at various levels. Managers should be seeking out their counterparts to learn what policy-makers are worried about, what kind of analysis would be useful to decision-makers, when it should be delivered, and even how it should be packaged. (1991, p. 85)

A similar view supporting close relations between intelligence consumers and producers is expressed by Betts. When a new administration enters office, he argues, it is the role of the intelligence analysts to market their products to their new and inexperienced consumers. This initiative should be taken at all levels and need not be done in formal discussions alone:

> Having lunch with, say, the appropriate NSC staff member is one way for an analyst to promote dissemination of papers beyond the ranks of other analysts. It also provides a chance to suggest issues to which the policymaker ought to give more thought—which could result in levying of more requirements upon the analysts. (1988, p. 188).

Betts, however, is well aware of the need to preserve the integrity of intelligence in this rather intimate relationship, and he emphasizes that compromising the intelligence product according to customers' needs "is not only illegitimate but ultimately self-defeating" (ibid.). Moreover, Betts does not ignore the problem of the impact of political biases upon intelligence estimates but rather suggests a mechanism to control it:

> If political-intellectual biases are inevitable, they should be organized intelligently, not suppressed, ignored, and left to pop up in unrecognized ways in the estimating process. Moreover, highlighting the contention between varying biases within the estimate

should make it harder for policymakers to glide over such differences
of opinion in their own deliberation. (1980, p. 126).

If the realists seek to increase the influence of intelligence on the
policymaking process, most of them implicitly accepting that they do so at
the cost of decreasing its objectivity and integrity, the professionals suggest
ways to increase these qualities even if doing so means decreasing their
impact. Although they agree with their adversaries that in the "real world"
intelligence cannot be completely isolated from politics, they nevertheless
regard this state of affairs as an unavoidable evil. Such a situation, they
argue, creates the conditions under which the intelligence product may get
compromised and distorted. Such a product becomes useless, even an
obstacle, for the conduct of high-quality policymaking. Hence, for the
sake of intelligence and policymaking alike, maximum separation between
intelligence and politics should be maintained. If the cost is a decrease in
the level of influence of intelligence on the policymaking process, this price
should be paid.

Earlier practitioners of the intelligence-policymaking relationship expressed this rather traditional view in simple terms. Thus, for example,
despite being known as "Wild Bill," General William Donovan, the
founding father of the Office of Strategic Services (OSS), maintained a
rather traditional view according to which "intelligence must be independent of the people it serves so that the material it obtained will not be
slanted or distorted by the views of the people directing operations" (quoted
in Hulnick 1986, p. 214).

Sherman Kent, another early practitioner, held a similar view. In his
influential book *Strategic Intelligence for American World Policy* (1949), he
took into account the advantages and disadvantages involved in keeping
intelligence and policy apart. On the one hand, he recognized that intelligence must enter into dialogue with policymakers and that during this
process each side will invade the domain of the other. This dialogue is
necessary. Without it the intelligence officer will be forced to operate in a
political vacuum, thus providing a product of little or no use at all. At the
same time, however, Kent firmly warned against too close a relationship
between the two, emphasizing that intelligence "is not the formulator of
objectives; it is not the drafter of policy; it is not the maker of plans; it is
not the carrier out of operations. Intelligence is ancillary to these; . . . it
performs a service function" (1949, p. 182). Being aware of the problematic
possibility that too close a relationship may drive the intelligence organiza-

tion into "prostituting itself," Kent adapted Walter Lippmann's formula for avoiding such behavior:

> The only institutional safeguard [for impartial and objective analysis] is to separate as absolutely as possible . . . the staff which executes from the staff which investigates. The two should be parallel but quite distinct bodies of men, recruited differently, paid if possible from separate funds, responsible to different heads, intrinsically uninterested in each other's personal success. (Ibid., p. 200)

Kent, of course, observed that such a high level of separation might prevent policymakers from guiding the intelligence services. His solution, though not very original, still emphasized the need to preserve the professional standards of the intelligence organization:

> The only way out of the dilemma seems to me to lie in the very compromise that is usually attempted: guarantee intelligence its administrative and substantive integrity by keeping it separate from its consumers; keep trying every known device to make the users familiar with the producers' organization and the producers with the users' organizations. (Ibid., pp. 200–201)

Twenty years later, after gaining additional experience as the chairman of the Board of National Estimates, Kent still took the same position: "If influence cannot be our goal, what should it be? . . . It should be to be relevant within the area of your competence, and above all it should be to be credible" (1969, p. 16).

It is interesting to note that, while writers who support the realist or activist school are mostly Americans, their rivals come from various national backgrounds. Thus, for example, R. V. Jones, the head of British Scientific Intelligence during the World War II believed that

> the intelligence officer's problem is to paint the picture that will best convey its intended content to the commander. Here, of course, he must be punctilious in making the picture as objective as possible, while inevitably emphasizing the points which *he himself* believes to be important; and he must not attempt to achieve

emphasis by suppressing justifiable doubts about the validity of any evidence on which he draws. (1989, p. 294; emphasis added)

Winston Churchill's experience during World War I led him to a similar conclusion: "The temptation to tell a chief in a great position the things he most likes to hear is the commonest explanation of mistaken policy. Thus the outlook of the leader on whose decisions fateful events depend is usually far more sanguine than the brutal facts admit" (quoted in Jones 1989, p. 290).

Probably because of similar national experiences, Israeli writers on this subject tend to adhere to the professional approach as well. Yehoshafat Harkabi, one of Israel's best intelligence experts and a former chief of Military Intelligence, warns that too close a relationship between the intelligence chief and the policymaker involves major setbacks for the intelligence process. Under such circumstances the intelligence officer

> loses perspective and his independent critical vision, and gradually succumbs to the conception of the policymakers. He is then unable to detach himself from festivities of policymaking just like the other self-gratified members of the court who bask in their connections with power. (p. 129)

Similarly, Michael Handel, one of the main proponents of the professional approach, suggests in his analysis of the intelligence-politics relationship that "it is imperative that intelligence professionals accept the standards of the ideal system [in which institutional integrity is preserved at the cost of political influence] in order to develop a professional 'super-ego' that may, in the long run, be the best check on the excesses of political interference" (1987, p. 13).

Altogether, then, professionals believe that the quality of the intelligence product is more important than its marketing. Robert Jervis summarizes this stand very well when arguing that, although the consumers' readiness to listen to their intelligence experts is an important issue, "perhaps the intelligence community has paid too much attention to [this] question . . . and not enough to how the community's internal structure and norms might be altered to enable intelligence to be worth listening to (1986, p. 41).

In between the realists and the professionals are what I term professional realists or traditional activists, who analyze the problematic nature of intelligence-policy relations but avoid taking a clear stand in favor of one school or another. Roger Hilsman, one of the earlier and most influential exponents of this view, tended to emphasize the need for a close relationship between intelligence makers and users. At the same time, however, he also emphasized the risk involved in the inertia of human and bureaucratic behavior that might wreck the boundaries between intelligence and politics. Hilsman nevertheless concluded that intelligence officers

> must orient themselves frankly and consciously toward policy and action—creating a frame of mind that is manipulative, instrumental, action-conscious, policy-oriented; recasting their thought to the context of action and adapting their tools expressly to the needs of policy. (1956, p. 182)

A similar, though more organizational solution, was suggested by Chester Cooper in the early 1970s. After reviewing the frustrating intelligence-policy relations, especially during the Vietnam war, he concluded that in order to gain more impact on the policymaking process "estimators must be brought out of their cloister into the real world." The best way to attain this goal is to get members of the Board of National Estimates to function as intelligence advisors in their field of expertise to senior policymakers. Cooper, however, was aware of the problem that intelligence integrity and impact might be eroded in this suggested policymaking milieu and emphasized two ways to avoid such erosion: first, intelligence experts should always maintain considered judgments and cool objectivity; and, second, their interaction with policymakers should be rather limited, since "indiscriminate participation in every policy discussion is likely to erode both of these precious attributes to the point where they are just one more group in Washington living by its wits in an atmosphere of advocacy and passion" (p. 235).

Finally, Thomas Hughes is rather pessimistic regarding the possibility of reaching a satisfying solution to the problem. The source of the problem, he convincingly argues, is human nature, particularly that "the typical policy-makers and the typical intelligence officer are inevitably a little of both. In practice their roles tend to merge" (1976, p. 7). And since human nature cannot be modified, it will always be the tendency of men who inhabit institutions "to defy the jurisdictional reforms, mock the machinery of government and frustrate the organizational tinkering" (ibid., p. 60). The optimal solution Hughes can offer, then, is the intelligence-maker type of an intelligence manager as the link between the intelligence and the policymaking communities.

All in all it is important to note that the various positions taken by the realists and the professionals, as well as those in between, are of a somewhat moderate nature. None of the realists maintains that intelligence and politics should be inseparable, that intelligence work should be done on the basis of motivated political biases, or that politics should make use of the intelligence product according to parochial political interests. Similarly, the professionals accept that the intelligence product is a means to an end, that it should be usable for policymakers, and that it should be produced in accordance with their needs. In this sense, despite the differences between them, the realist and the professional approaches stand quite close to each other, leaving wide margins at both ends of the intelligence-politics relationship spectrum, as described in Table 1.

Table 1.　Separation between intelligence and politics: A continuum of four approaches

Total separation	High level of separation	Lower level of separation	No separation
Idealistic approach	Professional approach	Realist approach	Totalitarian approach

Relatively close as they are in theory, however, in practice the differences between realists and professionals are nevertheless rather significant. They were best demonstrated during the 1980s when the professional approach, which traditionally dominated CIA-policymaker relations, was replaced by the activist policy. As had become rather clear towards the end of the 1980s, the results of this transformation were quite disastrous for intelligence officers and policymakers alike. This practical test for the theoretical debate will be discussed in the following section.

THE PRACTICAL TEST

With relatively few exceptions—the most significant of which was the "Bay of Pigs" episode—during its first thirty-five years of existence the CIA maintained high professional standards as far as its analytical duties were concerned. Typically, the motto selected in 1961 to decorate the agency's new headquarters at Langley, Virginia, was a quotation taken from St. John: "The Truth [not influence] Shall Make You Free." Most DCIs, as well as their subordinates, acted accordingly. It was in this environment that the CIA's analysts could produce high-quality products, the most important of which were the NIEs that "represented the broadest, most informed judgements available" (Leary, p. 69). What the CIA gained in quality, however, it lacked in influence. Interactions between senior analysts and policymakers were rather limited, and relations between presidents and DCIs—especially during the war in Vietnam—were kept at a low profile. This neglect led, in the long run, to a growing frustration on the part of both intelligence and policymakers, a frustration that incubated over time toward a more "active" policy.

The coming to office of the Reagan administration and, even more important, the nomination of William Casey (who had previously served as Reagan's presidential campaign manager) as the new DCI signaled the transformation from traditional to activist policy. Casey himself emphasized shortly before being nominated that his top priority was going to be what he regarded as the required improvement of the analytical estimates—the link between the agency and the White House (Woodward, p. 76). Ideas turned into action in 1982 with the reorganization of the Directorate of Intelligence aimed at making the agency's analysts far more active, aggressive, and supportive in their interaction with their counterparts in the policymaking community. It was in this environment of intensified intelligence-policy interaction that the distance between the two groups diminished and the boundaries between intelligence and policymaking—especially at the highest CIA echelon—were practically removed.

In late 1987 Robert Gates, then Deputy Director of Central Intelligence (DDCI) and a longtime driving force behind the establishment of the new policy, enthusiastically wrote about the result it had brought: "This has contributed enormously to improving the *relevance, timing* and *substance* of intelligence analysis and other CIA support" (1987/1988, p. 226). At about the same time, Arthur Hulnick, then Presentation Officer in the CIA Public Affairs Office, reported similar positive findings with regard to the outcome of the new policy: "Supervisors report that their analysts routinely become involved in 'networking' and the results should be products that are *timely* and *relevant*" (1987, p. 132).

Gates and Hulnick, however, talked publicly only about improvements in two components of the intelligence product—timing and relevance—avoiding any clear reference to the third and the most critical one: accuracy.

Indeed, as the evidence recently disclosed shows, during Casey's tenure as DCI some of the CIA's products in the most critical foreign policy issues reflected the worst possible combination: they were timely and relevant, hence very useful for policymakers, yet at the same time they were also highly inaccurate owing to motivated and unmotivated political biases, thus lending policymakers misleading support for wrongheaded policies. Casey, the most political director in the agency's history, had made no secret of his strong political beliefs before and during his tenure as DCI. And since he regarded himself as much a policymaker as an intelligence director, intelligence products in major areas had become driven by his policy agenda rather than the other way around.

The Iran-contra investigation committees and Robert Gates's Senate nomination hearings of September–October 1991 revealed some of the practices through which the intelligence process had been corrupted during this period. These, as senior analyst Melvin Goodman quite convincingly described, included:

- imposition of intelligence judgment not supported by evidence,
- suppression of intelligence that does not support the policy agenda,
- manipulation of the analytical process,
- misuse of the directorate of operations to influence the analytical work of the directorate of intelligence, and
- personal management that ensures responsiveness to policy interests.[4]

These practices were employed in the most critical foreign policy issues, among them: the balance of forces within the Iranian leadership and the likelihood of Soviet intervention in Iran after the death of Khomeini, which served as the analytical justification for the Iranian initiative in 1985; Moscow's Third World policy and her readiness and ability to further intensify investments and strengthen her positions in the Middle East, Africa, Latin America, and Asia; Soviet involvement in international terrorism, including allegations that the Soviets were directing such groups as the IRA, the Red Brigades, Baader-Meinhof, and the Japanese Red Army, and that Moscow was behind the 1981 attempt to assassinate the

---

4. Testimony of Melvin A. Goodman to the Senate Select Committee on Intelligence, pp. 2–3. It should be noted that, although Gates's counterarguments during his hearings had focused on denying his personal role in these activities, he nevertheless left little doubt that corruption of the intelligence process along these lines did take place during Casey's tenure as DCI. See *Hearings*, vol. 2, pp. 714–15.

Pope; possible use of Soviet chemical warfare in the war in Afghanistan; the magnitude of the Sandinista threat to American interests in Latin America; and the alleged instability of the Mexican regime. Political biases also colored the CIA's analyses of the most important issue in the postwar world—the dramatic changes in the USSR and the East European bloc that culminated in the collapse of the Soviet empire.

The debate over the extent of the corruption of the intelligence process during Casey's tenure as DCI, as well as other issues such as whether Casey simply misinformed the President or intentionally misled him, or the level of Gates's personal involvement in these wrongdoings, will probably go on and new findings will come out. Yet one conclusion may be reached now: never before in the history of the CIA was the intelligence process so systematically corrupted and the professional integrity of the organization so severely undermined as in the period when the "activist" policy triumphed over the "traditional" approach. Although the cost to the American national interest in this case was not catastrophic (mainly because of the collapse of the Soviet Union) future practitioners of activism should bear in mind that under different conditions the outcome could have been far worse.

Notwithstanding the practical damage that is likely to be caused by the policy of activism, two more points should be made here regarding such a policy. First, there is some exaggeration in the activist argument according to which intelligence analysts hardly know what interests policymakers and that without a close, even intimate, interaction this gap cannot be bridged. In fact, a daily reading of the *New York Times* or the *Washington Post* will tell analysts much of what they need to know in this regard. As for the rest, reality shows that when policymakers avoid tasking intelligence, this has less to do with them being unaware of the potential of intelligence for contributing to their policy and more to do with their being apprehensive that objective intelligence might cast doubt over their policy line. Hence the need for intelligence initiative to tighten relations with policymakers seems rather overstated.

Second, there is some exaggeration in the argument—also usually made by activists—that the time of the president is so dear and rare that he can hardly spare it on intelligence. The president is, after all, the master of his time. If he does not spend enough time on intelligence, it is not because of objective constraints alone but also because of his personal preferences. After all, during World War II Winston Churchill was at least as busy as, for example, President Reagan. Churchill, nevertheless, insisted on seeing every day not only intelligence estimates but raw material as well, and regarded high-quality intelligence intercepts as his "golden eggs" (Andrew 1989, p. 181). There is nothing wrong with intelligence advisors who try to attract the attention of the leader to their product; in fact, under certain circumstances this is precisely their duty. But a clear line should be drawn here between form and content. Activists like Gates, for example, frequently define their goal as supplying the president with "supportive intelligence." As long as "supportive" relates only to form, there is nothing unethical about it. Indeed, the product should be presented to leaders in the form that best suits their ability to understand it—be it in oral presentation, written prose, or a comic strip. One may suspect, however, that intelligence activists might also be inclined to change the content of their product to make it more attractive to the busy president and this, of course, is clearly unethical. As experience proves, it is also counterproductive.

METHODOLOGICAL CONCLUSIONS

The ongoing debate about the optimal tradeoff between the integrity of the intelligence organization and its level of influence on policymaking is rich and sophisticated. Yet, despite these qualities, the participants in this debate appear to share similar shortcomings.

First, all of them, but mainly the realists, fail to identify the direct link between lack of sufficient separation of intelligence from politics and intelligence action aimed at an alteration of policy by illegal means—action that is unacceptable even to the most ardent realist. Thus a major argument of this book is that this type of intelligence intervention in politics is the result of a growing lack of awareness by intelligence consumers and producers of the need to separate intelligence from politics. This argument will be tested through the case studies of this work and will be reexamined in the conclusions.

A second shortcoming is the failure of the participants in this debate to discuss the problem more systematically. This study suggests that the fundamental problem of intelligence-state interaction is insufficient separation between intelligence and politics. Since this difficulty is also the source of a fundamental problem in civil-military relations and since the latter field is far more developed academically, this book draws certain elements from it and applies them to the analysis of the relations between the state and its intelligence community. At the first stage the two fields are compared. At the second stage this study selects from the literature on civil-military relations two variables—"professionalism" at the bureaucratic level of analysis and "political control" at the state level—and argues that these two constitute the structural keys to understanding the problem of intelligence-state relations and its optimal solution.

Third, the present debate focuses only on the highest level of interaction between the state and its intelligence community. This, however, is inadequate since the behavior of political and intelligence institutions reflects not only functional imperatives but also societal ones, that is, the norms, beliefs, and ideologies of the society in which they operate. These factors channel the producer-consumer interaction into specific patterns of behavior that may be unique to each nation and explain differences in such interaction between one state and another. Although this book focuses on the intelligence-state relationship at the decisionmaking level, it nevertheless uses variables of political culture—the context in which this interaction takes place—in order to explain certain elements in the behavior of the intelligence officers and the politicians involved.

Fourth, most writers on the subject are Americans and tend to investigate the relations between intelligence and policymakers from an American perspective. This is so not only because their studies are policy-oriented but also because their knowledge and experience derive mainly from their own nation's history. However, since the problem is of a universal nature, it needs to be studied in the context of other national experiences as well. This book addresses this problem by comparing cases of intelligence intervention in politics not only in the United States, but also in Britain and Israel.

Fifth, students of the subject make little use of the wide body of empirical evidence that is available today. For the most part this evidence is integrated into their studies in anecdotal form, as a means to illustrate a point or to prove an argument. Although this inductive approach is understandable, there is also much sense in using a more deductive strategy in studying the problem. Hence this book constructs and analyzes four detailed case studies that are used both to answer principal questions and to test certain hypotheses in the subject of intelligence intervention in politics.

2

Civil-Military and Intelligence-State Relations

COMPARISON

Unlike civil-military relations, which is already a well-developed field of academic research, the study of intelligence in general, and intelligence-state relations in particular, is a relatively young domain. Given this state of affairs, this study intends to apply some of the accumulated knowledge of the former field to the latter.

As opposed to societies with a less-developed political culture, the core of the problem of civil-military relations in the modern democratic state is not the violent intervention of the armed forces in politics but the role of military expertise and advice in the national policymaking process. To a large extent, as has already been noticed, the same is true with regard to the interaction between intelligence and policymakers. On the surface, then, there should be no significant difference between the roles of these organizations and the roles of other professional groups, such as diplomats or economists, that also participate in the national policymaking process. And yet civil-military and state-intelligence relations are usually perceived as unique in their nature. This perception is mainly the result of a legacy of fear among large segments of society regarding the possibility of military or intelligence intervention in state politics. Such apprehension does not exist with regard to other professional groups, and it constitutes the main justification for studying the state's relations with these two organs separately from its relations with other national bureaucracies.

The sources of this fear can be traced to three unique similarities between the military and intelligence. The first of these three is *historical experience.*

Western democracies have rarely experienced violent military intervention in politics in the post-1945 era. However, such intervention has been part of their history in the past, and at present they witness the continuation of this phenomenon in most Third World countries. Intelligence intervention in politics and political intervention in intelligence were always more salient yet also more subtle issues. In recent decades many political scandals in Western-type democracies involved exactly this kind of problem. History, then, shows that both the military and the intelligence community have at least the tendency to intervene in politics, though in different ways and usually under different circumstances. At the same time, experience shows a similar tendency on behalf of politicians to intervene in military and intelligence affairs.

The second similarity that is unique to military and intelligence institutions is their *professional values*. There is a fundamental contradiction between the principles essential for efficient military and intelligence performance and those that are basic to the functioning of a democratic society.[1] Military institutions are built on authority, hierarchy, and discipline; intelligence is built on the basis of secrecy. The essence of the democratic open society, in contrast, is the belief in individual freedom and freedom of information. This contradiction is a major cause for the widespread perception in many liberal democracies that the military and intelligence agencies are sinister organs, alien to democratic values. This perception is enhanced by the nature of military and intelligence roles. Military professionals are identified with war and are believed by many to be the protagonists of armed conflicts. The same is true with regard to the intelligence community. For many this community embodies an intimidating combination of secret—and therefore uncontrolled and often illegal—activity combined with a high level of influence in state affairs.

While it is probably true, as some experts argue (e.g., Huntington 1959; Betts 1979), that the professional soldier is often less belligerent than other segments of society, the mere identification between the military and war enhances the belief that the stronger the military, the higher the likelihood of war. Similarly, while intelligence professionals might be rather reluctant to use their means—after all, they know better than others their limits and

---

1. Notably, there is also a fundamental discrepancy between military and intelligence values. The proper analysis process—the main task of intelligence organizations—demands intellectual freedom, openness, and divergence of opinion. These values diametrically oppose the strict hierarchical principles of the military. This is a major reason why the work of intelligence agencies within military organizations should be limited to purely military issues.

how dangerous they are to the freedom of their society—they are still widely considered (and on many occasions rightly so) as the main protagonists of the use of nondemocratic policy instruments.

The third common denominator that is unique to both military and intelligence institutions is their *ability to intervene in state politics*. This ability is the result of the monopoly or near monopoly that the military has on arms and intelligence agencies have on secret information and covert action. It is true that in politically developed democracies, where political institutions are well established and where there is a wide consensus regarding the legitimacy of the constitutional system, violent military intervention in politics is a remote problem. Yet the fact that the military has a monopoly on arms and is the most coherent, disciplined, and hierarchical organization within the state raises suspicion and fear regarding its behavior, especially in times of domestic crisis. The intelligence monopoly over information from closed sources is a less salient asset, but information is, no doubt, a commodity highly valued by all actors in the political arena. If power is the ability to get someone to do something he or she would not otherwise do, then the mere access to information unavailable to other professional groups is a major tool of persuasion available only to the intelligence community. When combined with its control of the means of covert action, the intelligence community has access to means of power that can be used to manipulate politics.

The legacies and possibilities of military and intelligence intervention in politics as well as their professional values establish the need to separate them as much as possible from the politics of the state. In the case of the military this task becomes more complex since the armed forces control and consume major human, economic, and technological national resources. Apprehension of the "military-industrial complex," on the one hand, and the need to take into account the military's legitimate requirements, on the other, add a dimension of tension and confusion to soldiers' interaction with civilians. Although this dimension does not exist in state-intelligence relations, two other features of this relationship make the separation of intelligence from politics no less problematic than isolating the military from civilian affairs.

The first of these features involves the authority of intelligence in the policymaking process. Soldiers are asked to advise politicians on military questions or other subjects directly related to military issues. In this sphere they enjoy a near monopoly of information. They also enjoy a high level of authority to interpret this information, since civilians recognize and trust their expertise in this rather narrow domain. Intelligence advice, in contrast, is requested in all areas of national policymaking, whether it be diplomacy, the military, the economy, technology, etc. Here intelligence officers may have some monopoly of information, but not enough authority in its interpretation. Since intelligence is requested to interpret information on issues in which it has no monopoly of expertise, politicians regard themselves as experts enough to challenge intelligence on a wide range of issues. This lack of authority creates a source of potential friction, a problem that is less likely to arise in civil-military relations.

If intelligence advice creates such a unique dilemma, then intelligence covert action is even more problematic, for here the special characteristic of intelligence—secrecy, responsibility for controversial operations, and "plausible denial"—may come into full expression. The military, of course, must maintain a high level of secrecy regarding some aspects of its activity, as a means to surprise the enemy. But although secrecy is essential for military success, it is only one component of the military way of thinking and behavior. For intelligence organizations, on the other hand, secrecy is the necessary condition for proper functioning, indeed a way of life; and unlike military action, the success of intelligence action is dependent to a large extent on its being kept secret even after it has been carried out.

The issue becomes even more problematic owing to the difficulty in making a distinction between *functional* and *political* secrecy. Any organization has its own political secrets. This obviously includes the military, which has a parochial interest in concealing its own failures, whether they involve gross mismanagement such as the C–5A scandal of the 1960s or operational flops such as the failure of a supersophisticated and costly "Stealth" fighter to hit undefended targets in the Panama campaign of December 1989. But given that in the intelligence community everything is kept secret and that, more than any other state organ, intelligence resorts to controversial means, it has both more political secrets to hide and better means to hide them. Given, moreover, that in many cases the line between functional and political secrecy is very fine, what intelligence officers may regard as functional secrecy is often considered by outsiders as purely political.

Nowhere does this problem of interpretation become sharper than in the sphere of intelligence responsibility for controversial actions and the subject of "plausible denial." When a policymaker wants a certain action to be taken, and this action—for example, intervention in the political process of a friendly nation or an arms deal with a hostile nation—contradicts fundamental ethical values and his own declared policy, he can hardly give direct orders to his intelligence officers to carry it out. Under such circumstances he may hint at his wish, but it remains up to intelligence to interpret it and take action. Responsibility for the act in case of failure or revelation usually becomes a bone of contention between politicians and intelligence makers.

As with other issues of intelligence and politics this problem is a very old one. The most famous example of ancient "plausible denial" is that of King Henry II asking his men: "Will no one revenge me of the injuries I have sustained from one turbulent priest?" Yet when Thomas à Becket, the "turbulent priest," was assassinated by the King's zealous knights, Henry II in person did penance for this action.[2] The differences between the way the problem was dealt with in the past and the way it has been dealt with today are of an administrative nature. First, unlike in the past, state institutions—the intelligence organizations—are now available for the conduct of such action. Second, a modern bureaucratic method to protect leaders and senior officials by isolating them from such actions, "plausible denial," is in use today. For some in the administration, plausible denial constitutes a sort of functional secret, a means without which instructions to conduct a necessary but unethical policy cannot be given. For others, mainly outside the administration, plausible denial is merely a political secret or a political lie—a means that enables politicians to escape responsibility for immoral aspects of their policies. This difference in interpretation takes place within the intelligence community as well, but whether or not intelligence officers accept plausible denial as a functional or political means, they must live with it. In any event, these unique features of intelligence work add another dimension of confusion, sometimes distrust, to intelligence-politics relations. This dimension is far less evident and influential in civil-military relations.

CONCLUSIONS

This discussion leads to three conclusions. First, there are enough similarities in the relations of military and intelligence institutions with the state

2. The Bible tells us of a similar episode that took place about two thousand years before Becket's murder. King David's captain of the host, Jo'ab the son of Zerui'ah, murdered Abner the son of Ner, a professional soldier and an opponent of the King. Although this elimination served his

to distinguish them from the state's relationship with other professional groups that directly participate in the national policymaking process. Hence we can justify studying these two subjects as an independent field of study. Second, unlike the military, which consumes major human, economic, and technological resources, the intelligence community does not. Hence we need to focus less on intelligence relations with society as a whole and more on this interaction at the decisionmaking level. Third, when compared to civil-military relations, the interaction between the intelligence community and the state involves potential sources of friction that exist, but to a lesser extent, in the relations between soldiers and civilians. Hence we cannot automatically apply solutions for the regulation of relations between the polity and the military to intelligence-state relations.

---

political interests, King David made all efforts to prove to his suspicious people that he was not involved in the murder. As the Old Testament tells us, he was very successful in this mission, "For all the people and all Israel understood that day that it was not the king to slay Abner the son of Ner" (2 Samuel 3:37). The blame remained with Jo'ab, and shortly before his death the King ordered his son Solomon to eliminate him, allegedly for this authorized action (1 Kings 2:5). A more conspiratorial mind would suspect that the elimination of Jo'ab was intended to prevent him from telling his own version of the episode once King David passed away.

3

Isolating Professionals from Politics

FORMULAS OF CIVIL-MILITARY RELATIONS: THE LITERATURE

Armed forces can be used either as instruments of foreign policy or as agents in partisan or nonpartisan domestic politics. In countries of less-developed political culture—whether they are "praetorian" or "garrison" states, or "nations in arms"—domestic use of the military is usually more common than its use in foreign policy. In the modern democratic state, the type termed by Rapoport (1962) "military-and-civic polity," soldiers are rarely used domestically, and their task is national defense against foreign threats. Indeed, as has been argued in Chapter 2, the crucial problem of civil-military relations in this type of society is not how to employ soldiers in domestic affairs but how to keep them out of this arena while at the same time maintaining their operational effectiveness.

During the last three decades the academic literature on civil-military relations has paid less attention to this relationship in Western-type democracies, focusing instead on the more dynamic relations between soldiers and civilians in Third World countries. Thus, even though the two most prominent works on civil-military relations in democratic regimes—*The Soldier and the State* by Samuel Huntington and *The Professional Soldier* by Morris Janowitz—were published by the end of the 1950s, they are still considered as the foundation for any discussion of this subject.

Although both studies were written at the same period of time and focus on the American military (Janowitz more than Huntington), there are major differences between them. Janowitz's book, as implied by its subtitle, is "a social and political portrait" of the American professional officer; Huntington's study is about "the theory and politics of civil-military relations." The advantage of Huntington's study for our subject derives not only from its more relevant focus but also from the fact that, apart from its empirical sections, his work offers an elegant framework for the study of civil-military relations in democratic regimes in general and the problem of mutual interference between the military and politics in particular.

Huntington's theory, in a nutshell, regards the military as a profession. As such, the argument goes, it has its own professional ethic. The professional soldier focuses all his energies on his military responsibilities and thus is left with no interest to interfere in civilian affairs. Hence the more professional the soldier and the higher his adherence to the military professional ethic, the less he will be inclined to intervene in politics. According to Huntington, the society that is most likely to enable the military to become professional is the "conservative" society,[1] where politicians avoid interfering with professional military affairs as long as there is no danger of military intervention in politics. In sum, then, Huntington's formula for separating the military from politics calls for maximization of military professionalism and avoidance of political control; it is a self-control system which he terms "objective civilian control."

Huntington's advocacy for objective civilian control has been challenged by Samuel Finer (1988; first published in 1962) and Janowitz (1964). Finer's main argument is that a high level of military professionalism yields, as reality shows, a higher level of military intervention in state politics. Hence professionalism leads not to the military's isolation from politics but exactly to the opposite result. Janowitz presents a similar argument when maintaining that the military develops an "anti-politics" outlook:

> Interest in politics goes hand in hand with a negative outlook and even hostility to politicians and political groups. It is the politics of wanting to be above politics. In fact it could be said that, if the military of the new nations has an ideology, it is distaste for party politics. (p. 65)

As an alternative to Huntington's professionalism, Janowitz suggests his own formula for the regulation of civil-military relations—the "constabulary

---

1. Huntington's "conservatism" is in fact an old-fashioned liberalism characterized mainly by its openness: "[C]onservatism . . . is not monistic and universalistic. It does not attempt to apply the same ideas to all problems and all human institutions. It permits a variety of goals and values" (Huntington 1959, p. 93).

control" system. In essence, this method advocates an integral military, on the one hand, and civil institutions more powerful than the military, on the other, as the best equilibrium between military effectiveness and effective political control. Under such a system

> [t]he constabulary officer performs his duties, which include fighting, because he is professional with a sense of self-esteem and moral worth. Civilian society permits him to maintain his code of honor and encourages him to develop his professional skill. He is amenable to civilian political control because he recognizes that civilians appreciate and understand the tasks and responsibilities of the constabulary force. (Janowitz 1964, p. 440)

Huntington rejects this solution, which falls into the category of what he terms "subjective civilian control," that is, "maximizing of the power of civilian groups in relation to the military" (1959, p. 80). According to his argument, such a method leads to competition between various civilian groups over who will gain more control over the military. The end result is not more effective civilian control but "civilianizing the military, making them the mirror of the state" (ibid., p. 83) or, in other words, making the military a tool of the strongest civilian group.

At least partially, however, the impression of a discrepancy between these arguments is mistaken. Janowitz's and Finer's alleged objection to Huntington's military professionalism as a means to isolate soldiers from politics derives from the fact that the locus of their studies was different from that of his. Whereas Janowitz and Finer focused on the investigation of societies with less-developed political culture or "new nations," Huntington's formula was suggested as a solution to the problem of civil-military relations in societies with a more mature political culture.[2] For their part

---

2. The level of political culture is defined by the level of public consensus regarding the legitimacy of the political system to rule the country. When such a consensus is wide and well established, the political culture of the society is high. When there is no such consensus, the political culture is low or underdeveloped. Finer ranks the level of political culture according to three criteria:

> (1) Does there exist a wide public approval of the procedures for transferring power, and a corresponding belief that no exercise of power in breach of these procedures is legitimate?
> (2) Does there exist a wide public recognition as to who or what constitutes the sovereign authority, and a corresponding belief that no other persons or centre of power is legitimate or duty-worthy?
> (3) Is the public proportionately large and well mobilized into private associations?

Finer and Janowitz were right when arguing that military professionalism in politically underdeveloped countries contributes to the tendency of soldiers to intervene in politics. This is so because, owing to the lack of highly professional and able civilian organs (which is a principal weakness of societies with a low level of political culture), the military perceives itself, and is perceived by large segments of the society, as the only body capable of governing the country. This fact does not contradict Huntington's argument but complements it, for in the politically mature society that is the subject of Huntington's study the military has no monopoly on professionalism and effectiveness, and civilian state organs are no less able to conduct state affairs. Moreover, they can conduct this role more effectively than the military precisely because there is a wide and well-established public consensus regarding their legitimacy to govern the country.

FROM CIVIL-MILITARY TO INTELLIGENCE-STATE RELATIONS

Can Huntington's model of "objective" control and Janowitz's system of "constabulary" control be applied to intelligence-state relations? Huntington's formula is, of course, an ideal solution. Its only problem is that it is hardly feasible with regard to the military and wholly infeasible as the sole means to isolate intelligence from politics. After all, the success of this system is dependent on the readiness of both soldiers and politicians to restrain their behavior. It is possible that the adherence of soldiers to their professional ethic will leave them out of politics. Yet, by the very nature of politics, politicians have hardly any ethic at all. The expectation that they will avoid interfering in professional military affairs simply because soldiers do not interfere in politics seems to be overly optimistic. When it comes to intelligence—a profession that is the "subject, object and instrument of power politics" (Ransom 1987, p. 25)—such expectations have no ground in reality at all. In this sense, given the ever existing urge of politicians to intervene in intelligence affairs in order to increase their power, professionalism per se will not suffice to defend intelligence from such intervention. And such intervention is only the beginning of a spiral process in which the

i.e., do we find cohesive churches, industrial associations and firms, labour unions, and political parties? (Finer 1988, p. 78)

professional level of intelligence agencies decreases and the boundaries between intelligence and politics become far more indistinguishable. Hence Huntington's objective control cannot fully be an answer to the problem.

Janowitz's model of "constabulary control" is not suitable for intelligence-state relations since its main foundation is the integration of the armed forces. Integration may be suitable for military organizations, where cohesiveness and centralized command and control systems are highly desired. It is not desirable for intelligence organizations since cohesiveness, conformity, and centralization come into conflict with essential norms of this profession—openness, divergence of opinion, and intellectual freedom. Hence, in order to prevent the monopoly of a single view, the intelligence community must maintain separate and professionally competitive agencies.

This rejection of the "objective" and "constabulary" control systems does not mean, however, that central elements from each of these methods cannot be incorporated together in order to construct an effective system of political control over intelligence. Hence I suggest that a feasible model of state-intelligence relations can be built on Huntington's principle of professionalism at the bureaucratic level and Janowitz's call for a control system that avoids intervention in professional work at the political (or state) level. The construction of this model according to these two components is the task of Chapter 4.

4

The Professional Dimension of Intelligence

THE CONCEPT OF PROFESSION

A classical definition of the concept of professionalism suggests that an occupation can be defined as a profession when it meets three criteria:

> First . . . is the requirement of formal academic training accompanied by some institutionalized mode of validating both the adequacy of the training and the competence of trained individuals. Among other things, the training must lead to some order of mastery of a generalized cultural tradition, and to do so in a manner giving prominence to an *intellectual* component—that is, it must give primacy of cognitive rationality as applied to a particular field. The second criterion is that not only must the cultural tradition be mastered in the sense of being understood, but skills in some form must also be developed. The third and final core criterion is that a full-fledged profession must have some institutional means of making sure that such competence will be put to socially responsible uses. (Parsons, p. 536)

Huntington also counts three criteria for the definition of professionalism, but his are somewhat different. The first of them, *expertise,* incorporates Talcott Parsons's training and skill. Expertise is a "specialized knowledge and skill in a significant field of human endeavor" that is acquired through a long period of general education and specific experience and study, and it is universal and intellectual in its nature. The second criterion, *social responsibility*, is similar to Parsons's, though its sources are more precisely explained. According to Huntington, responsibility derives from three qualities of the profession: its essentiality for the functioning of the society; the generality of its character; and the monopoly it has over this type of service. Huntington's last criterion, *corporateness*, is not found in the earlier definition. It is a sense of *Gemeinschaft* shared by professional group members in terms of training, type of work, and social responsibility—all of which combine to form a sense of unity among them. Together with the sense of social responsibility, corporateness leads the group member to establish written or unwritten professional ethical codes that set the standards of behavior within the group and with the outside world (Huntington, pp. 8–10).

In his definition Parsons highlights the formal requirements for becoming a member of the professional group. Huntington emphasizes the characteristics of the professional group once it is formed. But since there are no major discrepancies between the two definitions, the criteria used by both are incorporated here. Thus intelligence making can be defined as a profession if it incorporates: (1) formal education and the acquisition of specific skills, mainly as defined by Parsons; (2) social responsibility; (3) corporateness.

INTELLIGENCE: A PROFESSION OR A QUASI-PROFESSION?

Expertise as a Function of Formal Education

The expertise of the intelligence maker is the *management of information*[1] and includes three main functions: collection of information, its analysis,

---

1. Intelligence organizations are established precisely because of the need for information as a means to correctly perceive reality. Although many of these organizations also become responsible for covert operations, this type of action is not unique to intelligence agencies and, to some extent, is alien to the main tasks of the intelligence profession. Covert action uses rather than collects information and in many cases uncovers sources of information rather than protecting them. The main reason for designating the function of covert action to intelligence organizations is more bureaucratic than professional: both demand a high level of secrecy, and it is easier to maintain this secrecy in one organization.

and its distribution.[2] Intelligence officers have different fields of expertise such as military, political, or economic intelligence as well as the study of specific countries or regions. The more capable they are and the more experience they gain, the higher they can climb in the organizational hierarchy, thus becoming managers of information collection, analysis, and distribution.

As with some other professions, the skill demanded from intelligence makers is neither craft, nor art, but (to use Huntington's description of military skills) "an extraordinary complex intellectual skill requiring comprehensive study and training" (p. 13) that is universal in its nature. The intelligence manager need not be the best technical expert in his area of responsibility. Rather, he must be the best expert to manage the resources under his command in order to obtain optimal results.

As far as expertise, skills, and intellectual abilities are concerned, then, intelligence making meets the requirements set forth above. But it does not meet these criteria when it comes to formal education because of three shortcomings. First, unlike classical professions such as medicine or law, or even less typical ones such as military officership, there are hardly any specific formal education requirements for becoming an intelligence maker. Although the majority of intelligence officers today have an academic education, this education is of a general nature and constitutes neither a necessary nor a sufficient condition for becoming a member of the intelligence community. Thus, unlike other professionals who must pass formal examinations regulated by the state to have a formal degree in their professional field, the intelligence officer does not. Instead he gains his education within the organization, mostly in the form of "on the job training."

Second, unlike other professionals who specialize in a narrow field of expertise and climb to senior professional managerial positions in their narrow field, in the intelligence community the boundaries of specialization are more open, and horizontal movement is far more common. One can

2. The main difference between the intelligence maker and other professionals, such as the journalist—who also collects and analyzes information in order to describe reality—is not in the source of information (in both cases it can be open or secret), and not in the relevance of their profession to society (a free press is essential to democracy no less than intelligence), but in the identity and the needs of their masters. The intelligence maker serves the state and performs duties in defense of the national interest; the journalist is employed by a private organ and although he has obligations to society—given his professional service and the principle of freedom of information—he does not serve the state directly. Needless to say, this does not imply that journalism is not a profession.

hardly see an eye doctor becoming the manager of the Intensive Care Unit, but in the intelligence community it is quite ordinary to move an analyst who specialized for years in a given subject to a new position that has little to do with his or her earlier experience or to appoint a specialist in covert action to head an analysis section.

Third, unlike in other professions, promotion within the intelligence community is not limited to members of this group alone. One cannot be nominated to head a medical department in a hospital without being a physician; and one cannot command a military division without being a professional soldier. Yet directors of intelligence agencies can either rise up from within the organization or be brought in from outside,[3] and the same is true with regard to other senior positions within the community. This widely accepted norm of political appointments implies that intelligence is not fully recognized as work that can be done only by professionals. It is clear, then, that as far as formal education and promotion are concerned, intelligence making does not meet the criteria set for its definition as a profession. We shall return to this subject in the summary of this section.

Intelligence as a Social Responsibility

The social responsibility of intelligence is the defense of the state through the collection, analysis, and distribution of information relevant to its security. Like the military, the state is the sole client of the intelligence community and monopolizes all its activities—an arrangement that adds another impetus to intelligence's sense of responsibility. Intelligence officers are motivated by a love for their craft and by their social obligation to their country. This sense of patriotism is enhanced by the monopoly intelligence has over the essential means needed to ensure the state's security. Given this monopoly and responsibility, formal and informal codes to regulate behavior within the intelligence community and between this community and the rest of society are developed.

As is clear from this description, the social responsibility of intelligence officers is different from that of other professionals such as physicians in that the clients of the latter are individuals whereas the client of the former is

3. For example, out of fifteen directors of the CIA between 1946 and 1992, six came directly from the armed forces (four of them from the Navy), and three from business. Only three—Helms, Colby, and Gates—were professional intelligence makers.

society as a whole. In this sense the responsibility of intelligence is the same as that of the military: just as the military meets the criteria of social responsibility (Huntington, pp. 14–16), so does the intelligence community.

Intelligence Making and the Sense of Corporateness

As with social responsibility, intelligence making is very similar to the military when it comes to Huntington's criteria of corporateness. Both the military and the intelligence professions are public bureaucracies, and only their members are entitled by law to practice their respective professions. Both are distinct from the rest of society because of their professional craft and their social responsibility. This distinction is more evident for the military since soldiers wear uniforms; it is less salient for intelligence. It derives from a sense that only the members of the intelligence profession have, and should have, access to secret information that is relevant for the well-being of the nation. If uniforms are the bonding symbols among professional soldiers, secrecy is a major source of bonding among intelligence officers. Being aware of the need to keep information secret within the group, intelligence makers are encouraged to distinguish themselves from outsiders, in fact to compartmentalize themselves from the rest of society. In this sense, whereas in other professions isolation from outsiders is an unintentional result of mutual practice and social responsibility, in intelligence it is a functional imperative.

Conclusions

Intelligence making clearly meets two of the three criteria needed to be defined as a profession but not the third. Indeed, the fact that intelligence is not learned formally but on the job, that it does not involve formal state examinations to be passed before "certification," that specialization is not a condition for promotion within the organization, and that outsiders with no previous experience in this type of work can become professional managers in the intelligence community are all indications that intelligence is not a profession in the classic sense. Yet the difference between intelligence making and classic professions such as medicine or law does not lie only in the formal requirements of education and promotion. These requirements merely derive from the unique character of intelligence work: its multidisciplinary nature and the complex interaction it has with the political environment in which it functions.

The multidisciplinary nature of intelligence work derives from the fact (1) that its task is to gain maximal knowledge on a wide range of issues and (2) that it uses for this purpose methods and techniques from different disciplines. Although, as defined earlier, intelligence agencies collect only information relevant for the "national interest," the values that constitute this concept are broad enough that intelligence can collect almost any type of information. Alexander George and Robert Keohane (p. 224), for example, identify three fundamental values—physical survival, liberty, and economic subsistence—that make up the national interest. The information needed to defend these values involves almost any type of human endeavor, from military and political action to research in physics and computer science. Moreover, in processing this information intelligence uses a wide variety of methods, starting with psychology and sociology and ending with mathematics or chemistry.

The second problem that prevents intelligence making from being regarded as a classic profession involves the essence of intelligence work. Unlike technical professions, intelligence cannot make a scientific and "objective" analysis and prediction. In this respect it is similar to the social sciences and as such suffers from the same type of problems involved in social research. Unlike scientific disciplines such as physics or chemistry, the ability of the social sciences (with the possible exception of economics) to make high-quality predictions is very low.[4] Yet the main contribution of intelligence work to the state is measured precisely by its ability to make good predictions. Specifically, intelligence faces here one unique problem: unlike meteorologists who can forecast the weather but cannot influence it, or physicians who have no motivated biases to influence their diagnosis of the patient, intelligence officers and, even more so, policymakers have both the ability and the interest to intervene in the situation analyzed and predicted by the intelligence. They have the motivation since they have their own personal biases; and they have the ability because the elements of self-fulfilling and self-negating prophecy (or what Karl Popper terms the "Oedipus effect") exist in politics.

4. For an excellent discussion of this problem, termed by Popper as "the anti-naturalistic doctrines of historicism," see Popper 1957, pp. 5–34.

Consequently intelligence work cannot be defined as a profession. But since doing this work demands a high level of intellectual ability and training, it cannot be regarded as a nonprofession either. Hence, given its status between these two poles, we conclude that intelligence is a "quasi-profession."[5]

Yet the fact that intelligence is a quasi-profession does not imply that it has no professional ethic, since the establishment of this code does not exclusively derive from the requirement of formal training, as described in the following section.

THE INTELLIGENCE ETHIC

The Concept

The sources of the professional ethic are social responsibility and a sense of corporateness, as well as lengthy practice in professional work that produces professional thinking. As Huntington points out:

> People who act the same way over a long period of time tend to develop distinctive and persistent habits of thought. Their unique relation to the world gives them a unique perspective on the world and leads them to rationalize their behavior and role. This is particularly true where the role is a professional one. (p. 61)

The combination of values, attitudes, and perspectives that derive directly from the nature of a given profession is the "professional mind." Its ideal and abstract form incorporates only those beliefs that stem directly from the given profession. This ideal type of professional belief system is the *professional ethic*. Its scope, it should be emphasized, is determined by the essence of the given profession. Thus the Hippocratic code, which regulates the relations between doctor and patient, is limited to medical relationships alone. In intelligence the range of responsibilities is far more comprehensive. Hence the scope of the intelligence ethic is far wider than that of most other professions.

---

5. This book will continue, now and then, to refer to intelligence as a profession and to intelligence makers as intelligence professionals. This is done only for the sake of simplicity and in order to avoid a too cumbersome style.

The professional ethic is relevant to our subject for two reasons. First, it should constitute what Handel (1987, p. 13) calls the "professional super-ego," that is, an accepted way of thinking, or an ideal common denominator, that all intelligence makers should strive to achieve. Second, it can serve as a standard to measure how near or far the intelligence organization is from the ideal type of professionalism. The intelligence ethic as described below borrows selectively from Huntington's description of the military ethic (pp. 62–78).

The Intelligence Professional Ethic

The premise that human beings are complicated, selfish animals provides the rationale for the existence of intelligence. The professional intelligence officer is highly aware of the negative aspects of this premise, mainly of the readiness of human beings to resort to violence in order to fulfill their desires. But the intelligence officer is also aware of the other side of selfishness—the ability to satisfy needs by cooperation. Embracing the premise that human beings are complex creatures, intelligence officers accept that there are limits to their capacity to understand the rationality of others and doubt their own ability (despite endless efforts) to perfectly penetrate the minds of others. Hence motivation for the intelligence maker remains uncertain and can be ultimately understood only ex post facto.

Intelligence professionals believe that a healthy society is built on values of collectiveness, tradition, and unity, but also on open criticism, individualism, and originality. They also believe in morality. This derives not only from their personal beliefs but also from experience showing that extensive use of immoral methods can, in the long run, become counterproductive. For this reason they perceive a fundamental tension between intelligence effectiveness and immorality. They nevertheless accept that under certain circumstances, when the welfare of the state demands it, immoral methods can be selectively used. In this regard, like professional diplomats, they are ready to lie for their country but only as a last resort.

The values most highly esteemed by intelligence officers are truth, honesty, and trust. Although they are aware of the consumer's preference for reports that correspond to their own parochial political interests, they reject this need as a factor in the conduct of intelligence work. The belief in honest reporting as a norm that should never be violated derives from two sources. First, it is fundamental for intelligence work; without it there would be no value for the intelligence product. Second, the readiness of consumers to accept the intelligence product is determined not only by trust in the intelligence makers' professional qualifications but also by dependence on their impartiality and personal integrity. Trust and integrity are scarce resources in politics, and intelligence officers, who know that their ability to influence the policymaking process is dependent in the long run on these qualities, will never sacrifice them in order to achieve short-run influence.

History is a major source of learning for members of the intelligence community. In studying history the professional mind tends to emphasize failures rather than successes and draws more lessons from "Pearl Harbors" and "Barbarossas" than from "Ultras" and "Magics." The usefulness of historical lessons is limited since history is a description and explanation of the past, whereas the duty of an intelligence officer is to describe and explain the present and, if possible, also the near future. The principal lesson from history is that certainty never exists and that prudence is always necessary.

Intelligence officers regard the international arena as chaotic by nature, an environment in which no law except the "law of the jungle" exists. Moreover, they have very little faith, if any at all, in international organizations and international treaties as means to regulate this chaos. While perceiving the nation-state as the prime actor in this arena, analysts are also aware of the existence of other actors, such as multinational corporations or international terrorism. Hence the international environment confronts them with a wide spectrum of threats of which the most crucial ones are surprise attack and general war. Despite this emphasis on risks, intelligence officers being realists are aware that the international environment offers opportunities as well. For this reason they are permanently vigilant to receive not only negative but also positive signals.

In estimating threats intelligence makers take into account intentions no less than capabilities.[6] But since they know that nothing is certain, they are very prudent in this task. On the basis of the information available, their intellectual abilities, and their professional experience, they make educated assumptions about the intentions of friends and foes but only in terms of low and high probabilities. Moreover, they are always aware of the possibility of deception. Hence, unlike physicians, whose common wisdom is that

6. Here the intelligence officer clearly differs from the professional soldier. The latter emphasizes capabilities and is careful not to engage in estimation of intentions since this is clearly beyond his or her sense of responsibility. For this reason soldiers, more than intelligence makers, tend to engage in worst-case analyses.

"when one hears hoof beats, one should look for horses, not zebras," intelligence officers are always suspicious that the hoof beats that they hear are those of the zebra and that it is their opponents who want them to believe that the sounds are caused by a horse. Here, more than anywhere else, the Socratic principle of "I know that I do not know" serves as their guiding light.

Intelligence makers have a craving to maximize their means of collecting information. In this regard there is no limit to what further assets they would like to have, for their belief is that additional capabilities will enable them to better serve their country. Being aware of how crucial these means are to national security, they automatically object to any use of information that might reveal the existence of these means to the target state. Hence they tend to avoid action that may compromise their intelligence assets. Similarly, they tend to object to spectacular covert operations that cannot remain covert or that might put at risk their secret sources of information. Like the professional soldier, the intelligence officer "always favors preparedness, but never feels prepared" (Huntington, p. 69).

Despite their specialized knowledge in foreign affairs, intelligence makers are aware of the political limitations of their profession. Where policymaking is concerned, they know that they see only a part of the picture while their superiors, the top-level policymakers, comprehend more of it. Their role at this juncture is to ensure that the information and analysis in their possession are given to policymakers in the most accurate and objective way. Professional intelligence making does not directly involve advice on how to conduct policy (with the exception of covert action). Exactly for this reason professional intelligence makers believe that their role is not to "sell" the intelligence product but to give policymakers a product that reflects as much as possible "the truth, the whole truth, and nothing but the truth." This does not imply that intelligence makers have no interest in influencing the policymaking process. Since they are patriots who believe in the relevance of their product to policymaking, they have a professional interest in gaining influence. But, when having to choose between truth and influence, they will always choose the first.

Intelligence makers are aware of the potential presence of a "gray area" where intelligence and policymaking overlap. But since they are professionals, they try to minimize these unclear boundaries. They object to politicians' attempts to interfere with their professional affairs and themselves avoid any actions that might constitute intervention in politics. Consequently, they perceive a high degree of separation between intelligence and politics as the key to both effective political control and efficient intelligence performance.

Intelligence officers accept as a rule the supremacy of policy over intelligence, yet they are aware that there may be rare situations in which they cannot accept the judgment of the policymaker because of professional beliefs. Under such circumstances they should take any means necessary to bring to the attention of the policymaker their reservations, in an attempt to change policy. If no outlet remains, intelligence makers have the personal (but not collective) option of resignation as a kind of political protest.[7] Such occasions, as the prudent officer knows, are very rare. Other than these instances, intelligence work should be kept as distinct as possible from politics, for politics is the most damaging endeavor to professional intelligence making.

Conclusions

This portrait of intelligence ethics leads to two conclusions. First, in many of its features the intelligence ethic resembles the ethic of professional soldiers; in others it is more similar to the ethic of diplomats. It parallels the military ethic in that both perceive the international environment as chaotic, with power as the main instrument to regulate this chaos. They both believe in the realistic principle of "self-reliance," in the need to maximize military and intelligence capabilities, and in prudent use of the means available. More like diplomats, intelligence makers believe that relations between states are not built only on a "zero-sum" basis, and although they look for threats, they also seek opportunities for beneficial cooperation between states. Indeed, given the scope of their responsibilities, there is little wonder why intelligence makers develop a way of thinking that incorporates professional elements from the other two bureaucracies involved in foreign policymaking. All in all this mind-set can be character-

7. The right to resign is a principal feature that distinguishes democratic from nondemocratic societies. In a democracy professional intelligence officers relinquish only their careers when they resign. The cost of such an act of protest in nondemocratic regimes might go far beyond one's personal career, to include risk of personal freedom or even life. This principal difference in the personal cost involved makes it far more feasible for intelligence officers to follow their ethics in democratic societies.

ized as realistic, skeptical, prudent, nonmonistic, and, most important, containing a high level of personal integrity.

The second conclusion is more closely related to the main subject of this book. Professional intelligence officers, like professional soldiers and diplomats, accept the supremacy of the state, embodied in its political leaders, but resist political intervention in their own professional affairs. Since unclear boundaries between professional and political affairs are the most serious obstacle for the proper conduct of intelligence work, the intelligence officer has a crucial interest in maximizing the separation of the two. Thus the final conclusion that derives from this discussion is that the more professional intelligence officers are, the less will be their interest to intervene in politics and the higher will be their interest to prevent politicians from interfering in their professional work. Hence professionalism is a key variable for the separation of intelligence and politics. And the level of intelligence officers' professionalism may be measured by how well their professional belief system approximates the model of the intelligence professional ethic.

5

The Political Control
of Intelligence

Ancient writers were aware of the need to guard the guards. Aristotle raised this point in the context of state politics in *Politica* (1322a). The Roman satirist Juvenal alluded to this issue when discussing the low morals of the Roman wives of his times (*Satires* 6), and a generation ago a popular song used to ask "Who takes care of the Caretaker's daughter / when the Caretaker's busy taking care?"

Indeed, important as it is, professionalism by itself is not a guarantee for avoiding, in the long run, the corruption of the intelligence process. If the political environment blurs the boundaries between intelligence and politics and creates opportunities for political interference with professional intelligence work and abuse of its product, the intelligence community will inevitably follow suit. Hence the second variable that determines the quality of intelligence-state relations is the political environment in which intelligence functions.

Democratic societies, which grant individuals considerable personal freedom, encourage intelligence professionalism more than nondemocratic regimes, since the latter leave individuals insufficient room for discretion when professional and political considerations come into conflict with each other. Despite this advantage, both types of regimes need instruments to prevent the corruption of the relationship between intelligence and the state. Given the supremacy of politics over intelligence, such control systems must be political. What types of political control systems are possible, how to measure their quality, and how they interact with intelligence in reality are the subject of this section.

THE CONCEPT

Unlike professionialism, which is a universal and objective concept, political control, whether it is of the military or of intelligence, is far more difficult to define. Each country develops its own control mechanisms in its own image, on the basis of its political culture, national experience, balance of forces between opposing political groups, or security needs. And since the political control system reflects the politics of the country it serves, a system that may be suitable for one country may not be suitable for another.

The rapid increase of independent nations in the post-World War II era produced an increased number of patterns of civil-military relations and political control systems. Thus, for example, whereas Janowitz (1957) offered four types of civil-military relations and Rapoport (1962) suggested only three such models, Luckham (1971) counted nine categories—some containing subcategories—with each of them employing a different type of political control system over the military.

This great variance in civil-military relations is the result of the crucial role of military organizations in all aspects of societal life and of the many functions that the military can perform within society. Intelligence organizations, on the other hand, have a far more limited role, and when it comes to a democratic society, their only recognized task is to collect, analyze, and distribute information relevant for the defense of the national interest.[1] Thus political control over intelligence in democracies must meet two demands: preventing intelligence from interfering with politics and politicians from intervening in professional intelligence work; and enabling the intelligence community to maintain a high level of operational effectiveness.

The key to attaining these goals is the ability of the control system to establish a high level of mutual trust—within and between the intelligence community, the political system, and the general public—that intelligence and politics are, indeed, kept separate from each other. The ability of the system to establish and maintain this trust is obviously a function of its measure of success in actually reaching this goal. This, however, depends

---

1. Although it was argued earlier that the military's only role in democratic societies is the defense against external threats, at times of emergency the army can be used for other roles as well. For example, the Israeli army of the early 1950s played a major role and invested extensive resources in absorbing the massive wave of immigration to the country, a task that had no direct relation to the actual defense of the state. Intelligence organizations, owing to their far smaller size, cannot be used for any role other than their professional one.

extensively on the readiness of the actors involved—especially opposition parties in the political system—to trust that their opponents will avoid abusing their power. Thus the key criterion to measure the quality of any given control system is its ability to construct and maintain this confidence.

FOUR TYPES OF CONTROL SYSTEMS

The difference between control systems is, principally, the function of two variables: *participation*—which of the state's political institutions participate in controlling intelligence; and *means*—which way this control is maintained.

Two methods of participation are possible: *unilateral*—when a single institution controls intelligence; or *multilateral*—when at least two state institutions are responsible for this task. Given that intelligence is a part of the executive branch, control over the service devolves to this branch according to the unilateral method. In a more extreme form of this system, control over the service is exclusively maintained by a single, or very small, group within the executive branch. In the multilateral system, control is maintained by the executive and the legislative branches, possibly also by the judicial branch, as well as by informal groups such as the media, pressure groups, and public opinion. In political systems that do not practically maintain a system of distribution of powers, a limited form of the multilateral method may be employed through a division of control between various groups within the executive branch.

The means by which control is maintained may also be divided into two types: *personal,* in which individuals who are trusted to represent the interests of politicians are put in managerial positions in intelligence institutions in order to ensure that the agencies act in accordance with the policies outlined by these politicians; and *constitutional,* in which the regulation of control is maintained by state law.

Altogether the interaction between these variables yields four possible types of political control systems as shown in Table 2.

As with any theoretical model, these four methods represent ideal types that do not exist in a pure form in reality. Nevertheless, it is possible to identify the main characters of existing control methods and to categorize them according to these four ideal-type models. A short analysis of the four

Table 2.   Four methods of political control of intelligence

		PARTICIPATION	
		Unilateral	Multilateral
MEANS	Personal	Unilateral-personal	Multilateral-personal
	Constitutional	Unilateral-constitutional	Multilateral-constitutional

methods, how they function in reality and the way they interact with intelligence organizations, is presented in the next section.

POLITICAL CONTROL AND INTELLIGENCE

Of the four types of suggested political control systems the *unilateral-personal* method is the least likely to prevent the corruption of state-intelligence relations. Basically this system uses individuals selected by the executive branch for senior positions in the intelligence community as a means to ensure that the services act in accordance with the government's policy. Even if initially no abuse of this monopoly takes place, the fact that this method is regulated by persons rather than by law and does not allow the legislative branch formal access to intelligence makes its corruption unavoidable in the long run. Although such a method can ensure intelligence loyalty to the government in power, it cannot prevent the use of the intelligence community for parochial political interests, and it opens the way for parochial alliances between intelligence and politicians. Under such conditions it is impossible to establish a trustful relationship between the government and the opposition regarding intelligence policies. As for the intelligence community itself, even a very strong and highly professional service can fall victim to the deficiencies of this system, and if it lacks in professionalism, it is sure to become a partisan rather than a state instrument.

The unilateral-personal control model is the most widely used method to supervise intelligence organizations in countries with a low level of political culture. In such societies, where distribution of power does not exist, the most important factor in selecting heads of intelligence services is their loyalty to the single leader or junta in power. In some nondemocratic regimes personal loyalty combines forces with nepotism. In Syria, for example, the head of the special forces in charge of internal security used to be Rifaat Asad, the brother of the Syrian president, and in Rumania under Ceausescu key positions in the security services were held by members of the Ceausescu family.

Unilateral-personal control systems in their pure form are almost never found in democracies, where distribution of power is the foundation of political life. But even in such regimes this type of control can sometimes be used by ambitious politicians. For example, in 1981 Ariel Sharon, Israel's Minister of Defense (1981–83), nominated one of his cronies, Rafael Eitan, to head Israel's Science Liaison Bureau (Lakam), a top secret agency in the Defense Ministry that dealt with industrial and scientific espionage. Other politicians in Israel hardly knew of the existence of this agency, and the heads of Israel's intelligence community could do nothing to prevent Sharon's drive to obtain personal access into the intelligence system.[2]

Even a narrow opening for the use of the unilateral-personal control method can involve serious risks. The American control system, probably the most sophisticated system yet to exist, enabled President Reagan to appoint William Casey—who served earlier as his presidential campaign manager—to head the CIA. Obviously, the president's prime consideration in making this appointment was his desire to have his own man running the agency. Indeed, Casey's nomination was followed by White House pressures on the agency to adapt itself to new policies. In this case the damage to intelligence was limited since the CIA by the early 1980s was highly professional and strong enough to reject most of the pressure. This strength, it should be noted, derived largely from the fact that by this stage the American political control system was already of a multilateral-constitutional type.

In the *multilateral-personal* system, control is also employed by the appointment of outsiders to key positions in the intelligence services. Yet this system allows other groups that participate in the political process direct access to the intelligence community through representatives of their own.

2. The way the system worked in this particular case demonstrates some of its principal deficiencies. Lack of proper supervision enabled Eitan to break all norms of the Israeli intelligence community by recruiting Jonathan Pollard, an American Jew who worked as an analyst for Naval Intelligence. Pollard's capture in 1985 caused great damage to American-Israeli relations in general and to their intelligence cooperation in particular.

Although this method decreases the risk that intelligence will become a single party's instrument, it nevertheless increases the danger of political contention within the intelligence community, thus making it merely another arena of political competition. The less professional the community, the higher the likelihood that this danger will materialize.

It is difficult to find examples of this system in reality. In countries where the principle of distribution of power dominates, control of the intelligence system is usually maintained by law rather than by personal arrangements. In countries with a low level of political culture, the system employed is unilateral rather than multilateral. A system that partially resembles the method of multilateral control is the one used in the Soviet Union where, after Stalin's death, the selection of senior officials in the intelligence system involved a bargaining process between various opposing groups of the ruling Politburo. This bargaining process usually ended in a compromise that reflected the balance of forces within the Politburo. In Britain, where the intelligence services only recently have started to come out of the closet, ideas for some form of supervision by a variant of the multilateral-personal system are being put forward. In late 1992 the Home-Affairs Selected Committee suggested, unanimously, that it should oversee the activities of MI5, the British Security Service. Prime Minister Major and his security chiefs proposed, in response, the establishment of a five-man team of privy councillors chosen by the Prime Minister with cross-party agreement (*The Economist*, 24 July 1993, p. 37). To a limited extent this system is also reflected in the way the DCI is selected to his post in the United States: although the president has the prerogative to make the selection, the Congress has the right to veto it.[3]

The third method is *unilateral-constitutional*. In this system the executive branch has a de facto monopoly in controlling intelligence, but this is regulated by law or by institutionalized ethical norms rather than by personal means. Hence this type of control can be maintained only in politically developed societies. Employment of this control method demands that other participants in the political process have little interest in intelligence affairs or that they fully trust the executive branch not to abuse its excessive power. They would be motivated to act this way mainly by patriotism—the belief that secrecy is essential for effective intelligence conduct and that it cannot be maintained if other groups participate in control.

3. Section 102 of the National Security Act of 1947, which first established this arrangement, says: "The Director shall be appointed by the President, by and with the advice and consent of the Senate" (Leary 1984, p. 128).

The ability of this system to separate intelligence from politics depends on the readiness of the executive branch to restrain its power and on the professional level of the intelligence community. If both conditions are met, such a system can work. Its main test comes at times of crisis, when sharp cleavages regarding the use of the intelligence services arise within the executive branch or between opposing political parties, or both. Under such circumstances, especially when the services are not professional enough, the boundaries between intelligence and politics are very likely to collapse.

Although it was employed in the United States until the mid-1970s, this method is more likely to be found in parliamentary rather than presidential systems. In theory, parliamentary systems—where the government's ability to remain in power depends on its ability to maintain a majority in the parliament—create better conditions for shared control of intelligence. In practice, however, since members of the parliament are elected through a party system—thus becoming dependent on senior party members who hold key positions in the executive branch—the de facto situation is that the parliament is highly dependent on the government rather than the other way around. This dependency facilitates the creation of practical means—as is still the case, for example, in Britain and in Israel—that leave the legislative branch out of direct participation in the control of the intelligence services. The media are neutralized from monitoring these activities through practical arrangements as well. In Britain this neutralization is accomplished through the "D-notice" system in which the press accepts the authority of the executive branch to censor information (Palmer, pp. 227–49). In Israel the chief editors of the press are briefed on sensitive issues by the government on condition that they will not use this information.

Experience shows that the unilateral-constitutional control system is fragile and tends to break down under severe pressure (see the account of the Israeli and British episodes that follows). Hence, while this method suits democratic societies more than the previously described methods, its fragility makes it less desirable when compared to the fourth control method, the *multilateral-constitutional* system.

The implementation of this fourth method requires a consensus within the political system about principles, such as the ethical rules that the services should follow and the need to avoid the politicization of the intelligence community. If such a consensus is reached, the multilateral-constitutional system offers a method of checks and balances that prevents one branch from taking control over intelligence and a form of legal control that makes political intervention in professional intelligence work far more difficult. Under such a system the intelligence community can reach professional autonomy and, at the same time, reduce its ability and tendency to intervene in politics.

Multilateral-constitutional control systems can be established only in countries in which political culture is highly developed and in which intelligence organizations are highly professionalized. The system has been under trial in the United States since the mid-1970s, when competition intensified between the executive and legislative branches over who would control the CIA.[4] As a result of this debate, Congress's share in the oversight of intelligence activities became far more decisive. So, too, did monitoring by the media, which turned into an effective watchdog of the nexus between the administration and the CIA.

Antagonists of this system have argued before, during, and after its establishment that it would lead both to the politicization of the CIA and to a sharp decrease in its operational effectiveness and ability to keep functional secrecy. Yet, although there is no doubt that the growing involvement of Congress and the media in the CIA's affairs decreased the agency's freedom of action and, possibly, even its operational effectiveness, there is no indication that the CIA has become less professional in its main task—the collection, analysis, and distribution of information. Most important, the system revived congressional and public trust in the CIA—a necessary condition for its proper functioning—and limited the ability of the executive branch to pressure the CIA politically.

Successful as the multilateral-constitutional method can be, even this system cannot fully prevent frictions between politics and intelligence from arising since much depends also on the human factor—the readiness of politicians and intelligence officers to restrain their behavior and avoid intervention in each other's domain. Unlike the other control systems, however, this one provides optimal conditions for the prevention of such behavior. In this sense, of the four control systems discussed, the multilateral-constitutional system is the most desirable.

A concise summary of the interaction between the four types of control systems and professional and nonprofessional intelligence organizations is presented in Table 3.

4. For a concise description of how congressional and public faith in the CIA collapsed, see e.g. Jeffreys-Jones 1989, pp. 194–215, and Ranelagh 1987, pp. 584–626. For the DCI's perspective on this period, see Colby 1978, pp. 389–424.

Table 3. Interaction between control systems and intelligence organizations

Intelligence Organization	Control System			
	Unilateral-personal	Multilateral-personal	Unilateral-constitutional	Multilateral-constitutional
Professional intelligence		USSR (?) PRC (?)	Israel Britain	CIA since 1975
Nonprofessional intelligence	Third World countries		Britain in the 1920s; Israel in 1954	

CONCLUSIONS

Four points should be emphasized in concluding this section. First, an effective control system is a necessary condition to prevent the degradation of intelligence-state relations. Without it even a strong and highly professional organization is likely to lose its integrity in the long run. Second, political control systems reflect the societies they serve, their security needs, dominant societal values, political systems, and political cultures. Hence different societies develop different control systems, and a system that is suitable to one society cannot always be constructed in another. Third, in democratic regimes, control systems—whether they are unilateral or multilateral—are maintained by law. The multilateral-constitutional system offers a better equilibrium of effective control and intelligence performance than the unilateral system. Fourth, even the combination of a highly professional intelligence organization and an effective political control system cannot fully prevent the corruption of the system. It makes such a development far less likely, but ultimately whether such corruption occurs depends also on individuals and the level of their personal integrity and political ambitions.

Summary

This part of the book set the theoretical foundations. It began with the premise that intervention of intelligence and politics in each other's domain is a universal problem, a typical pattern of human behavior limited neither to a specific society nor to any one period of time. In analyzing the present academic discussion of this problem, I identified some of the shortcomings involved in the debate. The most important of these were: (1) the lack of a general theoretical framework for discussing the problem; (2) the reluctance of most participants in the debate to recognize the direct link between unclear boundaries separating intelligence from politics and serious cases of intelligence intervention in politics; and (3) the lack of comparative studies on this subject.

Given the unsatisfactory state of the literature on intelligence-state relations, I compared this interaction with civil-military relations, which is a far more developed domain of academic investigation. I concluded that, although the two fields deal with similar problems, there are unique features in the relations between intelligence and policymakers that prevent a full adaptation of a single theory from civil-military relations. Instead, after analyzing various aspects of the problem in both fields, I suggested the incorporation of two means to separate intelligence from politics: a high level of professionalism at the bureaucratic (or intelligence) level; and a multilateral-constitutional control system at the state (or political) level. Hence this theoretical introduction concludes with the proposition that a combination of these two will offer the optimal equilibrium between effective state control of intelligence and intelligence effectiveness.

Part II

Intelligence Intervention
in Politics

Introduction

THE GENERAL CONTEXT

Interaction between the tendency of intelligence to interfere with politics and the tendency of politics to intervene in professional intelligence work can yield four outcomes, as described in Table 4.

Table 4.   Intervention as the outcome of intelligence-politics relations

		Tendency of politics to intervene in intelligence	
		LOW	HIGH
Tendency of intelligence to intervene in politics	LOW	(1) Low intervention: Holland Denmark Switzerland	(2) Political intervention in intelligence: Nazi Germany Stalinist Russia
	HIGH	(3) Intelligence intervention in politics: United States—1961 Israel—1954 Britain—1920s	(4) Mutual intervention: Most Third World countries

The first outcome (number 1) represents the ideal type of relationship. In this situation the political level does not intervene in professional intelligence affairs, usually because intelligence is regarded as not very relevant to national security and therefore to politicians and also because there is a prevalent belief that intelligence should be politically neutral. Intelligence makers for their part perceive interference with politics as an undesirable action owing to their high level of professionalism and their adherence to the professional ethic. Moreover, from their perspective, intervention in politics is counterproductive because it may undermine the credibility of their product as representing a purely professional standard to policymakers.

This ideal model is most likely to exist in countries with a high level of political culture and a perception of a low level of external threat. Their political cultures determine the norm that intelligence and politics should be separate. The perception of their status in the international arena makes the use of intelligence warfare—except for defensive purposes—rather unnecessary and thus creates few opportunities for frictions between intelligence and politics. Small NATO countries such as Denmark or Holland, which used to protect themselves through membership in a defensive alliance and through the protective umbrella of larger powers rather than by using their own military power, were typical societies in which such a relationship could be maintained. The same is true with regard to countries such as Switzerland or Sweden, which enjoyed the same type of political culture but used neutrality as their main means of defense. Although these conditions do not exist in many other countries, which either lack a high level of political culture or resort to extensive use of intelligence or both, this type of relationship can nevertheless serve as a model that both intelligence and policymakers should try to achieve.

The fourth type of relationship represents the worst of both worlds. It is the situation in which there is mutual distrust between intelligence and the political echelon, which results in parochial alignments between intelligence officers and policymakers and the negligence of service to the national interest. As was mentioned before, this type of relationship is very typical of many Third World countries with a less-developed political culture.

Relationships between intelligence and politics in countries with a developed political culture and a high level of political interest in intelligence usually fall somewhere between the first and the fourth models. In such countries some level of interference between intelligence and policymaking is maintained. In some cases—as in the United States since the mid-1970s, during which time a high level of intelligence professionalism and an effective control system have been maintained—the situation is relatively better. In others, such as Israel, where the intelligence is professional but the control system is not as effective, the character of the relationship is somewhat closer to the fourth model.

The second type of relationship is typical of situations in which strong leaders prefer to be their own intelligence analysts and compel their intelligence organizations to accept their opinion. For example, Churchill during his service as First Lord of the Admiralty in 1939–40 limited the distribution of reports of Naval Intelligence that contradicted his own public statements (Handel 1987, pp. 8–9). In its more extreme form, when leaders have both unlimited power and a great belief in their "intelligence genius," the result is regular political interference in intelligence affairs and selective use of the intelligence product. Obviously, under such circumstances no intelligence community can preserve its professional standards. The relationship between Hitler and his Abwehr is one such example. The way Stalin ignored the numerous intelligence reports on the coming German attack in 1940–41, compelling his intelligence services to misrepresent the information they had obtained (Whaley 1973), is another.

The third outcome involves situations in which there is insufficient political control of the intelligence services and an insufficient level of professionalism within the intelligence community. At times of crisis these conditions may lead intelligence to intervene in politics. This type of behavior is the subject of this book.

INTELLIGENCE INTERVENTION IN POLITICS: DEFINITION AND TYPOLOGY

Intelligence intervention in politics may be defined in two ways. The first is an indirect definition, which considers any action taken consciously by intelligence makers in contradiction to their professional role as an intervention in politics. If the role of intelligence is defined as a combination of two tasks—first, to collect, analyze, and distribute information relevant to national security as objectively as possible and, second, to conduct covert action with the proper political authorization—any action by intelligence makers that consciously violates this definition constitutes an intelligence intervention in politics.

The alternative definition regards intelligence intervention in politics as any deliberate action taken by intelligence that derives from at least some parochial political motivations.

Intelligence intervention in politics includes such acts as concealment and manipulation of information over which the intelligence services have a monopoly, unauthorized use of intelligence assets, mainly the means of covert action, or conspiracy against political institutions. Usually such misbehavior involves different mixes of these methods. Hence a better typology of this type of behavior may be achieved by reference to the goal of the intelligence action. According to this parameter it is possible to identify two types of intelligence intervention in politics: the first, "intelligence to please," is the corruption of the intelligence ethic in order to support the policy of the government in power. The second, an action taken in opposition to the policy of the elected government, will be termed here as "alteration of policy." This second type of intelligence intervention in politics is the subject of the four case studies of this book.

THE CASE STUDIES: A FRAMEWORK FOR ANALYSIS

The empirical part of the book investigates, through detailed case studies, situations in which intelligence organizations and individuals intervened in politics in order to alter the policies of the government in power. Generally, these cases answer three questions: How and by what means do intelligence organizations intervene in politics? Why do they do it? And what conditions, at all levels of analysis, make it possible for them to behave this way? More specifically, the cases are used to provide empirical support for three interrelated propositions that derive from the theoretical discussion:

1. *That unauthorized intelligence attempts to alter the policy of the elected government are not isolated incidents but the culmination of a process in which the distinction between intelligence and politics becomes steadily less clear.* There is, in other words, a definite link between the failure of intelligence officers and politicians to clearly separate their respective domains and intelligence and political fiascoes.

2. *That there is a high correlation between a low level of intelligence expertise and the tendency of intelligence to intervene in politics.* Thus intelligence officers who intervene in politics are often more likely to demonstrate poor performances in professional aspects of their work, such as confusing ends and means, unrealistic estimation of threats and opportunities, selective use of information according to preconceived biases, and indulgence in best-case and worst-case scenarios. Moreover, empirical evidence will show that intelligence officers tend to intervene in politics precisely because they are unprofessional. This tendency is, then, the effect and not the cause of a poor level of

professionalism. Had the argument been the other way around, it would have been tautological.

3. *That the unilateral-constitutional control method, the one system that was employed in all the cases under investigation, is not sufficient to prevent intelligence from intervening in politics.* Consequently, it will be argued, a higher level of oversight by the legislative branch and the public—as embodied in the system of multilateral-constitutional control—offers a better chance to prevent intelligence and political fiascoes.

The independent variables in each of the case studies are the conditions at four levels of analysis—the structural (international system), the state, the bureaucracy, and the personal—that shape the likelihood of intelligence intervention in politics. The intervening variable is the tendency of intelligence either to intervene in politics or to avoid such action. The dependent variable comprises not only the outcome of this tendency—which, in the four cases selected, amounted to a conscious decision to intervene in politics—but also the way this decision was translated into action.

As a class the events covered in this book involve situations in which senior intelligence makers intervene in their own country's politics. As was noted earlier, these situations can be divided into two subclasses: first, intervention taken in order to please consumers; and, second, intervention taken in defiance of consumers' policy. The term "consumer" refers here to the leader of the country—the president in the American case and the prime minister in the Israeli and British cases. Focusing on this level of course does not exclude the possibility of cooperation between intelligence and lower-level policymakers. All of the four case studies selected come from the second subclass of events. In addition, since intelligence behavior is influenced by the type of regime the state has, this variance was limited also by investigating only second subclass events that took place in democracies.

The case studies were selected according to the following criteria:

1. *The level of intensity of the intelligence intervention in politics.* Within the second subclass of events this book distinguishes between three such levels: alteration of means—intelligence action in accordance with the leader's policy goals but by means not approved by him; alteration of ends—intelligence action in contradiction of the leader's policy goals; and alteration of government—intelligence action aimed directly or indirectly at changing the elected government. The Ameri-

can case study represents the first type, the Israeli case the second, and the British cases the third.

2. *Cross-country comparability.* A fundamental assumption of this book is that intelligence intervention in politics is a universal problem. Hence there is a need to study it on the basis of more than one state's experience. As already mentioned, countries were selected primarily according to their type of regime. Further selection was done according to the criteria listed below.

3. *The significance of the cases.* Each case represents a highly significant event in the history of the country involved. Although the British case of 1920 did not play a major role in Britain's history, it at least had the potential to do so.

4. *The availability of primary sources.* Given the controversy involving situations in which intelligence communities interfere with politics and the possible tendency of secondary sources to be biased in describing the events, the use of documentary evidence was considered to be highly necessary for the proper construction of the case studies. In the Israeli case, where documents were rather scarce, interviews with most persons involved in the events were used in order to bridge this gap. The need to use primary sources implies that more modern case studies could not be used.[1] Language was, of course, another technical parameter in selecting the case studies.

5. *Originality.* Although the American case of the "Bay of Pigs" and the 1924 British case of the "Zinoviev letter" have already received attention, the Israeli and the 1920 British cases have hardly received any. Given the potential interest of students of intelligence and politics not only in the theoretical aspects of this subject but also in the empirical evidence, these cases were selected in order to familiarize readers with previously unknown information.

---

1. The most interesting case of this type is the "Harold Wilson" plot in which, so it is argued, officers of MI5 and MI6 with colleagues from the CIA and BOSS conspired against the British prime minister (see Wright 1987, Pincher 1988, Leigh 1988, Dorril and Ramsay 1991). Yet the type and the quality of the data available at present on this case make it unsuitable for my type of research. Another possible case study is that of the CIA's involvement in the Iran-contra affair. Here the problem is just the opposite, namely, that too much evidence is available and new evidence comes to light frequently and will continue to do so in the future.

6

Alteration of Means:
The CIA and the Bay of Pigs

> Colonel Saito, have you a knife? I just realized the bridge has been mined.—British POW Colonel Nicholson to the commander of the Japanese POW camp, Colonel Saito, minutes before an important Japanese military train was to cross the bridge (*The Bridge Over the River Kwai*, the movie)

The humiliating failure of the 1961 American paramilitary operation to overthrow Castro's regime in Cuba received much attention in both academic and nonacademic literature. Usually known as the "Bay of Pigs" or "Operation Zapata," after the name of the proposed landing site of the Cuban exiles, it was dubbed by some scholars "the perfect failure." Indeed, all the bureaucracies involved in making, evaluating, and authorizing this venture—the CIA, the Joint Chiefs of Staff (JCS), the State Department, and the White House—failed to carry out their tasks properly, and each must bear its own share for the blame of what constitutes the classic failure of covert action during the Cold War era.

Some investigations of this episode focus on only one of its aspects. Johnson (1964), for example, studied it mainly from the perspective of the Cuban leaders of Brigade 2506, the invading force that landed at the Bay of Pigs in the early hours of 17 April 1961; Janis (1972) analyzed how President Kennedy and his close aides went about authorizing the project, concluding that their malfunction was to a large extent the result of "groupthink." Others (e.g. Wyden 1979, Higgins 1987) have made detailed studies of the episode in all of its many dimensions. The largest body of literature on the subject, finally, is to be found in the many academic, journalistic, and personal histories of the CIA following Watergate and its attendant congressional investigations of U.S. intelligence activities (e.g., Hunt 1973, Smith 1976, Phillips 1977, Prados 1986, Ranelagh 1987, and Jeffreys-Jones 1989).

This chapter will investigate the way in which the CIA interfered with the political process in order to implement the project, the causes of the agency's behavior, and the conditions that enabled it to act as it did. Because the many aspects of this operation are already well documented, I will refrain from repeating them. Instead, the first part of this chapter will focus on three issues. First, I look at how the CIA, after being authorized in March 1960 to carry out a specific program to overthrow Castro by a combination of political, psychological, and guerilla warfare, eight months later introduced and implemented a totally new concept of invasion without receiving the political authority to do so. Thus the CIA created a fait accompli for President Eisenhower, who authorized this change ex post facto during the last days of his administration. Second, I inquire into how the CIA convinced President Kennedy and his aides that its ambitious and hazardous plan was not just militarily and politically feasible but virtually fail-safe, even though many of the planners themselves did not really believe so. Third, I ask how, despite presidential instructions that under no circumstances would American forces intervene directly in the operation, senior CIA officers could assume that, if the invasion failed, such intervention would be inevitable. As Allen Dulles admitted later: "We felt that when the chips were down—when the crisis arose in reality, any action required for success [that is, direct American intervention] would be authorized rather than permit the enterprise to fail" (Vandenbroucke, p. 369). Needless to say, Dulles and his aides had never apprised the White House of their feeling.

The second part of this chapter will answer two questions. First, what could have motivated the CIA senior officers in charge of the Cuban project to behave as they did? Second, what factors enabled the CIA, whose role was supposedly limited to supplying information and advice to the President and implementing his covert action policy, to become an independent actor in the process of the U.S. foreign policy making?

THE CONCEPT AND ITS IMPLEMENTATION: JANUARY 1960–APRIL 1961

January 1960–January 1961: From SOE to D-Day

Cuba did not rank high on the Eisenhower administration's order of priorities through most of Castro's first year in power. Only towards the end of 1959 did the dimensions of the threat posed by the revolutionary regime in Havana to American hegemony in the Western Hemisphere become clear and the need to take firm action against Castro become evident. On 9 November 1959, consequently, President Eisenhower approved, on the basis of recommendations of Acting Secretary of State Christian Herter, a policy of discreetly encouraging inside and outside opposition to Castro, thus making him for the first time, officially though secretly, a prime target of American covert action (Higgins, p. 46).

While other agencies participated in the formulation of this policy, especially the State Department, which was engaged in generating Latin American support for the removal of Castro, the burden of getting rid of the Cuban leader by covert means lay with the CIA. Accordingly, in December 1959 plans to build a cadre of Cuban military forces were drawn up. Since this cadre was to be trained by American instructors on American soil, it was theoretically to be used only for the training of additional recruits in a Latin American country and was never itself to operate in Cuba. By such compartmentation the CIA hoped to conceal its involvement in the project (Operation Zapata, p. 56). At the same time, inner circles in the agency started suggesting Castro's assassination as the most effective means of putting an end to the Cuban problem.[1]

In early 1960 Allen Dulles, the Director of Central Intelligence, informed the Special Group[2] that his agency did "not have in mind a quick elimina-

1. Castro's elimination was first discussed in the CIA's top echelons in mid-December 1959, following a memorandum by the head of the agency's Western Hemisphere Division, J. C. King, who suggested that: "Many informed people believe that the disappearance of Fidel would greatly accelerate the fall of the present Government" (Alleged Assassination Plots, p. 92). The SNIE of December 1959 offered a similar assessment:

> Castro's elimination would have an immediate drastic effect on political stability. Raul Castro, his appointed heir, and Che Guevara, Raul's close associate, would probably assume control of the government. It is unlikely, however, that they would be able to maintain control for long, and Cuba would be in for a period of violent political upheaval and terrorism. ("The Situation in the Caribbean through 1960," SNIE 80/1–59, 29 December 1959, Declassified Documents Reference Service (from herein DDRS), 1984/001504, p. 5, para. 24)

Neither King's "suggestion" nor, obviously, the SNIE's was based on concrete plots to eliminate Castro. They rather reflect the way of thinking about the problem in late 1959, and they probably were based on the logic of the situation coupled with the CIA's modus operandi regarding "problematic" leaders.

2. The Special Group, known also as the 5412 Group, was a committee designated to consider and approve covert operations according to NSC Directive 5412/2 of 28 December 1955. It consisted of representatives of the rank of assistant secretary or above in the State Department and Department of Defense plus a representative of the president. The Special Group was renamed the 303 Committee in 1964 and again renamed the 40 Committee in 1970. Apart from its official

tion of Castro" and asked for approval of "actions designed to enable responsible opposition leaders to get a foothold" (*Alleged Assassination Plots*, p. 93). Following approval, the CIA established a Cuba Task Force (WH/4) as a fourth branch in King's Western Hemisphere Division. Under Jake Engler, the former CIA Station Chief in Caracas, the new branch in its first months of existence prepared various plans for the training of a cadre of guerrilla leaders and the disruption of the Cuban economy by sabotage (Prados, pp. 176–77).

It is not clear how aware President Eisenhower was of the agency's activities during this period, especially with regard to possible assassination plots. But in February 1960 he dismissed Dulles's sporadic efforts to sabotage the Cuban economy, demanding instead that the agency submit a more comprehensive plan to topple Castro (Wyden, p. 24). Although the CIA responded enthusiastically, it is important to note that Eisenhower probably never regarded the immediate removal of Castro as a high priority goal of his administration. Rather, his demand likely reflected the attitude of an experienced general staff officer who perceived the availability of contingency plans as a routine procedure for proper conduct of policy. For Eisenhower, Cuba remained one problem among many. For the CIA, it did not.

As often happens in bureaucracies headed by ambitious men, the comprehensive plan the President had requested was formulated not by the professional echelon of Engler and his WH/4 branch but by Richard Bissell, the Deputy Director for Plans and the second most influential man in the CIA during the early 1960s. Engler's men, who were to implement the new plan, learned of its existence only on 9 March shortly before it was submitted to the Special Group and the President for approval (Prados, p. 177).

Bissell's plan defined its objective as "the replacement of the Castro regime with one more devoted to the true interests of the Cuban people and more acceptable to the U.S. in such a manner as to avoid any appearance of U.S. intervention."[3] It outlined four courses of action:

1. The establishment of a "responsible, appealing and unified Cuban opposition to the Castro regime, publicly declared and therefore necessarily located outside Cuba. It is hoped that within one month a

---

functions, the committee also served as a buffer between the president and controversial U.S. covert operations, thus providing him with a convenient plausible deniability.

3. "A Program of Covert Action against the Castro Regime," 15 March 1960, White House Office, Office of the Staff Secretary Records, International Series, Box 4, DDRS 1989/000015, p. 1.

political entity can be formed in the shape of a council or junta." The plan estimated that this leadership under the slogan "restore the Revolution" could "serve as a magnet for the loyalties of Cubans" and would actually direct opposition activities. Taking into account the friction between various exile groups, the plan emphasized the importance of selecting "an eminent, non-ambitious, politically uncontentious chairman." In an attempt to distance itself from the unpopular Batista supporters, the CIA suggested forming a council based on three groups—the Montecristi, the Autentico party, and the National Democratic Front—many of whose members participated in the 26th of July Movement and became anti-Castro because of Castro's failure to live up to the movement's original platform. The junta's platform would denounce Castro for the establishment of a new dictatorship and call for a genuine democracy, realistic agrarian reform, the restoration of individual freedom, and the elimination of Sino-Soviet influence in Cuban domestic affairs.[4]

2. The development of a "gray broadcasting facility" to launch an anti-Castro propaganda campaign. The plan suggested that the radio station be located on Swan Island in the Caribbean and estimated that its construction could be completed within two months. The plan also called for the use of propaganda "broadcasting from U.S. commercial facilities paid for by private Cuban groups" as well as other means of the media. In addition, several prominent Cuban exiles were already mobilized to garner support for their activities in Latin America and others were to follow.[5]

3. The creation of a "covert intelligence and action organization within Cuba which will be responsive to the orders of the 'exile' opposition." Noting the activities of WH/4, the document added that some effort in this direction was already under way and warned that "such a network must have effective communication and be selectively manned to minimize the risk of penetration." It estimated that "an effective organization can probably be created within 60 days."[6]

4. The development "of an adequate paramilitary force outside Cuba, together with mechanisms for the necessary logistic support of covert military operation within the island." Noting that preparations to

4. Ibid., pp. 1–2, 3–4, appendix: *The Political Opposition*, pp. 1–2.
5. "A Program of Covert Action against the Castro Regime," p. 2, appendix: *Propaganda*, pp. 1–2.
6. Ibid., p. 2.

organize such a force had already started, the CIA estimated that this task could be completed in "a minimum of six months and probably closer to eight." There would be three stages: "[1] Initially a cadre of leaders will be recruited after a careful screening and trained as paramilitary instructors. [2] In a second phase a number of paramilitary cadres will be trained at secure locations outside of the U.S. as to be available for [3] immediate deployment into Cuba to organize, train and lead resistance forces recruited there both before and after the establishment of one or more active centers of resistance." At the same time, the agency's current air capabilities "for resupply and for infiltration and exfiltration" were to be expanded within two months.[7]

On the surface Bissell's plan appeared solid, comprehensive, and, perhaps most important, politically prudent. To a certain extent it resembled earlier covert-action programs such as the successful Guatemala project ("Operation Success") of 1954, and was built along the lines of the British Special Operations Executive (SOE) of World War II in that it combined political factors (leadership in exile), psychological warfare, the organization of guerilla forces within an occupied territory and their support from without into a single comprehensive effort.

Most important, however, the plan did not call for any immediate paramilitary action against Castro. Although establishing links with existing opposition groups in Cuba and supplying them with logistical support might begin with a relatively short period of time, the more direct and significant aspects of American involvement were still six to eight months away. Such a program appeared rather attractive given President Eisenhower's prudential point of view, for on the one hand it enabled him to prepare a military option—in addition to diplomatic and economic means—to deal with Castro, while on the other it did not require him to make any immediate, risky commitments.

It is not clear whether the program was intentionally tailored to Eisenhower's known preferences or whether it was devised solely on professional grounds. In light of later developments, however, it seems that its architects were at least partially motivated by their own bureaucratic considerations, namely, the need to get presidential support for a large-scale covert action as soon as possible. Yet in retrospect, as approved by Eisenhower on 17 March the plan was far from flawless from the professional perspective, its

7. Ibid., p. 3.

main deficiency being its dependence on factors that were mostly beyond American control.

This was obviously the case with regard to the development of opposition groups inside Cuba. By March 1960 there was only isolated domestic resistance to Castro, and a March SNIE of "Communist Influence in Cuba" had hardly anything to relate about inside opposition and its paramilitary potential, emphasizing instead that

> [u]nder the direction of Fidel Castro's brother, Raul, and under the influence of "Che" Guevara, the armed services, police, and investigative agencies have been brought under unified control, purged of Batista professionals as well as other outspoken anti-Communist elements, and subjected to Communist-slanted political indoctrination courses; a civilian militia composed of students, workers, and peasants is being trained and armed.[8]

This estimate patently contradicted the agency's far more optimistic assessment, according to which an effective connection between the CIA and a reliable opposition inside Cuba could be created by no later than mid-May. Indeed, as time passed and Castro's mechanisms of control became more effective—a trend already evident at the time the program was approved—the domestic resistance option became increasingly difficult.

There were similar limitations to CIA control over two other integral components of the program, the buildup of a unified and attractive junta of Cuban exiles and the training of a cadre of guerrilla leaders. The intrinsic tension of every covert-action project—the conflict between the needs for operational effectiveness and for political plausible denial—tends to become more problematic the larger the scale of the project. In this sense the CIA's earlier plans to mount sabotage acts against the Cuban economy were less ambitious but also more operationally feasible. Conversely, by increasing the need to avoid the appearance of American intervention—a necessary condition for the approval of any covert-action program—the CIA virtually ensured the "Cubanization" of the project.

Still, if the anti-Castro opposition had been an organized, unified, and effective group, the "Cubanization" of the project would have been viable. Such, however, was not the case: the establishment of a leadership accept-

8. "Communist Influence in Cuba," SNIE 85–60, 22 March 1960 (DDRS 1984/001513A), p. 1.

able to all factions divided over political and personal issues proved to be far more difficult than predicted. Although to a certain extent Bissell and his aides were aware of this problem, their estimate that the necessary political entity could be formed within one month did not receive nearly enough realistic criticism either within the CIA or by the political authorities who approved the program. Even a year later on the eve of the operation, the FRD (Frente Revolucionario Democrático) was far from being a unified, attractive, and effective leadership.[9]

Only one component of the program—the establishment of the means to launch a propaganda campaign—was under the CIA's full control. As things turned out, this was also the only element that was completed in time: "the station was able to go on air on May 17 [1960] . . . precisely on schedule."[10]

If the March plan was perceived as solid and attractive despite its intrinsic deficiencies, such was also the case with the team in charge of the Cuba project. Once the program was approved, branch WH/4 was de facto detached from King's Western Hemisphere Division and became part of a newly organized Cuba task force under DDP Richard Bissell. On the surface this was only an administrative step, justified by the agency's modus operandi. In fact, however, the creation of the new task force enabled the project's architects to select officers who supported the covert-action plan while neutralizing important figures within the CIA who objected to it.

Bissell's deputy in the Cuba project was Tracy Barnes, the chief of the psychological and paramilitary staff in the Directory of Plans. A daring operational officer, Barnes was nevertheless disliked and distrusted by many veterans of the DDP who regarded his rise to the top "as due to Dulles's weakness for an old friend and dashing figure" (Powers, p. 121). Under him were Jake Engler and his WH/4 branch. Engler had worked with guerrillas in the Far East during the World War II, later served as the chief of the agency's guerrilla training center in Georgia, and also had considerable experience in Latin American affairs, first as a Cuban desk officer and then as a station chief in Guatemala and Venezuela. As the only one of the project's architects with both extensive paramilitary experience and Latin American expertise, Engler regarded himself as "the 'cement' that was

9. The British Special Operation Executive faced similar problems (especially in Yugoslavia) during World War II. The source of the problem is, of course, the competition between the factions that comprise the leadership in exile on who would lead the country once the common enemy was defeated.

10. CIA report: "Brief History of Radio Swan," Annex no. 2 of the Taylor Committee Report, DDRS 1985/001562, p. 1. On the propaganda aspect of the Cuba project see Phillips, pp. 107–41.

supposed to hold [its] many elements together on behalf of the man who counted, Dick Bissell" (Wyden, pp. 19–20). At the submanagerial level was a group of CIA officers in charge of specific parts of the program: Gerry Droller (aka "Frank Bender") and Howard Hunt, who were to organize the political leadership;[11] David Atlee Phillips, in charge of propaganda; and some other mid-range planning officers of WH/4 in charge of the project's daily management.

Altogether the CIA team that was to handle the program consisted of highly motivated and operationally oriented officers who believed, at least initially, that the overthrow of Castro by covert action was both desirable and feasible. As such, and despite some internal disagreements, it was a very homogeneous group, many of whose members, among them Bissell, Barnes, Engler, Philips, and Hunt, had shared a similar experience in Operation Success in 1954. The composition of the group, however, was not inadvertent, for its members were selected exactly because they worked so well together. This was the result of the agency's bureaucratic modus operandi, according to which chiefs of the task force enjoyed a free hand in selecting their subordinates while the selectees had the unofficial prerogative of refusing to join a project they did not believe in. The advantage of this procedure was teamwork; its disadvantage was a sort of "team think."

In the case of the Bay of Pigs the result was that senior officers who were supposed to participate in the operation ex officio were excluded either because they did not believe in its feasibility or because they did not fit comfortably into the operational milieu created by Bissell, or both. The best example is Richard Helms, Chief of Operations (COP) and number two man in the Directorate of Plans. Helms was known to dislike large-scale paramilitary operations, believing that they could not be kept secret for long. He was well aware, moreover, of the long-term undesirable results of even successful operations like the Guatemala project of 1954. He and

11. The selection of Droller and Hunt for these positions was peculiar. Droller, who was picked for this post by Barnes, lacked any experience in Latin American affairs and spoke no Spanish; indeed, since he was German-born, even his English was hard to understand. He was hated by the more liberal Cubans and disliked by the conservatives. Hunt, who had served as the political officer of the Guatemala project in 1954, did speak Spanish and had considerable experience in Latin American affairs but had a reputation in the agency for consistently being wrong. Moreover, Hunt, who years later would become famous for his role in the Watergate affair, was a right-wing extremist whose decisions as the project's political officer were influenced by his political beliefs. Droller and Hunt did not get along together, and some in the CIA compared the selection of these two to handle the delicate political aspects of the operation to "sending Rosencrantz and Guildenstern to tame the Eskimos" (Wyden, p. 32).

others in the CIA believed that the price of the 1954 success was too high, both politically given the growing Latin American hostility towards the United States in general and the CIA in particular and professionally given the risk of compromising the agency's assets involved in such spectacular projects. But besides professional disagreements, personal aspects were involved as well. Helms, a natural candidate to become Deputy Director for Plans in late 1958, simply did not get along well with Bissell. The result was that, apart from a passive participation in the first meeting on the project in March 1960, Helms distanced himself from the project with Bissell's enthusiastic approval, leaving it entirely in the latter's hands (Powers, pp. 110–16).

Another example of the exclusion of a senior officer is the neutralization of King, the Western Hemisphere Division chief, who from March 1960 onwards ceased to be an active participant in the program despite the fact that his division was an integral part of the DDP. Here at least this policy could be partially justified on professional grounds, since King and his division officers—many of them ex-FBI men who had been in charge of counterespionage in Latin America during World War II—had so close a relationship with Batista's men that they could well have alienated the more liberal Cubans who were to make up the bulk of the operation (Smith, pp. 331–32).[12] Others in the agency such as "Henry," the chief of the CIA's propaganda support branch, preferred to keep away from the project mainly because they had grave doubts about its feasibility and serious apprehensions regarding the consequences of failure (ibid., pp. 329–33).

Compartmentation of the Cuba project, however, was effected not only on a personal basis but also along bureaucratic lines. Most significant here was the fact that from the project's start to end CIA analysts were prevented from assessing the likelihood of the operation's success. The result was a widening gap between the task force's estimate of the situation as presented to policymakers and that of the analysts, a gap that on the eve of the operation had grown to a veritable abyss.

A high level of coherence, homogeneity, and unquestioned motivation might be desirable in a group of soldiers at time of war or in a football team competing for a championship. It is, however, undesirable during the planning phase of a complicated, politically sensitive covert operation. In

12. It is not clear whether King believed that the Cuba operation was feasible, but it is quite clear, especially in light of his December 1959 memorandum, that he perceived the removal of Castro from power as a desirable goal. It is interesting to note that in 1954 King distanced himself from the Guatemala project because he did not believe that it was feasible (Prados, p. 100).

this sense Operation Pluto, as the Cuban venture was code-named after its approval, suffered from the start from two major interrelated deficiencies: overoptimistic planning and overzealous planners. These seeds of destruction, moreover, became evident soon after the beginning of implementation of the program.

Of the four tasks the CIA set for itself in the 17 March program, only the two over which the agency had a relatively high level of independent control were implemented according to schedule. Radio Swan became operational in mid-May,[13] and about a week later the first group of twenty Cuban volunteers arrived at the tiny Useppa Island off the south Florida coast for training as guerrilla leaders and radio operators. Later, owing to the State Department's objection to the conduct of such activities on American territory, arrangements to secure a training site in Guatemala were made. Not much, however, was achieved with regard to the other two tasks. A council of exiled Cuban leaders—the Frente Revolucionario Democrático— was formed on 11 May, but it remained fragile and ineffective. It had no control over any aspects of the operation, its members competed furiously among themselves for American political support and financial aid, and it never developed into the sort of unified responsible junta that could have attracted support inside Cuba.[14]

The most significant failure of the plan at this stage, however, did not involve its political aspects but rather the CIA's inability to nurture domestic guerrilla opposition within Cuba, which was the fourth task outlined by the 17 March plan. There is almost no evidence that the agency ever succeeded during April and May in even starting to build a covert-action apparatus on

13. Even so, bureaucratic frictions prevented it from functioning the way it was supposed to:
   3. Originally it was planned that Radio Swan would be a clandestine station . . . [three lines sanitized]. . . . just prior to inauguration, however, it was decided the station should be a commercial one. This was at the request of the Navy [whose logistic support was needed], which reasonably argued that should their participation of a black facility be known, explanations would be difficult. ("Brief History of Radio Swan," p. 1)
As a result of this decision the station had to "sell space" to various Cuban groups instead of using the CIA's own propaganda material. The ultimate result was that
   [t]oward the end of 1960, the effectiveness of Radio Swan began to diminish. Although great numbers of Cubans still listened to the station, its credibility and reputation began to suffer as the result of statements representing the selfish interests of the Cuban groups producing the various programs. (Ibid., p. 2)
14. For an official description of this subject, see "Chronology of the Development and Emergence of the Revolutionary Council," Annex no. 3 of the Taylor Committee Report, DDRS 1985/001552. Despite its buoyant title, this document (which was probably written at the State Department) serves as little more than bureaucratic camouflage for the failures and weaknesses of this part of the project.

the island.[15] The optimistic estimate that "an effective organization can probably be created within 60 days" thus proved by the end of May 1960 to be no more than wishful thinking. Although the June 1960 NIE noted that "in recent months there have been increasing signs of opposition within Cuba" and that "small-scale guerrilla activity has reappeared in Oriente Province," it also suggested that

> [w]ith the old-line political parties discredited and many of the propertied class in flight, much of the anti-Castro activity has until recently come from adventurers and embittered Batista supporters, operating from the Dominican Republic and the US. Such activity is beneficial to the Castro regime in that it tends to identify all opposition with the generally detested Batista dictatorship. Moreover, the activities in the US of those closely associated with Batista lend plausibility to Castro's anti-American campaign.[16]

Estimating the prospects for the formation of an opposition inside Cuba during the next six months, the June 1960 NIE said: "In sum, while opposition is growing, it is still relatively weak and disorganized. In particular, it thus far appears to lack a dynamic leader capable of bringing various groups together and of making an effective challenge to Fidel Castro for popular support."[17]

At the same time, Castro had extended his control within the military: "The armed forces, police and investigative agencies have been thoroughly organized by the regime to strengthen its control over them." The report admitted that because of (among other reasons) large-scale purges, the army's effectiveness had been reduced "except for guerrilla-type operations" but also noted a new development that added a further obstacle to the CIA's plan:

> The regime has also established a "people's militia" made up of students, peasants and urban and sugar workers, and numbering 100,000 of both sexes. It is as yet only partially armed and for the

15. It is possible, of course, that some success was achieved in this domain but that, owing to the need to protect its assets in Cuba, the CIA has rightly prevented any disclosures until now.

16. "The Situation in Cuba," NIE 85-2-60, 14 June 1960, DDRS 1984/001513, p. 6.

17. Ibid., pp. 6–7. It is interesting to note that the report refers to the formation of the FRD in mid-May and correctly estimated that "FRD activity has not gone beyond the initial organization stage" (ibid., p. 7).

most part poorly trained. At present it could be expected to contribute to Castro's control of the urban areas in event of major disorders and to conduct harassing and sabotage operations against anti-Castro forces.[18]

Altogether by mid-1960 the CIA task force must have realized that the materialization of the most critical component of its plan—the buildup of an effective opposition force inside Cuba—was highly unlikely. Moreover, Castro's tightening control of the military as well as other institutions, the improvement in the lower classes' standard of living, and the estimate that "real national income for 1960 will probably surpass last year's total"[19] could all serve as good indicators that the prospect for growing domestic opposition to Castro was low. Given the critical importance of this component, it could be expected that the CIA task force would reestimate the plan, perhaps even reaching the conclusion that it was not feasible. There are no indications, however, that such a reevaluation ever occurred. Instead, it was decided to compensate for the loss of local guerrilla opposition by building a paramilitary exile force.

Originally the cadre of Cuban guerrilla leaders and radio operators trained by the CIA outside Cuba was to number about seventy-five (Ranelagh, p. 358). By mid-May, however, Washington instructed the CIA head station chief in Guatemala to arrange housing facilities for an additional one hundred fifty Cubans. Although Bissell maintains that at this early juncture he did not pay much attention to the instruction (ibid., p. 359), the decision to increase the number of Cuban trainees in Guatemala so significantly was the first major deviation from the CIA's original plan. Three points should be made here. First, tripling the number of trainees was not merely a quantitative change but a qualitative one. The two hundred or so Cubans were supposed to serve not only as leaders and radio operators but also as regular fighters—a substitute for the unavailable armed resistance within Cuba. Second, the new policy ignored an important earlier restriction that no Cubans trained by American instructors would be sent into combat. Third, this change in plans originated within the task force and there are no indications that it was ever approved by any authority outside the agency.[20] While the CIA planners might have justified this change by

18. Ibid., p. 5.
19. Ibid., p. 8.
20. President Eisenhower became aware of these changes only on 29 June. A few weeks later chairman of the 5412 Committee, Gordon Gray, informed him of additional changes in the original

maintaining that the new instructions affected only incidentals, the significant increase in the number of Cubans involved had clear political as well as operational implications: in addition to deepening the perception of American commitment to the project and making it more difficult to abandon, the growing number of persons involved augmented the likelihood of security breaches that could compromise its covert nature.

The first Cubans, a cadre of 28, left Florida on 23 June and received eight weeks of extensive training in guerrilla warfare in the Panama Canal Zone. In the third week of August they were transferred to a new training site in Guatemala known as Camp Trax. Shortly afterward new recruits arrived in camp, and by early September their number had reached 160. Simultaneously 45 Cuban pilots and technicians arrived at the CIA's newly built air base near Retalhuleu, some thirty miles from Camp Trax, where a small air force—fifteen B-26 medium-range bombers and twelve C-46 and C-54 transports—was already assembled for training and logistic support missions.[21] Towards the end of September a group of 20 CIA contract personnel started training the Camp Trax recruits in guerrilla warfare (Johnson, pp. 37–49; Wyden, pp. 49–51; Prados, pp. 182–84).

The information out of Cuba between July and September 1960 was mixed in nature. On the bright side, some encouragement could be drawn from the growing alienation from the regime of student groups and the Church. Even more important were indications that in mid-August several hundred guerrillas were actually operating in the provinces of Camaguey and Las Villas, causing the government much concern.[22] According to an additional report of 8 September, a guerrilla group of some four hundred to five hundred men was operating in the Escambray mountains: "Although poorly armed and equipped thus far, this force provides a nucleus and a highly useful symbol which, with luck, may become increasingly effective in the future."[23] On the darker side, various intelligence reports since mid-July indicated that arms supplies from the Soviet bloc had started arriving in Cuba. These included small arms, artillery, tanks, and possibly even

---

plan, including expanded training, the use of bases in Guatemala, and the need for additional budget (Prados, p. 182).

21. The CIA had already started forming this small tactical air force in June 1960 (*Operation Zapata*, p. 5). Adding the bombers component to transport aircraft constituted an additional significant deviation from the 17 March plan and serves as a good indicator that thinking in terms of a more conventional warfare operation started in the agency earlier than was previously realized.

22. "Progress Report on Cuba," 24 August 1960, DDRS 1989/000399, p. 2.

23. "Progress Report on Cuba," 8 September 1960, DDRS 1989/000402, p. 2.

crated MIG fighters.[24] The obvious implication of this development was that Castro's increasing military power might make impossible any paramilitary action against him.

Assessing the situation toward the end of the summer, the CIA planners had no reason to be overly optimistic about the feasibility of their plans. Except for the psychological warfare aspect, nothing was going right. The exiles' leadership (FRD) was still riven with internal rivalry and was totally dependent upon the CIA's guidance and support; the number of Cuban trainees at Camp Trax and at the air base at Retalhuleu was small, morale among them was low, and the training was considered inefficient. And although there were some indications of a growing armed resistance in Cuba, the quality, efficiency, and ability of these splinter guerrilla groups to coordinate their actions with the American project were limited and various efforts to supply them with American logistical support had failed. Most important of all, Castro's ability to control the Cuban population kept improving, the regime continued to be generally popular, and Soviet bloc military assistance was steadily increasing the ability of the armed forces—by now genuinely loyal to the government—to deal with armed resistance within the island.

In light of all these difficulties, planners in the Cuba task force started reevaluating the feasibility of their already modified program. By the beginning of November they had reached the conclusion that all guerrilla options, either local or from the outside, had practically become obsolete and that a radical change in the project's concept was essential.

In theory, the project's architects had three options. The first was to abandon the military components of the program and focus solely on the buildup of an exile leadership and the continuation of psychological warfare against Castro's Cuba. This effort could supplement the already growing diplomatic and economic pressures on the Cuban government being applied by other departments in the administration. The main advantage of this option was that it involved minimal risks for the United States. Its main disadvantage, however, was that it significantly compromised the U.S. effort to overthrow Castro as soon as possible. At least from a bureaucratic point of view, moreover, accepting this option meant admitting the agency's failure to deliver the goods as promised in its 17 March program.

24. "Memorandum of [19 July 1960] Meeting with the President," 26 July 1960, DDRS 1986/000552; "Synopsis of State and Intelligence Material Reported to the President," 30 August 1960, DDRS 1986/001690; "Progress Report on Cuba," 14 September 1960, DDRS 1989/000403; "Progress Report on Cuba," 26 September 1960, DDRS 1989/000404.

A second option was to continue the buildup of a modest-sized guerrilla force, which could then be introduced into Cuba if conditions for such action became more favorable (for example, growing armed resistance inside Cuba, a decline in Castro's popularity, a sudden internal crisis, etc.). Again, this was a prudent option. It would have kept the project covert while leaving the political echelon the opportunity to use some force against Castro at a later stage. On the other hand, the guerrilla option was now regarded by the task force planners as too little too late given Castro's success in controlling the population and the rapid buildup of his armed forces.

The third option, which involved a radical change in the original program to overthrow Castro, was to abandon the guerrilla concept in favor of using a conventional assault force. In light of the information available in the fall of 1960 this must have been considered as a high-risk but low-chance course of action. For reasons that will be discussed below, this was the strategy adopted by the CIA. It was implemented effectively on 4 November 1960 by a cable from the task force in Washington to the project officer in Guatemala. *Inter alia* the cable instructed:

1. Plan employ not over 60 men for ref teams. Remaining trainees for assault force. . . .

2. Assault force will consist one or more infantry battalions each having about 600 men with three infantry companies, weapon company and HQS and service company.

3. Mission of assault force is seize and defend lodgement in target by amphibious and airborne assault and establish base for further OPS. Automatic sea and air resupply will be provided.

4. Assault force to receive conventional military training in sequence as follows: individual training, squad platoon and company training, followed by battalion field and command post exercises. . . .

6. Possibility using U.S. Army special forces training cadres for assault being pursued. Will advise. . . .

11. Plan use [probably guerrilla] teams now and during next two months as situation inside target permits. Conditions inside may dictate stretchout. Earliest team requirements are for Pinar del Rio Havana and Las Villas.

12. Assault of size now planned cannot be readied before several months. Do not plan strike with less than about 1500 men. Smaller force has little chance success in view situation in target. Suggest begin psychological preparation members strike force for intended training period. Can encourage them by prospect eventual bigger scale strike.[25]

The change in plan outlined in this cable was no doubt of a strategic nature and was treated as such at Camp Trax. According to the Cuban trainees, the 4 November cable "became the Bible of the training camp. From that date any talk in the camp about guerrilla warfare was regarded by the CIA as a sign of weakness" (Johnson, p. 54).

One would expect that the President would have been asked to authorize such a radical change in the largest "covert-action" project in U.S. history ever to reach such an operational stage. Even Allen Dulles, however, had to admit that he briefed Eisenhower on the new paramilitary concept only on 29 November, more than three weeks after it had gone into effect (*Operation Zapata*, p. 7). Dulles and Bissell, moreover, briefed the president-elect, John F. Kennedy, on the Cuba project on 18 November. As they themselves described it, however, at the center of this briefing was the project's old concept as approved by President Eisenhower in March 1960 and not the new one as outlined by the 4 November cable (Jackson, 3:117–18).

Under NSC Directive 5412/2 one would also expect the Special Group to be notified of the change in the project's concept prior to its implementation.[26] Again, such was not the case, and it is not even clear if the 5412

25. "Cable to the CIA [sanitized] Senior Project Representative in Guatemala, 4 November 60," Annex no. 4 of the Taylor Committee Report, DDRS 1985/001539.

26. Paragraph 4 of this directive states that the DCI be responsible for:

a. Ensuring, through designated representatives of the Secretary of State and of the Secretary of Defense, that covert operations are *planned* and conducted in a manner consistent with United States foreign and military policies and with covert activities, and consulting and obtaining advice from the Operations Coordinating Board and other departments or agencies as appropriate.

Paragraph 7 of the 5412 directive says:

Except as the President otherwise directs, designated representatives of the Secretary of State and the Secretary of Defense of the rank of Assistant Secretary or above, shall hereafter be advised *in advance* of major covert action *programs* initiated by CIA . . . and shall be the normal channel for giving policy approval for such programs.

National Security Council Directive 5412/2, 28 December 1955, on Covert Operations, Leary, pp. 146–49 (emphasis added).

Group ever officially authorized the new program. According to testimony by Dulles and Tracy Barnes, "Special Group references show that on 16 November 1960, the changing concept of the operation was noted by Undersecretary Livingston Merchant" (ibid., p. 59). Then on 8 December 1960 the new concept was presented in this forum and its members approved CIA requests for the use of officers from the Special Forces for training missions and the use of an air-strip in Nicaragua for supply missions (ibid., pp. 59–60). There is no indication that the Special Group was notified of the change in the Cuba project before 16 November. At best, then, the approval was de facto and ex post facto.

So it is clear that under the nose of their political superiors the architects of the Cuba project implemented a radical change that had potentially enormous implications for U.S. foreign policy. Why did they behave this way? A possible explanation is the one given later by the agency's leadership, that no further authorization was needed as long as no forces were put into combat. This, however, is a weak excuse. After all, what was approved in March was a guerrilla training program, not a conventional invasion of Cuba in which the U.S. role could hardly remain covert and which might well have triggered the need for an overt American intervention. The impression, then, is that the project's architects avoided informing the President and his aides of this shift until it had become a fait accompli because they suspected that it would not be authorized in advance. Indeed, they had ample reason to believe so, since professional considerations were squarely opposed to their new plan.

The Taylor Report describes the shift in the agency's program as the result of a gradual process. It started (probably in May or early June 1960) when the officers of the task force began considering the formation of a small infantry force (of some two to three thousand men) "for contingency employment in conjunction with other paramilitary operations" (*Operation Zapata*, p. 5). It ended with the radical shift in plans outlined in the 4 November cable that actually gave up the guerrilla option, thus making a conventional assault force the exclusive paramilitary means of overthrowing Castro. The Taylor Committee found the CIA explanation for this operational paradigm shift "ample": "The air drops into Cuba were not proving effective. There were increasingly heavy shipments of Communist arms to Cuba, accompanied by evidence of increasingly effective control of the civilian population by Castro" (ibid., p. 5).

The first CIA airdrops into Cuba were made in early October (Prados, p. 187), and the first reports indicating possible shipments of Soviet arms to Castro arrived no earlier than the second half of July.[27] It is extremely difficult to understand why the members of the Taylor Committee found the reports an "ample" explanation for the November change. After all, if forces now known to be loyal to Castro were getting new heavy weapons, challenging them by a numerically far inferior conventional force made no sense from a military point of view.[28] And if the new concept regarded the main aim of the assault to be the triggering of a general uprising against the regime, Castro's popularity and his firm control of the population were sufficient evidence that this strategy was based more on wishful thinking than on solid facts.

Indeed, the most logical decision at this juncture would have been to abandon the paramilitary components of the plan and instead concentrate on its political and psychological warfare aspects. The CIA also had another possible course of action, Castro's assassination, which had now become—given the reduced chances of success of the guerrilla option—even more justified on professional grounds.[29]

But by now foregoing the paramilitary plan involved serious difficulties for the agency. The dismantling of the Cuban force might not only have compromised the covert nature of the project but also have caused the exiles to give up all hope of overthrowing Castro. Certainly such developments would have had significant negative impact on the CIA's political and propaganda efforts. These drawbacks, however, could only have justified the continuation of the modest guerrilla option but not the far more ambitious new plan. So it seems that the task force's most important (though tacit) consideration at this juncture was not professional but bureaucratic. From the moment the CIA suggested its comprehensive program to overthrow Castro, a program whose heart was paramilitary action, the agency became committed to this plan. Giving it up, especially now when U.S.-Cuban relations were deteriorating further and the menace of Castro was even more clearly evident, would have meant that the agency could not stand up to its original promises.

27. The June NIE informed that: "To date no Cuba-Bloc arms agreement is known to have been concluded" (NIE 85–2–60, 14 June 1960, DDRS 1984/001513B, p. 5). For the first reports on Soviet arms to Cuba, see n. 24.

28. The same is true with regard to the small force of sixty men that was scheduled for guerrilla operations in Cuba according to the 4 November cable. Under the new circumstances in Cuba, sending this force had become too risky. At least here the CIA abandoned this mission.

29. Indeed, by mid-summer 1960 the CIA had moved from earlier plots to destroy Castro's public image (in which it had been engaged since March) to assassination plans. Bissell probably formulated the first plot, which later came to involve the Mafia, and took measures for its implementation in August 1960 (*Alleged Assassination Plots*, pp. 72–75, n. 3 on p. 74).

Even worse, admitting such failure now, without dramatic changes in the situation in Cuba taking place, would have meant that the plan to overthrow Castro by force had no solid basis from the start. In this sense there is no doubt that the architects of the project had a strong personal vested interest in maintaining their program. Needless to say, this could not serve as a justification for the new plan from the President's point of view and was probably the reason they avoided informing him about it before its implementation.

All in all the development of the Cuba project during its first year was influenced by three factors. First was the consolidation of Castro's power, a trend already evident in 1959 and one that intelligence estimates of late 1960 predicted would continue during 1961. The Cuban armed forces improved both in quantity and in quality; Castro's personal popularity did not decline and remained especially high among the lower classes; despite the regime's economic reform there was no economic crisis and the standard of living of the masses even improved. Thus, even if anti-Castro opposition became more widespread, it nevertheless remained ineffective in comparison to the regime's improved control.

Second, as U.S.-Cuban relations continued to deteriorate, the need to overthrow Castro became more evident. Owing to his consolidation of power, however, achieving this goal became increasingly difficult. During 1960 this dual trend led to a constant escalation in the CIA's paramilitary plans: from sporadic acts of sabotage up until March, to nurturing guerrilla resistance between March and May, to training a small infantry strike force in early summer, to building a conventional strike force as a means of triggering a general uprising in early November. Despite this constant growth in plans, however, the likelihood of toppling Castro by paramilitary means did not improve.

Third, the expansion of the agency's paramilitary program was initiated without proper political authorization despite the significant implications these changes had for overall U.S. foreign policy. Although the Special Group and the President were notified of these changes ex post facto, there are no indications they demanded that the CIA inform them of major alterations in plans before they were actually implemented.

January–April 1961: A Chain of Fools?

Once the architects of the Cuba project had concluded that their only chance of overthrowing Castro was by a conventional assault, the program's basic concept underwent no other major changes until its actual implementation in April 1961. This concept was summarized on 4 January 1961 in an intra-task force paper:

1. It envisioned "the seizure of a small lodgement on Cuban soil by an all-Cuban amphibious/airborne force of about 750 men." This "lodgement" was supposed to include an airfield and access to the sea, but there were contingency plans for air drops if these were not available.[30]

2. It planned on the destruction of Castro's air and naval forces on the day before the landing (D-1) and of other Cuban military targets later by air strikes. Cuban Exile Force (CEF) aircraft were to supply the landing force with close air support.[31]

3. After a beachhead had been secured, subsequent offensive operations were seen to be dependent on two political possibilities: (a) "It is expected that these operations will precipitate a general uprising throughout Cuba and cause the revolt of large segments of the Cuban Army and Militia." It was hoped that such a general revolt might "serve to topple the Castro regime within a period of weeks."[32] (b) If revolt did not materialize, "the lodgement established by our force can be used as site for establishment of a provisional government." A recognition of this government by the United States and other American states would then pave the way "for United States military intervention aimed at pacification of Cuba, and this will result in the prompt overthrow of the Castro Government."[33]

It is important to note two elements here. First, direct American intervention was explicitly considered, though it is not clear whether the President or his close advisors were aware of it. Second, by early 1961 the guerrilla option, the safety-net mechanism to prevent a total failure, was not yet part of the plan.[34]

In late January a new administration entered office and precipitated some

30. Memorandum for Chief, WH/4: "Policy Decisions Required for Conduct of Strike Operations Against Government of Cuba," 4 January 1961, Annex no. 14 of the Taylor Committee Report, DDRS 1985/001540, p. 1.

31. Ibid.

32. Ibid., p. 2.

33. Ibid.

34. The guerrilla option was mistakenly included in a summary of the 4 January paper in the Taylor Committee discussions (*Operation Zapata*, p. 72).

further changes. It is not clear if the CIA briefing given to leading members of the Kennedy administration on 22 January or the one given by Dulles to the President on 28 January, was at all detailed. As a result of these meetings, however, Kennedy instructed the CIA to intensify its propaganda, its exile leadership buildup, and its sabotage activities, and authorized the continuation of flight missions over Cuba for these purposes. As for the invasion plan, he demanded that the JCS and the CIA review the current program and report their conclusions.[35] Kennedy's demand was the first presidential instruction that directly involved the JCS in the Cuba program[36] and an obvious move given the military nature of the project.[37]

The concept of the plan submitted for JCS review on 31 January stated that the mission of the CEF was to:

a. Invade the Island of Cuba by amphibious and airborne assault.

b. Hold a beachhead long enough to establish a provisional govern-
ment, act as a rallying point for volunteers and as a catalyst for uprisings throughout Cuba.

c. Integrate with existing guerrilla bands and carry on guerrilla operations if driven from the beachhead area.[38]

This marked a divergence from the 4 January concept. The possibility of direct American intervention was abandoned (at least from official docu-ments) and the guerrilla option reinstated as a means of securing the operation from total failure.

Here, then, was the last transformation within the concept. From this

35. "President Kennedy's First Briefing on Operation TRINIDAD on 28 January 61," Annex no. 8 of the Taylor Committee Report, DDRS 1985/001542, p. 2.

36. Even though the CIA needed military support (Special Forces instructors, naval support, etc.) to carry out its conventional assault program, it nevertheless attempted to keep the military in the dark about its operational plans. See e.g. Wyden, pp. 78–80.

37. Kennedy may also have been motivated by his Secretary of Defense, McNamara, who a day earlier had received a JCS memorandum that criticized the CIA plan:

> The current [CIA] Political-Para-Military Plan does not assure the accomplishment of the above objective [Castro's overthrow] nor has there been detailed follow-up planning to exploit that plan if it succeeds or for any direct action [implicitly by U.S. forces] that might be required if the plan is found to be inadequate. (The Joint Chiefs of Staff: "U.S. Plan of Action in Cuba," Memorandum for the Secretary of Defense, JCSM–44–61, 27 January 1961, Annex no. 7 of the Taylor Committee Report, DDRS 1985/001541, p. 2.)

38. The Joint Chiefs of Staff: "Military Evaluation of the Cuban Plan," Memorandum for the Secretary of Defense, JCSM 57–61, 3 February 1961, DDRS 1985/001557, p. 4.

point on the project will be evaluated on the basis of three factors: the ability of the small CEF to seize and hold a lodgement on Cuban territory, the likelihood of a popular uprising triggered by the invasion, and the ability of the CEF to become a guerrilla force in case it lost the battle on the beachhead and no popular uprising materialized. Since each of these factors was considered a necessary condition for both JCS approval of the plan and White House authorization of its implementation, the rest of this section will discuss their progress between the end of January and the second week of April, when a tentative green light for the operation was given. This analysis will examine each factor separately, focusing on three questions: What was its status at various stages of the project? How was this status estimated by those involved in assessing the project? And how was it communicated to the President and his aides?

Factor 1: Military Feasibility

Each of the CIA's invasion plans was structured on the basis of three components: a ground force (Brigade 2506) to occupy and hold the beach-head; a tactical air force capable of destroying Castro's aircraft on the ground and supplying air support and material to the ground force; and a naval element capable of bringing the brigade to the beach and conducting the main logistical effort.

The military feasibility of these plans was analyzed by the JCS on three occasions and was summarized in three papers: JCSM–57–61 of 3 February; JCSM–146–61 of 10 March; and JCSM–166–61 of 15 March 1961.

JCSM–57–61: 3 February 1961

The JCSM–57–61 report was not only the first professional analysis of the project's military feasibility, it was also the most comprehensive one and the basis for all additional evaluations. The task of analyzing the CIA's invasion plan was entrusted to Brigadier General David W. Gray, who at an earlier stage headed the committee that prepared the JCSM–44–61 paper of 27 January (see n. 37). Under him were three colonels from the Army, Marines, and Air Force and a military intelligence specialist who had served in Cuba.

In contrast to usual military procedure, the CIA gave the Gray committee no documented report of the planned invasion project, probably because no such document was ever prepared by the task force. Instead, Gray and his colonels received an oral briefing that lasted for a few hours. On the basis of this briefing they themselves wrote the plan (known from this stage on as the Trinidad plan) and then set out to evaluate it (Wyden, pp. 88–89).[39]

According to CIA reports, the ground force of exiles under training in Guatemala totaled 826 personnel in late January. They were organized along the lines of a U.S. infantry battalion with a headquarters and support company, four rifle companies, one heavy gun company, and one M-41 tank platoon. The naval support unit amounted to about 40 men and twelve landing craft of various types. The CEF air element was comprised of 100 personnel of which 18 were pilots (including some Americans). The available aircraft were seventeen B-26 medium-range bombers, plus ten C-54s and five C-46s for logistical support. Other known friendly forces included a guerrilla force of about 1,500, of which about 660 were estimated to be in the area of Trinidad, the designated landing site. In expectation of additional support the CIA prepared arms for 1,500 volunteers.[40]

Castro's armed forces totaled an army of 32,000 and a militia of 200,000 to 300,000. Twelve hundred militiamen were estimated to be in the area of Trinidad, while 6,000 troops (including one infantry regiment, one artillery battalion, and one tank battalion) were located about one hundred miles from the designated beachhead. Castro's air force included eighteen fighters (three F-47s, one F-51, and fourteen Sea Fury), thirteen B-26 bombers, six TBM-38s, fifteen transport aircraft, and twenty-two helicopters of various types.[41] The Cuban navy totaled 5,000 personnel and had two frigates and about forty smaller crafts.[42]

---

39. Wyden's description of this episode contradicts a WH/4 officer who testified before the Taylor Committee that the Trinidad plan was written in January, presumably by the CIA task force, and submitted to the JCS on 31 January (*Operation Zapata*, p. 77). In light of Gray's detailed description of this episode and the task force's modus operandi, my impression is that Gray's version is far closer to the truth.

40. JCSM–57–61, 3 February 1961, DDRS 1985/001557, pp. 7–8, 15–17. The situation of the CEF as described in this document had improved significantly compared to four weeks earlier. In early January it comprised a ground force of 500 Cubans, an air force of ten B–26s, seven C–54s, and a few C–46s, and seven amphibious craft of different types. Although the status of the naval force was considered satisfactory in early January, this was not true of the assault force and the air element (Memorandum for Chief WH/4, 4 January 1961, DDRS 1985/001540).

41. It is not clear why this estimate ignored some T-33 jet trainers known to be in the Cuban air force. The T-33s armed with .50-caliber machine guns and rockets proved highly effective in the fighting during April. A possible explanation for this failure is that the Cuban air force was evaluated according to American standards. In other words, since the T-33 was not a fighter in America, it was assumed that the same was true with regard to Cuba, ignoring the probability that the Cubans would improvise in order to put into combat the only jets they had.

42. JCSM 57–61, DDRS 1985/001557, pp. 7, 11–14. It is not clear whether this information came from estimates from the military or the CIA.

Given Castro's enormous quantitative superiority, initial military success depended on the qualitative superiority of the CEF and on the achievement of surprise, which would enable the destruction of the Cuban air force and the isolation of the beachhead. On D-1 the operational plan of early February called for an air strike by twelve B-26s against Cuban airfields, naval patrol boats, communication facilities, and other military targets, a deceptive landing off the northwest coast of Cuba, and demolition by parachuted assault teams of three key bridges leading to the Trinidad area. On D-Day the task force was to invade amphibiously and by air, with the beachhead under close air support. It was expected that by night of D-Day the CEF would control the beachhead area, including a small air strip, and be resupplied with the necessary material by sea and air. Following this stage it was expected that up to 1,500 volunteers, for whom equipment was being prepared, would join the CEF. The brigade's mission was to defend the beachhead but, if driven out, to commence guerrilla operations in the Escambray mountains.

This was a most ambitious plan, a highly complicated operation for a small and relatively untrained force. Yet the JCS report favored the plan and concurred regarding the ability of the CEF to carry it out. It considered Trinidad as the best site for an invasion, the air plan "within the capability of the air units," and the airborne and amphibious assaults likely to "be successful,"[43] while calling for some modification of specific elements. It appears that the JCS's favorable assessment of the initial stage of the project was mainly the result of their belief that the qualitative balance of power tended heavily in favor of the CEF. They believed that Castro's armed forces lacked experience in large-scale offensive operations and that their combat readiness was low; the JCS report estimated that it would take Castro two days to assemble "substantial forces" in the combat zone and at least an additional two days to prepare a coordinated attack. Underlying this estimate were CIA reports indicating that the CEF was an effective force: "Reportedly, personnel of the Task Force are well-trained and willing to fight. Leadership is effective and reliable. . . . Reports indicate that personnel have reached a fine edge of training which they will lose if not employed in the near future for purpose intended."[44]

On the basis of such information the JCS gave a "favorable assessment . . . of the likelihood of achieving initial military success."[45] As their report

43. Ibid., pp. 4–5.
44. Ibid., p. 18.
45. Ibid., p. 2.

repeatedly noted, ultimate success depended on the degree of local Cuban support. Yet the final estimation of the whole project was that "[d]espite the shortcomings pointed out in the assessment the Joint Chiefs of Staff consider that timely execution of this plan has a *fair chance of ultimate success* and, even if it does not achieve immediately the full results desired, could contribute to the eventual overthrow of the Castro regime."[46]

How well did this JCS assessment reflect the actual military situation in early February? Quite well, probably, with regard to the quantitative balance of forces, but quite poorly regarding the qualitative dimension, especially that of the CEF.

Despite its numerical growth, the Cuban force under training at Camp Trax deteriorated in effectiveness to hit rock bottom in January. From the start the recruits were divided along political lines—the ex-Castro rebels, the ex-Batista soldiers, and the students—and relations among these groups were always tense. In January worsening relations with their American instructors and the Byzantine politics of the exile groups in Miami caused this tension to reach its peak. When some factions of the FRD demanded the nomination of a new commander to the brigade and the American instructors agreed, a mutiny broke out and 230 Cubans, including the entire Second and Third Battalions, resigned. Although the change of command was ultimately called off, about twenty of the leading "dissidents" were arrested and sent to prison until after the invasion (Johnson, pp. 60–63; Wyden, pp. 57–59).

Training was resumed only in February after the crisis was over, but its cost was not only in wasted time. From the CIA's perspective, the mutiny could have had disastrous consequences, even resulting in the possible termination of the project. For it revealed that instead of there being a cohesive unit, effective leadership, and close American control—all necessary conditions for the operation's success—the Cubans were sharply divided among themselves, their leadership was ineffective, and the degree of American control was badly limited. None of this was noted in the JCS report, however, probably because the CIA, the only source of information on the CEF, preferred to conceal its poor status from the professional soldiers who were to estimate its quality. Given that the mutiny in Camp Trax was no secret from Bissell's task force in Washington, it can be concluded that essential information was concealed from General Gray and his committee by the CIA.

46. Ibid., p. 2 (emphasis added).

Yet, even if the JCS lacked sufficient information about the real status of the CEF, they must have had enough expertise to judge its merits properly. The impression, unfortunately, is that they made little use of their expertise. For example, the assault force's manpower was increased from about five hundred to over eight hundred in the three-week period between early January and the end of the month. It is difficult to believe that the three hundred new recruits, most of them lacking previous military experience, could have reached "a fine edge of training" in such a short time. Also, while the JCS paper estimated that Castro could launch a counteroffensive only on D + 4, it neglected to estimate the chances of the invading force holding beyond that stage. Only later would General Gray admit that his committee "thought that the invasion forces could hold the beachhead about seven days" (*Operation Zapata*, p. 105).

Taking such considerations into account, it is difficult to understand how the report concluded that the plan had "a fair chance of ultimate success." Indeed, this was not General Gray's own conclusion. Instead it was the result of a typical compromise between him and his boss, Lieutenant General Earl Wheeler, who demanded that Gray give an overall estimate of the chance of success. When Gray refused, Wheeler suggested using the term "fair." As Gray argued fifteen years later, he and his boss "thought that other people would think that a 'fair chance' would mean 'not too good'" (Wyden, p. 89). In fact, Gray personally estimated that the plan had no more than a 30 percent chance of success.[47]

Little if any of this was known to President Kennedy and his aides. As is usual with busy policymakers, they were more interested in the final judgment of the professional soldiers than in learning how they arrived at it. Thus the term "fair chance" was interpreted by most of them as JCS support for the CIA plan. A short memorandum submitted by McGeorge Bundy to Kennedy prior to a discussion of Cuba on 8 February noted that, although the State Department might disagree, "Defense and CIA now feel quite enthusiastic about the invasion from Guatemala—at the worst they think the invaders would get into the mountains, and at the best they think they might get a full-fledged civil war in which we could then back the anti-Castro forces openly."[48]

Arthur Schlesinger, Kennedy's Special Assistant, interpreted the JCS

47. According to General Gray, 30 percent "was a general numerical guess. . . . I heard others saying that the chances might be 40 to 60, which is the highest guess that I heard" (*Operation Zapata*, p. 107).

48. McGeorge Bundy: "Memorandum for the President," 8 February 1961, DDRS 1984/000555.

report similarly. Aware, however, of the skepticism of some of the Joint Chiefs regarding the feasibility of the plan, Schlesinger treated the report suspiciously, concluding that it suffered from a "logical gap between the statement that the plan would work if one or another conditions were fulfilled and the statement that the plan would work anyway." His ex post facto explanation for this gap was that the Joint Chiefs were convinced, whether consciously or not, that once the operation got under way the United States could not risk failure and would have to intervene directly if needed (Schlesinger 1965, pp. 238–39). As he must have learned later, this was not the report's only deficiency.

Altogether, then, a hurried plan, prepared on the basis of partial and misleading CIA information and privately assessed by the same men who put it into writing as having about a 70 percent chance of ultimate failure, was regarded by the White House as a well-designed conception that the JCS had properly analyzed and given their professional blessing.

JCSM–146–61: 10 March 1961

Aware of their overdependence on CIA reports, the JCS announced in their 3 February paper their intention of making an independent inspection of the Cuban force and the CIA's operational plans. This was done on 26–27 February; the results were summarized in the JCSM–146–61 of 10 March. Yet, even after inspecting the force on site, Gray's experts had to admit that their investigation was not thorough enough and that much of the information obtained was not from the Cubans themselves but from their American instructors.

Generally, the 10 March report again employed a positive tone: "from a military standpoint, since the small invasion force will retain the initiative until the location of the landing is determined, the plan could be expected to achieve initial success."[49]

Unlike the earlier JCS report, however, the later one refrained from estimating the likelihood of the operation's ultimate success, noting instead that this depended on the ability of the invasion to serve as a catalyst for the "further action of anti-Castro elements throughout Cuba."[50] Specifically, it

49. Memorandum for the Secretary of Defense: "Evaluation of the CIA Cuban Volunteer Task Forces," JCSM–146–61, 10 March 1961, DDRS 1985/001558, p. 2.

50. Ibid., p. 2. From the JCS point of view, its reluctance to estimate ultimate success could be justified by the narrower scope of the 10 March paper. This meant, though, that the 3 February conclusion that the project had "a fair chance of ultimate success" remained valid.

estimated that by 15 March the air and the ground elements of the CEF would attain the military effectiveness to carry out their mission successfully.

The report was more critical of the logistical planning. It noted that the invading force had a marginal capability to sustain itself for as little as thirty days and that the logistical plans must be revised. Even worse, since preparations for an anti-Castro invasion were no secret and it was impossible to conceal the air lift that was to take the brigade from Guatemala to Nicaragua, the JCS estimated that the chances of achieving surprise were no more than 15 percent. This could have a devastating effect on the likelihood of even an initial success: "If surprise is not achieved, it is most likely that the air mission will fail. As a consequence, one or more of Castro's combat aircraft will likely be available for use against the invasion force, and an aircraft with 50 caliber machine guns could sink all or most of the invasion force."[51]

This prediction clearly contradicted the positive estimate of the operation's chances of initial military success. Although the JCS suggested that the CIA should change its plans so as to increase the possibility of achieving surprise,[52] they nevertheless failed to link this condition directly to their overall estimate. Thus once again the policymakers had the impression that the military was more favorable to the plan than the Joint Chiefs really were. This impression dominated the atmosphere during the 11 March meeting at the White House. Dulles warned Kennedy of the devastating political consequences if the project were called off, while Bissell, serving as the operation's staff officer, interpreted the recent JCS report in the most positive manner: "The Cuban paramilitary force if effectively used has a *good* chance of overthrowing Castro, or of causing a damaging civil war, *without the necessity for the United States to commit itself to overt action against Cuba.*"[53] Then Bissell presented four possible courses of action: covert landing; surprise attack; diversionary landing and surprise attack; and landing in a remote area with a slow buildup. After analyzing each plan, he finally recommended that the third course of action be adopted.[54] President Kennedy, perhaps under strong pressure from Assistant Secretary of State

51. Ibid., pp. 8–9.

52. Ibid., p. 1.

53. From Mr. Bissell's paper entitled "Proposed Operation against Cuba," which summarized action to 11 March 1961, Annex no. 11 of the Taylor Committee Report, DDRS 1985/001543, p. 12 (emphasis added).

54. Ibid., pp. 5–12.

Thomas C. Mann,[55] rejected this recommendation, instead demanding a less spectacular operation.

Within three days the task force came back with three new alternatives tailored to meet the President's demands. Evaluating them became the next JCS task.

JCSM–166–61: 15 March 1961

The JCS evaluation of the alternative CIA plans was done under pressures and in a hurry. The plans were considered by the Joint Chiefs for no more than twenty minutes (*Operation Zapata*, p. 267) and on the basis of the experience gained in the two earlier estimate processes.

The first CIA alternative suggested an amphibious landing in the Trinidad area, at night, without airborne landing and air strikes. The second formulated an evening airdrop to seize control of and isolate the main landing area at Preston on the north coast of Oriente Province in eastern Cuba. This was to be followed by a night landing of the remaining forces and the use of the available port and airstrip facilities for the continuation of operations. The third option called for an amphibious night landing in the Zapata area of southern Cuba, departure of ships by dawn, and air operations from a nearly airstrip the next day.

Overall the JCS concluded that "none of the alternative concepts are considered as feasible and likely to accomplish the objective as the basic para-military plan [Trinidad]." More specifically, the report decided that the first alternative's chances of ultimate success were "doubtful" and that the second was the "least likely to accomplish the objective." They were more positive about the third option:

55. Assistant Secretary of State Thomas Mann, along with Under Secretary Chester Bowles, were among the main opponents of the CIA plan in the State Department. In mid-February 1961 Mann estimated that the project had a poor chance of success for the following reasons: there was no likelihood of a popular uprising in Cuba; there were logistical problems in supplying the exile force if it were to become a guerrilla force; invasion would violate international treaties that permit the use of force only for self-defense; Castro could gain popular support, at home and in Latin America, if the United States was perceived to be behind the attack; Cuba was not a direct security problem for the United States; economic failures could lead to the overthrow of Castro by the Cubans themselves. Mann concluded therefore that "it would not be in the national interest to proceed unilaterally to put this plan into execution." Memorandum from Mr. Mann to the Secretary: "The March 1960 Plan," 15 February 1961, DDRS 1984/000943.

a. In the absence of significant enemy forces in the [Zapata] area, the invasion force can be landed successfully in the objective area and can be sustained in the area provided resupply of essential items is accomplished.

b. The area meets the requirements imposed including the availability of an airfield, suitability for a clandestine landing, and possibly suitable for extending operations to cause the downfall of Castro.[56]

The three alternatives, with a joint CIA-JCS recommendation to adopt the Zapata concept, were presented to President Kennedy immediately after the JCS concluded their analysis on 15 March. Despite the fact that Zapata was far less spectacular than the earlier Trinidad plan, the President continued to demand that the landing "appear as an inside guerrilla-type operation" and ordered a review of planning.[57] Others at the meeting were more impressed. McGeorge Bundy, for example, informed his boss:

I have been a skeptic about Bissell's operation, but now I think we are on the edge of a good answer. I also think that Bissell and [the officer in charge of military planning in the task force, Colonel Jake] Hawkins have done an honorable job of meeting the proper criticisms and cautions of the Department of State.[58]

The modified Zapata plan was approved, with some reservations, at a 16 March White House meeting. This marked the end of the JCS's role as professional estimators of military planning.

All in all, between late January and mid-March 1961, a widening gap was created between the JCS's "real" estimate of the military plan's feasibility and what Kennedy and his aides believed it to be. First, the original Trinidad plan was allowed about a 30 percent chance of success. This must have been reduced even further after the JCS experts conducted their independent inspection in late February, although the report of this inspection avoided an overall estimate. Then, when the JCS came to assess the Zapata plan in

56. Memorandum for the Secretary of Defense: "Evaluation of the Military Aspects of Alternate Concepts, CIA Para-Military Plan, Cuba," JCSM–166–61, 15 March 1961, DDRS 1985/001544, pp. 1–2, 10.
57. Summary of White House Meetings, 9 May 1961, DDRS 1985/001550, p. 2.
58. Memorandum for the President: "Meeting on Cuba, 4:00 P.M., March 15, 1961," 15 March 1961, DDRS 1984/000556, p. 2.

mid-March, their conclusions were relatively positive but also misleading; Zapata was judged better than the two other alternatives but inferior, as the report pointed out, to the Trinidad plan. Indeed, "the Chiefs apparently rated the chances of success for Zapata as something less than fair" (*Operation Zapata*, p. 247).

At the same time, the principal policymakers were exposed to diametrically opposed interpretations of these estimates. The plan that in February had "a fair chance of ultimate success" (that is, "not too good") was described by Bissell on 11 March as having "a good chance of overthrowing Castro." And five days later, ignoring JCS reservations, Kennedy and his aides heard from Bissell that on balance Zapata was "more advantageous than the Trinidad Plan" (ibid., p. 14).

As a result of the widening gap between these two estimates, operational plans with a diminishing chance of success were receiving growing support in the White House. Thus it happened that Bundy, who was skeptical of the invasion plan in early February, supported Zapata a month later, while the mere fact that in mid-March Kennedy authorized the CIA to continue preparing for the implementation of this plan is a clear indication that he was not aware of the JCS's true estimates of the project.

Factor 2: Local Support and General Uprising

A precondition for overthrowing a government by covert action is the existence of effective domestic, military, or civilian opposition to the regime. Such conditions had existed in two earlier CIA attempts to topple hostile leaders, in Iran in 1953 and in Guatemala a year later. The use of American money and British agents enabled the CIA and its British counterpart, the SIS (Secret Intelligence Service), to regain power for the Shah of Iran from the politically weak Mossadegh, who had only partial control over the military and the police. And though Arbenz was the democratically elected president of Guatemala, disagreements between him and his army paved the way for the CIA's successful countercoup in 1954.

The situation in Cuba in 1961, however, was fundamentally different. Since early 1959 the American intelligence community had emphasized the contrast between Castro's efforts to consolidate power and the growing opposition to his regime, but by the end of 1960 it was already clear that Castro was winning. His strategy was threefold: the rapid buildup of loyal security forces with emphasis on a large-scale militia as a means of tightening internal security; the elimination of institutions resisting the regime and their replacement by supportive ones; and populist foreign and domestic policy aimed at acquiring genuine support, especially from the lower classes.

Obviously, as every NIE from mid-1959 noted, Castro's strategy alienated the Cuban middle and professional classes. But these classes, the reports also noted, were relatively ineffective. Thus by the end of 1960 the Catholic Church, the only institution still opposing the regime (but also a traditionally weak one in Cuba), was considered no more than "a rallying point for the opposition," while the middle and professional classes—many of which had fled Cuba—were dismissed as "disorganized and leaderless." And though some guerrilla groups were operating in the Escambray mountains and Oriente Province, "the regime has reacted vigorously and has thus far been able to contain these bands."[59]

The prospects for a change in this situation were distinctly gloomy. By the end of 1960 the U.S. Intelligence Board (comprised of senior representatives of all civil and military agencies that deal with American foreign policy) concluded:

> We believe that during the period of this estimate [six months] Castro's control of Cuba will be further consolidated. Organized opposition appears to lack the strength and coherence to pose a major threat to the regime, and we foresee no development in the internal economic or political situation which would be likely to bring about a critical shift of popular opinion away from Castro. Any further erosion of Castro's base of popular support is likely to be offset by the growing effectiveness of the state's instrumentalities of control. The regime's capabilities for dealing with internal disturbances and foreign-based incursions are almost certain to improve. Effective government control over the institutions and daily life of the Cuban people is also likely to increase, making effective opposition more difficult and risky.[60]

In light of this and similar reports the question is whether the CIA chiefs misled their political superiors (and the JCS) about the prospects for a general uprising as a result of the planned invasion. The answer is negative if we are to believe the agency's chiefs themselves. Allen Dulles later

59. "Prospects for the Castro Regime," SNIE 85–3–60, 8 December 1960, p. 2.
60. Ibid., p. 4.

maintained: "I know of no estimate that a spontaneous uprising of the unarmed population of Cuba would be touched off by the landing" (Dulles, p. 157). In an unpublished version of a magazine article he wrote about the Bay of Pigs episode he further maintained that "the planners believed that the invasion might prompt anti-Castro revolts, but only after the brigade had proved its staying power by seizing control of solid beachhead" (Vanden-broucke, p. 367).

Richard Bissell elaborated on Dulles's positions. First, he argued that only after a week or so of fighting in which the brigade (and especially its aircraft) were to inflict heavy losses on Castro's armed forces, coupled with intensive psychological warfare and diversionary landings, "was it anticipated that internal resistance might begin to materialize, probably more in the form of guerrilla action than of an uprising." Second, "the president, or other policymakers, may have formed an exaggerated impression of the contribution to be expected from spontaneous rebellion on the island." And, third, "there is no support in the record for the view that the CIA indulged in or promulgated such unrealistic optimism" (Bissell, pp. 379–80).

Dulles's and Bissell's protestations are problematic. Even taken at face value, Bissell's arguments raise the question of why the CIA (in fact, Dulles and Bissell himself) avoided warning Kennedy and his aides that their expectations for a general uprising were highly exaggerated. It is probably true (though not all records are declassified and not everything said was recorded) that the CIA did not directly promulgate such optimism. But it is also true that there is nothing in the record to show that the agency did the opposite. Clearly, Dulles and Bissell, Kennedy's chief intelligence advisors on the project, failed to carry out their tasks properly. Expressing their opinion on such a critical matter was no less their professional duty than convincing the President of the benefits of the operation. But they did not do so—and probably not by mistake.[61]

The same thing happened with regard to the JCS. As far as local support and a general uprising were concerned, there were significant differences between the Trinidad and the Zapata plans. Taking place in a sparsely populated swampy area and in a less spectacular form, Zapata could not be expected to impress the Cuban masses or arouse the massive local support

61. Bissell's argument that the CIA did not indulge in expectations of a general uprising is simply not true. Equipment and arms for 15,000 men were carried aboard the supply ships, and equipment for an additional 15,000 volunteers was held at an Army depot in Alabama for subsequent shipment (Supply Data, Annex no. 24 of the Taylor Committee Report, 23 May 1961, DDRS 1985/001553).

that Trinidad could. Yet the impression of the JCS was that changing the invasion site made little difference. General Thomas White, the Air Force Chief of Staff, testified that the intelligence the Joint Chiefs were provided with indicated "that military uprisings were likely" in both cases. His Marine colleague, General David M. Shoup, understood Zapata to mean that "there were lots of people just waiting for these arms, that they would get them in the same manner as they would have in the Trinidad Plan" (*Operation Zapata,* pp. 255; 245). The CIA planners, so it seems, made little effort if any to dispute such impressions.[62]

Finally, if the CIA did not expect an immediate uprising, then the whole rationale of its military plan was falling apart. As will be discussed later, CIA reports on the eve of the operation indicated that Castro had significant forces that could reach the Zapata area within ten hours. Even if it took them much longer, it is still unclear how guerrilla activities, which (according to Bissell's own estimate) would have reached no more than an embryonic stage by $D+7$, could have prevented a defeat at the beachhead. After all, according to JCS estimates, the brigade had no chance of holding off Castro's forces for more than three days.

So three facts become quite clear here. First, since the requisite conditions had not materialized in Cuba prior to the invasion, there was little chance if any that it would trigger a general uprising. Second, the civilian and military policymakers were too optimistic about this factor despite NIE reports that firmly indicated the opposite. Third, the architects of the Cuba project did nothing to bridge this gap by warning their political superiors and the JCS that they were indulging in wishful thinking.

Factor 3: The Guerrilla Option

Every military operation conducted by a small force against a larger one without feasible course of retreat involves a high risk of total failure. Two courses of withdrawal were theoretically available to the invading brigade: evacuating by sea or going guerrilla. The first option involved a highly complicated military operation obviously beyond the limited independent capabilities of the CEF. It was clear that in order to succeed such an

---

62. Neither General White nor General Shoup directly accused the CIA of misleading the JCS. Yet there can be hardly a doubt that the intelligence they received, perhaps indirectly, came from the CIA itself, either in the form of written documents or in verbal briefings.

operation would demand overt American intervention, something ruled out from the start by both President Eisenhower and President Kennedy.

Left only with the guerrilla option, the CIA planners as well as the JCS promoted it as a highly reliable means of securing the operation against total failure, that is, the destruction of the invading force on the beachhead by Castro's military. Ex post factum, however, they admitted that the guerrilla option was never really feasible, especially under the Zapata plan. The sparsely populated swampland offered no concealment for a large invading force, especially against Castro's helicopters, and the guerrilla zone in the Escambray mountains was seventy miles away from the landing site at the Bay of Pigs. Given that the same logic of the situation existed also during the planning stages, one may wonder if the planners ever believed in the real feasibility of this option.

But even though Trinidad was only a few miles from the Escambray, and thus within reach of any brigade survivors in case of defeat on the beach, the feasibility of large-scale guerrilla operations from this region is also rather doubtful. To begin with, as a CIA apologia had to admit, "At no time did the Brigade once organized [that is, after 4 November 1960] receive training to fight as a guerrilla force."[63] Yet this document emphasized that the original cadre of the brigade, 375 officers and NCOs, received extensive guerrilla training in excess of thirteen weeks prior to the change in the project's concept in early November.[64] Even taken at face value, these figures show that most of the brigade, over a thousand men, were expected to become a guerrilla force without any prior training. Nor were they equipped for such warfare; most of their heavy gear, including M-41 tanks, 4.2 mortars, tracks, and jeeps, would have had to have been left behind, and there was little to make up for it. This, indeed, raises the question of the CIA's ability to support the CEF logistically once it had gone guerrilla. Given that the failure of small-scale air drops to local guerrilla groups during 1960 was one of the main reasons for the abortion of the guerrilla option, one can only wonder how the CIA hoped to succeed on a far larger scale by using the same logistics.

The possibility of going guerrilla in case of defeat in the Zapata area was

---

63. Paragraph F. of Memorandum dated 22 May 1961: "What Briefing If Any, Was Given the Brigade or the Brigade's Staff on Going Guerrilla?" 31 May 1961, Annex no. 17 of the Taylor Committee Report, DDRS 1985/001554, p. 2.

64. Ibid., p. 1. Guerrilla training at Camp Trax did not start before the last week of September, so it could not have lasted for more than six or seven weeks. The Cubans themselves rated the quality of this training as very poor (Johnson, pp. 48–49).

even more remote, especially for the Cubans who themselves knew only too well about the actual conditions in this zone. Indeed, discussions of the guerrilla option "did not cover the Zapata area specifically for security reasons, but covered the other feasible areas to include the Escambray, Pinar del Rio and the Oriente."[65] Explaining the lack of preparations for going guerrilla in the Zapata area by citing "security reasons" should have been too far-fetched even for the writers of this report. Nor could they explain how the brigade was supposed to reach the mountains in the first place without a magic carpet or the equivalent thereof.

We must therefore conclude that the guerrilla option was never a real one for the CIA. Nobody expressed this better than the agency's officers themselves:

> In summation it must be stated that little interest or enthusiasm was displayed by the Brigade personnel concerned for any aspect of the plan that involved retreat and defeat, to include this contingency for guerrilla operations plan. It was generally recognized and openly stated by the key officers that any military force involved in an airborne/amphibious landing and subsequent field operations against an enemy defending his homeland would have an extremely difficult time assuming a guerrilla role in any substantive force subsequent to defeat in the field. *Defeat itself implied that the enemy in close combat had surrounded or ruptured and destroyed the Brigade as a military force, thus allowing only a fraction of its combat effectiveness to escape to assume a role as escapees and evaders with a limited potential for later guerrilla operations.*[66]

The report does not specify the "key officers" who "openly stated" that the guerrilla option did not exist. Certainly they were not the chief architects of the project, who evidently never expressed such views to the JCS or the White House. Indeed, the opposite is true. As McGeorge Bundy testified before the Board of Inquiry on the Bay of Pigs (the Taylor Committee), "The President repeatedly indicated his own sense that this [guerrilla] option was of great importance, and he was repeatedly assured that the guerrilla option was a real one" (*Operation Zapata*, p. 178). Needless

---

65. "What Briefing If Any, Was Given the Brigade or the Brigade's Staff on Going Guerilla?" p. 1.

66. Ibid., p. 5 (emphasis added).

to say, this was Bundy's impression as well (ibid.). Defense Secretary Robert McNamara, who stated that the guerrilla option "was certainly in the President's mind," testified that if a general uprising did not occur it was expected that the brigade "would be split up into a guerrilla force and moved into the Escambrays" (ibid., p. 202). The President's brother Robert Kennedy was briefed in his office a few days before the invasion by Richard Bissell:

> He told me at that time that the chances of success were about two out of three and that failure was almost impossible. . . . [E]ven if the force was not successful in its initial objective of establishing a beachhead, the men could become guerrillas and, therefore, couldn't be wiped out and would be a major force and thorn in the side of Castro. (Schlesinger 1978, p. 443)

As for the military, their understanding was precisely the same. "If there were opposition and they [the brigade] could not hold," Admiral Arleigh Burke, the Navy Chief of Staff, believed, "they would slip through and become guerrillas (*Operation Zapata*, pp. 111–12).[67]

On 29 March President Kennedy decided to postpone the tentative D-Day from 5 April to 10 April. On 4 April he held a meeting at the State Department. After a briefing by Bissell, the President demanded the opinion of each of the relatively large number of participants. Except for the chairman of the Senate Foreign Relations Committee, Senator William Fulbright, who was participating in such a discussion for the first and the last time, nobody openly objected to the operation.[68] A day later the idea of a preliminary air strike by fake Cuban defectors as a means of concealing the U.S. role in the air operations was discussed with the President, who was receptive but demanded a more detailed plan.[69] This plan along with

67. One can understand how Kennedy and his aides, who lacked sufficient military experience, could fail to comprehend the absurdity of the guerrilla option, especially in the Zapata plan. It is more difficult to understand why the JCS failed here as well. The only reference, probably on the basis of CIA information, to the possibility of guerrilla warfare in their 15 March report was that Zapata "has been an historically suitable guerrilla area" (DDRS 1985/001544, pp. 8–9).

68. For a good description of this meeting, see Wyden, pp. 146–51. Schlesinger, the only one among Kennedy's advisors to clearly object to the operation, was present but was not asked by the President to express his opinion. He did so later (see n. 71), arguing convincingly but with little success (Schlesinger 1965, pp. 252–55).

69. This idea was first suggested by McGeorge Bundy in his memorandum of 15 March (DDRS 1984/000556).

some other operational details was discussed again on 6 April. At the end of this meeting 17 April was approved as the new tentative D-Day, with the first air strike to occur on 14 April and a diversionary landing a day later. Bissell informed the President that cancellation of the invasion was possible until noon of 16 April.[70]

What is striking is that during these lengthy discussions (especially on 4 April) the main focus of debate was not the feasibility of the operation but rather the ethical, legal, and foreign policy problems it involved plus the operational changes needed in order to satisfy Kennedy's demand for maximal plausible deniability.[71] It certainly looks as if cognitive barriers such as groupthinking helped to create an atmosphere bordering on that of a fool's paradise. But this does not sufficiently explain such behavior on the part of highly qualified and intelligent policymakers who all seemed to believe that the operation was militarily feasible, that there was a fair chance for a general uprising, and that even if it failed in its initial mission the brigade could still go guerrilla and thus avoid a total failure. These impressions were not solely the result of distorted cognitive processes. First and foremost, they were created and advocated by the CIA chiefs who participated in these meetings and were considered the ultimate authority on the project's likelihood of success. That within the task force itself there were grave doubts regarding the existence of the three necessary conditions for success was never brought to the attention of Kennedy and his advisors.

Thus all during the period under discussion, but especially toward its end when political decisions with operational implications had to be made, the CIA chiefs took ever greater risks by concealing vital information from policymakers in order to get the operation under way. If during Eisenhower's last year in office they avoided informing their political superiors of significant changes in the project until they became faits accomplis, during Kennedy's first months in office they avoided alerting the administration to possible total failure of the mission despite growing concern that such a result was likely. In this sense between January and early April 1961 the

70. Memorandum for Record: "Summary of White House Meetings," 9 May 1961, DDRS 1985/001550, pp. 3–4. This memorandum summarized all White House meetings on the Cuba project during the Kennedy administration and was written following the failure of the operation.

71. The main exception is Schlesinger's 5 April memorandum to the President in which Kennedy's Special Assistant pointed out both the main weaknesses of planning and the impossibility of American plausible deniability and of a general uprising in Cuba as the sources of his objections to the operation (Schlesinger 1965, pp. 251–55). He did not vent these reservations, however, during the discussion of 4 April in which he participated.

CIA chiefs consciously indulged in encouraging an unexperienced President to support a foreign policy venture he would otherwise have rejected by supplying him with incomplete and biased information.

12–17 April: Keeping the Momentum at All Cost

On 12 April 1961 the final version of Operation Zapata was presented to President Kennedy. He approved the continuation of operational activities, including the embarkation of the brigade onto vessels in Nicaragua that had already started on 11 April. While not giving his final approval of the invasion itself, Kennedy was informed of two coming deadlines: 12 A.M. on 14 April (Friday) for a diversionary landing in Oriente Province and 12 A.M. on 16 April for the main landing. Limited air strikes by planes disguised as Cuban were approved for 15 April (*Operation Zapata,* pp. 16–17).

Kennedy's refusal to give final approval until twelve hours before the main invasion, while at the same time authorizing a diversionary landing and first air strikes, initiated the climactic stage of the CIA's efforts to attain the result it so desired. Attaining it, however, became more and more complicated. For, on the one hand, as time passed without the President indicating any intention to veto the operation, the likelihood of its implementation increased; but, on the other hand, as activities commenced, there emerged new operational and political problems that indicated how infeasible the whole operation was from the start. Walking this tightrope, the CIA chiefs avoided any action that might have caused Kennedy to call off the operation at the last moment. This behavior meant not only concealment of important information, and on isolated occasions even the supply of misleading information, but also operational decisions that significantly compromised the ability of the Cuban exiles' brigade to succeed in its mission. How desperate these efforts were became evident in five events taking place between 12 and 17 April.

Colonel Hawkins's Military Evaluation

Still doubtful about the ability of the brigade to carry out its mission successfully, the President demanded a final evaluation of the CEF. Probably suspecting that the Cubans had been led to believe that American forces would intervene, Kennedy specifically demanded to know what they knew about the designated American role (see Robert Kennedy's description in Guthman and Shulman, p. 241). The mission of finding this out was assigned to Colonel Jack Hawkins, the task force's officer in charge of the brigade (and, obviously, a biased estimator). He received it in an emergency cable on 13 April while in Puerto Cabezas in Nicaragua, where the Cubans were in the process of embarking the vessels. His reply, which arrived the same day, is so unique that it deserves to be quoted almost in its entirety:

> (a) My observations the last few days have increased my confidence in the ability of this force to accomplish not only initial combat mission but also *the ultimate objective of Castro's overthrow*.

> (b) Reference . . . arrived during the final briefing of the Brigade and Battalion commanders. They now know all details of the plan and are enthusiastic. These officers are young, vigorous, intelligent and motivated with a fanatical urge to begin battle which most of them have been preparing in the rugged conditions of the training camps for almost a year. I have talked to many of them in their language. Without exception, they have utmost confidence in their ability to win. They say they know their own people and believe after they have inflicted one serious defeat upon opposing forces, the latter will melt away from Castro, who they have no wish to support. They say it is Cuban tradition to join a winner and they have supreme confidence they will win all engagements against the best Castro has to offer. *I share their confidence*.

> (c) The Brigade is well organized and is more heavily armed and better equipped in some respects *than U.S. infantry units*. The men have received intensive training in the use of their weapons, *including more firing experience than U.S. troops would normally receive*. . . .

> (d) The Brigade now numbers 1,400; *a truly formidable force*.

> (e) I have also carefully observed the Cuban Air Force. The aircraft are kept with pride and some of the B-26 crews are so eager to commence contemplated operation that they have already armed their aircraft. . . . [Name sanitized] informed me today that he considers the B-26 squadron *equal to the best U.S. Air Force squadron*.

(f) *The Brigade officers do not expect help from U.S. Armed Forces.* They ask only for continued delivery of supplies. This can be done covertly.

(g) This Cuban Air Force is motivated, strong, well trained, armed to the teeth, and ready. I believe profoundly that it would be a serious mistake for the United States to deter it from its intended purpose. [72]

Colonel Hawkins's estimate was about as unbiased as that of a dishonest salesman. Parts of his cable were simply lies. For example, the 13 April briefing discussed the operation only in general terms; the brigade's senior officers were not even informed that their destination was the Bay of Pigs. The final and more detailed briefing was actually given a day later (see below). Moreover, as the commanders of the CEF described it later, most of them believed that American forces would back them if needed (Johnson, pp. 74–76).

As for the quality of the brigade, some of its soldiers had been recruited only in late March or early April and had never used weapons until they boarded the ships en route to Cuba (ibid., p. 99). But even the better-trained Cubans were hardly an elite. A more sober estimate of their combat effectiveness was that of the Marine colonel who served on General Gray's inspection committee and spent some three weeks with the brigade. When asked by the Taylor Committee to compare the Cubans with American troops, he answered that "in a fight it would be like putting our Marines against Boy Scouts" (*Operation Zapata*, p. 155). And even if the brigade had been as good as the best American unit, no sober-minded general would have sent his troops on such a mission without ensuring that the whole American army was ready to back them.

Was Colonel Hawkins simply mistaken, or perhaps exaggerating a little but genuinely confident that the quality of the brigade ensured success? Probably not, for on 8 April, just five days earlier, he and WH/4 chief Engler had come to Bissell's house to inform their boss of their wish to resign. They expressed many reasons, political as well as operational (for example, the B-26s were too slow and had too short a range), for believing that the mission was doomed to fail. Although they were convinced by

---

72. Memorandum for General Maxwell D. Taylor: "Evaluation of Brigade for Action, 13 April 61," Annex no. 18 of the Taylor Committee Report, 26 April 1961, DDRS 1985/001546, pp. 1–2 (emphasis added).

Bissell to remain on his team, this was out of personal loyalty rather than any conviction that the project was feasible after all (Wyden, pp. 159–60).

There can thus be little doubt that Colonel Hawkins had consciously misled his supreme commander. So did Bissell himself, who upon receiving Hawkins's cable made sure that the President saw it right away (ibid., p. 169). What is most striking, however, is that President Kennedy, though possibly aware of Colonel Hawkins's bias, was highly impressed by his estimate. As the President's brother put it two years later, "this Marine colonel came back and gave a briefing and also wrote a memorandum, which I think was the most instrumental paper in convincing the President to go ahead."[73]

The Brigade's Briefings

When briefing the Cubans on the eve of the operation, their American instructors faced the delicate dilemma of whether or not to give an accurate intelligence picture; since this was so gloomy, it could have discouraged the exiles from going into battle. According to Dulles, CIA intelligence available just before D-Day indicated that "[t]he nearest enemy combat forces numbering about 6,000 men are located at Santa Clara, about 70 miles northwest of the target area. It is composed of one infantry regiment, one tank battalion, one artillery battalion" (*Operation Zapata*, p. 351).

According to this report, additional forces of about 6,500 men as well as another tank force could have reached the combat area within ten hours (ibid., pp. 351–52). Altogether, then, more than 13,000 soldiers equipped with tanks and artillery could have reached the Zapata area no later than D + 1.

But the briefing given to the commander of the Cuban brigade and his officers on 14 April never furnished these impressive figures. Castro, the

73. Robert Kennedy's interviews with John Bartlow Martin, 1 March, 13 April, 30 April, and 14 May 1964 (Guthman and Shulman, p. 241). Although Robert Kennedy's description of this episode is wrong in some details (for example, there is nothing in the record to show that Hawkins gave any briefing), there is no doubt that the mission RFK described was that of Colonel Hawkins and that the memorandum he mentioned was Hawkins's cable. Robert Kennedy's frustration over the failure of the Bay of Pigs and his interest in defending his brother's decision might have influenced his description of this incident. But even if Hawkins's telegram did not play such a decisive role in the President's decision to launch the operation, two facts remain valid: this estimate was based on motivated biases and the President took it into consideration when making his final decision.

Cubans were told, could not react within seventy-two hours, his forces were highly disorganized and lacked efficient communications, his aircraft and most of his tanks would be destroyed before reaching the Zapata area. More than 500 guerrillas, moreover, were waiting to assist the brigade while an additional 5,000 Cubans, equipment for whom was aboard the ships, were expected to join the force within two days. The intelligence picture was so promising, indeed, that the leaders of the brigade were told that, although the Americans were behind them all the way, they would need no further assistance; with so many volunteers all that was left was for them simply to march into Havana (Johnson, pp. 84–85).[74]

The Cubans themselves avoided asking any questions at this briefing. Partly it was because they believed the Americans and lacked the professional experience needed to challenge such an overly optimistic picture. But it was also because they were too polite. As the brigade commander admitted later, "We didn't want to ask these men we knew any embarrassing questions" (ibid., p. 85).

The Naval Rules of Engagement

Since the brigade had no effective means of defending itself on the voyage from Nicaragua to Cuba, and since early warning might possibly alert Castro's forces to locate and destroy the vessels carrying it,[75] supplying the brigade with naval protection was an important task. The original concept of Operation Crosspatch—the U.S. Navy's code name for the Cuba project, later changed to Bumpy Road—"was to ensure that when once embarked this operation must not fail."[76] Thus on 1 April the JCS approved rules of

74. The description of this briefing is based on the testimony of some of the brigade officers. Although it is possible that they exaggerated a bit, there is no good evidence to contradict them. Dulles said he believed that the CIA intelligence report he used was also employed to brief the brigade (*Operation Zapata*, p. 351). This means that at least technically the report could have been available to the CIA officers who conducted the briefing. Whether Dulles knew it was not used is a question I cannot answer, although I assume he did not know.

75. Castro already had ample information about the coming invasion from press reports and probably from informers in Guatemala, Nicaragua, and Miami as well as Soviet intelligence sources. He did not know, however, when and where the invasion would take place. There was a real risk that informers in Nicaragua could have supplied him with this information. This was the main reason why the CIA held its final briefing until the last possible moment. The embarkation of the troops on the vessels, however, was more difficult to conceal and involved the real risk that the timing of the invasion would become known to Castro.

76. A memorandum to Admiral Dennison, 13 April 1961, in "U.S. Navy Rules of Engagement, Operation BUMPY ROAD," DDRS 1985/001524, p. 1.

engagement according to which two American destroyers were to escort the CEF ships on D-2 and D-1, with naval aircraft conducting air patrols on D-1. The escorting U.S. forces were "to warn off any approaching Cuban aircraft or ships and if the Cuban aircraft or ships persisted in their approach the U.S. forces were to open fire when the Cuban aircraft or ships reached a position to attack or attacked the CEF ships."[77]

Then in two White House meetings on 5 and 6 April President Kennedy made it clear to the JCS and CIA that, if American forces were required to defend the CEF ships by fire, the operation would be aborted. As a result, the rules of engagement were changed. If earlier the primary role of the U.S. Navy was to protect the Cuban ships, now the most important element was to ensure that "premature U.S. intervention not occur which would be the cause for cancellation of this highly important and desirable operation."[78] Accordingly, the escorting destroyers were instructed to maintain maximum practicable range from the CEF ships during daylight and were not permitted to approach within twenty miles of the Cuban coast. In contrast to the earlier instructions, moreover, U.S. forces were allowed to intervene only if the CEF ships were fired upon.

The new rules implied a CIA and JCS readiness to take additional risks in order to prevent a last-minute abortion of the operation. It seems, however, that the task force chiefs were more concerned with the possibility that the Navy admirals might be trigger-happy than with the safety of the brigade. Thus the Deputy Director of the CIA, General Charles P. Cabell, was sent to the JCS on 13 April to discuss again the rules of engagement. According to a Navy report, "He was particularly concerned that the U.S. naval forces might intervene before seriously needed, thus forcing abandonment of the operation."[79] In line with this concern, Admiral Robert Dennison, the Commander in Chief, Atlantic (CINCLANT), received a cable summarizing the JCS's stand: "hope is that over all operations will not repeat not need to be aborted because of U.S. military intervention and to this end CEF prepared to take substantive risks."[80] Needless to say, the Cuban commanders of the CEF never knew of these rules of engagement, and the reference to the CEF in the cable meant the chiefs of the CIA. The only result of this additional warning was that EW (Early Warning) destroy-

77. Memorandum from G. A. Mitchell, CDR, U.S. Navy (no date), ibid.
78. Memorandum to Admiral Dennison, 13 April 1961, ibid.
79. Ibid., 2.
80. Ibid.

ers were now to stay at least thirty miles from Cuban territory, thus minimizing their ability to alert the CEF from incoming air attacks.

As it turned out, no Cuban ships or aircraft detected or attacked the CEF. But the CIA insistence on limiting U.S. protection of the brigade as much as possible despite serious apprehensions that it might be attacked constitutes further proof of how far the architects of the project were prepared to go in order to launch their operation.[81]

The Failure of the Diversionary Landing

According to the CIA plan as approved by the President, a diversionary landing in Oriente Province thirty miles east of the American Navy base at Guantanamo was planned for the night of D-2 (14–15 April). It was hoped that this landing of 164 men would convince Castro that the CEF's main effort was not in the Zapata area but hundreds of miles to the east.

However, this diversionary landing, the project's very first operational event, never took place. The commander of the force detected some Cuban soldiers on shore and concluded that his mission, which he considered of secondary importance, was not worth the risk (Wyden, p. 171). The Taylor Committee concluded differently:

> The landing failed to take place, probably because of weak leader-ship on the part of the Cuban officer responsible for the landing. This failure may have had a considerable effect on the main landing as the diversion was intended to draw Castro's forces to the east and confuse his command. (Operation Zapata, p. 18)

Although this failure became known to the task force at least twenty-four hours before the main invasion, there is no indication that it was ever reported to the President. If this was indeed the case, the CIA withheld important information that might well have affected Kennedy's final deci-sion. Was it simply because the CIA felt there was no need to tell a busy decisionmaker of every detail of the operation? Probably not. President Kennedy was personally involved in the decisionmaking process concerning various operational aspects of this project, which was, after all, the first

81. On the same day that General Cabell came to the JCS to demand additional limitation on CEF protection, the Cuban commander of the brigade was assured by his American case officer that close U.S. protection would be given to the force on its way to Cuba.

major foreign policy initiative of his administration. The architects of the project, moreover, made sure that encouraging information (such as Hawkins's telegram) was brought to Kennedy's attention. They did not act similarly in this case probably because the failure of this mission not only further minimized the project's likelihood of initial military success but also served as a good indication of the real quality of the Cuban force and its leadership. And this was exactly why, according to the rationale of the project's architects, such crucial information needed to be concealed from the President.

The Abortion of the Second Air Strike

The complete destruction of Castro's air force had to be considered crucial to military success. Already in early January 1961 CIA planners warned that "[t]he Cuban Air Force and naval vessels capable of opposing our landing must be knocked out or neutralized before our amphibious shipping makes its final run into the beach. If this is not done, we will be courting disaster."[82]

Foreseeing the political dimension of this issue, namely, the difficulty of plausibly denying U.S. involvement in massive air strikes, the memorandum recommended:

> (1) That the air preparation commence not later than dawn of D minus 1 day.
>
> (2) That any move to curtail the number of aircraft to be employed from those available be firmly resisted.
>
> (3) That the operation be abandoned if policy does not provide for use of adequate tactical air support.[83]

The first air strike by fake Cuban defectors was carried out according to plan at dawn on D-2 (Saturday, 15 April). Although initial pilot reports indicated impressive success, subsequent U-2 photographs showed that only five aircraft had been destroyed and a few others damaged (*Operation Zapata*, p. 18). At least some of Castro's aircraft (including T-33 and Sea Fury

---

82. Memorandum for Chief WH/4, 4 January 1961, DDRS 1985/001540, p. 6. For a similar JCS warning see JCSM–145–61, 10 March 1961, DDRS 1985/001558, p. 10.

83. Memorandum for Chief WH/4, p. 6.

fighters as well as B-26 light bombers) remained undamaged. Under these circumstances the second air strike, planned for D-day at dawn, became even more crucial.

On the evening of 16 April, about five hours after President Kennedy gave the final go-ahead signal for the invasion and less than five hours before it started, the CIA officer in charge, DDCI Cabell,[84] called Secretary of State Rusk on his own initiative, and against the advice of the task force officers present, to receive final approval for the second air strike. Rusk, aware that the fake defectors' cover-up story had already been exposed, had consulted some time earlier with Bundy and the President. Following their telephone discussion, President Kennedy ordered the second air strike cancelled unless there were "overriding considerations" (Wyden, pp. 195–99). Accordingly, upon receiving Cabell's call, Rusk informed the DDCI of the President's decision and invited him and Bissell to his office to present their counterarguments.

In the discussion that followed Rusk explained the political rationale for Kennedy's decision, maintaining that the need to conceal American involvement should now override the military demands. Cabell then presented the operational implications of the decision. One or more of the CEF ships might be destroyed by Castro's aircraft, he argued; such an event "would be serious but not catastrophic" if unloading had proceeded on schedule, as was somewhat unlikely. Also the brigade itself could expect to suffer heavier air strikes, although in light of the inefficiency of Castro's air force this probably "would be damaging . . . but not decisive." Even further, the ability of the CEF B-26s to isolate the beachhead would be significantly reduced. This, Cabell emphasized, was the "most serious effect" of the President's decision. Finally, he argued that the late change would reduce the general efficiency of the operation.[85]

While not regarding these as "overriding considerations," Rusk neverthe-

---

84. Allen Dulles left on Sunday (16 April) for Puerto Rico to give a lecture on how to do business with the Soviet bloc. This had been planned months ahead and now helped to create an atmosphere of business-as-usual as cover-up for the operation. His absence, while typical of his managerial style as well as of the trust he had in Bissell as the man in charge, was nevertheless peculiar. One would expect Dulles to feel the need to be in Washington during this time when critical decisions might be required.

85. "Mr. Bissell's and General Cabell's Memo of 9 May 61, re Visit to Secretary Rusk's Office on 16 April," Annex no. 21 of the Taylor Committee Report, DDRS 1985/001551, p. 2. According to Cabell, he was informed of the decision to veto the air strike only at 9:30 P.M. But other sources (e.g. Wyden, p. 199) maintain that he and Bissell were in Rusk's office by 7:00 P.M. The time element is crucial here, given that abortion of the invasion might still have been feasible two or three hours before H-Hour (midnight of 16–17 April). My impression is that Cabell's timetable is wrong.

less suggested that the two CIA men speak with the President. Cabell and Bissell saw no point to it, being "impressed with the extremely delicate situation with Ambassador Stevenson and the United Nations and the risk to the entire political position of the United States, and the firm position of the Secretary."[86]

Given the crucial importance of a second air strike to the military success of the operation, Cabell's behavior throughout this episode and even more so Bissell's seem strange. Their most logical course of action, surely, would have been to inform both Rusk and the President that calling off the air strike probably meant a death blow to the whole operation. This was certainly the belief of the task force's officers and the JCS when they learned of the decision.[87] Ex post facto Bissell himself would argue again and again that the abortion of the second air strike was the main cause for the operation's failure (e.g., *Operation Zapata*, pp. 112–13). Yet, face to face with Rusk, Bissell remained uncharacteristically passive, letting the inept Cabell do most of the talking. Even more strange, though aware that the President regarded him highly and despite their relatively warm relations,[88] Bissell preferred to avoid talking with Kennedy when Rusk suggested he do so.

Leaving Rusk and the President with the impression that the air strike was important but not crucial was a grave mistake. The Taylor Committee concluded as much (ibid., p. 38) and so did Bissell himself (Bissell, p. 379). What is not clear is why the chief architect of the project avoided expressing his opinion at the most crucial moment and when it was most needed. Although any answer involves more speculation than hard facts,[89] my impression is that Bissell declined to press Kennedy because he suspected that, faced with such a dilemma, the President might choose to abort the whole operation. Such an option, indeed, was still technically feasible, given that the earlier diversionary landing never took place and that no actual landing on the shores of the Bay of Pigs was expected to start for at

86. Ibid., pp. 2–3. For a similar explanation by Cabell and Bissell see also Jackson, 3:124–25.

87. Following the decision, Engler wrote a letter of resignation dated 2:00 A.M. 17 April (Wyden, p. 203). General Lemnitzer, the chief of the JCS, considered total air control (which had become unattainable following the decision) as "absolutely vital for success" (*Operation Zapata*, p. 326).

88. Shortly after entering office, the President made it clear to Bissell that he was his candidate to replace Dulles on 1 July 1962 (Wyden, p. 96).

89. General Taylor's scenario of what might have gone through Bissell's mind in Rusk's office is that Bissell lacked the experience to fully grasp the operational implications of aborting the second air strike and felt embarrassed about telling the President how crucial this mission was after being lectured by Rusk on the need to keep the whole operation as quiet as possible (Wyden, pp. 321–22).

least two hours. Although it would have involved significant difficulties, the CEF would have had ample time (at least seven hours) to turn around and get out of Cuban territorial waters by dawn.

It can be speculated, however, that Bissell behaved as he did not only because he was emotionally committed to a project in which he had invested all his energies for such a long time but also because he feared that if the operation were called off the President might, in the aftermath of this failure, learn how he had been misled by his intelligence advisors, first and foremost by Bissell himself. On the other hand, if the operation were carried out and ultimately succeeded, no questions would need to be asked. If this was the choice facing him, Bissell's reluctance to speak with the President was perhaps his greatest gamble. Unfortunately for everybody involved in the project, above all himself, he lost.

The Nature of the CIA's Misconduct

The CIA's conduct between early 1960, when the agency assumed full responsibility for overthrowing Castro by covert-action means, and mid-April 1961, when Operation Zapata was launched, was essentially the product of three factors: the professional quality of the officers in charge; the political demands; and the bureaucratic imperative, that is, the project officers' personal and organizational need to succeed.

These factors play a part in any operational planning. What characterizes the CIA's conduct at every juncture of the Cuba project, however, is the dominance of the third factor—the impulse to carry out the operation at all costs while ignoring the fundamental conflict between operational and political requirements.

The dominance of the bureaucratic imperative can be seen in the task force's consistent tendency to first escalate the project and then advocate its implementation as early as possible despite negative intelligence information. The plan was adopted and maintained merely because other courses of covert action were considered worse alternatives. To be sure, it is evident that time was working against the CIA and that small-scale activities against Castro (except for his assassination) would be fruitless. But the simple truth is that, when the CIA was formulating its first plans, Castro was already too strong to be toppled by any covert-action means. Yet this professional consideration, though clearly evident to some in the agency as early as

January–February 1960, never impinged on the project's architects because of the dominance of the bureaucratic imperative. And as time passed and the conflict between operational and political demands became even more evident, this factor became increasingly dominant, forcing the CIA planners to desperately foster a plan that was operationally infeasible under the given political constraints.

Thus during 1960 it was decided to abort the original guerrilla option because it was thought to be too little too late. But, instead of admitting that Castro was already too strong, the project's architects opted for a third alternative, escalating their operation into a conventional assault that professionally and politically was even less feasible and more risky. Since the political echelon might have objected to this new concept on professional and political grounds, moreover, considerable efforts were made to conceal it until no time was left to reverse it.

Then under the Kennedy administration the task force's problem was not how to conceal the project, which had become a fait accompli, but rather how to sell it to the President and his advisors. Here the CIA's chief planners used various techniques to convince the White House and the JCS that the project was militarily and politically sound and was provided with the fail-safe strategy of going guerrilla. In doing so, they exploited their image as experts in covert operations, Cuban affairs, and guerrilla warfare, while the real experts (such as the agency's Cuban analysts) were never brought onto the scene, probably because they would have contradicted their chief's optimistic estimates. At the same time, the new administration's lack of expertise in the conduct of foreign policy, as well as the reluctance of the JCS to take firmer responsibility for the operation, enabled the CIA planners to compound their salesmanship.

The influence of parochial bureaucratic interests reached its peak on the eve of the operation when the need to prevent President Kennedy from aborting the project at the last minute, coupled with an attempt to keep the CEF as enthusiastic as possible about their mission, compelled the CIA planners to mislead both their superiors and subordinates. Kennedy was thus led to believe that the CEF was far better than it really was; was probably not informed of the failure of the diversionary landing; and was kept ignorant of the operational risks involved in the decision to minimize cover for the CEF vessels, probably because of his warning to abort the project if the U.S. Navy had to intervene. Finally and most critically, there was no serious effort to explain to him the devastating effect of his decision to call off the D-Day air strike. At the same time, the CEF was fed with false assurances of the likelihood of military success and was led to believe that the United States was committed to victory. In reality, however, last-minute operational changes so severely crippled the brigade's ability to succeed that when it finally landed at the Bay of Pigs it had no chance of obtaining even its most minimal operational goals.

At this final stage the planners' own interests—their selfish need to carry out the operation at any cost—utterly overwhelmed any professional or political considerations. Like the Red Queen in Alice's looking-glass world, they found themselves running faster and faster just to keep in the same place. Still, the questions remain: Were the project's officers honestly mistaken and unconsciously motivated by the force of the bureaucratic imperative? Were they just not professional enough and too blinded by cognitive barriers to understand how marginal the chances of success really were? Or were they aware, at least partially, of what they were doing and why?

Certainly at the submanagerial level of Engler and his men at the CIA headquarters in Washington there was a definite awareness of the project's deficiencies. Probably no one was more aware of them than Engler himself, the only officer among the project's architects who had sufficient expertise in covert operations and Latin American affairs. Indeed, Engler did not keep his doubts to himself and at least twice expressed his concerns. In March he considered resigning when the invasion site was changed from Trinidad to Zapata (Wyden, p. 101). Then, as D-Day drew closer and the project's operational shortcomings became more evident, Engler became more decisive until on 8 April he and Colonel Hawkins came to Bissell's house to resign but were persuaded to withdraw their resignations.

The day after this incident the problem arose again. This time Richard Drain, a task force officer who had been part of the project since its inception, brought up the possibility of a collective resignation as a means of compelling Bissell to reconsider the whole operation. He did it informally, over lunch in a Washington restaurant with about a dozen task force officers present. Even though no collective action was taken, the impression is that everybody there agreed with Drain that the operation's prospects of success were poor. Interestingly enough, it was Engler himself, probably the most pessimistic officer present, who quelled the short-lived "mutiny" by appealing to his colleagues' sense of loyalty to Bissell (Phillips, pp. 131–32).[90] A

90. Wyden seems to be wrong in asserting (pp. 158–59) that this episode took place before Engler and Hawkins came to see Bissell. The testimony of Phillips, who participated in this "last lunch," seems to be more accurate.

week later, when they learned of the President's decision to abort the second air strike, they could only regret that they had not followed Drain's suggestion.

Thus the evidence is clear that some of the men best able to judge the operation's prospects were aware that these were rather slim. But they were kept in the dark about what Dulles and Bissell told the President behind closed doors, and they were strongly motivated by a deep sense of loyalty to and admiration of their chiefs. In this sense the WH/4 officers, with the exception of Hawkins and his report of 13 April, did not conspire to mislead the supreme political echelon but were merely pawns in a more complex game.

The same, however, cannot be said of Dulles and especially of Bissell, the project's main architect. Even if they were more optimistic than their subordinates about the prospects, they still knew only too well that President Kennedy had been misinformed about every component of the plan when he finally authorized it on 16 April. Indeed, they themselves admitted this ex post factum. In the drafts of his unpublished article about the Bay of Pigs, Dulles argued that one of the main reasons for the operation's failure was that the President "had views of [the plan] that were not consistent with the realities of the situation" (Vandenbroucke, p. 368). Bissell even enumerated the President's four most important misconceptions: the belief that "the covert character of the operation could be maintained"; the failure to understand "the absolute essentiality of air command and of effective air cover for the success of an amphibious operation"; the belief that the guerrilla option was available in case of defeat on the beachhead; and the expectation that "successful landing would promptly detonate internal revolts within Cuba," which would ultimately lead to the overthrow of Castro's regime (Bissell, pp. 377–78).

Bissell maintained that the CIA shared no responsibility for Kennedy's misconception of the covert nature of the operation and the possibility of an uprising, that the agency was partially responsible for not sufficiently emphasizing the need for a second air strike, and that it was most responsible for the misconception about the guerrilla option (ibid., pp. 378–80). But even while admitting this minimal responsibility, Bissell saw no serious ethical problem with his behavior or that of his colleagues:

> If there are to be operational plans in government, or elsewhere, there have to be enthusiastic people to conceive them, develop them, submit them for approval, and become advocates in the

process. For these people to put their best foot forward in policy discussion, so long as the facts and the assumptions on which the projections rest are honestly and accurately presented, does not constitute the willful misleading of the policymakers who must finally decide whether the plans are to be carried out. (Ibid., p. 380)

Dulles was ready to admit more responsibility:

> [We] did not want to raise these issues in an [undecipherable word] discussion—which might only harden the decision against the type of action we required. We felt that when the chips were down—when the crisis arose in reality, any action required for success would be authorized rather than permit the enterprise to fail.
>
> In a sense we were right. If only half the military help had been made available to get the brigade and its equipment safely ashore, that was later shown in trying to rescue and later liberate the brigade, there would have been a good chance of success. (Vandenbroucke, p. 369)

Both Dulles's and Bissell's explanations are based on professional and ethical arguments that are either inadequate or disingenuous. If, indeed, the CIA chiefs behaved as Bissell maintains they did, then their own mistake was professional. But as has already been demonstrated, this was not the case. Not only did the CIA planners actively mislead the President (as with Hawkins's cable) and also, quite cynically, the Cuban brigade (as with the intelligence briefing of 14 April), they consciously, if passively, misled the President about every other major component of the plan by not informing him that he was totally misconceiving reality.

Such behavior cannot be justified by any degree of enthusiasm, as Bissell tries to do. No policymaker can conduct successful policies on the basis of false information, and the role of describing reality, even an unpleasant one, lies first and foremost with the policymaker's intelligence advisors. Dulles as the DCI, and Bissell as the man whom Kennedy intended to make the next DCI, ostensibly served as the President's chief intelligence advisors on the Cuba project but actually served only what they, not Kennedy, considered to be the national interest as well as their own purposes. They enjoyed Kennedy's confidence but used it in order to deliberately mislead him. In this sense, certainly, they committed a serious ethical crime.

Dulles and Bissell also made serious professional mistakes. Their gravest one was their belief that the President would authorize any action, including direct intervention, in order to ensure victory, despite his reiterated pledges to the contrary. But this was not only a professional mistake, it was also an ethical one. For it is ethically wrong to plan an operation on the basis of such assumptions while not informing the President of what he is expected to do when "the chips are down." Even more than wars, after all, covert operations are the continuation of politics rather than ends in themselves. And just as generals are expected to conduct wars in accordance with political directives, so must the architects of covert operations.

This was certainly Kennedy's understanding of the relations between intelligence and politics. Had he known that his intelligence advisors were behaving according to a different code, however, one that accorded supremacy to operations over politics at times of crisis, he would probably have vetoed the Cuba project from the start. Dulles and Bissell consciously tried to compel their supreme commander to choose a policy line he wanted to avoid, and in the most crucial and delicate area of foreign policy, too. There is thus little doubt that their conduct of the Cuba project constitutes one of the most significant cases of intelligence intervention in the process of foreign policy making in American postwar history.

THE CIA OUT OF CONTROL: HOW COULD IT HAVE HAPPENED?

Previous explanations for the Bay of Pigs episode have focused mainly on the political and operational aspects of this venture. Such political studies as Janis (1972) attempted to answer President Kennedy's famous question: "How could I have been so stupid to let them go ahead?" The causes of the operational failure were the subject of other investigations, the most important of which was the official inquiry of the Taylor Committee, whose sanitized report was published in 1981 (Operation Zapata).

In this examination of the episode I seek to answer two questions. First, what motivated the CIA, especially Bissell, to resort to unlawful methods in order to bring about the implementation of such a defective operation? Second, what enabled Bissell and the rest of the CIA officers to succeed, or, in other words, why did the system fail to prevent the CIA from taking over the conduct of U.S. foreign policy?

To a certain extent, however, the answers to these questions also explain what caused the operation to fail, for the Bay of Pigs episode reveals the close connection between intelligence intervention in politics and humiliating operational failures. The fundamental cause for the project's failure was the unbridgeable gap between its ends—overthrowing Castro's regime—and its means—covert action. This gap, at least partially evident to the project's architects, was artificially bridged by them through the supply of selective information to inexperienced policymakers, who were thus not aware enough of its existence until it was too late.

It is obvious, but should nevertheless be emphasized, that the CIA planners did not conspire to mislead the military and the political echelons from the start. But as the project escalated, so did its architects' commitment to its implementation. In this sense, as other scholars have already emphasized, the project's own momentum became an independent factor, impelling the planners to sacrifice long-term goals for short-term ones. Such situations in which means become ends are not rare. But in this case the opposite was also true: in the crisis that developed following the Bay of Pigs landing, President Kennedy's avoidance of direct intervention preserved his long-term policy at the cost of an immediate failure.

The first part of this section will explain what drove the CIA to use unethical methods in order to get the operation under way. Given that the project was created in Bissell's own image and after his own likeness—for it was he who evolved the original concept in February–March 1960, then transformed it into a conventional assault-type operation, and later "sold" it so successfully to President Kennedy and his advisors—I believe that the key to understanding the CIA's behavior in this venture lies first and foremost with his personality. The possible motivations of the other CIA officers involved will then be discussed, and the second part of the section will analyze the conditions that kept the American system of checks and balances from preventing the CIA's wrongdoing.

The Motivation

Bissell: The Impact of an "Action Intellectual"

Born to a wealthy family, an elitist with an Ivy League education and a bright academic career, Richard Bissell combined two qualities: superior intellect and outstanding managerial ability. Bright minds are not rare in

Washington, nor are skillful managers; their combination, however, is far less frequent. Nowhere are these virtues more appreciated than among Washington policymakers, frustrated by their limited ability to control and direct the cumbersome bureaucracies under their command that often seem to acquire a life of their own. Indeed, what policymakers need most are men and women who not only know what to do but are also capable of getting it done. Such "action intellectuals" are scarce and therefore also very powerful. Henry Kissinger was this type of a person; it seems that his power in the Nixon administration derived less from his high intellect than from his ability to implement policy despite bureaucratic obstacles. Richard Bissell was much the same.

Described by his colleagues as a "human computer" and "a genius," Bissell was blessed with an impressive talent for grasping the essence of complicated problems, analyzing them, and emerging with the most feasible solutions. A master of effective management, he commanded the ability to maximize and centralize his own control of any given project and to communicate on a face-to-face basis with minimal paperwork, thus obtaining the power to implement his plans with minimal bureaucratic friction and outside intervention. His CIA task forces, whether for the U-2 plan, the intelligence reconnaissance satellite program, or the Cuba project, were typically and totally isolated from the agency's other activities and the influence of other senior CIA officers. A perfectionist and a complete individualist, he demanded, and usually received, the utmost loyalty from his subordinates.

Nobody is perfect, however, and some of Bissell's other qualities were less attractive. He was impatient with and scornful of the opinions of others, which he rightly, in most cases, considered to be inferior to his. Even more important, Bissell tended to take risks, some less calculated than others, being confident of his ability to get out of any deadlock situation (Wyden, pp. 10–19).[91]

91. Bissell was also known for his fidgety habits such as twisting paper clips and playing with a small rubber ball during meetings. One of his ex-CIA colleagues brought up, in this connection, Captain Queeg of *The Caine Mutiny* whose trademark was the clicking of metal balls (Wyden, p. 324). Bissell, of course, was no Queeg but rather the opposite; the captain of the Caine was motivated by a severe inferiority complex, whereas the architect of the Cuba project had a strong superiority complex. Nor was Bissell a Dr. Strangelove-type, as Wyden (ibid.) correctly points out. Possibly more than those of any other fictional character, Bissell's deeds during the Cuban venture resemble those of Colonel Nicholson, the proud British battalion commander whose men, prisoners of war of the Japanese, built the bridge on the River Kwai. Unlike Bissell, however, Colonel Nicholson realized at the last minute that he was sacrificing ends for means and took the right course of action.

As an elitist Bissell divided the world into technicians who follow orders and decision makers who give them. He had no doubt where he himself stood: "I admire and believe in the use of power," he once said, "when it is available, *for purposes that I regard as legitimate*" (ibid., p. 13, emphasis added). He did not see it as his responsibility, moreover, to make sure that his judgment coincided with the policy of his superiors. That was their problem. According to Marchetti and Marks:

> Covert action operations are generally aimed at short-term goals and the justification for the control machinery is that bias of operators to the short run can be compensated for in the review process. Mr. Bissell can conceive of no other way to force greater attention to long-range costs and values. One alternative is that caution will lead to ineffectuality. "Operational types" will be risk takers; the counter weight is, and should be, applied by the other agencies in government. ("The Bissell Philosophy," p. 339)

In line with these beliefs it was Bissell's own judgment—not that of his superiors inside or outside the agency—that served above all else to guide his behavior. And Bissell's private system of checks and balances could have worked, but in order to function effectively the "other agencies"—mainly policymakers—had to receive true information, which is exactly what Bissell failed to supply them, not only during the Cuba project but also during earlier ventures (see below). Whether he perceived such a modus operandi as justified by the need to make his "judgment" more imperative is not clear.

Bissell was brought to the CIA in 1954 as a special assistant to DCI Dulles after demonstrating his abilities as the driving force behind the Marshall Plan. Lacking military and intelligence background did not prevent him from successfully playing a major role in the 1954 Guatemala venture, which gave him his first operational experience. But his masterpiece (at least until the Cuba project) was the U-2 program, the CIA's most significant achievement during the 1950s. Within two years Bissell managed to bring in under budget and in utmost secrecy the reconnaissance aircraft that the Air Force had claimed would take eight years and far more money to build.

Yet, as director of the U-2 flight program over the USSR, Bissell also revealed some of the professional deficiencies that would become even more evident in the aftermath of the Bay of Pigs. Typically, it was his personal decision that the first U-2's flight would take it over the most sensitive areas of the Soviet Union. Dulles learned of this only when the plane was already in the air, and even President Eisenhower, who had personally authorized the first flight, knew nothing of its course. Bissell explained after the fact that the effect of surprise on the Soviet air-defense system would result in a low state of alert and prevent an effective reaction. Whether he accepted this rationale or not, Eisenhower decided that in the future he would authorize not only each flight but also its course (Ambrose, pp. 266–67; 272).

But although the President kept tight control over the program, he was unaware of some of its main deficiencies. Bissell and Dulles promised him that in case of a crash within Soviet territory no evidence of the mission's true nature would remain since the pilot would commit suicide (and could probably never survive such a crash anyway), while his plane would be destroyed by explosives it carried precisely for that purpose. They avoided telling Eisenhower, however, that the pilots were not ordered to commit suicide, that they were equipped with parachutes and getaway gear, that the small amount of explosives could hardly destroy the airplane beyond recognition, and that the films the U-2 carried could always survive as incriminating evidence (ibid., pp. 277–84; Beschloss, pp. 8, 152; Kirkpatrick 1968, p. 208).

In a way Bissell's solutions to the conflict between operational and political problems in the U-2 program and in the Cuba project were alike. To bridge the gap between the risks involved in the mission and the motivation of those who were to carry it out, he supplied both the U-2 pilots and the Cuban brigade with a chance of survival in case of failures. The main difference was that the American pilots received a real chance, whereas the Cubans were only supplied with false information. At the same time, in order to obtain political authorization for both missions, Bissell concealed these "technical" details from the presidents involved. He acted, indeed, according to his elitist philosophy, believing that he knew best what needed to be done and how to do it. In both cases, of course, he made mistakes that cost Eisenhower and Kennedy dearly.

What traits in Bissell's personality might have caused him to commit such grave professional and ethical mistakes during the Cuba project? To begin with, he was simply not professional enough to grasp how unrealistic his whole plan was. He had never planned conventional assault operations, never participated in any, and in fact had no experience at all with this type of activity. It is thus very possible that Bissell related to the plan in abstract terms, ignoring its concrete difficulties. His judgment, moreover, was warped by his belief in his own superior ability to successfully plan and carry out a highly complicated venture. This was probably also the reason why he declined to accept the sober reservations of Engler, Hawkins, and possibly others. In addition, it is not unlikely that the many risks involved appealed to Bissell, who was a gambler by nature; what others had judged to be unacceptable chances were for him an essential part of the game. Indeed, the word "game" may be appropriate here, since to some extent Bissell regarded the project as a maxi-max gamble in which he had to play not only against Castro but also against suspicious Joint Chiefs and a reluctant President.

If such was the case, it also provides us with a partial explanation of Bissell's ethical wrongdoing. From his point of view, success was probably measured by two results: first, the mere implementation of the project and, second, its outcome. Loyal to his belief that operators must act to solve immediate problems while it was the role of others to see that this action coincided with the general policy, he was ready to take any measures to get his operation under way, leaving it to the JCS, the State Department, or the White House to determine if he was acting according to a different code from theirs. But although this approach could work for years in the U-2 program (until the plane crashed), in the Bay of Pigs episode it became obviously inadequate in the first hours of the operation.

Bissell was aware of the possibility of failure but believed that, once the invasion had started, the other American actors involved, first and foremost the White House, would have to accept the new logic of the situation and intervene directly in order to ensure ultimate success. This belief, which was shared by others including Dulles and possibly the Joint Chiefs, was a sort of psychological defense mechanism against the possibility of total failure. It was supported by the experience gained in "Operation Success" in Guatemala, when at the critical moment President Eisenhower removed some restrictions on direct American intervention in order to obtain operational success. Kennedy, however, was not Eisenhower. Moreover, the extent of American military intervention required to save the Cuban venture was far greater than in Guatemala seven years earlier.

Bissell's ability to overcome obstacles cannot be explained, however, only by his impressive personal qualities. If he had not enjoyed an exceptional accessibility to the Kennedy administration, he could never have convinced the President and his advisors of the merits of such a defective plan. But Bissell had the necessary connections. For example, Kennedy's National Security Advisor, McGeorge Bundy, and his older brother Bill, who worked on the Cuba project as Kennedy's Deputy Assistant Secretary of Defense for International Security Affairs, were among Bissell's students at Yale and had learned to admire their professor. So did Walt Rostow, McGeorge Bundy's deputy, who had served as Bissell's assistant in the Department of Economics at Yale when his future boss was a student there. And Bissell had a direct link to the President through the columnist Joseph Alsop, a close and influential friend of Kennedy who had been Bissell's best friend in childhood.

These "old boy" connections were complemented by the fact that Bissell was a Democrat who began his government career under President Truman and had offered Senator John Kennedy assistance in his election campaign. Indeed, Kennedy himself was so impressed with Bissell that he considered him not only the future DCI but also "probably one of [the] four or five brightest guys in the whole administration" (Wyden, p. 95). This was certainly a significant remark coming from a President who wanted only the best and the brightest to work for him.

Altogether, then, Bissell was a very powerful actor. His superior mind and managerial skills, his past successes and personal connections with the President and some of his senior advisors, made him one of the most influential figures in Washington, far beyond his formal role as DDP and number-three man in the CIA. Combining influence with ambition and relatively low ethical restraints, Bissell was the main power behind the Cuba project and the person most likely to succeed in convincing the President to launch it despite its many defects.

Yet, regardless of his dominant position, Bissell alone could not have succeeded if it had not been for the support he received from DCI Dulles and the task force officers. Their role will be discussed next.

The CIA Chiefs and the Task Force Officers

It is possible to understand how a single quasi-amateur qualified man can make grave professional and ethical mistakes. It is more difficult to understand why similar mistakes were made by CIA professionals who by the early 1960s had gained significant experience in conducting covert operations and in managing the agency's relations with the White House.

Neither Dulles nor his deputy were qualified enough or motivated enough to oversee Bissell's project. Dulles was an intelligence professional but not a military expert. His operations in Switzerland during World War I and II, though affording him the reputation of a "Master Spy," had hardly prepared him for this type of mission. An operational-type officer to whom ventures such as the Cuba project had a special appeal, a DCI both loyal to his men and admired by them, Dulles lacked the ability to conduct an objective analysis of the operation. Besides, at the age of sixty-eight and coming to the end of his career, he might have regarded the Cuba project as the final triumph of his successful tenure as DCI; calling it off was no doubt a personal defeat for him. Also, as the U-2 episode demonstrated so well, Dulles had full confidence in Bissell and was reluctant to intervene in his projects.[92] During that episode, moreover, he had demonstrated defective professional ethics by backing Bissell's misleading arguments about the possibility that incriminating evidence of the U-2's true nature might survive in case the airplane crashed. All in all, Dulles was an amateur in military planning who adored covert operations and trusted Bissell to the point of covering up his wrongdoing, thus lacking both the ability and the will to restrain his subordinate.[93]

Like Dulles, DDCI General Cabell, though a professional soldier, had no experience in military operations of this type. True, as an Air Force career officer during World War II he had planned strategic bombings, but he had never had to deploy old bombers with an insufficient range to supply close air support for a small force fighting a numerically superior one. Moreover, within the CIA Cabell was not even considered an intelligence professional, having been nominated for the post of DDCI in 1953 for political reasons. The task force officers, perhaps including Bissell and Dulles, had little respect for him. Lacking influence and the necessary professional qualifications, Cabell like his boss had neither the ability to assess the project's chances nor the power or the will to stop it.

As is often the case with large organizations and complicated planning, some of the task force officers were professionally more capable than their superiors of estimating the operation's chances. In fact, Engler, with his vast Latin American and paramilitary expertise, concluded that the project

92. Like Bissell, Dulles preferred to work independently. During World War II he declined an offer to serve as a senior officer in London, saying that he did not want to work "with a lot of generals looking over my shoulder" (Ranelagh, p. 74).

93. The relations between Dulles and Bissell resemble the link between DCI Casey and Colonel North in the Iran-contra affair. Despite the differences (for example, North was not a CIA man and obviously not as intelligent as Bissell, and the target of their cooperation was not the President but the Congress), the chemistry between the operational-type directors and the ambitious action officers seems largely the same.

was too risky. So did the Marine officer in charge of the invasion, Colonel Hawkins, who despite his lack of experience in the conduct of small amphibious operations joined Engler in expressing his reservations to Bissell a week before D-Day.

Other officers, as we have seen, reached similar conclusions. Yet, with the exception of Engler and Hawkins,[94] they all failed to challenge Bissell on professional grounds. The main reason for this failure was that, like their bosses, they were overcommitted to the operation and its implementation. This commitment was partly psychological and social, the result of investing so much of their energies in the project for over a year. But as one CIA officer who was not a member of the Cuban task force argued, they also had a strong vested interest in it—the prospect that its success would lead to personal promotion (Smith, pp. 328–29) and that its abortion might mean the opposite.

Challenging Bissell, moreover, was a very hard task for these officers precisely because they believed in his intellectual brilliance and were influenced by his impressive record of past successes. Thus they acted according to administrative norms that allow some criticism but then demand compliance with the final order. Such norms are well suited to military organizations in which hierarchy and obedience are predominant but not to intelligence organizations that conduct special operations and call for more open and constructive criticism.

For these reasons none of the task force officers found the courage to break the bonds that held the group together and warn other senior officers in the agency, or even outside officials, that the emperor was naked. By avoiding such action, they like their superiors betrayed the ethical ingredient of their professional responsibility.

To be sure, we need to separate Dulles's misbehavior from that of the task force officers; as the DCI for eight years and one of the few survivors of the change of administration, Dulles had the graver ethical and professional responsibility. But the task force officers also failed to function as they should have. If they did not grasp how infeasible their operation was, then they failed as experts; if they grasped its real prospects and nevertheless failed to express their views vigorously enough, then their failure was ethical.

All in all, this discussion shows how motivated and unmotivated biases

---

94. Although it is true that Engler and Colonel Hawkins protested to Bissell, they nevertheless played a major role in making the operation possible, Engler in averting the 9 April call for collective resignation and Hawkins in his false report of 13 April.

led the CIA's key officers to eagerly support the Cuban operation and abuse their power in order to accomplish its implementation. It is now time to look at the conditions that prevented the policymakers from taking the opposite action.

The Conditions That Made the Project Possible

The commitment of the CIA task force to the implementation of its invasion plan played a decisive role in President Kennedy's decision to launch the operation. But, given that the project was defective from the start, it could have been expected that the JCS and the State Department, less involved in it and therefore less committed to it as they were, would have been in a better position to estimate its chances properly and warn the White House about its infeasibility. Furthermore, President Kennedy's advisors, the best and brightest brains in Washington, were exactly the men who should have seen how absurd the project's concept was. Yet with a few exceptions they did not object to the CIA plan after it was first discussed by the new administration in late January 1961. This section will address some of the causes for this behavior.

Structural Factors

The most fundamental problem facing American policymakers when they came to deal with Castro was the gap between the need to take action against him and the lack of sufficiently feasible policy options. There was a general consensus that Castro constituted a serious threat to the national interest: the mere success of his revolution combined with the fragile structure of the other Latin American regimes had made his declared policy of exporting the revolution to neighboring states a real danger that demanded an active American response. It was felt that without such a response not only might pro-American regimes in the Western Hemisphere be endangered but U.S. prestige as a determined anti-Communist world power as well.

On the other hand, political factors (mainly U.S. nonintervention commitments to the OAS) as well as strategic considerations (such as the need to avoid a provocation that might lead to a Soviet reaction elsewhere) made the potential costs and risks involved in a direct military action against Castro too high. Diplomatic pressures demanded that the invasion be firmly supported by the Latin American states, but many of their leaders "felt they would be overthrown by their people if they took a public stand, since Castroism had made great inroads, particularly among the poorest classes of their people."[95] Although some diplomatic action was nevertheless taken, it proved insufficient to curb the Cuban leader, as did economic sanctions.

For U.S. policymakers determined to topple Castro but aware of the dangers involved in military action and the insufficiency of diplomatic and economic pressures, covert operations seemed to offer the most practical course of action, since past experience had shown that the CIA was capable of overthrowing anti-American regimes without the risks of direct American intervention. Other alternatives that were either less appealing (such as doing nothing) or too risky (such as direct American attack) made covert action a particularly attractive option and made it difficult for policymakers to see its main weakness, namely, that Castro was already too strong to be overthrown by such means. Indeed, the opposite was true: Castro's growing power served as a major incentive for launching the operation as early as possible. All policymakers were aware of the danger that by mid-1961 the Cuban army's absorption of modern Soviet-made weapons (especially MIG fighters) would make the use of paramilitary means even less effective.

On the whole, then, structural constraints made the use of covert action appear the most rational option. Obviously, there was one other alternative: simply avoiding the use of power. This alternative, however, was not considered attractive partly because of domestic political constraints.

State-Level Factors

The strong anti-Communist sentiment that dominated American public opinion at the height of the Cold War made it difficult for any president to avoid action against a new revolutionary regime settled at the heart of the U.S. sphere of influence. This sentiment became even more influential owing to the presidential elections of November 1960.

The Cuban problem played a major role in the Nixon/Kennedy election campaign of late 1960. At least partially responding to the popular anti-

---

95. Memorandum of Conference with the President, 29 December 1960, DDRS 1980/445A.

Castro sentiment of the American public, Senator Kennedy promised "to strengthen the non-Batista democratic anti-Castro forces in exile and in Cuba itself who offer eventual hope of overthrowing Castro." Using this issue as an additional means of attacking his opponent, Kennedy added that "[t]hus far these fighters for freedom have had virtually no support from our Government."[96] While Nixon called his opponent's proposals "probably the most dangerously irresponsible that he's made in the course of this campaign" (*New York Times*, 22 October 1960, p. 1), nobody knew better than the CIA planners that the Vice President was in fact the most determined supporter of their plans in Eisenhower's administration.[97]

From the CIA's perspective, it made little difference whether Kennedy knew at the time about the agency's operational plans or not. The more salient factor was that both candidates were now committed to the Cuba project. It is very possible that this served as an important impetus to Bissell's escalation of his plan into a conventional assault-type operation in early November. Certainly Kennedy's public commitment to support paramilitary action against Castro was later effectively used by the CIA as leverage. During the 11 March discussion of the project at the White House, for example, Dulles emphasized that, if the President decided to abort the invasion plan, the disappointed Cuban recruits would expose not only CIA operations but also "how the United States, having prepared an expedition against Castro, then lost its nerve" (Schlesinger 1965, p. 242).

Dulles did not have to elaborate on the impact of such allegations on the President's popularity with the public; Kennedy was sophisticated enough to understand it on his own. It is quite probable, indeed, that when giving the final go-ahead to the invasion in mid-April, he was motivated by the need to minimize the potential damage at home no less than by his conviction that the operation stood a good chance of success. Unlike his predecessor, who did not have to prove that he was a real American patriot, Kennedy was still viewed by large segments of the American public as a big talker who carried a small stick.

Other factors involved in the change of administration also helped advance the high-level acceptance of the Cuba project. The fact that President Eisenhower avoided aborting it despite his concern about its

96. "Text of Statement by Kennedy on Dealing with Castro Regime," *New York Times*, 21 October 1960, p. 18.

97. In a talk with Howard Hunt of the CIA task force, Brigadier General Cushman, Nixon's military aide, defined his boss as the "project's action officer within the White House" and promised any help needed to get the anti-Castro operation under way (Hunt, pp. 39–40).

feasibility can be attributed at least partly to his realization that the future of the operation would have to be decided by another president. While Eisenhower was no doubt concerned about the menace of Castro, he was nevertheless uncommitted to the CIA project, regarding it as only a "program" (Ambrose, p. 315). Yet, when discussing foreign-policy issues with President-elect Kennedy a day before leaving the White House, "President Eisenhower stated in the long run the United States cannot allow the Castro Government to continue to exist in Cuba."[98] Although he never specifically referred to the CIA plan, the impression Eisenhower left his heir was that at least he did not object to it.

In addition, the CIA was assisted in its efforts to implement the project by Eisenhower's and Kennedy's different managerial styles. Eisenhower's remote-control style of covert operations enabled Bissell and the task force to change the nature of the project radically without a presidential veto because for Eisenhower the final, most critical, and almost the only decision was whether or not to launch the operation. Kennedy's personal involvement in the operation from the early days of his presidency may have created a personal committment to it that was fueled by the many discussions about it he had with Dulles and Bissell.

More crucially, as a young and inexperienced president responsive to the advice of capable men with a similar lack of experience, Kennedy was highly impressed by the CIA chiefs. A more mature president, especially one who had already suffered at the hands of his intelligence advisors, would have behaved differently. Kennedy's decision following the failure of the Cuba project to have his brother keep a close eye on the agency shows the impact of his earlier inexperience on the decision to launch the defective operation.

Altogether, then, the changing of the guard at the White House created a convenient environment for the CIA that was effectively used by Dulles and Bissell. The contribution of other agencies to their success will be discussed next.

Bureaucratic Factors

Bureaucratic competition played a significant role in the CIA's drive to implement its project. Once it was authorized in March 1960 to prepare its

98. Robert McNamara: "Memorandum to the President," 24 January 1961, DDRS 1985/ 001563, p. 2.

anti-Castro program, the agency's need to demonstrate its ability to stand up to the challenge became an important impetus for the project's architects. Bureaucratic imperialism, moreover, drove it to minimize the role of other agencies, especially that of the JCS. In acting according to bureaucratic imperatives, the CIA planners made extensive use of compartmentation to prevent essential information from reaching non-CIA officials. This tactic was used by Bissell within the agency. We have already seen the neutralization through compartmentation of CIA opponents to the project such as Helms, and the same fate befell the agency's intelligence branch under Robert Amory. Reflecting on the abortive Bay of Pigs operation, Schlesinger found this intrabureaucratic compartmentation most irritating:

> The Bay of Pigs Operation . . . was tightly held within a small CIA faction; even the CIA intelligence branch was never brought in—a fact which was not clear to the Kennedy White House at that point—though its estimate of the probable reaction of the Cuban people to an invasion of exiles might have been instructive.[99]

Secrecy was used by the project's architects for three purposes. First, to protect their plans from the real enemy—Castro's Cuba and the Soviets. This was a functional secrecy. Second, to prevent outsiders within the national bureaucracy from being able to criticize the program. Third, to preserve their monopoly on purveying information to the President. These last two uses of secrecy were political. A high level of secrecy and compartmentation, always characteristic of Bissell's projects, reached a new level of absurdity in the Cuba venture. For our purposes, though, what is important is that this enabled him to carry out his plans with minimal outside intervention.

Interbureaucratic considerations and parochial interests also helped determine the behavior of the JCS. Attempting to avoid frictions over a program the Joint Chiefs did not regard as their own, JCS military experts preferred to keep a low profile, thus playing directly into the hands of the CIA. The result was a lukewarm professional criticism of the CIA's defective opera-

99. Statement of Arthur Schlesinger, Jr., former Special Assistant to President John F. Kennedy, in *U.S. Intelligence Agencies and Activities: Risks and Control of Foreign Intelligence*, Hearings before the Select Committee on Intelligence, U.S. House of Representatives, 94th Cong., 1st sess., p. 5, 11 December 1975, p. 1847. Notably, lack of experience on the part of the President and his advisors, who did not have the sense to ask the CIA analysts for their own estimate, facilitated the way for the success of the task force's tactics of compartmentation.

tional plans instead of the far harsher tone they really deserved.[100] It is also likely that the JCS believed (as Schlesinger argues) that once the operation was launched the President could not let it fail because of what they considered the national interest.

It would be a mistake, however, to explain the JCS's behavior only by such considerations. Despite the fact that the operational parameters of the CIA plan were analyzed by their military experts, the truth is that the Joint Chiefs themselves lacked sufficient experience in the conduct of small-scale operations. So, while each of them was capable of analyzing the prospects of a third world war with the Soviets (which was their main task), none had the experience required to properly understand how low the chances of the Cuba operation really were. And, in any event, like the President and his advisors, the JCS were misled by the CIA into believing better of the CEF's military capabilities than they really deserved.

The State Department never utilized its potential to prevent the operation. Its failure to do so was partly the result of the CIA's successful compartmentation policy. When, for example, the State Department's Director of Intelligence and Research, Roger Hilsman, inadvertently received some information about the CIA plan, he asked his boss to let State's Cuban analysts estimate the likelihood of a popular uprising against Castro. Rusk's answer was no—the project was "too tightly held" (Hilsman 1967, p. 31).

In light of their growing competition with the CIA over the conduct of U.S. foreign policy, it might have been expected that State Department officials would have objected to the agency's new venture more forcefully. But like Hilsman these officials were neutralized from the project not only because of Bissell's successful compartmentation policy but also because of their relative weakness in comparison to the CIA. By 1961 the CIA's budget exceeded the State Department's by 50 percent (Schlesinger 1965, p. 427), its professional manpower was superior, and its prestige higher. Under such conditions State was unable to control the CIA to any significant extent.[101]

100. A conspiracy theorist might argue that the JCS had a vested interest in the implementation of the CIA plan and its subsequent failure, for this could have led to one of two results: total CIA failure and thus an improvement in the JCS position due to the zero-sum nature of the interbureaucratic competition, or, even better, a failure that would call for direct American intervention, a situation clearly demonstrating the contribution of the military to the U.S. national interest. I do not think that such considerations played any role in the JCS thinking about the project.

101. For a good postmortem of CIA-State Department relations following the Bay of Pigs, see Arthur Schlesinger: "Memorandum to the President on the CIA Reorganization," 30 June 1961, DDRS 1988/002808, pp. 3–4.

The abuse of the CIA's Standard Operational Procedures regarding secrecy has already been discussed, but the impact of other SOPs with the agency should also receive some attention. The first of these involves how the agency constructed its special task forces. As was described earlier, manpower for such groups was selected not only according to the ability of the available officers to succeed in their assignments but first and foremost according to their personal identification with the task force's particular mission. By definition this increased the possibility that, consciously or not, such task forces would perform according to predominant biases, and certainly the result of such a selection process in the case of the Cuba project was deeply destructive. Had the agency been more aware of this problem, it could have formed a control group composed of officers known to be less enthusiastic about the project yet not regarded as "devil's advocates" with institutionalized biases that could allow them to be ignored. This might have kept a minimal measure of control over the task force's action; but there was no possibility of constructing such a group when the task force it was supposed to control was headed by Bissell.

A second defective procedure within the agency involved learning from past events. It is not clear whether, or how well, the lessons of Iran in 1953, Guatemala in 1954, and Indonesia in 1957 were ever formally studied within the agency. But even if they were, the project's architects seem to have reached the wrong conclusions. Most relevant for their task was the Indonesian venture, which failed simply because Sukarno, like Castro, was too strong to be toppled by a local group supported by the CIA. The impression, however, is that Bissell and his men mainly stressed the less relevant Guatemalan experience, from which they then drew all the wrong conclusions: that violations of international treaties hardly mattered as long as the operation succeeded; that it was possible to maintain "plausible deniability" even in complicated operations with substantive American participation; that any diplomatic action initiated by the OAS was ineffective; and, above all, that policymakers were apt to loosen restrictive orders when an operation was already under way and the chips were down (Etheredge, p. 8). They failed, however, to learn the most important lesson, that even against the weak president of Guatemala their chances of success had only been marginal and that similar operations against stronger leaders had a still lower likelihood of success.

The last factor within the agency that hampered the chance of military success was the quality of the intelligence information available and its analysis by the task force's officers. Lyman Kirkpatrick, the CIA Inspector

General who conducted a thorough internal investigation of the failure, concluded that "inaccurate intelligence was the basis for the Bay of Pigs disaster. . . . Much of the intelligence came from the Cuban resistance, which was not always an objective intelligence source." This inaccurate information, moreover, was assessed by the "operators running the operation" and "not by the intelligence directorate, where it should have been done" (Kirkpatrick 1972, pp. 39–40). As a result the agency failed in making "cold, hard appraisals at recurring intervals of the chances of success of major covert projects" (Jackson, 3:129).[102]

General Pathologies

The factors set forth above explain to some extent how and why an operation of substantial importance to the American national interest could be planned on fundamentally absurd assumptions and be authorized by policymakers without any of them ever becoming cognizant of its extreme weaknesses. But, given the extent of this gap, the explanation that these factors afford us is not enough, and therefore two additional factors need to be discussed. These two factors are groupthinking and low level of professionalism.

Janis's study (1972, pp. 14–49) of the role of "groupthink" in shaping the behavior of Kennedy's close advisors during the Bay of Pigs episode supplies us with a fine analysis of why the best and the brightest failed to realize how defective the CIA plan was. In a nutshell, Janis concluded that this failure

> can be at least partially accounted for by the group's tendency to seek concurrence at the expense of seeking information, critical appraisal, and debate. The concurrence-seeking tendency was manifested by shared illusions and other symptoms, which helped the members to maintain a sense of group solidarity. Most crucial were the symptoms that contributed to complacent overconfidence in

102. Kirkpatrick's critical report of the CIA's performance in the Bay of Pigs episode was unanimously and categorically rejected by the agency's officers responsible for the fiasco. Wayne Jackson, a CIA officer who composed in the early 1970s an inner (and very biased) secret history of the tenure of Allen Dulles as CIA director, summarized his discussion of the Kirkpatrick Report as follows: "It is the writer's [Jackson] belief which was shared by Cabell and other knowledgeable [sic] officers, that Kirkpatrick used the survey as an instrument to make a case to the incoming Director and to the President's Board for the appointment of a chief of staff, so as to further his own ambitions" (Jackson, 3:141).

the face of vague uncertainties and explicit warnings that should have alerted the members to the risks of the [ill-conceived] clandestine military operation. (Ibid., pp. 48–49)

But, as Janis himself notes, his explanation is only partial. Without underestimating the impact of groupthinking on Kennedy and his advisors, it should nevertheless be emphasized that, if they had had adequate and fully accurate information about the project—information that was, at least partly, available to the CIA but was never presented to the White House—their decision would probably have been different. In this sense groupthinking was a necessary but not a sufficient condition for the authorization of the Bay of Pigs operation.

At the same time, groupthinking appears to have played a major role in the dynamics of the CIA task force. Their belief in the project despite the superior information they had, together with the fact that regardless of their apprehensions none of them stood up to challenge the operation with any vigor, most likely indicates the impact of this particular factor. The task force, indeed, displayed most if not all of Janis's groupthinking symptoms. The illusion of invulnerability—the belief that with a strong, competent, lucky leader and internal consensus nothing can prevent success—can account for the task force officers' conviction that Bissell with his unique capabilities was bound to lead the project to political validation and ultimate operational triumph. Members of this group also believed that they were superior to outsiders, whether these were friends (the Pentagon generals, State Department officials) or foes (Castro and his armed forces). The illusion of unanimity and the decay of individual critical thinking came into expression in the group's reluctance to formulate personal apprehensions about the feasibility of the plan and to express them forcefully enough to their leaders when they finally did so. They acted this way despite the conviction of many of them that under the given circumstances the operation was quite likely to fail.

The source of this symptom, meanwhile, as well as of the task force officers' tendency to put aside their personal doubts after expressing them, was their sentiment of commitment to the group itself and to its leaders, Bissell and Dulles, who "could not do wrong." The role of self-appointed mindguards was played by Bissell (when suppressing Engler's and Hawkins's reservations) and then in turn by Engler (when averting the call for collective resignation). Bissell's leadership style and personal dominance of the task force's dynamics was also reflected in his group's tendency towards docility.

Altogether the impression is that group pathologies played an important part not only among Kennedy's advisors but also in the CIA team in charge of the operation. And since, unlike the civilian policymakers, the task force's officers had better information as well as experience and were thus more capable of estimating their project's chances, it is possible that groupthinking symptoms were as significant in their behavior as in that of the President's advisors.

Finally, a low level of professionalism serves here as the last factor that dominated the ill-conceived Cuba project and the process that led to its implementation. As is clear by now, the architects of the project failed to act according to their professional code during most stages of preparation for the invasion. What should be emphasized here is that the level of their expertise—the special knowledge acquired by prolonged education and experience—was very low in the specific operation under discussion. Of all the CIA planners, only Colonel Hawkins had good formal and practical experience in the conduct of amphibious operations. But this was limited to large-scale invasions backed by the whole might of the American armed forces, not to mini-invasions supported by a small number of old bombers with insufficient range against a numerically superior enemy. Neither Dulles nor Bissell and the rest of his task force had any expertise in this type of warfare (most of them lacked sufficient expertise in any type of warfare), yet they took it upon themselves to plan and carry out this highly complicated venture. Similarly, the Joint Chiefs, despite years of formal and practical education, knew little about the specific demands of small operations, something they had seldom if ever experienced in their long careers. The same holds true for the task force's expertise with regard to Cuba. The real professionals on this subject, the CIA and INR analysts, were replaced by amateurs who believed that their mental qualities could substitute for years of experience in studying Cuban affairs. In the case of the Bay of Pigs, what made this insufficient professional experience so critical was that despite this deficiency the CIA planners as well as the military generals were mistakenly regarded by the other relevant actors as genuine professionals.

7

Alteration of Ends: Israel's "Unfortunate Business" of 1954

> Friends, I want to be sure, or at least I hope, that the future historian, when taking upon himself the mission of solving the mystery of this affair . . . will first of all abandon the hope of understanding the matter thoroughly, and of discovering the truth in all its winding and twisting.—Moshe Sharett's speech at the *Mapai* Party Center at the height of the Lavon affair, 4 February 1961 (Sharett Diary, p. 778)

Few affairs, if any, were as traumatic and as significantly influenced the history of Israel as the intelligence mishap of 1954. Euphemistically called the "unfortunate business," this Directorate of Military Intelligence (DMI) operation was aimed at preventing a major change in the Arab-Israeli balance of power—a change perceived by some in Israel as inevitable owing to the imminent conclusion of Anglo-Egyptian negotiations on the withdrawal of British forces from the Suez Canal Zone. Less than six weeks before the agreement was initialed in Cairo, the chief of the DMI estimated in a special report that the evacuation of British forces from the Canal Zone would mean, from the Israeli perspective, that:

1. The British military buffer zone between Israel and Egypt will be removed.

2. The Egyptian military potential will be significantly improved.

3. American military assistance will be given to Egypt. . . .

4. The main obstacle for the joining of Arab countries in a regional defense pact will be removed.[1]

In order to prevent this grave development, a network of Egyptian Jews in Cairo and Alexandria was activated. The network, in existence since mid-1951 and headed by an Israeli agent, perpetrated some acts of sabotage against Egyptian and American installations in Cairo and Alexandria. These were to show that the Egyptians were incapable of maintaining law and order in their own country, and thus to demonstrate the risks involved to Western security interests in withdrawing from the strategically important Canal Zone and relying on Nasser's shaky regime.

The improvised and amateurish operation proved highly unsuccessful. The first act of sabotage was executed on 2 July 1954 and was followed by two others on 14 July. During an attempt to conduct a third wave of sabotage acts on 23 July, one of the homemade bombs exploded in the hands of an agent. He was immediately caught by Egyptian security men, and within less than a month the whole network collapsed. Two agents were sentenced to death and executed on 10 February 1955. Six others were sentenced to long prison terms—four of them were released only in the POW exchange between Israel and Egypt following the 1967 war. Two Israeli intelligence officers were sentenced to death in absentia, and a third, who was not part of the network but was caught in connection with its collapse, committed suicide in jail during his trial. Another Egyptian Jew, mistakenly suspected as a member of the network, committed suicide in jail as well.

As is usual with humiliating failures, nobody among the Israeli military and political leadership was ready to take responsibility for this debacle. Moreover, revealing the truth about the "unfortunate business" proved highly difficult and complicated. The chief of the DMI, Colonel Benyamin Givli, admitted that he gave the order to carry out the operation but argued that he received instructions to do so from the Defense Minister, Pinhas Lavon. The latter denied any responsibility for the operation, blaming Givli for acting on his own initiative. Neither mentioned any involvement on the part of either Prime Minister Moshe Sharett or Chief of Staff Moshe Dayan.

Given the sensitivity of the affair—the use of crude provocations in order

---

1. From Chief of Intelligence Branch GHQ to Defense Minister and Commander-in-Chief IDF: "The Renewal of Negotiations on the Evacuation of the Canal Zone," 16 June 1954. *Israel's State Archives*, Foreign Office (henceforth *ISA*, FO), 130.02/2419.2.

to damage one state's relations with another, the death of Egyptian Jews and an Israeli officer that resulted from this hazardous and Machiavellian plan, the risks it involved to the whole Jewish community in Egypt—Israel never officially admitted her responsibility for the operation for almost two decades. Between 1954 and 1960, however, at least six attempts were made by various investigative committees to clear some of the fog that surrounded the question "Who gave the order?" None of these attempts proved totally successful.[2]

Apart from its apparent victims—the agents in Egypt who paid with their lives and freedom—the failure in Cairo cost some others in Israel dearly and influenced, directly and indirectly, the course of events in the Middle East. Its first effect was felt simultaneously in the military and political echelons: when the trial of the network members was over, Colonel Givli and Lieutenant Colonel Benzoor, the commander of Unit 131 of Military Intelligence, to which the network in Egypt belonged, were removed from the DMI to relatively low positions. More significant was the aftershock in the upper political echelon: in February 1955 Defense Minister Pinhas Lavon was compelled to resign. His replacement by David Ben-Gurion signaled not only a major weakening in Sharett's personal status as prime minister but also the beginning of the end of his policy of "diplomatic activism"—a policy aimed at reaching a settlement with Egypt through political means. Indeed, a few days after Ben-Gurion returned to the Defense Ministry, the Israeli Defense Force (IDF) carried out the Gaza retaliation act in which thirty-eight Egyptian soldiers were killed. According to the Egyptians, this constituted proof that no political settlement with Israel was possible and motivated Nasser to sign his first big arms deal with the Soviet bloc, a deal that changed the face of the Middle East in the years afterward.

Then in 1959, following the revelation of new evidence that Lavon thought proved his innocence, the former Defense Minister demanded that Ben-Gurion (who by now was also Prime Minister) clear his name. The

2. The first and the most important of these investigations was conducted by Major General (ret.) Ya'acov Dory, the chief of staff of the IDF during the 1948 war, and Itzhak Olshan, a Supreme Court judge. They were nominated for this role by Sharett, shortly after the first revelations of the Egyptian operation came to his knowledge, in order to find out whether the instruction to activate the network was given by Defense Minister Lavon or without his knowledge. The Olshan-Dory investigation committee conducted the most comprehensive and thorough investigation of the affair, but its work was hampered by false testimonies of the intelligence officers involved in the project and possibly by Lavon himself. Concluding that it could neither prove that Lavon gave the order nor that he did not, the committee has been known since then as "the stalemate committee."

latter's principal objection to this demand led to a continuous political struggle within the leadership of the ruling party in Israel, Mapai, a struggle that lasted until the mid-1960s. Isolated at the top, Lavon had to resign again in 1960, this time from his position as the General Secretary of the Histadrut, Israel's national trade union organization. Yet Lavon's continuous struggle for rehabilitation led to the collapse of Ben-Gurion's government in 1961 and at a later stage—though indirectly—to Ben-Gurion's final resignation from the government in 1963.

Even more significant than the personal fate of those involved were the political developments triggered by what has been known since the late 1950s as the "Lavon affair." Highly dissatisfied with the way his predecessor, Levi Eshkol, managed the crisis, Ben-Gurion left Mapai in 1964 together with many of his supporters (among them Moshe Dayan and Shimon Peres) and created a new party, Rafi, which challenged the right of Mapai's "old guard" to govern Israel. In a chain reaction new parties and political alignments were created on the right and the left. On the left the "Labor Alignment" between Mapai and "Ahdut Ha'Avoda" was created in 1965, at least partially as an answer to the new challenge set by Ben-Gurion. On the right the "Liberal party," just created in 1961, combined forces in 1965 with "Heruth," Israel's right-wing party, thus presenting for the first time a serious challenge to the hegemony of socialist rule in the country. In the long run these developments facilitated the ability of the Israeli right to lead the country for the first time in 1977. To a limited extent, then, the Likud could have never come to power if it had not been for the "unfortunate business" of 1954.

Significant as they are, these developments are secondary to our subject. Instead, the focus of this chapter is the 1954 intelligence mishap and the two questions it invokes. The first is: what actually happened in 1954 and, more specifically, did the DMI really try to conduct an independent foreign policy and if so by what means? Or, in the words of that recurring question in Israel's politics, "Who gave the order?" The first part of this section will thus describe the background to the "unfortunate business," and the second part will address the DMI's responsibility for the venture by tracing its complicated developments between the beginning of April and mid-August 1954. The last part of the section will then discuss the implications this intelligence operation had, and could have had, on Israel's foreign policy as pursued by Prime Minister Sharett. My main conclusion, which will be elaborated later, is that the order to launch the operation was given by the chief of the DMI, Colonel Givli, who tried to cover himself by obtaining instructions from Defense Minister Lavon at a stage when the operation was already under way. Even if Lavon approved the operation at a later stage, therefore, this approval had no effect at all on the course of events initiated and conducted independently by the DMI.

The second question to be answered involves the conditions under which such an event could take place. More specifically, at which level of analysis—the international, state, bureaucratic, or personal—can we find the variables that best explain this crude intervention by the DMI in Israel's foreign policymaking process at one of its most crucial junctures? After analyzing the various conditions at these four levels of analysis, I conclude that the critical variables are to be found at the state and the personal levels. When discussing this subject I will also address, though more in the form of speculation, an interrelated question: what could have possibly motivated the DMI's chief to resort to an independent line of action that was clearly beyond the scope of his responsibilities? Here I will argue that Colonel Givli's personality best explains the initiation of the operation that led to the most serious political crisis in Israel's history.

THE "UNFORTUNATE BUSINESS": HOW DID IT HAPPEN?

The Background

In order to understand how this security mishap could have happened, some background on Israel's intelligence system is needed. Hence the first part of this section will briefly discuss the organizational history of the Israeli intelligence community in its first years. The second part will describe the establishment of Unit 131, one of the DMI's special operations units, and the buildup of its Egyptian network. Since the "unfortunate business" was closely connected to the personnel changes in Israel's political and military leadership in 1953–54, this subject will be discussed in the third part of the section. Finally, since perception of reality influences policy, the fourth part will describe the information that arrived in Israel during 1953–54 with regard to the Anglo-Egyptian negotiations on the British evacuation of the Suez Canal, how it was interpreted by the Foreign Office and the DMI, and what courses of action they suggested in order to forestall the conclusion of the negotiations.

The Israeli Intelligence Community: 1948–1953

The post-Mandate intelligence community in Israel was established on 30 June 1948.[3] The need for a reform in the young state's intelligence system was made obvious by the first round of battles between the Israeli Defense Forces and the Arab regular armies that invaded the country on 15 May 1948. Lack of coordination between the various collecting, processing, and operational intelligence organs, as well as the absence of a central military intelligence organization, left military and political leaders dissatisfied with regard to intelligence performance during these first stages of the regular war (Gelber, pp. 417–19).

As a result, a new intelligence system was established. It combined three main organs: (1) Military Shai (Shai stands for Sherut Yediot, or Information Service), headed by Lieutenant Colonel Isser Be'eri, which later became the Military Intelligence Department in G (General Staff), Branch GHQ and in 1953 the I (Intelligence) Branch GHQ, or the DMI; (2) Domestic Shai, which was under the responsibility of Isser Harel (Halperin) and became known later as the SHABAK (initials of *Sherut Bitahon Klali*, or the General Security Service); (3) Foreign Political Shai, headed by Reuven Shiloah. Simultaneously, a new intelligence department—the Political Department—was established in the Foreign Office under Borris Guriel. This intelligence organ had an operational unit of its own, established during the war. Titled as Heker Beth ("Research B"), this unit was to operate outside Israel's territory, mainly in order to plan and execute operations against the Arab military effort at time of war (Harel 1989, p. 172). Shiloah received responsibility for the Political Department as well, thus becoming the senior person in Israel's intelligence community.

These changes did not put an end to friction and competition between the different intelligence organs. The main rivalry, which focused on domains of responsibility and resources, was between the Military Shai and the Political Department of the Foreign Office. Moreover, the system was shaken by various crises, the most important of which—"The Tobianski affair" (see below)—ended in Be'eri's trial. Even earlier, in December 1948, and on the background of some other incidents, Be'eri was removed from Military Intelligence and was replaced by Haim ("Vivian") Herzog (Israel's president between 1983 and 1993).

The need to better coordinate intelligence activities and solve disagree-

---

3. For a good description of some of the activities of the pre–1948 Shai, see Dekel 1959.

ments between the various services led in April 1949 to the establishment of a new organ, the Supreme Inter-Service Coordination Committee, which was built according to the British model. It was chaired by Shiloah, and its members were the heads of Military Intelligence, the Political Department, the Security Service, and the Israeli Police, as well as their deputies. But even this new organ could hardly control the community's intrabureaucratic competition.

According to the June 1948 agreement, the Foreign Office's Political Department was to be the sole supplier of information from non-Arab countries. Yet it could never satisfy the demand of the IDF for high-quality intelligence. Moreover, the IDF argued that this failure was not incidental but a function of the Political Department's lack of professionalism as well as the low priority it gave to military information. Under these conditions Herzog's deputy in Military Intelligence, Lieutenant Colonel Benyamin Givli, succeeded in breaking the Political Department's monopoly on intelligence activities in the non-Arab world. In December 1949 he sent Major Haim Gaon of Military Intelligence to Europe as its independent representative. Gaon's mission was to recruit new sources and agents in Europe that would be operated directly by Military Intelligence and not through the Political Department. During 1950 Military Intelligence expanded its activities in Europe, and its competition with the Political Department intensified (Eshed 1988, pp. 129–30; Black and Morris, pp. 78–86).

Then in February 1951 Ben-Gurion and Shiloah recognized the army's demand for better information as legitimate and acknowledged the risks involved to Israel's international image and status because of the Political Department's activities by dismantling this organ and transferring its responsibilities to a new organization, the Institute for Intelligence and Special Roles (HaMossad le'Modi'in ve'Tafkidim Meyuhadim, known since as the Mossad), which became part of the Prime Minister's Office. The new organ started functioning on 1 April 1951. For the first five months of its existence it was headed by Shiloah, but in September 1951 Harel replaced him while functioning at the same time as head of the Security Service. When in March 1953 Shiloah resigned from the chairmanship of the Supreme Inter-Service Coordination Committee, Harel replaced him in this role as well (Eshed 1988, pp. 131–40).

Taken as a whole, the history of Israel's intelligence community from 1948 to 1953 was characterized by bitter bureaucratic and personal rivalries, intense competition, and rapid organizational changes. These naturally left their marks on the community's intrabureaucratic modus operandi in the years following and hampered efforts by the various intelligence organizations to cooperate and coordinate their activities. Its most significant impact, however, was probably at the personal level. Cooperation between Harel and Givli—who replaced Herzog in mid-1950 as the head of Military Intelligence—lasted only as long as Shiloah was the senior person in the intelligence community as the two shared an interest in undermining his status in order to strengthen their own. Once Shiloah left, however, new tensions arose between Harel, who perceived himself as the new senior in the community, and Colonel Givli, who was not ready to replace one superior with another. As will become clear later, this personal and bureaucratic rivalry played a major role at a critical juncture in facilitating the conditions under which the "unfortunate business" took place.

Unit 131 and the Buildup of the Egyptian Network: 1948–1954

Towards the end of the 1948 war Military Intelligence was organized into eleven branches: Shin.Mem. (Sherut Modi'in, or Intelligence Service—hereafter IS) IS–1 (combat intelligence); IS–2 (the SIGINT unit); IS–3 (field security); IS–4 (military censorship); IS–5 (national basic research center); IS–6 (topographic research); IS–7 (central intelligence library and research of non-Arab armies); IS–8 (technical branch); IS–9 (military attachés' branch); IS–10 (collection from open sources); and IS–18 (special operations branch, or the operational unit of Military Intelligence) (Gelber, pp. 428–29; Black and Morris, pp. 54–56).

Combat intelligence was the heart of the organization's activities and demanded most of its human and material resources. The SIGINT unit—being the only one of its kind in the community—gave Military Intelligence a monopoly in this important field and a significant advantage over its competitors in the community's intrabureaucratic rivalry. But it was the special operations branch, IS–18, which was in charge of operations in the Arab world and in which the story of the "unfortunate business" began.

IS–18 was based, to a large extent, on a unit named HaShahar ("the Dawn") that was created in 1942 as the combat intelligence organ of the Palmach. It comprised some dozens of Jews of Arab origin who were planted in Arab populations, mainly in Palestine but also in the neighboring states. Nicknamed "the Arabists of the Palmach," they dealt simultaneously with intelligence collection and special operations, such as sabotage, deception, elimination of leaders, and psychological warfare. In August 1948 this unit became an official part of Military Intelligence, known as IS–18 (Dror, pp. 11–13).[4]

IS–18, however, was not the only special operations unit in the young IDF. The embryonic Israeli navy of 1948 had a unit of its own, combined of veterans of the sabotage unit of the Palyam (naval Palmach), which successfully carried out sabotage acts and other special operations during the war. Some of these were conducted in collaboration with members of IS–18. This unit, later known as the Naval Commando of the Israeli Navy, or Shayetet (Fleet) 13, is still operational today.

The success of the Naval Commando operations during the war, combined with the experience gained by the "Arabists of the Palmach," led in 1949–50 to an attempt to build a similar unit in the air force. Very much like its sister in the navy, the air force commando unit was designed to use unorthodox warfare methods, in this case to compensate for Israel's inferiority in the air. Titled "Air Force 13," this unit was to be mainly composed of veterans of HaShahar who would serve as light-plane pilots trained in sabotage operations. During wartime they were to fly at low altitudes to Arab airfields, land near them, and infiltrate them in order to destroy key installations and planes. The initiative to build this unit came mainly from

---

4. Up to now information regarding IS–18's activities in Arab countries during the war and the immediate postwar period has been scarce. The little information available can give some impression regarding the unit's goals and modus operandi.

In the spring of 1948 a network of six members of the Palmach's "Arabists" (later to become Unit IS–18) was planted in Beirut and supplied with explosives and a radio communication setup. In addition to providing information, these Israeli agents devised plans for future operations: the elimination of Kaukji, the commander of the Arab Liberation Army, who was a neighbor of one of the agents; the blowing up of refineries in Tripoli; and the sabotaging of bridges and main roads. Only one of the plans—the blowing up of a yacht that had belonged to Hitler and was being renovated for military purposes—was approved by Israeli authorities and was carried out successfully (Dror, pp. 190–200). Then in 1950 the original members of the network were replaced by a new team (p. 230). Also in 1948 a second network was established in Damascus. Unlike their colleagues in Lebanon, the agents in Syria were only used for acquisition of intelligence. It is not clear when Israel disbanded this second network, but it is known that in late 1949 some of its agents were activated in order to obtain information on Syrian strategic installations, including air fields near Damascus and deep in Syrian territory, a mission that was successfully completed (pp. 201–10).

Not all the operations of IS–18 were as successful: two of its agents were caught and executed in Gaza by the Egyptian military authorities in mid-1948, and a third was executed in Jordan about a year later (pp. 217–24). The agents caught in Gaza admitted in their investigation that they were sent to poison local wells with dysentery microbes. Although Israel officially denied it in 1948, in 1993 some Israelis connected with this episode admitted that the Egyptian accusations held more than a grain of truth (*Hadashot*, 13 August 1993).

members of the Naval Commando, supported by some air force personnel. But after initial preparations took place in late 1950, the idea was rejected by the air force orthodox elite, who believed that all resources should be devoted to winning the next war in the air rather than on the ground.

The establishment of special operations units was initiated mostly by young officers from different branches of the military but with similar operational backgrounds. They gained training and combat experience either with British assistance during World War II or on their own in the different Jewish underground movements, first in fighting the British army during the late Mandate years and then during the war with the regular Arab forces. Basically their thinking was influenced by three key elements. First, years of service in the underground taught them that stratagem is the best weapon of the weak against the strong. Second, the success of British special operations units, especially in the Western Desert during World War II, highlighted the potential of such instruments in the Arab-Israeli arena. Third, and most important, in the early 1950s the IDF lacked a strategic arm capable of hitting targets deep within the enemy's territory. Until the Israeli army could acquire such a capability in the form of long-range fighter-bombers (which did not occur until the mid-1950s), special operations units were considered the only reasonable alternative.

Although the initiative to develop such units came mainly from lower-ranking officers, senior officials in the Israeli intelligence community were thinking along similar lines. Indeed, in late 1950, at approximately the same time the IAF (Israeli Air Force) rejected the idea of "Air Force 13," and following demands by Colonel Givli, it was decided to transfer the operational unit of the Political Department ("Research B") to Military Intelligence. This decision was followed by Ben-Gurion's decision in February to dismantle the Political Department. In May 1951, while these organizational reforms were under way, the Political Department's "Research B" unit suffered one of the most serious failures in the history of the Israeli intelligence community.[5]

5. In May 1951 an agent of the Political Department's special-operations unit was caught by Iraqi security along with another Israeli who was the chief organizer of the Jewish emigration from Iraq. Lack of compartmentation between the activities of the two organizations brought about the total collapse of the second organ. Dozens of Iraqi Jews were arrested, small arms caches that had been prepared for self-defense were confiscated, and Zionist activities in Iraq were almost totally halted. Following a public trial, two Iraqi Jews were executed and some others, including Yehuda Tajar of "Research B" unit (who had received the rank of captain in the IDF following the transfer of his unit to Military Intelligence), were tried and sentenced to long prison terms (Harel 1989, pp. 176–77; Hilel, pp. 325–42; Black and Morris, pp. 86–95. Details of the trials of the Jewish

Most members of "Research B" unit joined the Foreign Office, the Ministry of Defense, and the newly established Mossad. Only a very few preferred to enter the DMI. Thus the manpower required for the new Military Intelligence unit came mainly from its sister units in the Navy and the Air Force. Quite naturally, then, the special operations unit was titled "Intelligence 13." It comprised two sections, No. 1 and No. 2, which shortly afterwards became Unit 131 and Unit 132. Unit 132 dealt with tactical psychological warfare and constituted Military Intelligence's operational unit in peacetime. Unit 131, with which IS–18 was combined, was to serve as Israel's strategic arm and was to operate only in times of war.

The concept behind the creation of Unit 131 is somewhat controversial. Harel, for example, argued that the unit was aimed at carrying out special operations behind enemy lines, mainly in the field of psychological warfare (Harel's testimony before the Olshan-Dory investigation committee, Harel 1982b, p. 22). Veterans of the DMI maintain, however, that the unit was not built as a psychological warfare instrument but as Israel's strategic arm in time of war. Thus Major General (ret.) Yehoshafat Harkabi, who replaced Givli between April 1953 and April 1954 as the acting chief of the DMI, explained that Unit 131 was a substitute for the long-range bombers that the IAF lacked at the beginning of the 1950s and was instituted to carry out sabotage acts against strategic targets in the Arab hinterland in wartime (Harkabi interview). Alouph Hareven, Givli's military assistant from June 1954, argued much the same (Hareven interview). The command of Unit 131 from late 1951 to the end of 1954, Lieutenant Colonel (ret.) Mordechai Benzoor, defined the mission of his unit as follows: "To plant agents in Arab states. These agents were to be 'sleepers,' to keep in constant communication with headquarters, and to supply early warnings. If the need arose, these agents were to have the capability to conduct sabotage acts according

---

underground in Iraq are found also in a special document prepared in connection with the Cairo trial of 1954–55 titled "The Baghdad Trials" ISA, FO 130.02 2387/7).

How Tajar received his freedom from an Iraqi jail is a fine example of the strange relations that can be created between countries during wartime. In early 1954 the DMI planned a daring operation for the rescue of its agent from jail. However, Harel, the head of Mossad, vetoed this plan, which he considered too hazardous. Following the 1956 Sinai Campaign against Egypt, however, Mossad developed an excellent working relationship with the Iranian intelligence service, and Harel himself became the personal friend of his Iranian counterpart Timmur Bakhtiar. In the late 1950s Mossad delivered to President Quassem of Iraq several warnings of Egyptian plans to eliminate him. On one occasion the warning was delivered through Bakhtiar, who told the Iraqi president of the source of his information. The Israelis used this debt in order to ask for Tajar's freedom. Through Bakhtiar's mediation he was returned to Israel in 1960 (Harel 1989, pp. 177–78).

to instructions from Israel" (Benzoor interview). Major (ret.) Avraham Dar, the man who recruited the Egyptian network—the main asset of Unit 131 until its collapse in July 1954—had a somewhat different concept: the local recruits were to make preparations for future operations (that is, to build caches of arms and explosives or to collect the information needed for carrying out sabotage acts). These facilities were to be used by Israeli special operations units (such as the Naval Commando) but not by the local Jews themselves, in order to carry out sabotage acts against strategic installations in wartime (Dar interview).

These different and to a certain extent conflicting views can still lead to some initial conclusions. First, Unit 131 was established in order to compensate the IDF for the lack of long-range strategic arms that were unavailable to Israel at the beginning of the 1950s. Second, although the prime object of the unit was the conduct of sabotage acts against strategic installations in wartime, at least some of the unit's agents were also to collect information. Third, and most important, except for intelligence gathering (which was never the task of local recruits), the unit was to operate only in wartime.

Unit 131 had to be built from scratch. It had neither agents nor any other assets in the Arab world when it was created: most of the men who had been planted in neighboring countries had by then returned to Israel and new ones were not readily available. Indeed, locating, recruiting, and training fresh manpower was the top priority of the new unit. Recruitment was done on an informal basis, mainly using personal connections. But the recruitment policy was highly controversial. Isser Harel maintains that in the early 1950s the heads of the DMI believed that it was

> possible to make use of the desire of criminals and others with criminal records to become rehabilitated by volunteering for danger-ous and difficult national missions. According to this concept, the tougher the criminal, the more daring the missions that can be assigned to him. . . . It was a belief—a wrong one—that when carrying out a special mission, one done in the national interest, all positive characteristics, even in the negative type of person, will come out. This belief ignored the serious risk that in the critical moment, negative characteristics such as adventurism, lack of discretion, greed, lying, boastfulness, lawlessness and even disre-spect for human life, might come out. (Harel 1980, p. 299)

There is no doubt that some in the DMI, such as 131's commander, Benzoor, were actually infected by this "Dirty Dozen" syndrome that received its professional blessing from Dr. David Rudi, a psychologist who participated in formulating the unit's selection policy. Accordingly, some of the personnel recruited did have criminal records. Others maintain that the use of criminals was not the result of free choice but was done since no better candidates were available. Harkabi, for example, explained that it was almost impossible to find suitable volunteers who would accept risky missions in enemy territory purely out of idealism (Harkabi interview). Whether it was a matter of necessity or choice, however, the fact is that the DMI took considerable risks in recruiting criminals as new agents. Nowhere else would this become more evident than in the case of the "unfortunate business."

While recruitment and training were at their initial stages, Unit 131 launched one of its earliest operations. The mission was to examine the conditions for intelligence activities in Egypt, and the chosen agent was Major Avraham Dar. He entered Egypt in April 1951, using a British passport under the name of John Darling, a salesman of electrical equipment for a factory in Gibraltar (Golan 1976, pp. 28–29). In his four-month stay in Egypt, and in defiance of his instructions from Israel, Dar not only examined conditions for Unit 131's activities in Egypt but also recruited six young local Jews from Cairo and Alexandria for future operations. He thus laid the infrastructure for the first Unit 131 network in an Arab country. Unknowingly, he also planted the seeds for the "unfortunate business" that would take place three years later.

In his recruitment mission Dar was assisted by two workers from the Institute for Illegal Immigration,[6] Dr. Victor Sa'adiya and Ovadia Danun. The six recruits were Dr. Mussa Marzouk and Victorine Marcelle Ninio ("Claude") from Cairo and Shmuel Azar ("Jacques"), Victor Levy ("Pierre"), Robert Dassa ("Roger"), and Philip Natanson ("Henri") from Alexandria. Given that Israel had had no human assets in Egypt since the 1948 war, and that earlier DMI attempts to obtain such assets had failed, the

6. The Institute for Illegal (or B) Immigration was established during the early 1940s in order to organize illegal Jewish immigration to Palestine. It also dealt with acquisition of arms and their smuggling to the Yishuv. The Institute continued to organize all underground Zionist activities in Arab countries after the state of Israel was born and was dismantled only at the end of 1951. Its Hebrew name was HaMossad le-Aliyah Beth, known as HaMossad. It is important not to confuse this organization with the Institute for Intelligence and Special Roles (Mossad), which was created shortly before the other organ was dismantled.

mere fact that infrastructure for intelligence activities there was established through Dar's mission was regarded at the time as "a significant coup" (Harkabi interview, Dar interview). Yet the mere use of this asset was highly controversial. Upon Dar's return to Israel in August 1951 a serious debate began within the DMI and the IDF over whether or not to use the newly recruited Egyptian Jews, a debate about professionalism and principles that also stemmed from internal politics and personal roots.

The principal controversy focused on two issues. First, conservative officers argued that, since the IDF was so small and its resources so scanty, the army could not afford to take upon itself new missions such as the conduct of warfare in the enemy's hinterland. According to these conservatives, moreover, the newly assembled units involved serious risks, including the eruption of hostilities at times and conditions unfavorable to Israel. Hence, they maintained, all resources should be devoted to conventional means of defeating the enemy on the battlefield. Opposing them were officers such as Chief of Staff Yigael Yadin and his deputy Mordechai Makleff, who replaced him in late 1952. They favored the relatively small investment needed to build up the new means, which might prove highly useful in wartime (Golan 1976, p. 46).

The second principal issue involved the question of whether or not to use local Jews in intelligence operations in Arab countries. On the one hand, local Jews were available for recruitment, their motivation was regarded as high, and they were far more reliable than any local Arabs who might have cooperated with Israeli intelligence organizations either because they were being blackmailed or because of financial temptation. On the other hand, there were the risks to the local Jewish community if any of its members were caught red-handed participating in such activities. Indeed, for an Israel that perceived herself as the representative and defender of Jews all over the world and especially in the hostile Arab countries, the mere use of Arab Jews for intelligence purposes meant a grave responsibility. In this sense the activities of Unit 131 were among the most sensitive issues in the nation's foreign and defense policy.

The Israeli political and military leadership was aware of this delicate problem. Hence, against the background of the early 1950 debate between Military Intelligence and the Political Department, an agreement was reached at the time Unit 131 was established according to which a committee of two was set up: Shiloah, as the senior person in Israel's intelligence community and a close advisor to Prime Minister Ben-Gurion and Foreign Minister Sharett; and Major General Makleff, the head of the

G (General Staff) Branch GHQ to which Military Intelligence belonged until 1953. This committee was supposed to ensure combined civilian and military supervision of the unit's activities (Harel 1982b, pp. 17–18; Eshed 1979, pp. 39–40). However, once its two members assumed new positions some months later, it ceased to exist for all practical purposes. With the resultant lack of proper supervision, Major Dar, a relatively low-ranking officer in the DMI, could count on a fait accompli when recruiting local Egyptian Jews on his own initiative.

At the professional level there were doubts about the operational reliability of the Egyptian Jews recruited by Dar. Although Benzoor had to accept the network as part of his unit upon entering office, he opposed the recruitment of local Jews, not on grounds of principle but of competence. Having experienced almost two years' service as an agent in Iraq (between 1945 and 1947), Benzoor believed he knew first hand the capabilities of local Jews and did not regard them as adequate to the needs of his unit (Benzoor interview). Others in Unit 131 were worried about using agents whose reliability was not sufficiently known and who thus might— mistakenly or under pressure—reveal their secrets and jeopardize not only themselves but also other DMI assets in the target country.

The internal debate within the DMI had some power politics and personal aspects as well. Obviously, Dar was the natural candidate to become the new network case officer. Yet, despite his many qualifications, he was not considered a suitable choice by his superiors, mainly because he was notorious for his inability to keep secrets. Benzoor, who personally disliked him, objected to Dar's independent control of the network. His demand was quite clear: either Dar should be removed to a different position or the whole network should be eliminated from Unit 131 (ibid.). Dar, for his part, refused to work under Benzoor, whom he considered as "not clever . . . and not suitable" to head Unit 131 (Teveth 1992b, pp. 21–22). It is quite probable that considerations of power politics played a significant role at this juncture as well. If Dar was to become the network's commander, direct linkage might have been established between him and the head of Military Intelligence, Colonel Givli, leaving Benzoor a commander without troops.

It is not clear at what level the decisions were made and whether or not civilian decisionmakers were involved in making them. In the question of whether or not to use local Jews, those who favored their use won, and it was decided not only to maintain the new network but also to train its members in Israel. Accordingly, between September 1951 and October 1953 five agents—four who were recruited directly by Dar and a fifth who joined the network later—received training at the DMI's facilities in Israel. They arrived in Israel via France and their training included enciphering and deciphering methods, use of radio communication systems, composition of explosives, and sabotage techniques. In addition, they received some traditional military training: navigation, topography, and the use of small arms. Most of the instruction was done on an individual basis and lasted from a couple of weeks to a few months (Golan 1976, pp. 41–57).

This training period also enabled the experts of Unit 131 to judge both the quality of the young recruits and their ability to conduct their missions. The general impression was fairly good. As Benzoor put it: "Individually they were fine. They could carry out their missions, if they had a suitable commander. The problem was with command. And of course, there was a problem with means, that is, explosives" (Benzoor interview).

Indeed, as time passed and the trainees started returning to Egypt, finding a suitable commander became a pressing problem. Because of his known weakness, and under Benzoor's pressure, it was decided to remove Dar from the network's activities. The only other available candidate, then, became Unit 131's only active agent in Egypt, Major Max Binnet ("David"). Binnett had considerable experience; before his assignment to Egypt at the beginning of 1952 he had successfully completed missions in Iran and Iraq. During the 1951 trials of the Jewish underground in Iraq, however, it became known that his cover was blown when the prosecutor referred to him as the head of an Israeli intelligence network. Lame from a wound suffered in the 1948 war, Binnet used his handicap to pose as the representative in Egypt of a German firm manufacturing prostheses. He was sent there mainly for intelligence gathering and was to act on his own, and in this sense his mission had little to do with the network. Compelled by the need to find a commander to head it, however, Colonel Givli wanted his only available agent in Egypt to fill this role as well. So, despite Benzoor's objections, mainly on grounds that a link with the network could endanger him, Binnet was instructed to make contact with Marcelle Ninio in Cairo. Through her he met other members of the network. But upon learning the nature of their mission and recognizing the amateurish nature of their activities, Binnet was permitted to disconnect himself from the network. He maintained links only with Ninio, who became his liaison officer and radio operator[7] (Golan 1976, pp. 50–51; Benzoor interview).

7. In spite of his many qualifications, Binnet was a poor radio operator and his "wireless fingerprints" could be easily recognized owing to the slowness of his transmissions (Biberman

In October 1953 the last member of the network, Philip Natanson, completed his training in Israel and returned to Egypt. He brought with him instructions for his colleagues to intensify their training and start manufacturing homemade explosives. Yet by early 1954 the network was very far from reaching an operational status. It still had no commander, its means of communication with Israeli headquarters were slow and inefficient, and its members had not been supplied with false passports and getaway routes. Most important, they still lacked effective explosives needed to carry out the missions they were trained for. There were two reasons for this situation. First, although Unit 131 was in charge of the network, other sections in the DMI were responsible for supplying it with false documentation, means of communication, etc. These sections had a different order of priorities and had rejected or ignored Benzoor's demands for supplying his men with the necessary means. Second, and even more important, according to the DMI's plans the network was not scheduled to become fully operational until 1956–57 (Benzoor interview).

But plans are made to be changed. As Benzoor was to discover very soon, his planning lagged behind developments within the Israeli political and military leadership and between Egypt and the Western powers. These developments ultimately led to the activation of the network at least two years ahead of schedule.

The Israeli Decisionmaking Apparatus: 1953–1954

In December 1953, after heading the state of Israel for over five years as Prime Minister and Minister of Defense, David Ben-Gurion retired to Sdeh Boker, a new kibbutz in the Negev desert. His departure left a major vacuum in Israel's power structure, since none of his colleagues could boast the same kind of authority in the ideological, political, and military realm that Ben-Gurion had obtained through his many years of leadership, first in the Yishuv under the British Mandate and then as the state's supreme decision-maker.

His successor as prime minister was Moshe Sharett, who was elected to this post by Mapai's leadership over Ben-Gurion's objections. The source of the retired premier's reluctance to support Sharett was less personal than

---

interview). This was probably the reason why a local radio operator was assigned to him. Before using Ninio, Binnet held radio communications with Israel at least a few times.

political, for although Sharett had undoubtedly been the number two man in Mapai for many years, he represented an alternative approach to Ben-Gurion's tough foreign and defense policy. Yet it is important to note that there was no disagreement between the two regarding the ultimate goal of Israel's foreign policy—reaching a stable settlement concerning the Arab-Israeli dispute. Moreover, the two rejected categorically any attempts to reach such an agreement on the basis of ceding land to the Arabs, maintaining that Israel's territorial integrity should be preserved under any political settlement. Still, on many occasions in his capacity as the Minister of Foreign Affairs, Sharett had challenged, on both practical and ethical grounds, the tactics used by Ben-Gurion and his close aides. The dispute between them, therefore, was over the means rather than the ends of Israel's foreign policy.

On his side, Sharett professed what became known as the "political activism" approach to Israel's defense and foreign policy. Simply put, this school of thought maintained that Israel was too small and too weak to challenge the Arab world on a long-term basis all by herself. Sharett and his followers maintained that, without the support of the outside world and especially of the United States, Israel could hardly survive in the hostile environment of the Middle East. The political implications of this line of thought were two. First, Israel should avoid as much as possible any confrontations and frictions with the main global powers. Second, Israel should exhaust all practical options to reach a political settlement with her Arab neighbors, first and foremost with the strongest of them, Egypt. The "political activism" school of thought thus objected to any acts, above all in the military realm, that might endanger the nation's relations with her potential supporters and reduce the likelihood of reaching a political settlement. Instead, it maintained that demonstrating Israel's willingness to solve the conflict through diplomatic means was the key to obtaining both support from the Western nations and the reduction of Arab hostility towards the Jewish state.

Opposing the "political activism" approach was Ben-Gurion's so-called "military activism." While not denying the value of outside, mainly Western, support, Ben-Gurion and his followers maintained that diplomatic activism by itself would not suffice to reach the final goal of a political settlement to the Arab-Israeli conflict. Instead, they maintained, Israel should also show her "teeth"—her ability to cause her Arab neighbors pain if they continued to conduct hostile acts against her and refused to come to the negotiating table. Politically, the "military activism" school of thought recommended a considerable use of force in reaction to Arab hostile acts. This translated, for the most part, into a policy of military retaliation against acts of infiltration and sabotage conducted from the neighboring Arab states. The logic behind this policy was twofold: first, to show the Arabs that the continuation of hostilities towards Israel could cost them dearly; and, second, to demonstrate to the outside world that Israel was ready to use brute force in order to defend her interests and that she had the ability to do so successfully. This use of force was also an implicit means of obtaining Western support, since in the tight bipolar competition of the early 1950s it was believed that a strong and somewhat aggressive Israel was far more attractive to the West than a state that relied on political means and on foreign aid alone. The theory of "military activism" thus considered the use of force rather than diplomacy as the best means of maintaining Israel's security in the short run and in the long run of bringing her to the negotiating table in a position of strength.

No two persons could have represented these two competing schools of thought better than Ben-Gurion and Sharett. Ben-Gurion was a man of deeds rather than words; his personal history recapitulated the national history of the Yishuv and that of the Israeli state. At every point he intuitively understood, often far earlier than his colleagues, where the central problem lay and how to focus all his energies on solving it. Thus in the 1930s, when the Yishuv's main problem was establishing the basis for an independent Jewish community in Palestine, Ben-Gurion served as the general secretary of the Histadrut—the main instrument for acquiring land acre by acre and building Jewish settlements one by one. In 1942, already foreseeing such global developments as the decline of the British Empire, he announced that the foundation of an independent Jewish state was now the practical goal for the Jewish community in Palestine. Then early in 1947, perceiving that the independence process would be accompanied by an Arab military offensive against the Yishuv, he devoted all his energy to preparing the new nation for war, acquiring weaponry and training the manpower that would be needed to weather this test. Thus the IDF, which was formally established during the 1948 war, was to a certain extent the personal creation of Ben-Gurion.

Following the establishment of the state of Israel, Ben-Gurion served not only as Prime Minister but also as Minister of Defense. In this latter capacity he was perceived as the ultimate authority in military affairs by his civilian colleagues and military men alike. Regarding youth as the major guarantee for a dynamic and active policy, Ben-Gurion pushed young officers up in the ranks at a rate unknown in any other military organization. He nominated Yadin, who was only 29, to head the IDF, recommended Makleff as his replacement at the age of 32, and chose the 38-year-old Dayan to replace Makleff. He similarly made Shimon Peres Director General of the Defense Ministry, the largest and strongest ministry in Israel, at the age of 29. Obviously, this policy had some disadvantages: by advocating the nomination of young men to senior positions, Ben-Gurion gained the opposition of the older generation of Israeli leadership, mainly on the grounds that the young were not yet ready for such roles. Yet so long as he was Premier and Defense Minister, there was a general consensus that the younger generation's lack of experience was compensated for by Ben-Gurion's enormous personal experience and authority. This situation changed dramatically when Ben-Gurion left the government at the end of 1953.

In comparison to Ben-Gurion, the new prime minister had far less authority in national security affairs. From the mid-1940s throughout the early 1950s Sharett had only limited access to the military. Instead, he had focused his attention on foreign affairs, first as the Yishuv's acting Foreign Minister and then as the Minister of Foreign Affairs of the young Jewish state. Indeed, if the army was Ben-Gurion's personal creation, Sharett's was the Ministry of Foreign Affairs and the diplomatic service. Highly intelligent, a superb linguist, and a born diplomat, Sharett was a gifted statesman. Yet, once he replaced Ben-Gurion as Prime Minister, his rather dovish approach to state security and his lack of personal authority over the young and aggressive IDF officers corp severely limited his ability to direct military affairs successfully.

If Sharett had been able to count on a defense minister who was both loyal to his chief and respected by the IDF elite, controlling the army could have been much less problematic. Unfortunately, the man chosen for this post by Ben-Gurion lacked both of these qualities. Pinhas Lavon was a man of notable intellect and good education; an excellent orator with a sharp mind and tongue, he was head and shoulders above the average Israeli politician. But Lavon was also exceptionally arrogant and ambitious, and he tended to underestimate the ability of others, friends and foes alike. Before entering the Defense Ministry in late 1953, Lavon had filled only minor posts in the government, had no experience in security affairs, and held rather dovish views. Once he became Minister of Defense, however, he went through a dramatic transformation. The moderate dove became a predatory hawk who pushed the already aggressive army into new ventures and adopted what even those around him considered "wild plans for military operations." In order to overcome Sharett's objection to this line, the ambitious Lavon simply ignored his Prime Minister. Sharett, hesitating to fire a Defense Minister who had been nominated by Ben-Gurion and attempting to avoid a confrontation that might lead to a political crisis, tried to "teach" Lavon the elementary rules of orderly administration. On the whole, however, he failed. Typical of these attempts was an understated note he wrote his Defense Minister at the end of May 1954:

> The manner in which security affairs are reported to me does not work properly. Things are happening without my being informed. I hear reports in *Kol Yisrael* [the Israeli radio station], and read about them afterwards in the press, without knowing their true background. It's only right that I should know the facts—whenever possible—before the official version for outside consumption comes out. In any event, I must know the facts. It seems to me that such an arrangement is possible, but you should initiate it. (Sharett Diary, p. 514)

Even following the Military Intelligence mishap of July 1954, after which Lavon's status in Sharett's government became rather shaky, the Defense Minister did not relinquish attempts to conduct an independent policy by ignoring the one pursued by the Prime Minister. Thus on the eve of sending an Israeli ship to pass through the Suez Canal as a test of Egypt's readiness to allow free navigation there—obviously a matter of foreign rather than defense policy—Sharett had to warn his subordinate in writing:

> Since I know in advance that you might object to my opinion, I have to add for the sake of clarification that I regard the sailing of the ship in the Suez Canal as an independent operation of foreign policy and not as a security matter. The Defense Ministry serves here only as a performing instrument, but it does not make the policy.[8]

Others in the Israeli hierarchy were well aware of the poisonous relationship between the Prime Minister and his Defense Minister and its implica-

---

8. Sharett's personal communication with Lavon, *ISA*, FO 130.02 2446/11.

tions for Israel's security. Isser Harel, for example, described the situation as "shocking," explaining that:

> I returned to Israel at the end of May 1954. . . . I found things that have shocked me with regard to the relationship between the army and the Defense Ministry and the Foreign Ministry and the Prime Minister. . . . There were operations on the border of which the Prime Minister was not informed ahead of time and when they were reported *ex post facto,* they were false.[9]

Lies, deception, and concealment, then, were the instruments Lavon used to bypass a rather helpless Prime Minister in order to push his personal and national goals. Just as important was the fact that Lavon made no effort to conceal his contempt for Sharett. His close aides, as well as high-ranking officers in the army and senior officials in the Defense Ministry, were well aware of his attitude towards his superior, and this obviously influenced their attitude not only towards the Prime Minister but also towards Lavon himself.

Under Lavon were Moshe Dayan as Chief of Staff and Shimon Peres, the Defense Ministry's Director General. Both had their own ambitions, both attempted to pursue their own policies, and both had a deep loyalty to Ben-Gurion—the man who had nurtured them and raised them to their present positions—rather than to their immediate superior. Although Dayan and Peres were themselves advocates of "military activism," they regarded Lavon's interpretation of this policy as too extreme. Other bones of contention existed as well.

Dayan's relationship with Lavon was highly complicated. On the one hand, the Chief of Staff used Lavon as a shield under which he could pursue military operations that contradicted Sharett's policies. Dayan explained this behavior quite frankly in his testimony before the Olshan-Dory investigation committee:

> There are operations to which I am sure Sharett would object, while I am certain that they should be done. . . . If the Defense Minister tells me that the matter is in his political and constitutional authority and if the matter [that is, the operation] is to be avoided, it would be better avoided between Lavon and Sharett. (Eshed 1979, pp. 40–41)

9. Harel's testimony before the Olshan-Dory investigation committee, Eshed 1979, p. 44.

On the other hand, Dayan had ethical and professional disagreements with Lavon. He did not accept Lavon's policy of consulting with other senior military officers without his knowledge. Regarding this policy as an expression of lack of trust in his judgment, Dayan demanded that his superior use the appropriate channels of command. When Lavon continued to ignore this demand, Dayan used one such incident in June 1954 to submit his resignation, knowing that Lavon was in no position to accept it. He agreed to back down only after Lavon apologized for his behavior, mainly on technical grounds. The problem, however, remained unsolved. There were also many disagreements between the two regarding the purchase of new equipment for the IDF, but since Dayan had more military experience and the support of most of the General Staff, he usually succeeded in imposing his opinions and pursuing his goals.

Lavon's policy of direct interference in professional and operational military affairs found its best expression in his relationship with the chief of the DMI. This was at first Lieutenant Colonel Harkabi, who served as acting chief of Military Intelligence until Colonel Givli's scheduled return to Israel in April 1954 from studies in the United States. The direct link between the Defense Minister and the chief of the DMI could be partially explained by the latter's responsibility for the military aspects of Israel's armistice and the subordination of the IDF spokesperson to the DMI. On these policy-oriented issues Lavon's direct contact with Harkabi, and then Givli, was considered legitimate and appropriate. Lavon, however, did not limit himself to these issues alone. In discussions with the chiefs of the DMI he showed a considerable interest in the organization's operational capabilities and plans. The focus of his attention was Unit 131, and according to evidence submitted to the Olshan-Dory investigation committee, Lavon demanded that he directly supervise the unit's activities (ibid., p. 39).

Supervision of Unit 131 thus became another bone of contention between Lavon and Dayan. In this struggle, however, they had a common enemy: Isser Harel. The senior person in Israel's intelligence community, Harel regarded himself as the legitimate heir to Shiloah, whom he replaced in 1952. He had been briefed by Shiloah on the 1950 arrangement to supervise Unit 131's activities but had to neglect the issue because of more pressing matters. Then in 1953, after learning from Harkabi of some of the unit's operational plans, he demanded that the acting chief of the DMI return to the agreement of 1950. As Harel explained it after the collapse of the Egyptian network, he was worried for two reasons. First, he considered the plans hazardous and amateurish, involving as they did a grave risk to the lives of non-Israeli Jews. Second, he was convinced that the Prime Minister knew nothing about these plans, which contradicted his foreign policy. Being directly subordinate to the Prime Minister's office, Harel regarded himself as the only channel through which Sharett could learn about what the DMI was planning right under his nose (Harel 1982b, pp. 17–18; Eshed 1979, pp. 39–41).

Harel's demand was discussed in a special meeting devoted to development plans for Unit 131 held in Lavon's office on 18 February 1954. Both Lavon and Dayan rejected it. To the Olshan-Dory investigation committee, Dayan explained that his position in this matter was a function of his general approach to Sharett:

> I was against cooperation with Isser [Harel]. First, because the matters we dealt with involved only the construction of the unit and there was no question of operations, and second, since Isser is subordinate to the Prime Minister. Letting Isser in means letting the Prime Minister in. (Eshed 1979, p. 40; Harel 1982b, p. 17)

Lavon objected to Harel's demand on the ground that its acceptance would bring about "a condominium of offices that opens the door to a lack of responsibility by any one minister." Instead, he demanded exclusive responsibility for the unit's plans and operations (Eshed 1979, p. 41). Thus, following this meeting, he informed Harel in writing:

> 1. It is the head of the DMI's responsibility to inform you of what is done in 131 and to ensure coordination between the Authority [that is, the Mossad and SHABAK] and 131.
>
> 2. The military hierarchy, according to which the Unit is subordinate to the chief of the DMI and through him to the Chief of Staff, will remain in effect.
>
> 3. No other management forums will be established. (Harel 1982b, pp. 17–18)

About a week later in a meeting with Lavon, Harel tried to convince the Defense Minister to reverse his decision. Harel's argument was that since the original agreement was between the Defense Ministry and the Foreign Ministry, Lavon was not authorized to cancel it unilaterally. Ignoring this procedural argument, Lavon insisted on preserving the new arrangement that excluded Harel—and Sharett—from Unit 131's affairs. In early March 1954 Harel left Israel without having had an opportunity to inform the Prime Minister of these developments (Eshed 1979, p. 41). Upon returning to Israel in early May, he found that Colonel Givli was back heading Military Intelligence and that the relations between the Mossad and the DMI had deteriorated to a new low (Harel 1982b, p. 18).

Colonel Givli had considerable experience in intelligence affairs. Charismatic, energetic, and an excellent organizer, he had many of the qualities needed to head the DMI and increase its power. Yet he was not without shortcomings. Unlike Harkabi, Colonel Givli was not an intellectual but a man of action. In this sense he regarded the contribution of his organization to national security more in operational terms than in the ability to give a clear and accurate national estimate. Ambitious and creative, Givli had brilliant ideas. But he lacked discretion, rarely considering the risks involved in carrying out his ideas and the potential negative results of an intelligence operation once it was started.

Givli's status in the IDF's leadership was somewhat shaky. Unlike the other young Israeli generals, he lacked the combat experience of field commanders. His entire career was spent in the Israeli intelligence community, first in the SHAI, next as a senior officer in the DMI, and then as its chief. Moreover, Givli had a dark spot in his past. While serving as the chief of SHAI's Jerusalem District during the 1948 war, he was extensively involved in the trial and execution of Meir Tobianski—an officer of the Hagana who was suspected of being an informer in the pay of the British officers of the Arab Legion. After an investigation committee concluded that Tobianski's guilt was not adequately proved and that his trial was not conducted in accordance with the proper legal procedures, it was Givli's superior, Colonel Isser Be'eri, who paid with his career. But in mid-1950 Ben-Gurion, who kept a close eye on the IDF, objected to the nomination of Givli as the new chief of the DMI mainly because of his role in the Tobianski affair. Ben-Gurion accepted this appointment only under pressure from Yadin, then Chief of Staff. Givli received, however, only the title of acting chief of the DMI, and Ben-Gurion saw to it that Harkabi joined the organization as Givli's deputy, somewhat in the role of a personal "watchdog" (Harkabi interview; Hareven interview; Teveth 1992a, pp. 143–45).

Upon returning to Israel in late March 1954, Givli found a different state of affairs from the one that existed a year earlier. First, Military Intelligence had become an independent branch in the IDF's GHQ. As its head, Givli now had direct access to the Chief of Staff. Second, Givli had a close relationship with the new Chief of Staff, Dayan, though not as close as other high-ranking officers (Harkabi interview; Hareven interview). Third, and most important, instead of Ben-Gurion, who distrusted him, Givli found a new man at the head of the Defense Ministry, Pinhas Lavon. The two soon created a close working relationship that was not necessarily based on personal chemistry; for Givli, Lavon and his behavior remained an enigma (Hareven interview). Still, the two shared similar perceptions of Israel's national security problems; even more important, not only was their diagnosis of the situation similar but their prognosis as well.

Givli's close relationship with Lavon ensured him a position of strength in professional matters as well as in bureaucratic politics. Backed by the Defense Minister, Givli could easily rebuff the attempts of his main competitor in the intelligence community, Harel, to interfere with DMI affairs, especially those involving Unit 131. Furthermore, Lavon supported many of Givli's creative projects. And without someone around to warn against the potential risks involved in such projects—Harkabi had recently left for studies in Paris—there was little to prevent the head of the DMI from initiating high-risk intelligence operations.

All in all, in mid-1954 the Israeli hierarchy resembled almost a caricature of an effective decisionmaking system. An effective hierarchy is based on instructions from the superior level to the subordinate one and their implementation by the latter. In an effective hierarchy, moreover, the superior level controls the implementation of its instructions by receiving timely and accurate reports from subordinates on how its instructions are being carried out. None of this existed in the Israeli hierarchy in 1954. Instead of a multilevel activation and control system, all relevant lines of command were broken. In the Defense Ministry and the IDF the norm was false reporting, the deception of civilian superiors by subordinates, and the pursuit of independent policies rather than policies formulated by the Prime Minister. Officially the system was headed by Sharett, but in reality the security apparatus under him rejected his authority and ignored his policy, opting instead for an opposing one.[10] This situation as it bears on the specific issues in our case study is outlined in Table 5.

As is evident from the table, the only lines of command that functioned properly were those between the head of the Mossad (who had no influence

10. For a very good analysis of this subject and its impact on the Egyptian operation, see Hareven, pp. 7–9.

Table 5.   Israel's decisionmaking system and the Egyptian network in mid-1954

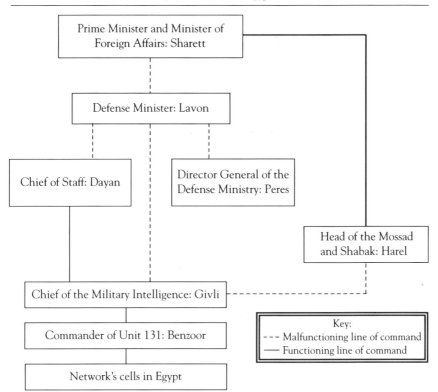

on the affairs of Unit 131) and the Prime Minister and those within Military Intelligence. Meanwhile, decisions were being made at the levels of Prime Minister, Defense Minister, Chief of Staff, and chief of the DMI, but with the exception of that between Givli and Dayan all relevant lines of command and control within and between these levels were malfunctioning. Once Dayan had left for a long visit abroad in July 1954, furthermore, the chain of command between his replacement and the chief of the DMI became distorted as well.

No organization can function efficiently under such conditions. Yet, if it does not confront fateful national decisions, such pathologies can survive for a long time. This was not the situation in Israel, however, in the first half of 1954; her regional and international position was at its lowest since the 1948 war. To begin with, room for maneuverability in the tight international bipolar system of the early 1950s was significantly reduced under the Eisenhower administration's growing inclination towards the Arabs. Then, too, the army was desperately looking, without much success, for sources of the modern weapons needed to defend the country in the foreseeable second round of battles. At the same time, intensifying infiltration from neighboring Arab countries constituted a major challenge for the IDF, which had to find an effective means of both patrolling the long borders of the young state and deterring the Arab regimes from violating these borders.

The most serious and pressing problem Israel had to confront during the first half of 1954, however, was the resumption of Anglo-Egyptian negotiations on the evacuation of British forces from the Suez Canal Zone. It was this development, regarded by the defense establishment as the gravest of threats to the state's security, that the DMI attempted to prevent by circumventing proper political channels to activate its Egyptian network.

The Anglo-Egyptian Negotiations as Perceived in Israel: 1953–1954

This section will not describe the Anglo-Egyptian negotiations themselves. Instead, it will focus on two issues: First, the information received in Israel through various channels regarding the main developments in British and Egyptian negotiations; second, the DMI's and the Foreign Office's diagnoses of the available information and their subsequent prognoses. Assuming that perception of reality rather than reality itself is the basis for action, this section will provide a partial explanation for Colonel Givli's decision to activate the Egyptian network in order to prevent, or at least postpone, the conclusion of the negotiations. It is important to note, however, that this explanation is based on partial information, mainly from the files of the Israeli Foreign Office and the British Public Records Office; there may well be other relevant documents, especially Israeli—in the DMI, IDF, and the Prime Minister Office's archives—that have not yet been declassified.

The Information

First alert regarding British intentions to reach a comprehensive accord on the evacuation of all combat forces from the Canal Zone arrived in Israel as early as December 1952. Reuven Shiloah, in his last days as an advisor for Special Roles, warned the DMI and the Foreign Ministry that, according to

British sources, Churchill's government considered the political, military, and financial cost of defending the Middle East to be too high. Accordingly, the British Prime Minister had decided to demand that the United States take responsibility for the region, a demand he intended to discuss during his upcoming visit to Washington. According to Richard Crossman, a pro-Zionist British Member of Parliament and one of Shiloah's informers, the implication of this decision was that either British units would be evacuated from their bases in the Canal Zone or they would be replaced by American forces. It was quite clear to London that Washington would refuse to keep forces in the Suez Zone in peacetime and hence that the only possible solution for the British was to reach an agreement with Naguib, the Egyptian president, to enable him to maintain the Suez bases until war erupted and the transfer of Western forces to the Canal Zone would become feasible.[11]

The DMI's estimate, on the basis of additional information, was less alarming than Shiloah's. On 2 January 1953 its research branch noted that reaching an actual decision on evacuation would be dependent upon two conditions: Egypt's joining the MEDO (Middle East Defence Organization); and Britain's supervising logistic installations in the Suez Zone. Neither of the two problems was even close to being solved. Hence the DMI estimated that "Britain will not evacuate the Canal Zone within the near future [that is, next year]," that "there is no intention of evacuating the RAF from the Suez under any circumstances," and that, therefore, any evacuation "will be only a partial one" with the intention of preserving British combat forces in the area.[12]

The problems outlined by the DMI research branch were indeed the main obstacles to reaching an Anglo-Egyptian compromise and the reason negotiations continued throughout 1953. Britain's main incentive to conclude an accord was twofold: to ease the financial burden of maintaining her strategic assets in the Canal Zone (which amounted to 50 million pounds annually) and to alleviate American pressures to reach an agreement, something the State Department believed would free Egypt to join a regional defense pact. In October 1953, however, faced with an uncompromising Egyptian position and a growing number of attacks on British troops in the Zone, London broke off negotiations with Cairo. This move was doubtless influenced by heavy pressure from the hardline wing of the

11. From Shiloah R. to Katz K. and Colonel Givli: "Britain and the Defense of the Middle East," 22 December 1952, ISA, FO 130.02 2403/12.
12. From Katz K. to Shiloah R.: "Britain and the Defense of the Middle East," 7 January 1953, in ibid.

Conservative party in Parliament; these "Suez rebels" objected to the evacuation of the British forces from the Zone on principle.

As time passed, however, the impasse in the negotiations became a major dilemma for Britain. In a cabinet meeting held in late December 1953 the Prime Minister expressed his belief that Britain could not allow the situation to continue indefinitely and that the government must choose between reaching the best possible agreement and breaking off the negotiations.[13] Although it was clear that without an accord Britain could still control the Canal Zone and evacuate her troops according to her own timetable, such a situation was not considered desirable because it would involve significant problems in logistics. Even worse, if provocations against British forces intensified, or if the Suez Canal was sealed off, military means would probably have to be employed.[14]

In fact, plans for a military operation named RODEO had already been prepared. Its operational goal was the occupation of Cairo, and the possible reason for its implementation was the protection of British subjects in Egypt in case the negotiations collapsed. Responding to the possibility that RODEO might be implemented, the commander-in-chief of the Middle East Land Forces (MELF) demanded early in 1954 that two infantry brigades be dispatched to the Canal Zone before any definite action was taken.[15] In the first week of January 1954 British experts estimated that implementing RODEO would become almost inevitable if negotiations broke down. Obviously, though, the military option could also be used to pressure the Egyptians. In early 1954 Sir Ralf Stevenson, the British Ambassador in Cairo, held this view, which was also supported by the head of the British Middle East Office, Sir John Strendale-Bennet, who suggested that "[t]he *threat* of occupying Cairo—if conveyed privately to the Egyptian Government—might . . . deter the Egyptians both from victimizing British subjects and from harassing our forces in the Canal Zone. The operation itself would then be unnecessary."[16]

If threats failed, however, Strendale-Bennet estimated that the implementation of operation RODEO might be necessary, since

13. Chiefs of Staff Committee—Joint Planning Staff: "The Military Implications of Three Possible Courses of Action in the Event of Failure to Reach an Agreement with Egypt," 6 January 1954, *The Public Record Office* (henceforth PRO), FO 371/461, p. 2.

14. Ibid., p. 3.

15. Ibid.

16. Secretary of the Chiefs of Staff Committee: "Likely Developments in the Event of a Breakdown of Defence Negotiations in Cairo," 11 January 1954, Flag A, in ibid. (emphasis in original).

we should inevitably be driven to seal off the Canal Zone, and no Egyptian Government could stay in office if they failed to react violently to what would appear as an annexation of their territory. In these circumstances the purpose of the operation would be: (i) to neutralize Egyptian military opposition; or (ii) to deal with chaos in the Delta (not to change the Egyptian Government).[17]

In his concluding remarks on the conditions for implementing operation RODEO, Sterndale noted that "[t]he only other factor besides (b) [successful threats] likely to prevent a breakdown of the talks from developing into an occupation of Cairo is international action directed against ourselves by the United States and other powers to refrain from the operation." All things considered, he estimated that "we should be extremely lucky to avoid the operation in these circumstances."[18]

In Israel, however, the British decision to break off the talks was regarded as purely tactical. During 1953 it became clear that a final British evacuation of the Canal Zone had become a matter of when rather than if. Some Israeli policymakers were even ready to indirectly support the Egyptian bargaining position in order to improve relations with Cairo. In early spring 1953, for example, when British-Egyptian tensions reached one of their periodic peaks, Israel indicated to Cairo that Egyptian troops might be safely withdrawn from the Israeli-Egyptian border if they were needed to confront British forces at home.[19]

In 1954, however, the dominant view in Israel held that the conclusion of the accord would weaken Israel's regional strategic position. Yet preventing it was never considered a realistic option by Prime Minister Sharett and his close aides. Instead, Foreign Office officials were looking for ways to compensate Israel for the potential losses. Among the suggestions made were demanding that Egypt officially end her state of war with Israel and obliging the United States and Britain to sell Israel arms in case British military installations in the Canal Zone were handed over to the Egyptian army. It was also suggested that the West make arrangements to store heavy arms and engineering equipment in Israeli territory as a replacement for

17. Ibid.
18. Ibid.
19. From Colonel Herzog (the Israeli Military Attaché in Washington) to the DMI and the Ambassador: "A Talk with the Egyptian Military Attaché," 12 March 1954, ISA, FO 130.04 2477/ 20. The Israeli answer came in response to Naguib's inquiry (Segre interview), although the channels through which the dialogue was conducted are not known.

British installations in the Canal Zone. This equipment was to be used only in case of an international crisis, but Israeli cadres were to be trained to operate it. Another suggestion was for Western assistance in developing civilian industry that in an emergency could be used for military purposes as well.[20] As some Israelis noted, however, such demands were excessive and unrealistic.[21]

The establishment of Western military bases in Israel as a replacement for British installations in the Canal Zone was not, however, an idea supported in Israel alone but, paradoxically, in Cairo as well. Following a visit there in January 1954, Richard Crossman reported to the Israelis that Nasser had told him he had no objection to the British making Israel their base.[22] Crossman himself concluded that "[t]he obvious reason why they [the Egyptians] should want British troops in Israel is that this would give them an alibi [for not attacking Israel] and enable them to drop the demand for a change of frontiers."[23]

Egyptian willingness to tolerate British bases in Israel was not the only surprise that Crossman encountered during his short stay in Cairo. Talking to Sir Ralf Stevenson, Crossman asked what would happen if the negotiations broke down, and "to my surprise, he stated categorically that there would be no military difficulty about a re-occupation of Cairo, since the Egyptian character has not changed, and they would support the winner."[24] Given Crossman's well-known pro-Zionist views, one can only wonder if Stevenson's remarks were not aimed at Israeli ears as well. It is quite probable that the British had an interest in letting the Israelis know that a military option existed in case the situation in Egypt deteriorated. Although there is no sign in Israeli declassified documents that such an option was seriously discussed by Israel's policymakers, it is a fact that information the British were thinking in military terms did reach Israel in January 1954. Whether the Israelis specifically knew about Operation RODEO, however, remains an unanswered question.

During the first months of 1954 civilian unrest in Egypt and the instability

20. From Raphael G. to Foreign Minister Sharett: "Guaranties to Israel with the Conclusion of a New Agreement between Britain and Egypt," 19 January 1954, ISA, FO 130.02 2403/12.

21. See e.g. M. Gazit's remarks to Raphael's memorandum, 28 January 1954, ISA, FO 130.04 2447/19.

22. Richard Crossman's diary: "African Journey," 21–24 January 1954, ISA, FO 130.02 2403/12, p. 3.

23. See Crossman's personal note to Ambassador Eilat, 3 February 1954, in ibid.

24. Crossman diary, in ibid.

of the Egyptian leadership delayed the renewal of negotiations. An even more serious obstacle was the small-scale guerrilla-type operations conducted by regulars and irregulars against British troops in the Canal Zone that reached their peak in mid-March 1954. In response to questions, the British Foreign Secretary, Anthony Eden, informed Parliament on 22 March that "the condition of order and security in the Canal Zone deteriorated very seriously in the past week. There was a number of incidents in which four British officers and men have lost their lives, several others have been wounded and two have disappeared." Eden added that

> Her Majesty's Ambassador has on my instructions further made it clear to the Egyptian Government that in the present conditions, which are due to their failure to take the necessary steps to maintain order, a resumption of discussions on the future of the Canal Zone Base is not possible. . . . The Egyptian Government have repeatedly asked us to have confidence in them. It is for the Egyptian Government to show by their actions that they are prepared to create the necessary conditions for such confidence.[25]

The stand Eden took publicly was also privately communicated to the Egyptians. In early May 1954 Charles Mott-Radclyffe, the Conservative chairman of the Foreign Affairs Committee in Parliament, briefly visited Cairo and held a talk with Fawzi el Mulki, the Egyptian Minister for Foreign Affairs. Fawzi's argument was that an agreement about the Suez Canal would be in Egypt's and Britain's mutual interest. The British MP replied that recent Egyptian moves, "including murder of British troops, . . . had all combined to produce the worst possible atmosphere in England." When the Egyptian official asked what could be done to improve that atmosphere, Mott-Radclyffe replied that there were three essential conditions to be fulfilled as a sign of good faith. The second and the third involved the cooperation of Egyptian authorities in investigating attacks on British troops and the cessation of anti-British propaganda in Egypt's mass media. But it was the first condition that is most significant here:

> (1) No attacks on British troops (excluding petty pilfering) for at least a number of weeks before an agreement was concluded. I added that if, for instance, *a bomb exploded in a cinema*, killing a

25. A. Eden's reply to Parliamentary Question no. 85, 22 March 1954, PRO, FO 371/453.

large number of troops, including women and children, the likelihood of the British public accepting any agreement was nil.[26]

These and other warnings probably had considerable effect on Egyptian policymakers, since during April and May 1954 operations against British soldiers in the Canal Zone slowed down. After Nasser replaced Naguib as Prime Minister in April, moreover, it became clear that Egypt was now headed by a strong man who could not only make decisions but also carry them out. Thus towards the end of May the possibility of resuming negotiations became more promising, whereupon the first secretary in the Israeli embassy in London asked an official in the African Department of the Foreign Office whether rumors about the reopening of the talks were true. The British answer was negative. Yet when the British official inquired whether Israel wanted to see a positive end to the negotiations, it is interesting to note that the reply was affirmative, even though it went on to outline the negative aspects of the accord from Israel's perspective.[27]

The pressure to reach an agreement increased during June, but the atmosphere was not yet positive enough for such a move since Egyptian attacks on British troops continued. The failure of Egyptian authorities to prevent such incidents despite strong protests led British military authorities in the Canal Zone, worried about further deterioration of the situation, to start demanding a more active policy. According to the commander of British troops in Egypt, General Festing, the source of the problem was the presence of the chief of Egyptian Military Intelligence in Ismailia, who was presumably directing anti-British activities in the Canal Zone. The general therefore suggested that there be issued

(a) an authoritative warning to the Egyptian Government from Her Majesty's Government of the consequences of the failure to maintain law and order in the Canal Zone, or

(b) a request by the B.D.C.C. [British Defence Coordination Committee] for Ministerial approval to evacuate the Egyptian Army Intelligence Headquarters from Ismailia by force.[28]

26. From the British Embassy in Cairo to the African Department in the Foreign Office: "Record of Conversation between Major C. Mott-Radclyffe, M.P., and Doctor Fawzi," 4 May 1954, PRO, FO 371/453 (emphasis added).

27. From M. Gazit to the Ambassador: "The Anglo–Egyptian Negotiations—A Talk with G. E. Millard of the African Department," 27 May 1954, ISA, FO 130.13 2593/17.

28. C. A. E. Shuckburgh: "Egypt: Recent Incidents," 8 June 1954, PRO, FO 371/450.

The BDCC's position was less extreme, acknowledging as it did that an agreement with Egypt was still the British government's first priority, that perhaps the Egyptian government was unable to exercise full control in the Canal Zone, and that elements hostile to the regime may have been responsible for the incidents. The BDCC suggested that personal and private representations to Nasser

> should make the point that the failure of the Egyptian authorities to exercise control so far leads logically to the conclusion either that they condone such incidents or that they are powerless to control them and in that event cannot be regarded by us as an effective government for negotiation purposes.[29]

If even the strongest representations failed to make the point, the BDCC concluded that "a serious situation would arise and the British military would be forced to take action. The consequences of that might be serious but the responsibility would lie upon the Egyptians."[30]

Two points should be made here. First, in early June 1954—approximately at the time when initial preparations to activate the Egyptian network were under way—the British were again considering military options. Second, if the supporters of the Egyptian operation in Israel had been asked to explain the logic behind their venture, they could hardly have chosen better words than those of the BDCC.

British Foreign Office officials, however, rejected the idea of using force. The use of such means, they maintained, would only complicate matters and would constitute another obstacle to the reopening of negotiations. Moreover, Assistant Under-Secretary of the Foreign Office, Evelyn Shuckburgh, emphasized: "[T]he fact is that these incidents are not the real reason why we do not renew negotiations. We have to overcome difficulties of a different order at home."[31] Among the difficulties he referred to was the opposition to the record of the conservative wing of the Conservative party. In any event, in June 1954 the Foreign Office continued to support the political rather than the military option.

In accordance with this policy, the British ambassador in Cairo met with Prime Minister Nasser and Foreign Minister Fawzi on 7 June 1954. Nasser

29. Ibid.
30. Ibid.
31. Ibid.

and Fawzi argued that they were doing their best to maintain order in the Canal Zone, and Stevenson was quite convinced: "My general impression is that the Egyptian Ministers are genuinely anxious to prevent incidents, but their position in the country is not strong enough for them to take overt action against those guilty."[32] British press reports on the meeting emphasized that Egypt shared Britain's interest in resuming negotiations as soon as possible.[33]

Press reports about a possible rapprochement were supplemented by reports from other sources. General Neville Brownjohn of the Ministry of Defense, for example, informed the Israeli military attaché in Britain on 9 June 1954 that the British military was pressing the Foreign Office to reach an agreement, mainly because the generals did not believe the Canal Zone was worth the efforts needed to maintain it. Brownjohn added that the British military estimated that a future world war would be decided in the European theater and hence that all efforts should be devoted to this region rather than to the Middle East.[34]

During the second half of June Israel obtained a growing number of indications that Britain had decided to resume negotiations with Egypt. A British journalist with good sources in the Foreign Office told an Israeli diplomat in London that an intensive effort to conclude an agreement would probably take place following the imminent return of Churchill and Eden from talks in Washington. He speculated that, since Eden was so worried about the reaction of the "Suez rebels" in Parliament, he would press for signing the accord before Churchill's expected retirement.[35] Another British source maintained that the Egyptians were expecting the conclusion of an agreement within days and were ready to give up some of their demands to guarantee it.[36] A source with access to the British cabinet informed Ambassador Eilat at the end of June that negotiations were to resume soon and that the Foreign Office, under some pressure from the

32. From Sir R. Stevenson to Foreign Office and Whitehall: "Canal Zone Incidents," 8 June 1954, *PRO*, FO 371/450.

33. See e.g. *Manchester Guardian*, 9 June 1954.

34. From Colonel Shalmon K. to the Chief of the DMI: "Report on a Talk with General Brownjohn," 9 June 1954, *ISA*, FO 130.13 2593/17. General Brownjohn, the chief staff officer in the Ministry of Defense, was pro-Zionist (see Sharett diary, p. 229), and it is possible that the information he gave was not ex officio.

35. From Arnon M. to the Ambassador in London: "The Anglo-Egyptian Negotiations," 23 June 1954, *ISA*, FO 130.13 2593/17.

36. From Arnon M. to the Ambassador in London: "The Anglo-Egyptian Negotiations—A Talk with Lord Stansgate," 27 June 1954, in ibid.

military, was now ready to make new concessions to the Egyptians that both Eden and Attlee supported, although Churchill was less enthusiastic.[37] On 30 June the DMI was informed by a reliable source that in early July Britain would submit to Egypt a new evacuation plan that had received an American blessing during recent talks in Washington between Churchill and Eisenhower (Eshed 1979, p. 66).

As indicated by these reports, during June the atmosphere in the Canal Zone did in fact become somewhat more positive. On 19 June 1954 the GHQ-MELF reported to the Ministry of Defense that

> while it is not yet possible to point to concrete results from H. M. Ambassador's representations there are hopeful signs of progress along the lines of these representations. Police co-operation is better. The tone of the Press has improved. Gang leaders are lying low and some of them may have even left the Zone.[38]

Despite this improvement, the military did not support an immediate reopening of the negotiations and suggested that the British ambassador "should keep up the pressure along existing lines." Yet the GHQ-MELF was well aware that time was not working in favor of the British: "Delay increases the risk of another serious incident which at this juncture might make resumption of negotiations impossible."[39]

According to the British press, the likelihood of concluding an agreement increased even further during the first half of July. The *Daily Mail* reported that a settlement of the Anglo-Egyptian dispute over the withdrawal of British troops from the Canal Zone "is expected to be announced this month or early in August." Officially, Parliament was informed that the Foreign Office hoped for resumption of the negotiations "within the relatively near future." Even more significant, though, was the fact that the British 16th Parachute Brigade, which had just withdrawn from the Suez, would not be replaced.[40] If the Israelis were still expecting a British military operation, the reduction of British combat forces in the Canal Zone probably indicated that the military option had ceased to exist.

By mid-July the British press was reporting that a conclusion to the

37. *ISA*, FO 130.02 2483/2. No other details were given.
38. From GHQ: "Middle East Land Forces to Ministry of Defence, London," 19 June 1954, *PRO*, FO 371/450.
39. Ibid.
40. *Daily Mail*, 6 June 1954.

agreement was now "closer than anybody thought" and that an official announcement might be expected even "today."[41] The opening of debate on the issue in Parliament on 15 July confirmed the press reports. It also revealed that Churchill was now supporting the agreement and that the "Suez rebels" were the only minority that still objected to it. A day later an Israeli diplomat in the London embassy reported to Jerusalem that "if nothing unforeseen occurs—and of course there is always that possibility in the Middle East—the heads of the agreement may soon be ready." At the end of his report he added some more positive information: according to "HaJogev"[42] the Egyptians were ready, if Britain pressed them, to consider "something like a declaration of peaceful purposes towards Israel."[43] About the same time the DMI received a report from a reliable source that the agreement might possibly be signed on 23 July—that is, within a week (Eshed 1979, p. 67).

Towards mid-July, then, Israeli policymakers were well aware of the almost certain possibility that an agreement would be reached within a matter of days, and on 27 July 1954 the agreement was in fact initialed. For our purposes, however, the relevant questions at this juncture are two. First, how did the Israeli decisionmakers estimate the implications of the agreement of Israel's security? Second, what possible courses of action did they consider in order to prevent or at least delay it or, alternatively, how did they attempt to compensate for the probable deterioration in Israel's regional status following the conclusion of the agreement?

Diagnosis and Prognosis

The upcoming agreement was discussed in both the Ministry of Foreign Affairs and the Defense Ministry. Foreign Minister (and Prime Minister) Sharett conducted the Foreign Office's final discussion on the subject in his chamber in Jerusalem on 19 July 1954. After describing the current state of negotiations, Gideon Raphael, a senior official at the ministry, maintained that there were no longer any significant disagreements between the Egyp-

41. *News Chronicle*, 14 July 1954.

42. "Hayogev"—"the farmer"—was the code name given to Abd Ghani al-Karmi, who served as King Abdullah of Transjordan's Chief of the Royal Cabinet between 1945 and 1948. He was an informer of the Israelis since at least the mid-1940s and was considered a reliable source with good access (see Bar-Joseph, pp. 40, 111).

43. From Avner G. to Lourie A.: "Anglo-Egyptian Negotiations," 16 July 1954, ISA, FO 130.13 2593/18.

tians and the British. Summarizing the agreement's main implications for Israel, Raphael noted four: "(1) Israel's isolation would be increased; (2) the military balance would change in favor of the Arabs; (3) Arab and Western political pressure on Israel would intensify; (4) Arab hostility towards Israel would increase."[44]

Taking the agreement as a fait accompli, the leaders then went on to discuss how Israel might minimize the damage to her strategic regional position. Among the demands suggested were: free navigation for Israeli ships in the Canal; guarantees that the installations transferred to Egypt under the agreement would not be used against Israel; and a request for Western arms sale to Israel. Summarizing the discussion, Sharett proposed that Israel demand that the West not supply arms to the Arabs until there was peace in the Middle East or, alternatively, that if arms were supplied to the Arabs they should be supplied to Israel as well; that she insist that the agreement facilitate the transfer of oil to Israel via the Suez Canal; and that she launch a major propaganda campaign whose main theme would be a request for Western guarantees of Israel's existence and security.[45]

The impression is that neither Sharett nor his top aides in the Foreign Office believed that the conclusion of the agreement would constitute an immediate threat to Israel's security. While there was a consensus that the new accord posed significant problems, none of the participants suggested forestalling them by any means other than diplomatic ones. This consensus reflected, in part, the way of thinking of diplomats. But it also reflected the belief of the participants that diplomacy could be effective even in such a dire situation.

This, however, was not the view of the DMI. On 16 June 1954 Colonel Givli submitted to his superiors a memorandum on the reopening of the Anglo-Egyptian negotiations. Given that there were no significant changes in the agreement's details over the next month, it can be assumed that the document also represented Givli's estimate in mid-July.[46] The memorandum's first section summarized the information available to the DMI in mid-

44. "Summary of Consultations on the Evacuation of the Suez Canal Zone Held at the Foreign Minister's Chamber," 19 July 1954, ISA, FO 130.20 2483/2.

45. Ibid.

46. In a discussion on 3 August 1954 in the Foreign Office in which the chiefs of the DMI participated, Colonel Givli said: "On January 5, 1954 we issued the first document on the evacuation of the Suez Zone and its implications, and nothing had been changed since then. The second document was issued on June 16, 1954 as a warning that an agreement was imminent." See "Summary of a Meeting on the Anglo-Egyptian Agreement on the Evacuation of the Suez Canal Zone," 3 August 1954, ISA, FO 130.13 2593/18, p. 2.

June. On the basis of this information Givli determined that "the time needed for concluding the negotiations is about three months if Nasser's regime survives that long."[47] The implications of this development for Israel were summarized as follows:

1. The British military buffer zone between Israel and Egypt will be removed.

2. The Egyptian military potential will be significantly improved.

3. American military assistance will be given to Egypt (unofficially the sum agreed to between the two nations was $20 million).

4. The main obstacle for the joining of Arab countries in a regional defense pact will be removed.[48]

The improvement in the Egyptian military potential was doubtless the issue that most worried the DMI and the defense establishment. While the 16 June memorandum only touched upon this, a more complete picture of the DMI's concerns was evident at the 3 August meeting at the Foreign Office in which Colonel Givli and his recently appointed deputy, Lieutenant Colonel Yuval Ne'eman, participated. According to Givli, the agreement gave the Egyptians new military options in the immediate future and even better ones in the long run, after the British evacuation from the Canal Zone was completed. The most important change involved Egypt's air capabilities: having eleven new airfields plus maintenance facilities located some fifty miles west of the present ones meant that the flight to Israel would be one hundred miles shorter and hence that enemy planes would be able to stay over Israeli territory for an additional fifteen minutes. This could also improve the Egyptian air force's ability to defend the populated region of the delta. If the British radar system in the Canal Zone was transferred to the Egyptians, moreover, they would be able to cover all Israeli territory south of Haifa, leaving only one airfield to the north uncovered. According to Givli, this change might eliminate Israel's ability to operate from the rest of her airfields.[49]

Lieutenant Colonel Ne'eman added that the new situation in the air

47. From Colonel Givli to the Defense Minister and the Chief of Staff: "The Reopening of Negotiations for the Evacuation of the Canal Zone," 16 June 1954, ISA, FO 130.02 2419/2.
48. Ibid.
49. "Summary of a Meeting on the Anglo-Egyptian Agreement on the Evacuation of the Suez Canal Zone," 3 August 1954, ISA, FO 130.13 2593/18, pp. 2–3.

would also enable Egypt to block Israeli flights over the Mediterranean and into Egypt's hinterland. This meant, Ne'eman claimed, that Israel's two jet squadrons would no longer suffice and more jets would be needed. In any event, Israel would have to change all her operational plans, and reaching the Egyptian airfields in wartime would become far more difficult.[50]

A second reason for grave concern was the equipment that might be left behind by the British. Even if only logistical equipment and spare parts reached Egyptian hands, it could significantly increase the Egyptian military potential. Material in the Suez Zone, according to the DMI's estimates, was enough for eighteen divisions. Since the Egyptian army had only three divisions, this would enable it to continue fighting a future war far longer than before. Since the DMI expected the Egyptian army to undergo revolutionary changes within the next two or three years even without the additional British equipment, Israel's existence could be seriously endangered once the process of British evacuation was completed and a massive quantity of new equipment reached Egyptian hands.[51]

All in all, the DMI's estimate of the situation was far more pessimistic than the Foreign Office's. The gap between them widened even more on the question of what response to make. As we have seen, the Foreign Office supported the use of traditional diplomacy in order to minimize the damage from what had been perceived as a fait accompli since at least January 1954.[52] In this sense no dramatic change had occurred in the Foreign Office's views for at least half a year.

In contrast, Colonel Givli was not ready to accept the agreement as a fait accompli even in mid-June 1954. The last section of his 16 June memorandum discussed the possible course of action Israel could take: "It is doubtful whether we can absolutely prevent the agreement on evacuation of the Canal, by force alone. But by action on our behalf, with the cooperation of other factors, we can delay it or at least make it harder to achieve."[53] Seeing how little time remained, the chief of the DMI recommended the following:

50. Ibid.
51. Ibid., pp. 4–6.
52. See e.g. from Raphael G. to Foreign Minister Sharett: "Guaranties to Israel with the Conclusion of a New Agreement between Britain and Egypt," 19 January 1954, ISA, FO 130.02 2403/12; M. Gazit's remarks on Raphael's memorandum, 28 January 1954, ISA, FO 130.04 2447/19; and from M. Gazit to the Ambassador: "Our Demands at This Stage of the Anglo-Egyptian Negotiations," 3 March 1954, ISA, FO 130.04 2447/19.
53. From Colonel Givli to the Defense Minister and the Chief of Staff: "The Reopening of Negotiations for the Evacuation of the Canal Zone," 16 June 1954, ISA, FO 130.02 2419/2, pp. 1–2.

a. *The transport of a ship through the [Tiran] Straits or the Canal.*

The Egyptians have two general courses of action in reaction to the ship's transport.
1. To stop it.
2. To let it pass.

If Egypt stops the ship, she will be in danger of an Israeli political-military reaction. As was proved last year, an immediate reaction would come from those who object to the agreement in the British Parliament. As a result, the agreement may be delayed. If Israel takes over the Canal Straits[54] in reaction to Egypt's stopping the ship, the whole of regional security would be undermined and this will not be an appropriate situation for signing the Anglo-Egyptian agreement. Even if an agreement is reached, control of the Straits would give us a good bargaining position.

If the Egyptians—for political and military considerations—let the ship pass, Israel should be prepared to immediately transport additional ships with every type of cargo. If the Egyptians let them pass, it will constitute a significant breakthrough in the Arab blockade and serious damage will be done to Egypt's relations with other Arab states.

b. *Propaganda activity in Britain* with the cooperation of those who object to the agreement. It should be emphasized that the British are evacuating the forces to the Far East, so that they can be replaced [in Egypt] by the Americans.

c. *Propaganda activity in the USA*, emphasizing the instability of the military regime [in Egypt] and the drift of factors within the [Egyptian] military towards Communism.

d. *Coordination of policy with France*, who objects to the agreement and understands our apprehensions.

e. *Psychological warfare within Egypt* in order to explain the clandestine commitments made during the negotiations, to demonstrate that Egypt has abandoned her comfortable neutral position, that evacuation is actually nothing but a change of uniforms and that

54. Givli referred to the Sharm-el-Shaiq (Tiran) Straits, through which Israeli ships could make their way to Eilat, and not to the Suez Canal.

the American factor will be added to the British factor already present in Egypt.[55]

Givli's recommendations were too sweeping for Chief of Staff Dayan. In his remarks on the memorandum Dayan rejected Givli's mildly optimistic "[i]t is doubtful whether we can absolutely prevent the agreement . . . by our own force alone" with the blunt assessment: "It can be assumed that we do not have the power to block the agreement all by ourselves" (Eshed 1979, p. 65). To Givli's recommendation that Israel send a ship through the Tiran Straits, Dayan added "on the condition that Israel is ready to take military action in case her ships are blocked by the Egyptians" (ibid., pp. 65–66). We do not know Dayan's opinion of Givli's recommendation to launch a psychological warfare campaign in Egypt, but it is obvious that he was aware of the fact that his DMI's chief supported this option. Yet whether or not he knew in mid-June about Givli's instruction to activate the Egyptian network for a far-reaching purpose—an instruction that was given no later than early June (see below)—is a question we cannot answer.

In any case, during the 3 August discussion at the Foreign Office the chiefs of the DMI abandoned most of these courses of action. One reason was that by then the agreement had been initialed and its prevention was thus no longer on the agenda. A second obvious reason was that Givli's "psychological warfare" campaign within Egypt had failed; by the end of July it was already known in Israel that the Egyptian network had collapsed and that the operation ended in a fiasco. A third reason may have been the forum in which the discussion took place: in 1954 the Foreign Office constituted the main opposition to the aggressive policy pursued by the IDF and was obviously not the appropriate place to suggest hazardous new plans.

Yet even under these constraints Givli and Ne'eman presented a daring proposal for preventing changes in the military balance of power in favor of Egypt. As in the mid-June memorandum, Givli again raised the issue of sending a test ship to be passed this time not through the Suez Canal but the Tiran Straits. The result, however, was to be just the same. Once the ship was intercepted and taken into Egyptian custody, Israel must react:

> There are two possibilities: the first is to submit a strong complaint
> to the Security Council. This has no actual value since we have

---

55. From Colonel Givli to the Defense Minister and the Chief of Staff: "The Reopening of Negotiations for the Evacuation of the Canal Zone," 16 June 1954, *ISA*, FO 130.02 2419/2, p. 2.

already seen its reaction when ships are stopped. Then the question arises of how to prevent the Egyptians from taking the ship and how to show world opinion that the situation cannot remain anarchical. We, the military men, have one way which might be considered rather strange by the rest of the world. In my personal opinion, their detention of the ship must be followed by us taking control of the Straits, since only in this way can we obtain any bargaining chips.[56]

Givli's deputy, who had earlier been the head of the Planning Department of the IDF, showed the Foreign Office officials a map of the Straits Zone, maintaining that

taking control of the [Tiran] Straits zone is in fact not only a solution to this Straits' problem but also to the problem of the Suez. If we look at the map, we can see that there is a single strait leading to Eilat and one which leads to the Suez, and hence all that we are prevented from in Eilat, we can prevent in the Straits of Suez. From that moment [when Israel controls the Tiran Straits] we constitute a threat to the Suez. Militarily, we need to take over Tiran Island or part of the Sinai Peninsula. This is an operation we have planned in the Operations Department and all we need is a prior notice so that we can have enough time to prepare the equipment. Militarily, such an operation is feasible. . . . There is no chance the Egyptians will arrive there in time to stop us, and even if things become more complicated it is better now than waiting for a war later.[57]

From this discussion as well as from Givli's memorandum it is clear that in 1954 the DMI believed time was working against Israel, that political solutions were not enough, and that Israel should launch a war with Egypt as soon as possible and before the Egyptians took the initiative. In this assessment the chiefs of the DMI obviously deviated from their scope of responsibility; they were supposed to provide information and estimates, not initiate wars. To the extent that none of the Foreign Office officials present at the meeting raised this point, the discussion in the Foreign Office exemplifies the atmosphere in which the Israeli decisionmaking process took

56. "Summary of a Meeting on the Anglo-Egyptian Agreement on the Evacuation of the Suez Canal Zone," 3 August 1954, ISA, FO 130.13 2593/18, p. 12.

57. Ibid., pp. 13–14.

place in mid-1954. It was only in such an atmosphere that the chief of Military Intelligence could have launched an operation aimed at changing the face of the Middle East, probably without the knowledge of the Chief of Staff, certainly without the knowledge of the Defense Minister or the Prime Minister, and without considering that what he was doing was especially unusual.

There are three main conclusions for this section. First, Israel obtained good information on the course of Anglo-Egyptian negotiations through open, diplomatic, and intelligence sources. The Israelis knew that the British were considering the use of force in case the talks collapsed, even if they did not know the exact operational parameters of operation RODEO. The logic of the situation could further convince some Israelis that under certain conditions the agreement could be prevented. There are no indications, however, that the Foreign Office considered Anglo-Egyptian military confrontation as a real option. During June and July 1954 the Foreign Office regarded the conclusion of the negotiations as a fait accompli; the DMI had a similar evaluation but estimated that some action by Israel could still prevent or at least delay it. Chief of Staff Dayan did not believe that this was a viable option.

Second, the Foreign Office and the DMI differed on the implications of the agreement for Israel. While both regarded the conclusion of the agreement as a negative development, the DMI's estimate was far more pessimistic. Thinking mainly in terms of a worst-case scenario, the DMI estimated that after the completion of the planned British evacuation Egypt could gain a decisive strategic superiority over Israel. The Foreign Office, on the other hand, regarded the situation as grave but not so serious as to threaten the very existence of Israel. In retrospect, the Foreign Office evaluation seems closer to reality than that of the DMI. The main source for the difference between them was probably the tendency within the DMI and the defense establishment towards "military activism," whereas the Foreign Office and the Prime Minister tended towards "political activism."

Third, the philosophic gap between the Foreign Office and the DMI, as well as their different *Weltanschauungen*, led to highly different views on how to forestall the new threats. Before the agreement was concluded, the Foreign Office perceived it as a fait accompli and regarded diplomatic activity as the best means of compensating Israel for her losses. In contrast, the DMI under Colonel Givli believed that preventing the accord was still feasible up until the time it was actually concluded. Following the signing of the agreement, the Foreign Office and Sharett again supported diplomatic means in order to minimize damages, whereas the DMI regarded the use of military means (taking control of the Tiran Straits) as the only practical way to forestall the deterioration of Israel's strategic position in the Middle East.

Under normal circumstances Sharett in his capacity as Prime Minister had the final word on Israel's handling of this delicate issue. But, as we have seen, in mid-1954 the Israeli hierarchy was far from normal. It was this anomaly that forms the background for Colonel Givli's initiative to pursue a foreign policy of his own in opposition to Israel's official policy and without the knowledge, let alone the authorization, of his superiors.

The Order

The Preparations: March–May 1954

The change of command at the DMI at the end of March 1954 was the event that triggered the "unfortunate business." When Colonel Givli returned to Israel in late March, his deputy, Lieutenant Colonel Harkabi, left to study in Paris. Harkabi and Givli did not get along. Givli was mainly an operations-type intelligence chief, whereas Harkabi was more of an intellectual, whose analytical mind could see the pros and cons of every plan. When Harkabi left, a vacuum was created at the top echelon of the DMI. Without him nobody near Givli could adequately criticize the operations the new DMI's chief initiated, the most important of which was the activation of the Egyptian network.

Immediately upon his return Colonel Givli started reviewing the operational status of the units under his command. One of his first meetings was with Lieutenant Colonel Benzoor, the commander of Unit 131. Upon learning of the operational status of the Egyptians network, Givli instructed Benzoor to reorganize radio communications with the cells.[58] Thus on 13

---

58. Three miniature communication sets were smuggled into Egypt by Max Binnet. Two were delivered to Marcelle Ninio ("Claude") in March or April 1954 for the network's use and the third was used by Binnet. See al-Gumhuria, 22 December 1954. The Egyptian paper's article, which was based on Ninio's and Binnet's interrogations, was translated into Hebrew by Branch 5 of the DMI on 10 January 1955 (ISA, FO 130.02 2387/7).

The communication sets were of the "Zamir" ("Nightingale") type developed by the IDF Signal Corps for the use of the DMI. In tests conducted in Israel the "Zamir" proved to have sufficient range and to be very reliable and easy to operate (Biberman interview).

April 1954 a coded letter containing a questionnaire regarding the location and the status of the network's radio sets was sent to Victor Levy in Egypt. The answer from Egypt did not contain the required information. This only enhanced Givli's conviction that the network urgently needed an Israeli commander (Eshed 1979, pp. 50–51).

Selecting a commander for the network posed a serious problem for Givli and Benzoor. Since early 1954 Unit 131 had had two agents in Egypt. One was Max Binnet, who at an earlier stage had made contacts with some members of the network but was later disconnected from their activities. The other agent had arrived at the end of December 1953 and had since succeeded in building a cover as a German businessman representing various German firms in Egypt. His name was Avraham (Avri) Zeidenberg (El-Ad), known in Egypt as Paul Frank.[59]

Even if El-Ad was not entirely typical of Unit 131's recruiting policy, which maintained that it could get the best results out of agents with criminal records, he still had a shady past that the DMI used as leverage to recruit him. In his autobiographical account of the "unfortunate business" and the "Lavon affair,"[60] El-Ad portrayed himself as a patriot who devoted himself to Israel's defense. According to his own account, he had only slipped up once: in 1950 he was tempted by what he describes as an *agent provocateur* to replace an old refrigerator in his house with a better one that he pilfered from his military unit. He was tried for the theft, sentenced to eighteen months in prison, and lost his rank as a major in the IDF. A higher court waived his imprisonment, but he was still forced to leave the army (El-Ad 1976a, pp. 22–24). This, according to El-Ad, was the incident that changed his life, making him a potential recruit for Unit 131.

In reality, however, the "refrigerator episode" was only one among many similar incidents in El-Ad's past. In 1942 he was dismissed from the "German platoon" of the Palmach when it was found that he was stealing from his comrades; towards the end of the war he was caught stealing again while serving as a military driver (and not as the commando trooper he claims to have been in his memoirs). During the 1948 war he dealt with the black market while serving in a rear-area unit (and not as a front-line

59. Avraham Zeidenberg was born in Austria in 1925 and known by at least six names. His *nom de guerre* in Unit 131 was El-Ad Zarhi, his cover name in Egypt was Paul Frank, and the network members knew him as "Robert." After returning to Israel he changed his name to Avraham (Avri) El-Ad (using officially his *nom de guerre*). In Israeli press reports about the "unfortunate business" he was nicknamed "the third man."

60. A. El-Ad, *The Third Man*, Special Edition (Tel Aviv, 1976).

commander of the Palmach as he portrayed himself in his book). In 1949 he was dismissed from the first Israeli paratrooper battalion when it was discovered that he had no previous experience as a paratrooper (Harel 1980, pp. 61–72).

When El-Ad was recruited for Unit 131 in late 1952, the DMI was aware of some of these incidents. Yet his recruitment could be justified on the basis of lack of alternatives since other Israelis were rarely willing to take the risk of conducting intelligence missions in an Arab country. As a precautionary measure, however, it was decided after the completion of El-Ad's training that he would only operate as a "lone wolf." It was thus hoped that the risks he represented to other intelligence assets would be minimal (Harkabi interview, Benzoor interview).

After completing his training in Israel, El-Ad left for Germany in March 1953 to build himself a cover as a German businessman. Because of a lack of DMI resources in Europe he had to be assisted by the Mossad's facilities there. Very soon, however, his superiors in the DMI found out that El-Ad constituted a very serious security risk and an additional cause for their already strained relations with the Mossad. While the nature of his mission required El-Ad to distance himself from any contacts with Israelis, he not only met with many of them openly but also told them about his mission. Following complaints by the Mossad, Lieutenant Colonel Mordechai Almog, the organization officer of the DMI, was sent to Europe in October 1953 to check El-Ad's activities and the feasibility of his mission. Prior to his meetings with El-Ad, Almog was sent a letter by the commander of Unit 131 in which El-Ad's many security breaches were discussed. Benzoor apologized for

> all the shame this man [El-Ad] has caused us, for our trusting and for his personal failures. El-Ad neglects all security. . . . In my view the man is lost. Perhaps nothing has happened from a security perspective and nobody knows about him. But if nothing has happened yet, something will happen in the future. As far as I am concerned, you can send him back to Israel immediately. (Harel 1980, pp. 76–77; Teveth 1992b, pp. 47–48)

Despite this critical assessment, it was decided to give El-Ad a second chance. Almog was instructed to warn him and to order him to settle his business in Germany and leave for Egypt within a month. Against all instructions, however, El-Ad arrived in Egypt only at the end of December after conducting additional security violations including the adoption, without authority, of a new cover (Harel 1980, pp. 77–82). The impression we get is that with no better prospects in view the chiefs of the DMI hesitated to terminate El-Ad's employment. Moreover, ending El-Ad's mission could also have been perceived as a failure of Unit 131's recruitment policy, a failure that could have lost Military Intelligence points in its intracommunity rivalry with the Mossad.

El-Ad's first mission in Egypt lasted two weeks, and at the beginning of March 1954 he returned to Cairo for an additional month. According to his instructions, his only mission was to establish a solid reputation as a German businessman. On his own initiative, however, and immediately upon his arrival he started to collect information as well. The information collected related mainly to the activities of German experts in the Egyptian defense establishment and seems to have made quite an impression on his superiors in the DMI.

But El-Ad's success in Egypt was eventually revealed as one of the DMI's biggest failures. For according to all indications the Egyptian security services suspected him of being an Israeli agent from the start, exposed his cover, and turned him into a double agent. El-Ad was probably recruited by them during his second trip to Egypt in March 1954, when communication with him broke down for a few weeks (Eshed 1979, p. 53). Isser Harel, who investigated the case and analyzed El-Ad's own accounts of this period, concluded:

> An analysis of El-Ad's behavior and activities, an analysis which examined his way of life from various angles, proves beyond any doubt that he exposed the network he commanded to the Egyptians. It was clear that El-Ad's identity had already become known to the Egyptians at the time of his first mission to Egypt, and that his activities were initiated and instructed by the Egyptians themselves. (Harel 1980, p. 205)

In April 1954, when this Egyptian intelligence coup was as yet unknown, available data on El-Ad's past performance were still sufficient to conclude that his employment constituted a serious security risk. By any professional standards the only sensible course was to adopt Harkabi's instruction to isolate him from all other intelligence activities. Indeed, in spite of the valuable information El-Ad had supplied—some of which would prove to be useless in the future (Teveth 1992b, p. 50)—Benzoor maintains that he objected to El-Ad's nomination as the case officer of the Egyptian network.[61] Yet when evaluating the pros and cons of this appointment Givli had very little room for maneuverability. Besides, some justification for his choice could be found in the report of Lieutenant Colonel Almog concerning his October 1953 meeting with El-Ad in Paris. Almog concluded that the source for most of the allegations about El-Ad's security breaches was the intrabureaucratic rivalry between the Mossad and the DMI. At least in part these conclusions enabled Givli to appoint El-Ad as the network's commander despite objections (Benzoor interview).

Givli's decision was made no later than 10 May 1954.[62] In accordance with it Benzoor left on 26 May 1954 for Paris to meet some of Unit 131's agents, not only from Egypt but also from other Arab countries. Benzoor summarized his meetings with the Egyptian agents in three separate reports. The most authentic of the three (see a discussion below) is the 5 October report. In this report, under the title "A Report on the Events in Egypt: July-September 1954," Benzoor wrote:

> Towards the possibility of activating the cells in Egypt I was ordered to examine the situation and it was found that [we have]:
>
> In Cairo—a commander [Marzouk] + 2 men.
>
> In Alexandria—a commander [Levi] + 5 men of which 4 were trained in Israel.
>
> In addition: 1. David [Max Binnet] in Cairo + signal operator [Marcelle Ninio ("Claude")].
>
> 2. El-Ad in Cairo—independent.
>
> In light of the unclear situation of the Cairo cell, it was decided to examine the issue with the commander, who was to arrive in Europe in connection with personal matters.

61. This is Benzoor's version according to an interview I conducted with him. Other officers from Unit 131, who preferred not to be identified, maintain that Benzoor had no objections whatsoever to this appointment. According to their version, Benzoor considered the termination of El-Ad's employment following his security breaches in Germany but became very impressed with the information El-Ad brought back from Egypt once he started his mission there. This version makes sense, especially when taking into account that, upon the end of El-Ad's training in Israel, Benzoor himself became his case officer. It is hard to believe that Benzoor would have undermined his own status by arguing that his agent was a security risk when at the same time this agent had already demonstrated that he was very capable.

62. In the network trial in December 1954 Victor Levy testified that he received a letter sent on 10 May 1954 informing him that a "new friend" whose name was "Robert" was scheduled to arrive in Egypt. Robert was the code name by which the network members knew El-Ad. See al-Ahram, 4 December 1954, translated by Branch 5 of the DMI on 26 December 1954, ISA, FO 130.02 2387.

In view of the possible activation of the cells it was decided to put them under the command of El-Ad, whose personal character suited the mission better than David's.

I invited El-Ad and David for a meeting in Europe and organized a meeting with the Cairo commander. I went abroad on May 26, 1954.

Between May 28–31, I conducted some talks with the Cairo commander at the end of which I found that we have nothing there. I ordered him to return his communication set, to close his accounts and to break all links with us. He returned to Cairo in order to sell his late father's house and then intended to emigrate to Israel.

Between May 31–June 3, 1954, I conducted some talks with El-Ad in which I explained the mission to him. In addition I explained about the [network] men, their nature, training and past, and how he should make his contact with the Alexandria cell.

The cell's missions were:
a. To immediately establish radio contact.
b. To prepare 25 Kg. of home-made explosives.
c. To reconnoiter some targets suitable for the operation.

El-Ad's missions were:
1. To make contact with the cell while *observing* maximal security.
2. *To activate its members in order to carry out their mission.*

The mission as explained to me by the chief of the DMI was: To undermine Western trust in the existing regime by causing public insecurity. [To conduct] acts which will bring about arrests, demonstrations and revenge by totally concealing the Israeli factor and directing suspicion to any other possible factor. The goal—preventing Western economic aid and arms to Egypt. The considerations for selecting targets was given to the man in place [El-Ad], who was to select them according to the potential result of each act.

We did not discuss elimination of personalities or mass murder acts, but sabotage operations which will invoke unrest and public confusion.[63]

---

63. From a photocopy of the original report in Eshed 1979, p. 100 (emphasis added).

This report is of critical importance to my argument. Given that other reports by Givli and El-Ad contradict this one, the reasons for using this specific account of events should be made clear.

Benzoor summarized his meetings with his Egyptian agents in three separate reports. The first was written on 1 August 1954, a few days after the DMI learned about the collapse of the network; the second was written on 5 October 1954. A third report, focusing on the instructions Benzoor gave El-Ad in Paris, has disappeared from Unit 131's archives (The Cohen Investigation Committee, quoted in Eshed 1979, p. 209). Although the two available reports are quite similar, the 5 October report is more useful than Benzoor's earlier version. It is more detailed and it includes information that was not yet known on 1 August. Most important, it was written under a direct order from Chief of Staff Dayan on the same day Colonel Givli left Israel to deal with the legal defense of the network's members. It can thus be reasonably assumed (Teveth 1992b, pp. 72–73) that Dayan ordered Benzoor to write the report precisely on that date in order to prevent pressures on Benzoor by his superior officer. In this sense Benzoor's 5 October report is probably the most authentic one available, as well as the most genuine account on the subject written by any of the DMI's officers who were directly involved in the operation.

In addition to Benzoor's reports, Colonel Givli and Avri El-Ad wrote their own official versions of the events in Egypt in connection with the first investigations of the "unfortunate business." These reports, however, are partial and obviously false. Givli's reports (earlier version in Eshed 1979, pp. 106–7; final version in Teveth 1992b, pp. 76–77) only describe events from 16 July—the day he allegedly received from Defense Minister Lavon the order to activate the network. It is obvious that Givli had an interest in concealing his responsibility for orders he gave prior to this date and therefore omitted all activities conducted before 16 July. El-Ad's report (a partial photocopy of the original is available in Eshed 1979, pp. 192–93) is clearly false. It only describes events after 4 July—the day on which, according to El-Ad, he first made contact with the network. But after the network members were returned to Israel (in 1968), it became clear (Golan 1976, p. 63) that first contact had already been made by the end of June. In fact, 4 July was two days after the first sabotage act in Alexandria. El-Ad admitted later that he wrote his false report in accordance with Givli's and Benzoor's requests.

It has also been argued that Benzoor's report on 5 October is false. Benzoor himself testified before three different investigation committees that he added the sabotage acts conducted on 2 July and 14 July in order to receive credit for his unit and himself, that is, to show that the operation was not a total failure and that some sabotage acts were done before the network collapsed (Eshed 1979, p. 120). This testimony, however, cannot be taken at face value. Benzoor met El-Ad in mid-August 1954 upon the latter's return to Israel and received a detailed report of the operation, including the 2 July and 14 July sabotage acts. At the beginning of October 1954, moreover, the dimensions of the mishap in Egypt were already well known in the government and the defense establishment, and attempts were already being made by the DMI to conceal its responsibility for the acts conducted before 16 July. Benzoor was familiar with these attempts and was under pressure by Givli to conceal (as Givli himself did) the DMI's initiative in launching the operation without authority. Under these circumstances it would have been irrational for him to take credit for acts that could only prove Givli's and his own guilt.

A second defensive argument presented by Givli and Benzoor before the various investigation committees was that the instruction given to El-Ad—"2. To activate . . . [the network members] in order to carry out their mission"—was only a preparation order, that is, that El-Ad was to ensure that all preparations for the operation were made but that no sabotage act was to be carried out before receiving the "green light" from Israel. The fact that acts were committed before 16 July was explained by confusion in communications between headquarters in Tel Aviv and the cells in Egypt. Years later Benzoor compared his orders to El-Ad in Paris to the others given the IDF on the eve of the 1967 war. Just as the IDF was ready to carry out its operational plans when given the code word "Red Sheet" on 5 June 1967, the network in Cairo was to start the operation when the signal was given from Israel (Benzoor interview). Again this argument does not hold water. If this was Benzoor's intention in the briefing he gave El-Ad in Paris, he could have simply used the word "prepare" instead of "activate" in his 5 October report. The fact that he wrote "to activate" when the failure was already known and the search for those responsible was already under way can only mean that orders to start the operation were given by the DMI no later than early June 1954.[64]

_____

64. Thus concluded also Lieutenant General (ret.) Ya'acov Dory, one of the two members of the committee that was the first to investigate the "unfortunate business." On the basis of his military experience he gathered that Benzoor's orders to El-Ad in Paris "were more like operation rather than alert orders." The Cohen investigation committee, which investigated some aspects of the episode in 1960, concluded similarly (Teveth 1992b, pp. 125, 335).

The "Unfortunate Business": June–August 1954

Less than three weeks after receiving his briefing from Benzoor in Paris, El-Ad returned to Egypt. He had been scheduled to arrive there earlier[65] but delayed his return because of personal business in Europe. Between the end of June, when El-Ad first established contact with the network, and the beginning of August 1954, when all the network members were arrested and inquiries about the responsibility for the operation had started in Israel, there were many developments, and much of the testimony regarding them is contradictory. For our purposes the most important subject during this period is the sequence of events, which is why they are described in this section chronologically. The sources for the description of events in Egypt include: the testimony of the network members at their trial (Foreign Office documents); their testimony in Israel after returning from Egypt (Golan's book); El-Ad's account of the events as presented in his book; and El-Ad's account of the events as documented in two secret diaries he kept from the beginning of 1954.[66] The sources for the description of events in Israel are mainly the testimony and documents presented to the various committees that investigated the affair.

June 28, 1954: El-Ad arrives in Alexandria and makes first contact with the network through Philip Natanson, whose address he received from Benzoor in Paris (El-Ad 1976a, p. 130). After meeting Natanson he sends a cable to Israel (via Europe) informing the DMI that "the consignment is possible," that is, that he successfully made contact with Natanson and preparations for carrying out the missions have started (Benzoor's 5 October report, Eshed 1979, p. 100).

June 29: El-Ad meets Victor Levy through Natanson and appoints him to command the Alexandrian cell. Levy gives a pessimistic report of the network's ability to carry out sabotage owing to a lack of explosives and experience (El-Ad, pp. 131–32). El-Ad delivers to Levy new crystals for the radio communication set and new radio frequencies, together with a new code book based on a paperback edition of *Moby Dick* (Golan 1976, p. 64). From this point on all communication between El-Ad and Israel is done

65. The Alexandria cell received a letter from Paris saying that "Robert [El-Ad] will come to visit Henri [Philip Natanson] on June 18" (Golan 1976, p. 63).

66. In his investigation in Israel in 1958 (after being suspected of having contacts with the Egyptian intelligence), El-Ad claimed that all facts written in these diaries were true and that they were to help him in making his reports for the DMI. One diary contained only points of reference as a means to reconstruct his activities, while in the other El-Ad elaborated on daily events (Harel 1980, p. 97).

through Levy and Natanson (Levy and Natanson's testimony to Harel, in Harel 1980, p. 107). According to El-Ad, he delivers a request to Israel to supply the network with explosives and escaping passports the same night (El-Ad 1976a, p. 132; in light of Levy and Natanson's testimony, this is probably not true). Lieutenant Colonel Benzoor ends his European trip and returns to Israel (Eshed 1979, p. 51).

1 July: El-Ad meets Levi in Cairo and informs him that he has received instructions from Israel to start the operation immediately. The two return together to Alexandria and meet another member of the network there, Shmuel Azar. El-Ad briefs the two on the first target he has chosen: the central post office station in Alexandria (Golan 1976, p. 66). According to El-Ad, they then conducted their first radio communication with Israeli headquarters and received "a green light to start the operation" (El-Ad 1976a, p. 134). This is probably false since radio communication with Israel started only on 5 July (see below).

2 July: This is when the first act of sabotage is carried out. In the morning Levy, Natanson, and Dassa prepare three fire bombs from chemicals bought in a local pharmacy, and Dassa plants them at noon in two post office boxes in the central post office station at Alexandria. Two bombs explode in the boxes, setting them on fire. The fire brigade is called and extinguishes the fire within a few minutes. A third bomb explodes in the hands of a local worker, causing him superficial wounds.[67] El-Ad maintains that he supervised the act without the knowledge of the network members (El-Ad 1976a, p. 135), but this is an obvious lie.[68]

3 July: El-Ad arrives in Alexandria from Cairo, receives a report from Levy on the previous day's sabotage, and instructs him to start preparations for the next act—the sabotage of the libraries in the American culture centers in Cairo and Alexandria (Golan 1976, p. 68).

5 July: Radio communication is established with the network in Egypt (Benzoor's report of 5 October in Eshed 1979, p. 100). El-Ad instructs Levy to begin preparations for the sabotage of the American libraries.[69]

67. Golan 1976, p. 67. For testimony of the participants and Egyptian post office workers, fire brigade, and policemen in the network trial, see *al-Ahram*, 4, 19, 26 December 1954, or *ISA*, FO 130.02 2387/7.

68. According to El-Ad, Levy and Natanson planted the bombs, but Levy himself testified that Dassa planted them.

69. Levy's testimony in the network trial (*al-Ahram*, 4 December 1954; *ISA*, FO 130.02 2387/7). It is quite possible that the instructions were given two days earlier and that Levy was mistaken in his testimony. In any event, the exact date is of little importance.

7 July: First wireless transmission according to the new timetable is received from Israel (El-Ad's elaborated diary, in Harel 1980, p. 119). In the short version diary El-Ad notes: "start of work" (ibid., p. 118).

9 July: According to El-Ad, he receives instructions via Kol Yisrael (the national radio station "Voice of Israel") to act against British objects and a confirmation that a report on the 2 July act was received in Israel (El-Ad 1976a, pp. 139–40). Given that (a) he did not refer to this message in his secret diaries and (b), according to Benzoor's report, transmissions via Kol Yisrael started only on 11 July (see below), El-Ad's account cannot be taken at face value.

10 July: According to El-Ad, he meets Levy in Cairo and instructs him to operate against the American libraries on 14 July (El-Ad 1976a, p. 140). There is no reference to this meeting in Levi's account of the events.

11 July: First message to the network is transmitted via Kol Yisrael (Benzoor's report of 5 October in Eshed 1979, p. 100).

12 July: IDF Chief of Staff Dayan leaves Israel for a five-week visit to the United States and France (he returns on 19 August 1954). The acting chief of staff during this period is Major General Yosef Avidar.

14 July: Natanson and Levi met El-Ad in Cairo, prepare a number of small homemade fire bombs packed in spectacle cases in his car, and plant them in the American library in Cairo. Azar and Dassa plant two similar bombs in the American library in Alexandria. The two bombs in Alexandria and at least one in Cairo explode, setting the libraries on fire. While extinguishing the Cairo blaze, firefighters find some unexploded bombs.[70] Only one Egyptian paper reports the incident, attributing it to an electrical short circuit (Golan 1976, p. 70).

15 July: Following the weekly meeting of the IDF General Staff with Defense Minister Lavon, Colonel Givli confers with Lavon privately. The subject of their discussion is probably what might be done to delay the conclusion of the Anglo-Egyptian talks. Later that day Givli informs Lavon that the only remaining practical option is direct action by the DMI's operational units (Eshed 1979, pp. 67–68, 70).

16 July: At 3:00 P.M. Colonel Givli meets tête-à-tête with Defense

---

70. Golan 1976, pp. 69–70; *al-Ahram*'s account of the network trial, 13, 26 December 1954; *ISA*, FO 130.02 2387/7. According to the testimony of Egyptian security men during the network trial, the spectacle cases formed the starting point of an investigation that could have led to the exposure of the network members even without the accident that happened to Natanson on 23 July. This testimony might have been aimed at concealing the main source of Egyptian security's information—El-Ad himself.

Minister Lavon at the latter's house. According to Givli, in this talk Lavon ordered him to activate the DMI's operational units, including the Egyptian network, in order to carry out sabotage acts that might prevent, or at least delay, the conclusion of the Anglo-Egyptian agreement on the evacuation of the British forces from the Canal Zone (Givli's testimony before the Olshan-Dory investigation committee, ibid., p. 71; letter to Dayan in Teveth 1992b, pp. 76–77).[71] Following this meeting, Givli invites Lieutenant Colonel Benzoor and Lieutenant Colonel Rehavia Vardi, the commander of the DMI's unit in charge of handling agents of an Arab origin (KATAM) to a meeting at his home. The three convene at about 5:30 P.M. and after a short discussion Benzoor is ordered to activate the Egyptian network (Benzoor's testimony before the Olshan-Dory investigation committee, in Eshed 1979, p. 68; Benzoor interview).[72]

17 July: At 10:00 A.M. Benzoor and another officer of Unit 131 encode operational instructions for the Egyptian network. One message, enciphered as a food recipe, is to be broadcast by Kol Yisrael on 18 July at 12:50 P.M.

---

71. The question of whether or not Lavon gave Givli instructions to carry out the operation has no definite answer. The Olshan-Dory investigation committee, which conducted the most thorough inquiry into the affair, decided to focus mainly on this issue. It is clear that this decision was partly the result of misleading testimony and forged documents supplied by the DMI under Givli's instructions in order to show that the operation began only after 16 July. A second reason was probably the critical importance Olshan and Dory as well as Sharett (who personally appointed them) gave to Lavon's behavior as Defense Minister rather than to that of Givli as head of the DMI. The committee concluded that it was not convinced that Givli received instructions from Lavon on 16 July. But at the same time it could not conclude positively that Lavon did in fact give the instructions (Sharett, pp. 658–65; Olshan, p. 276).

It seems, however, that Lavon did indeed give Givli the "green light" to start the operation (without knowing that it was already under way) during their 16 July meeting. As Olshan and Dory concluded, had Lavon given no such instruction at all, he would have demanded a thorough investigation once the collapse of the operation became known in order to find out how such a delicate and important project was launched without his knowledge (Sharett, p. 661; Olshan, p. 273). The fact that Lavon avoided such action is the best evidence (though only circumstantial) that he approved the operation on 16 July. Moreover, Lavon's secretary, Ephraim (Ephi) Evron testified before the Olshan-Dory investigation committee that Lavon did not deny that he gave the order (Olshan, p. 268). This is supported by additional evidence: in a talk with Avraham Dar, the DMI's agent who recruited the network members in 1951, Lavon admitted that the 23 July sabotage acts did not surprise him because he knew of the plans. He was surprised, though, to find that additional acts were conducted prior to this date (Dar interview).

72. Coincidentally, on 16 July Colonel Givli also conferred with Prime Minister Sharett (Sharett diary, 16 July 1954, p. 556). This meeting probably took place in the morning before Givli conferred with Lavon. Obviously, the chief of the DMI avoided even mentioning the activation of the Egyptian network, a possibility discussed a day earlier in his talk with the Defense Minister. In any event, if Givli was looking for an opportunity to inform Sharett of the operation, this meeting was clearly a good one.

on the Israeli radio program "The Housewife's Corner." After decoding, the message reads: "Act against the British in order to prevent the Cairo agreement. Public places, casualties, mere noise and local leaders. Action can also be in Alexandria and the Canal Zone" (Eshed 1979, p. 69; Teveth 1992b, p. 58). A second message, transmitted by shortwave radio, orders:

> One: Start acting immediately in order to prevent or delay the Anglo-Egyptian agreement. The targets are: One, cultural and propaganda institutions; two, economic institutions; three, official representatives, their cars, British representatives, or other Britons; four, everything else that can bring about the break-off of diplomatic relations.
>
> Two: Inform us about the possibility of operations in the Canal Zone.
>
> Three: Listen to us everyday at 7:00GMT on frequency G.[73]
> (Eshed 1979, p. 69; Teveth 1992b, pp. 58–59)

Since no prearrangements were made for the transmission of messages on Saturday, which is July 17, this message was scheduled for transmission on Sunday.[74]

In Cairo, El-Ad meets Levy, who has arrived from Alexandria, and briefs him on the next wave of sabotage scheduled for 23 July against five targets. The two reconnoiter the area of the Cairo targets—two cinema houses and the central railway station (Golan 1976, pp. 71–72).

18 July: Orders to activate the network—the orders prepared the day before—are transmitted for the first time by Kol Yisrael and the DMI's shortwave transmission facilities (Eshed 1979, p. 69). There is no indication in El-Ad's diaries that he received either of the messages (Harel 1980, p. 134). A coded letter is sent from Rome to Max Binnet, ordering him "to do

73. These instructions were different from the original instructions given by Benzoor to El-Ad in their Paris meetings. It is quite possible that the goal of original plans was more general—to stir up turmoil in Egypt as a means to create Western distrust in the ability of Nasser's regime to maintain law and order in the country—while the 17 July instructions were more specific, aimed at preventing the conclusion of the Anglo-Egyptian accord. In this sense the "unfortunate business" was possibly composed of two operations rather than one, which were carried out by the same agents with the same means in order to reach a similar (but not identical) goal. None of the persons whom I interviewed, however, suggested that this indeed was the case.

74. According to Benzoor's report of 5 October (Eshed 1979, p. 101), this message was transmitted to Alexandria on 17 July without knowing if the network received it. There is no indication that the message was received.

something" in order to prevent the conclusion of the evacuation agreement (Eshed 1979, pp. 69–70).

19 July: Preparations for the next acts of sabotage are under way in Egypt (Golan 1976, p. 73). Colonel Givli sends a letter to Chief of Staff Dayan, who is still in the United States, informing him of the decision to activate the Egyptian network (Eshed 1979, p. 71).[75]

20 July: The activation order is transmitted to the Alexandrian cell (Benzoor's report of 5 October). There is no indication that it was received in Egypt.

21 July: Binnet receives the 18 July instruction to act against the British. From his immediate reply it is clear that he does not take the new order seriously and he does not make any attempt to carry it out (Eshed 1979, p. 70).

22 July: A second activation order is transmitted by Kol Yisrael (ibid.) and is received by El-Ad (El-Ad's secret diaries, Harel 1980, p. 140). This is the first positively identified message to be received in Egypt since at least 16 July, the date Lavon allegedly gave the order to activate the network.

23 July: Under Givli's authorization a cable is sent from Paris to Egypt to inquire why the network's communication set does not operate (Benzoor's report of 5 October, Eshed 1979, p. 101). The third wave of sabotage takes place in Cairo and Alexandria. Dassa and Azar arrive in Cairo from Alexandria and plant one bomb in the central train station and two fire bombs in two movie theaters. Only one of them—a movie theater bomb—explodes. In Alexandria a fire bomb ignites in Natanson's trousers when he tries to enter another movie theater, and he is immediately arrested. Levy, who was to plant a bomb in a different movie theater, sees what has happened to Natanson and abandons his mission (Golan 1976, pp. 73–83). Natanson's arrest signals the collapse of the network.

24 July: Victor Levy is arrested in Alexandria (ibid., pp. 83–85). El-Ad sends a coded telegram to an emergency address in Germany, warning his superiors to stop all contacts with the network (Eshed 1979, pp. 78–79). The first reports of the collapse of the network are broadcast by Radio Damascus at 8:15 P.M. (ibid., p. 78).

---

75. In the original letter Givli wrote: "*We activated the 'boys' of 131*, though it was clear that prevention of the agreement was possible." Later the text of the letter was changed to say: "*According to Lavon's instruction* we activated the 'boys' of 131 though . . ." (Eshed 1979, p. 71, emphasis added; Teveth 1992b, pp. 105–7). This was one among a few documents forged by the DMI in order to prove that Lavon was responsible for the operation.

25 July: El-Ad's warning telegram arrives in Israel (ibid., p. 79). Robert Dassa is arrested in Alexandria (Golan 1976, pp. 89–90).

26 July: The first reports of the collapse of the Egyptian network, based on Arab sources, appear in the Israeli press (Ha'Aretz, 26 July 1954).

27 July: Egypt officially announces the arrest of Natanson, Levy, and Dassa (Golan 1976, p. 103). Prime Minister Sharett learns for the first time, probably through the press, that Jews arrested in Egypt are suspected of conducting sabotage acts under instructions from Israel (Sharett diary, p. 560).

29 July: Sharett receives additional information on the Egyptian fiasco and instructs Isser Harel to find out who is responsible for it (ibid., p. 562). When Harel questions him, Colonel Givli answers that "there were planning instructions but not implementation ones." Later Givli informs Harel that Defense Minister Lavon has forbidden him to say anything more (Harel 1982b, pp. 18–19).

31 July: Shmuel Azar is arrested in Alexandria (Golan 1976, p. 104).

1 August: Benzoor writes his first report on the operation (text of the report in Harel 1982b, pp. 125–28).

5 August: Mussa Marzouk is arrested in Cairo and Meir Meyuhas, who was connected with the network but never participated in the acts of sabotage, is arrested in Alexandria (Golan 1976, p. 104).

7 August: Marcelle Ninio is arrested in Cairo (ibid., p. 106). El-Ad leaves Egypt (El-Ad 1976a, pp. 161–62).

14 August: El-Ad arrives in Israel. He is received at the airport by Benzoor (El-Ad 1976a, p. 163).

For our purposes the most important fact in this sequence of events is that the first time El-Ad received activation instructions following the 16 July meeting in which Lavon allegedly gave Givli a "green light"[76] was on

---

76. One of the mysteries that still surround the "unfortunate business" is why Givli insisted that Lavon ordered him to activate the network on 16 July, two weeks after first acts of sabotage had been carried out. His insistence on this date is even more intriguing given the testimony of Lavon's private secretary before the Olshan-Dory investigation committee that during May or early June 1954 Givli discussed with Lavon plans to activate the cells and Lavon authorized him to review these plans (Teveth 1992b, pp. 96–98). Givli could use this testimony quite convincingly to argue that the order was given no later than early June.

It is quite probable, however, that Givli insisted on 16 July as the date he received the order because of his relations with Dayan rather than with Lavon. Had he admitted that he received the instruction to activate the network and that he acted upon it without even informing Dayan, he would have had to face the one man in Israel he probably feared most. But Dayan, it will be recalled, left Israel on 12 July. By arguing that he received the order on 16 July Givli could have at least avoided a confrontation with his chief of staff.

22 July. Prior to this date, however, the network had already acted twice (2 July and 14 July), and preparations for the 23 July wave of sabotage had been completed. There can thus be no doubt that the additional instruction—if it was indeed given—had no impact on the network's activities and that the operation started and continued and would have been carried out as planned even without it. The question of whether or not Lavon instructed Givli to activate the network is therefore irrelevant since the only applicable operational instructions were those given to El-Ad in Paris by Benzoor. These were Givli's orders, given to Benzoor without the knowledge, let alone the approval, of Chief of Staff Dayan, Defense Minister Lavon, or Prime Minister Sharett.

It could be argued, though, that the operation was not Colonel Givli's sole responsibility. After all, it is possible that El-Ad operated the network on his own or on behalf of his Egyptian operators, or that Benzoor instructed him to launch the operation without receiving the proper authorization from Givli. An analysis of the available information shows, however, that neither El-Ad nor Benzoor acted without Givli's orders.

There are four arguments against the possibility that El-Ad launched the operation without authority. First, in two separate reports (of 1 August and 5 October Benzoor admitted that he instructed El-Ad to activate the network during their meetings in Paris in late May and early June 1954. Second, if El-Ad had activated the network on his own initiative, or—a possibility that makes more sense—on the instructions of his Egyptian operators, this could have raised serious suspicions in the DMI about his bona fides as an Israeli agent. Third, neither El-Ad nor the Egyptian security service would have benefited from initiating the operation without instructions from Israel. Fourth, Givli and Benzoor never raised the question of why the network was activated by El-Ad prior to 16 July.

It is also not possible that Benzoor acted on his own or misinterpreted Givli's original instructions for the following two reasons. First, according to his 1 August report, Benzoor instructed El-Ad to activate the network. If this was without Givli's knowledge, the chief of the DMI—to whom the report was submitted—would have inquired why Benzoor acted without authority. There are no indications, however, that Givli ever raised the question. Second, according to Benzoor's 5 October report, Givli personally gave him the instructions before Benzoor left for Paris. Although Givli later expressed dissatisfaction with this report (which actually incriminated him), he never argued that he did not give Benzoor the instructions.

Given all the available information, then, there can be only one explanation for the activation of Unit 131's Egyptian cells in July 1954: it was done on Colonel Givli's instructions of May–June 1954. The order allegedly given by Lavon in mid-July had no impact at all on the way the operation started and the way it ended.

The Implications

Givli's Egyptian operation of 1954 is a clear-cut case of the crudest type of interference in the conduct of national foreign policy by an intelligence organization. Unlike cases where intelligence organizations use means not authorized by policymakers in order to reach the same goals (such as "The Bay of Pigs"), the DMI's operation in 1954 was carried out not only by means that Sharett never knew of and would have objected to but also in blatant opposition to his foreign policy. Givli's attempt to decide the fate of Israel looks especially grave, furthermore, when one considers exactly what that foreign policy was.

The fact is that since the July 1952 Egyptian Revolution Israel had been secretly trying to establish a direct dialogue with Cairo. Some success was achieved and a few communication channels were established between the Israeli and the Egyptian leaderships through special emissaries in Paris. Although direct links between the two states were only at an embryonic stage, Sharett suggested, probably in late 1953, that the following subjects might be discussed in future negotiations:

1. The cessation of hostile propaganda.

2. Reaffirmation of the undertaking of nonaggression.

3. Lifting of restrictions on the free passage of shipping through the Suez Canal to and from Israel.

4. Assistance by Israel to attain economic aid for Egypt and the mobilization of public and official opinion in support of her legitimate national demands [that is, the British evacuation of the Suez Zone] among the friends of Israel.[77]

77. "Draft Reply to Gamal Nassar's Communication by Sar [the Minister of Foreign Affairs, Sharett]"; no date is given (ISA, FO 130.02 2453/20). Nasser's emissaries were Colonel Okasha, the Egyptian military attaché in Paris, and Abdul Rahman Sadek. Their Israeli counterparts were Shmuel (Ziama) Divon, the Israeli charge d'affaires at the embassy in Paris, and Dan Avni Segre, the press secretary in the embassy (Segre interview).

Certainly the necessary condition for nurturing these secret links and upgrading them into an open or at least substantive dialogue was mutual trust between Sharett and the Egyptian leaders. From Nasser's perspective, however, the "unfortunate business" probably proved that the Israelis could not be trusted. After all, Israel had first promised him support in Egypt's struggle against the British presence on her soil and then, behind his back, launched a secret operation aimed at preventing the withdrawal of the British forces from the Canal Zone. It is hard to believe that the Egyptians were aware at the time that the operation was carried out without Sharett's approval, let alone his knowledge. But in light of the events of July 1954 Nasser could have only reached one of two conclusions: (1) if Sharett knew about the operation, he could not be trusted; or (2) if Sharett did not know about the operation, then any negotiations with him were quite useless. The mere conduct of such an operation without his knowledge, after all, could only prove that the Israeli Prime Minister had very little control over Israel's foreign policy and hence could hardly deliver the goods he had promised. In this sense the Egyptian operation, whether Givli was aware of it or not, could only destroy the chance of a possible improvement in Israel's relations with Cairo.

Yet, despite the damage caused by the DMI's operation to Sharett's top-secret connection with Egypt, direct links between him and Nasser were resumed in December 1954 during the trial of the network members in Cairo. Nasser's readiness to resume this connection despite what he already knew about the Israeli operation is proof that he was sincerely interested in preventing a deterioration in Egypt's relations with Israel, at least until solving more pressing problems at home.

The initiative to resume the secret dialogue was doubtless Israel's. In response, Nasser sent his special emissary Sadek to Paris on 15 December 1954 with a verbal reply to an earlier message from Sharett.[78] The Egyptian leader informed his Israeli counterpart that Egypt still wanted to reach a peaceful settlement to her dispute with Israel and was ready to privately discuss any practical suggestions to improve the tense relationship between the two states. The Israelis on their side used the opportunity to explain to Sadek that the immediate and most serious problem threatening that relationship was the possible outcome of the network's public trial in Cairo.[79]

78. A cable announces Sadek's planned arrival in Paris in *ISA*, FO 130.02 2453/20.
79. From Raphael G. to Sharett, 19 December 1954, in ibid.

Upon receiving this news from Paris, Sharett answered Nasser in writing, again emphasizing the importance Israel attached to the outcome of the Cairo trial:

> I cannot emphasize too strongly the gravity of the issue which hangs there in the balance for our future relations. I fervently hope that, whatever the guilt established, no death sentences will be passed, for their execution would lead to dire results: it would inevitably produce a most violent crisis, kindle afresh the flames of bitterness and strife, and defeat our efforts to curb passions and lead our peoples into ways of peace.[80]

The Egyptian emissary took Sharett's letter to Nasser and on 31 December delivered a written but unsigned answer in which the Egyptian leader informed Sharett that he was "very glad that you realize the efforts spent from our side to bring our relations to a peaceful solution. I hope they will be met by similar efforts from your side, thus permitting us to achieve the results we are seeking for the benefits of both countries."[81]

Verbally, Sadek added that the Egyptian government could not intervene in the trial but guaranteed proper legal procedures, explaining that in contrast to the "Muslim Brotherhood" trial of only a few weeks earlier the accusations against the network members were very grave. Yet Egypt avoided using the trial for propaganda purposes.[82] Indeed, unlike the massive Israeli propaganda campaign whose main theme was that the Egyptian accusations against the network members were false, a top-secret evaluation of the trial prepared by the Foreign Office confirmed Sadek's guarantees:

> From the procedural perspective the trial was conducted in proper order . . . except for minor deviations. . . . The trial received detailed but not noisy publicity. . . . No anti-Israeli propaganda was conducted inside or outside the courthouse at the time of the trial. . . . An attempt was made to emphasize the fair impartiality of the Egyptian Government towards Egyptian Jewry and to discon-

---

80. From Sharett HaMisrad [the Office], Jerusalem, to MemIsrael Paris, 19 December 1954, in ibid. Similar notes were sent to Paris on 20 and 21 December (ibid.).

81. From Ziama [Divon] MemIsrael Paris to Sharett, Raphael, personal, HaMisrad, Jerusalem, 31 December 1954 (ibid.)

82. From Divon, Palmon MemIsrael Paris to Sharett, Raphael, Hamisrad, Jerusalem; arrived on 1 January 1955 (ibid.).

nect the group [that is, the network members] from the Jewish community. The accused were not photographed as "chained criminals" like the accused in other recent political trials in Egypt.[83]

One can speculate whether the policy pursued by Sharett had a real chance of success or whether it was doomed to fail. It is evident, however, that in the summer of 1954 Nasser was ready to take practical measures to improve his relations with Israel. In addition to the exchange of notes between him and Sharett, there was Egypt's policy of maintaining quiet along her border with Israel. As documents captured by the Israelis following the 1956 Sinai campaign and the 1967 war show, Egypt consistently stopped spontaneous infiltration from the Gaza Strip, a policy that changed only in response to the massive Israeli retaliation raid on Gaza in late February 1955 (Ya'ari, pp. 12, 16). Moreover, the DMI was aware of this policy. A Military Intelligence report from 22 March 1955 noted:

> The second half of 1954 and the beginning of 1955 were marked by relative quiet along the armistice line, especially following the actions taken by the Egyptians to block infiltration and to restrain elements disturbing the Egyptian authorities (the Muslim Brotherhood and the Mufti's men). On the whole the regular Egyptian forces avoided entangling themselves in serious clashes with our forces.[84]

The policy pursued by Sharett was thus not based merely on wishful thinking but on some tangible evidence of Egypt's behavior. The DMI's initiative, therefore, was an unprovoked act against a neighboring state attempting to stabilize her relations with Israel.

Finally, while this discussion focused mainly on one aspect of the affair—the DMI's intervention in Israel's politics—its professional aspects deserve some attention as well. For apart from his interference in politics Colonel Givli also made some grave professional mistakes. The most basic one was probably his naive belief that it was possible to reverse such historical trends as the British withdrawal from the Middle East.[85] Indeed,

83. From Ariel D. to Eithan V.: "The Alexandrian Trial," 28 December 1954, ISA, FO 130.02 2387/7.

84. ISA, FO 2454/5; quoted in Cohen, p. 125.

85. Major General (ret.) Yehoshafat Harkabi, who served as acting chief of the DMI before Givli's tenure and as the DMI's chief after Givli left, considers the classic question of "Who gave

even Givli himself expressed deep pessimism about the likelihood of ultimate success when the operation was already under way. In his 19 July letter to Dayan he noted that, "though it is clear that an agreement cannot be prevented, even if the objections of the Young Conservatives [in the British Parliament] increase, Lavon believes that its delay is possible and this may bring some political benefit" (Eshed 1979, p. 71). The head of the DMI added: "With all apprehensions, this [the activation of the network] would be a test, even in small-scale operations" (ibid.). The first sentence casts a dark shadow over Givli's political judgment; after all, if the chance of success was so low, why was such a high-risk operation ordered? Certainly "some political benefit" is not a sufficient answer. The sentence that follows casts an even darker shadow over Givli's moral judgment: an intelligence exercise is obviously no grounds for risking the lives of young men who volunteered to serve the Israeli state. All in all, Givli's behavior in spring 1954 certainly raises questions regarding his professional standards. As Ya'acov Dory told Givli when the Olshan-Dory committee investigated him: "You certainly had to resist using and endangering 131, which was built as a wartime instrument. Not necessarily for political reasons . . . but because of the risks to the DMI's precious instrument" (Teveth 1992b, p. 114).

Had the chief of the DMI taken all possible steps to guarantee the success of the operation, perhaps a "live" exercise could have been accepted. But in his eagerness to carry out the operation Givli made these additional mistakes. Each in itself was sufficient to ensure the operation's failure, and when taken together they brought about its total defeat. First, Givli put El-Ad in command of the operation despite his well-known weaknesses, early warnings that he constituted a security risk, and an initial policy of isolating him from the DMI's assets. Indeed, as was revealed only years later, El-Ad betrayed the DMI and probably turned over the network members to the Egyptian security service. Second, Givli activated the network at least two years before it was scheduled to become fully operational. An integral component of its combat readiness was the availability of the means—most importantly effective and reliable explosives—to successfully carry out its missions. Without these means the network members had to use the only

---

the order?" as far less important than the principal question surrounding this episode: "How was born the idea that some small explosions by primitive means could bring Britain to refuse evacuating her bases in the Canal zone?" (Ha'Aretz, 4 December 1992). It should be noted, however, that when asking this question Harkabi was hardly aware of the British preparations to use military force if negotiations with Egypt broke down (Operation RODEO) and that they delivered warnings in this regard to the Egyptians (from a personal talk with Harkabi).

available explosives they could get—unreliable homemade bombs. The result was the accidental explosion of a fire bomb carried by Natanson, a mishap that led directly to his and his friends' capture. Third, the network was activated without the elementary preparations—such as preplanned escape routes, false passports, or safe houses—needed in case of failure. When one failure occurred, therefore, the fate of the rest of the network's members was decided as well.

Colonel Givli was an experienced intelligence officer. He must have known that his decisions could cost human lives. Under what conditions and why he decided to initiate and launch the Egyptian operation is a subject to be discussed later. At this stage it is important to point out one interim conclusion: there is a direct and positive correlation between making political and professional mistakes. In other words, as was the case in the "Bay of Pigs," when an intelligence operation is pursued so eagerly that it has to be concealed not only from foes but also from friends, the ability to judge its merits on purely professional grounds decreases significantly. When it was decided to launch the operation without even considering that it had a very slim chance of success, the result, as we know, was a total defeat, properly nicknamed the "unfortunate business."

THE "UNFORTUNATE BUSINESS": HOW COULD IT HAVE HAPPENED?

The "unfortunate business" was the result of complex conditions, of which some were unique even to the Israeli polity of 1954. To a large extent, then, existing decisionmaking theories are hardly applicable to this case. Thus, if we take the three classical decisionmaking models—rational actor, organizational process, and bureaucratic (or government) politics—none of them can sufficiently explain the events that took place in Israel during the first half of 1954.

The rational-actor model, for example, asserts that "governmental behavior can be usefully summarized as action chosen by a unitary, rational decisionmaker: centrally controlled, completely informed, and value maximizing" (Allison 1971, p. 67). Israel in 1954, however, was anything but a rational unified actor. Her foreign policy was not centrally controlled, and Prime Minister Sharett was not informed of significant initiatives of his state's foreign and defense apparatus.

The same is true of the organizational-process model. Its basic premise is the existence of Standard Operations Procedures (SOPs) that direct the behavior of the various bureaucracies involved in the decisionmaking process. This model accordingly assumes that governmental behavior can be understood "as *outputs* of large organizations functioning according to standard patterns of behavior" (ibid., emphasis in original). Neither the DMI nor the IDF nor the Israeli Defense Ministry, however, functioned in 1954 according to standard operating procedures, unless bypassing higher authorities, misleading superiors, and ignoring their directives can be so considered. In addition, this model implicitly asserts the existence of a bargaining process between the various bureaucracies involved, a process that ultimately yields policy outputs. But the most important characteristic of the Israeli decisionmaking process in the 1954 affair is that no such bargaining process ever took place since the decision was made and implemented at a single low organizational level. For this reason the bureaucratic-politics model, which explains governmental behavior as a function of the bureaucratic bargaining process, is not applicable to this case either.

Yet to a limited extent the existing body of literature on the decisionmaking process, such as research into its psychological constraints and studies of belief systems and images (e.g., Jervis 1976; George, pp. 25–80), can be very useful for understanding the behavior of the individuals involved in the 1954 affair. Scholars who have studied the role of organizational behavior and bureaucratic politics in the making of foreign policy, furthermore, have identified some of the distorted outcomes that result from such policymaking systems. Two of these seem highly relevant: "contradictory" or "leaderless" policy, "when different parts of the executive branch pursue conflicting courses"; and "paper" policy, "when a policy is officially promulgated but lacks support within the executive branch needed for effective implementation" (George, p. 114).

But explanations such as "leaderless" or "paper" policy are only partially helpful. The goal of this section is to explain, as comprehensively as possible, what caused the 1954 Israeli decisionmaking system to function the way it did. I will therefore analyze the conditions under which it operated at four levels of analysis: international (structure), national (state), bureaucratic (including interbureaucratic, bureaucratic, and intrabureaucratic), and personal. Finally, I will argue that the best explanation for the "unfortunate business" lies at the state and the personal levels.

The Structural Explanation

Geopolitical conditions have always placed severe limits on Israel's room for maneuverability in the international arena. In 1954, with a territory of about 21,000 square kilometers surrounded on all sides but the west by belligerent Arab states, with a Jewish population of about a million and a half and an annual budget of less than $250 million, with almost no natural resources and a high level of dependency on outside Jewish and American aid, Israel had to confront a hostile Arab world with enormous territory, population, and natural resources.

Israel had managed to compensate for these fundamental disadvantages in her first years of independence, but in 1953 came significant global political changes. Under the "new look" of the Eisenhower administration the doctrine of massive retaliation was formulated, a necessary condition for which was the availability of American military bases close to Soviet borders so that U.S. strategic bombers could reach targets deep within Soviet territory. Obtaining such facilities became a high-priority goal of the administration's foreign policy, and geopolitical conditions made the Middle East a prime area for providing them. From an Israeli perspective, the dire result was an increase in American political, military, and economic support for the Arab countries and a decrease in American support for Israel. The goal of this policy was to convince the Arabs to form a pro-Western pact in the Middle East.[86]

Simultaneously, and probably for the same reasons, the USSR took a similar line in Middle Eastern affairs. It is true that Soviet-Israeli relations had been frigid since the end of the 1940s. Now, however, Soviet moves— expressed mainly in two vetoes of moderate pro-Israeli resolutions in the U.N. Security Council (January and March 1954)—made it clear that Moscow was increasing her support of the Arabs, thus placing additional constraints on Israel's foreign policy.

Against this background the resumption of Anglo-Egyptian negotiations

86. Perhaps its clearest expression as far as Israel was concerned was put forth in two speeches given in the first half of 1954 by Henry Byroade, Assistant Secretary of State for Near Eastern, South Asian, and African Affairs. Byroade called on Israel to refrain from additional retaliatory acts and ease Arab fears of massive Jewish emigration to Israel. He explicitly suggested that Israel should become an integral part of the Middle East and "cease to perceive herself as a center for different peoples with a common belief." This last comment was perceived by the Israeli public as a direct attack on the whole concept of Zionism.

on the evacuation of the Suez Canal Zone, and the direct and indirect implications the agreement had for Israel's security, constituted an additional grave threat. As we have already seen, different policymakers tended to perceive the threat in different ways. Certainly, however, it comprised a major challenge to Israel's foreign policy and constituted the concrete external stimulus for the Egyptian operation.

But although this challenge could be dealt with by different strategies and there was deep division within Israel as to how to react to it, the international level of analysis can afford no explanation of the way Israel responded. These explanations lie, then, in the substructural levels.

The State-Level Explanation

Any attempt to understand Israel's 1954 foreign and defense policy in general, and the Egyptian operation in particular, is doomed to fail if it is filtered through the prism of a modern Western-style decisionmaking process. No one understood this better than the man who headed Israel in 1954, Sharett himself. In February 1961, while serving as secretary-general of Mapai, he made a speech during a debate that ended in Lavon's dismissal from his position as secretary-general of the Histadrut. In his opening remarks Sharett described what the future historian would consider to be the fundamental source of the 1954 tragedy:

> He will say, probably, that this state paid a dear price for her youth; that back then, the proper procedures for public life were not yet consolidated; that she sometimes suffered from untruthful reporting; that she suffered from improper discipline procedures, from a refusal to delve into the issues of statehood and public responsibility, from a lack of a tradition which teaches people to restrain themselves at difficult times; from giving too much freedom to warring inclinations; from lack of regular standards of behavior; [and] also from personal relations which had become too personal and not enough aware of being aware of their civic and national responsibilities.
>
> And as a result of all this, she paid such a dear price. (Sharett diary, pp. 778–79)

Sharett's remarks bring to light many of the distorted procedures and norms that dominated Israel's politics under his rule and yielded the most serious security mishap in the state's first decade of existence. What he described, however, are only the "rules of the game" of governmental politics without explaining their sources. Even more important, he did not explain why these distorted norms dominated Israeli politics under his rule but not under Ben-Gurion's.

The explanation lies, first and foremost, in the coexistence of two political systems in Israel during the early 1950s.[87] The first was the formal distribution of power; the second was the informal distribution, rooted in the Israeli elite's political culture.[88] Simply put, according to the formal distribution the center of power in Israel is the prime minister. Although he is only the first among equals, it is he who creates the government, chairs its meetings, and directs its discussions. Most important, his resignation automatically causes the government's dismantling. Until 1967, moreover, the prime minister always carried an additional portfolio. During Ben-Gurion's tenure he was also the defense minister, and the same was true of Eshkol when he replaced Ben-Gurion in 1963. As for Sharett, during his tenure as prime minister he was also the minister of foreign affairs. The result of this arrangement was that the premier enjoyed, at least formally, very strong personal power since he always served in two out of the three roles—prime minister, foreign minister, defense minister—that largely determined the national foreign and defense policy.

The formal system of government in Israel, then, alloted Sharett no less power than it had Ben-Gurion. Yet, as we have already seen, unlike Ben-Gurion, Sharett failed to control Israel's foreign and defense policy. It can thus be assumed that the explanation for his inability lies not with the formal distribution of power but rather with the informal one. In order to

87. This discussion focuses only on Israeli politics of the early 1950s. It does not imply that informal norms of behavior did not dominate the state's politics in later periods. Indeed, such norms dominated Golda Meir's tenure as prime minister (for example, Golda's "kitchen cabinet" of the early 1970s) and Menahem Begin's cabinet in the late 1970s and the early 1980s. Obviously, such norms are not unique to Israel and can be found in the politics of other nations as well. But the tendency of Israeli leaders to avoid any systematic decisionmaking process, especially in the most crucial issues, is exceptional. For some fine examples of this tendency, see Ben-Meir, pp. 85–117.

88. Political culture is defined here as "the set of attitudes, beliefs, and sentiments which give order and meaning to a political process and which provide the underlying assumptions and rules that govern behavior in the political system. It encompasses both the political ideals and the operating norms of a polity. Political culture is thus the manifestation in aggregate form of the psychological and subjective dimensions of politics. A political culture is the product of both the collective history of a political system and the life histories of the members of that system, and thus it is rooted equally in public events and private experience" (Pye 1968, p. 218).

understand the nature of this informal system, we must look briefly at the sources of the Israeli elite's political culture during that period and at some of its main characters.

The Israeli political elite of the early 1950s was comprised mainly of individuals who came to Palestine immediately before or after World War I. Most of them were born in Eastern Europe (mainly in Czarist Russia or Poland), rebelled against their parents and the traditional Jewish life of the Diaspora, and came to Palestine in order to build a new Jewish nation. Within a relatively short period of time, about three decades, they accomplished the unbelievable, experiencing both revolutionary successes and disasters such as the buildup of an organized Jewish community in Palestine (the Yishuv), the return of Jews to productive manual work, the creation of a Jewish military force, the Holocaust, the establishment of the state of Israel, the victory of the 1948 war, and the huge increase of the Jewish population in Israel during her first five years of existence. Altogether the record of these people

> was probably unparalleled in modern history, for these old veterans . . . had not only revolutionized their society but also to a large extent created it. Israel had come into being contrary to all prevailing reason in the course of their lifetime, on a new territory, through a modern *Volkerwanderung* of outcasts and ideals. (Elon, pp. 11–12)

The core of the Israeli ruling elite in the early 1950s was the leadership of Mapai, people like Ben-Gurion, Sharett, Golda Meir, Zalman Aranne, and Levi Eshkol. They had worked together for many years, and their experience had left its marks on their personal and collective world views and ways of thinking. The most important of these included a pervasive disrespect for a formal chain of command, for the advice of experts, and for orderly staff work. Their substitutes for an institutionalized decisionmaking process were improvisation and intuition. They thus accepted, as is usual during great revolutions, the dominance of one charismatic leader who displayed these qualities in abundance. They also tended to identify the good of the state with the good of their party; in this sense elements of Bolshevism influenced their thinking as well as their behavior. As for relations within this group, its members were influenced far less by their formal roles and far more by their many years of collective work, which yielded an intricate emotional web of personal love and hate, respect and disrespect, admiration and contempt.

The result was a unique political culture that created an informal distribution of power. At the top of the pyramid, high above all others, stood Ben-Gurion. His charisma, determination, political genius, and sharp instincts qualified him to lead his people for more than two decades and through some of the most serious challenges known to modern history. Ben-Gurion's overall success, the atmosphere of revolutionary change, and, not least important, the heritage of the Diaspora—all contributed to a belief shared by ordinary people as well as by senior politicians that he was somehow the new Jewish messiah.[89] Certain patterns of behavior in the close circle around him at the height of his career indeed resemble rabbinical Hassidic courts in which the rabbi is regarded as a preternatural phenomenon without whose presence and guidance life cannot go on. Even if not all of Mapai's leaders shared this feeling, a consensus within the party elite viewed Ben-Gurion as Israel's best available leader at the time.

So long as Ben-Gurion served as premier and defense minister, then, there was a high correlation between the formal and the informal distributions of power. In theory his colleagues accepted his decisions because of his governmental roles, but in practice they followed him because of his exceptional personal authority. But once Ben-Gurion left the government in late 1953, a gap between these two sources of power was immediately created. As time passed and the gap widened, it became clear that the source of real power lay not with Sharett and his government but rather outside the formal political system, in Sdeh Boker where Ben-Gurion was now living. Most of Mapai's veterans avoided exploiting this gap in order to enhance their personal status and political ambitions: ministers such as Eshkol, Golda Meir, and Aranne remained loyal to Sharett in spite of his political weakness either because of personal friendship and sympathy or because of their sincere support of his policies. Other ministers did not feel themselves strong enough to challenge Sharett without the backing of Ben-Gurion. This, however, was not the case with Defense Minister Lavon, as was described earlier and will be elaborated on later.

State-level variables such as the formal and informal distribution of power

89. Typically, when Secretary of the Government Zeev Sharef was asked to explain Ben-Gurion's retirement in late 1953, he answered: "The Messiah came, gathered the exiled Jews, defeated the surrounding gentiles, conquered the land, established the Temple, renewed holy worship—and then he had to sit in a coalition" (Bar-Zohar, p. 951). Sharef obviously did not mean this literally. Yet his words reflect the genuine beliefs of many of Ben-Gurion's supporters at the time.

and the Israeli elite's political culture of the early 1950s, therefore, provide us with the framework in which the "unfortunate business" took place. Substate variables, especially the personal ones, will explain why the system functioned the way it did.

The Bureaucratic Explanation

For our purpose the bureaucratic level of analysis is composed of all levels between the state and the individual and is divided into three sublevels: interbureaucratic, bureaucratic, and intrabureaucratic. Although it is certain that variables at this level had some impact on the making of the "unfortunate business," it is important to note that they were only partially independent, since to a great extent they were the result of two other sources: the conflict between the formal and informal distribution of power at the state level; and the beliefs, ways of thinking, and ways of behavior of the individuals who headed the various organizations—variables from the personal level of analysis.

At the *interbureaucratic* level two variables above all influenced the developments that facilitated the "unfortunate business": (1) the high level of tension that existed between the defense establishment and the Ministry of Foreign Affairs; and (2) the rivalry within Israel's intelligence community, especially between the DMI and the Mossad.

The conflict between the defense establishment and the Foreign Office focused on which of these organs would dominate Israel's foreign and defense policy. Very simply put, the defense establishment considered its role superior to that of Israel's diplomats. Believing, at least since 1953, that the availability and use of military power were not only the essential means of guaranteeing Israel's national security but also the only tangible method of compelling the Arab states to come to the negotiation table, the defense establishment regarded the Foreign Office's function as limited to propaganda (that is, explaining abroad the IDF's reprisal policy) and assistance in obtaining the needed weaponry.

Israel's diplomats, headed by Sharett, rejected this approach, adhering instead to the traditional axiom that military power should serve foreign policy rather than the other way around. But since the ability to use military power rested exclusively with the defense establishment, and since distorted norms already dominated the Israeli decisionmaking apparatus, the IDF could simply ignore the Foreign Office when making and implementing its decisions. Upon becoming Prime Minister, Sharett attempted to change this pattern of interbureaucratic relations (Sharett diary, pp. 340, 345–46, 373). His success, however, was negligible, and throughout 1954 the tension between the two organizations intensified significantly, partly because the defense establishment under Lavon perceived Sharett more as a diplomat than as prime minister.

The interbureaucratic rivalry between the DMI and the Mossad has already been discussed. Its most direct impact on the "unfortunate business" was the decision to isolate the Mossad from any activities directly linked to the Egyptian operation. As preparations for the operation developed, this decision was expressed in two ways. First, at the organizational level it neutralized the only still-functioning line of command between the Prime Minister and his intelligence community. Second, at the professional level it led to the absence of sound advice and criticism at a time when they were so much in need, thus freeing Givli to make grave professional mistakes.

It is important to note, however, that Lavon's unilateral decision (supported by Dayan and Givli) to isolate the director of the Mossad, Harel, from Unit 131's activities could have occurred when distorted norms of behavior were already dominating Israel's decisionmaking apparatus. The personal ambition of Lavon, Dayan, and Givli, moreover, contributed significantly to the making of this decision. In this sense the better explanation for this unilateral decisionmaking can be found in the state and personal levels of analysis rather than in interbureaucratic relations.

It is probable that variables at the *organizational level* of bureaucracies such as the army, the Foreign Office, or the Mossad[90] had some impact on the

90. Since malfunctions in the performance of the Defense Ministry under Lavon, the IDF under Dayan, and the Foreign Office under Sharett have already received attention, it is important to note that Harel's Mossad of the early 1950s was not free from defects either. Two points should be made here, both with regard to Harel's performance. First, his reports to his superiors were sometimes unnecessarily alarmist. For example, following the CIA coup in Guatemala (May–June 1954), he warned Ben-Gurion that the Americans might attempt a similar operation in Israel. As Ben-Gurion soberly pointed out, there was no basis for comparing the situations in Israel and Guatemala (Bar-Zohar, p. 1031, based on the diaries of Ben-Gurion and Argov).

Second, Harel was involved directly and consciously in Israel's domestic politics. He was an active member of the Mapai party, and many of his discussions with Sharett (and probably with Ben-Gurion) on intelligence and national security issues also involved pure party politics. Typically, in July 1954 he demanded that Sharett dismiss Lavon immediately before he caused serious damage to Mapai in the coming elections (Sharett diary, p. 559). In another meeting Harel complained to Sharett about negligence in Mapai's preparation for the coming elections and alerted him that activity in other parties was already in high gear (p. 692).

These examples serve only to emphasize how distorted norms and lack of separation between

case under discussion. But since the impact was mainly expressed at the level of interbureaucratic relations, the focus of our analysis at this level will be limited to the nature of the DMI in the early and mid-1950s.[91]

For our purposes two characteristics of Israel's Military Intelligence are particularly relevant. The first is what Harkabi, who headed the DMI before and after Givli's tenure, defined simply as "wild intelligence" (Harkabi interview). The DMI, especially under Colonel Givli, was creative and opted for a variety of operational plans but at the same time lacked both the professional discretion to distinguish between the possible and the impossible and the political discretion to distinguish between the desirable and the undesirable. To a large extent this was the result of the organization's youth and lack of experience, a situation neither rare nor necessarily negative. Some amateurism and "fresh blood" can improve the performance of any organization, as was certainly the case with the British intelligence community during World War II. Amateurism is constructive, however, only so long as it is balanced by professionalism, experience, and discretion. This was not the case with Israeli Military Intelligence in 1954.[92]

A second component of the DMI's reprehensible behavior in the Egyptian operation was its bias towards worst-case analysis, or what Laqueur so well termed the "Cassandra syndrome" (Laqueur, p. 280). It seems that, whenever the DMI had to assess regional and global developments, its analysis reflected a hypersensitivity to possible threats. For example, it warned that a Jordanian military operation was highly probable after the Jordanian army concentrated forces near the Israeli border following the Qibia raid in October 1953. Since this assessment did not take into account that there was no political or military rationale behind such an action, it was thus mainly based on analysis of capabilities rather than intentions. As Sharett correctly interpreted, the Jordanian moves were of a purely defensive nature

---

intelligence and politics dominated not only relations between the DMI and Lavon but also the upper echelon of the Mossad.

91. The first and so far the only academic analysis of DMI activities in the first half of the 1950s is Cohen (1988). Although in general he did a fine job, especially in his use of formerly classified documents, his article still suffers from some factual and interpretative errors, mainly in its discussion of the 1954 Egyptian operation.

92. Even the failure of the Egyptian operation did not improve the situation. During the Cairo trial of the network members, Colonel Givli made some hazardous plans to rescue DMI agents held in Egypt, including the hijack of Egyptian hostages form the Gaza Strip, Cyprus, and Europe. At the same time, the DMI prepared plans to hit the Egyptian embassy in Jordan in case any of the network members were executed. As was usual at the time, these plans were made without the knowledge of Prime Minister Sharett, who learned of them through Isser Harel (Sharett diary, p. 654).

(Sharett diary, p. 71). About three months later the DMI alerted the government that Iraq was behind the recent turmoil in Damascus and might very soon use the opportunity to take over Syria. The political and military implications were clear: Israel should take military countermeasures in order to avert the imminent threat on her northern border. This time, unlike in the Jordanian case, the DMI's assessment was not based on capabilities (since there were no indications of Iraqi military movements) but rather on "the logic of the situation." But as the DMI had to admit about a month later, the Iraqis were not involved in the Syrian coup.[93]

It can be concluded from these episodes that the DMI tended to perceive Arab capabilities and intentions through the prism of a worst-case analysis and used the information it had, or lacked, to support this perception. This tendency can be partially explained by Israel's military vulnerability during the early 1950s.[94] Moreover, being part of the army, the DMI was probably influenced by the military way of thinking that, especially in the case of Israel in the first half of the 1950s, was biased towards worst-case scenarios. We cannot ignore the possibility, however, that in submitting such alarmist reports the DMI was motivated also by a desire to serve the cause of the hardliners in the defense establishment who urged a policy of preemptive war, especially against Egypt, since they believed that time was working against Israel.

For our purposes it is important to note the effect of the "Cassandra syndrome" on the DMI's assessment of the military implications of a British withdrawal from the Suez Zone. As we have seen, these estimates were highly pessimistic, perhaps even justifying some drastic action. When combined with the "wild" nature of the DMI in 1954, this alarmism serves as an additional explanation for Givli's unilateral decision to launch the Egyptian operation.

Many of the *intrabureaucratic* factors that contributed to the implementation of the operation are not yet known, but from what is known we can identify three such catalysts: first, the high level of compartmentalization

93. For a thorough description of these cases, see Cohen, pp. 111–15. See also Sharett diary, pp. 44, 58, 65, 68–71, 333, 403–4; and Bar-Zohar (quoting from Ben-Gurion's diary), p. 983.

94. In 1950 the research branch of Military Intelligence conducted its first comprehensive analysis of Arab ability to launch a surprise attack against Israel. This research, which was updated in 1951 and 1952, was summarized in a volume titled *"Mikreh ha'Kol"* ("The All-Out Case") and postulated a scenario in which all Arab states launched a well-coordinated surprise attack against Israel (Granot, p. 34). Given that this work constituted the DMI's analytical masterpiece in the early 1950s, it can be reasonably assumed that it influenced the way the chiefs of Military Intelligence estimated threatening signals from Arab states.

within the DMI; second, Unit 131's inability to bring the Egyptian network to operational status before mid-1954 because of a lack of cooperation by other sections of the DMI; third, the amateurish nature of the network, and especially the lack of compartmentalization among its members.

Compartmentalization within the DMI caused Givli to overestimate the true capabilities of his Egyptian network. It appears that his main source of information on this subject was Benzoor's reports and that he avoided discussing them with other officers in the DMI in general and in Unit 131 in particular. Benzoor for his part behaved similarly, never thoroughly discussing with any of his subordinates either the ability of the network to reach its operational goals or the fateful decision to appoint El-Ad to head the operation.[95]

This extreme level of compartmentalization cannot be explained on professional grounds alone. Another explanation, certainly, was the need to keep the operation as secret as possible for political reasons. Yet another derives from the tense relations between Benzoor and some of his officers, who believed that their commander was deficient in expertise and apt to commit grave professional errors.[96] It is also possible that because Givli and Benzoor were themselves skeptical about the operation's likelihood of success they, intentionally or not, employed a defense mechanism to prevent outsiders from comprehending their mistakes.

A major cause for the operation's failure was the poor operational status of the Egyptian network. As we have already seen, no documentation, safe houses, or escape routes were prepared for getting the agents out of Egypt in case the operation failed. One objective reason for this deficiency is that the network was not scheduled to become fully operational before 1956–57 (Benzoor interview). A second reason is a lack of cooperation by other sections of the DMI; as Benzoor argued later, he had no authority to compel others in the organization to contribute their share to the goals of his unit (ibid.). There is little doubt, however, that Benzoor's poor performance as Unit 131's commander contributed significantly to this failure.[97]

The final relevant factor at the intrabureaucratic level of analysis is the

---

95. This information is based on interviews I held with some of the officers who served in Unit 131 before and during the "unfortunate business." For various reasons these persons preferred to remain anonymous.

96. The source of this information is the same as in the previous note.

97. According to one source of information that cannot be identified, Benzoor barely knew what sort of passports were requested and was, indeed, entirely unaware of the need to prepare plans and facilities that would enable his agents in Egypt to get away in case of emergency.

lack of compartmentalization within the Egyptian network, which probably contributed to its quick collapse. I use the word "probably" here since there is sufficient evidence that El-Ad betrayed the network to the Egyptians. Even if he was not a double agent, however, the results of the operation might have been just the same considering that the network members knew each other much too well. Once one of them was captured, therefore, the fate of the rest could well have been decided also.

The Personal-Level Explanation

Structural variables constituted the external stimulus for the Egyptian operation. State-level variables explain the environment in which the decision and its implementation became possible. Factors at various levels of bureaucratic politics explain many of the professional defects and mistakes that made the project a total failure. But the individual level of analysis is where all these factors can be combined into a full explanation of the conditions that enabled the DMI to launch its operation. It was individuals with emotions, beliefs, and political ambitions, after all, whose actions and lack of actions decided the fate of the "unfortunate business."

In discussing the relevant factors at this level, I limit my analysis to those persons who directly composed the chain of command from Israel's top leadership to the agents in the field: Prime Minister Sharett, Defense Minister Lavon, IDF Chief of Staff Dayan, the head of the DMI Givli, the commander of Unit 131 Benzoor, and the commander of the network El-Ad. In order to explain their behavior I will utilize relevant components of their belief systems and operational codes.[98] It should be pointed out, though, that while in some cases sufficient information is available regarding the personal thinking and motivation of the individuals involved (for example, Sharett), very little is known about others—especially Givli, who to a certain extent is the main focus of my interest.

---

98. "Belief system" is the term used to describe a decision maker's fundamental beliefs about: "(a) the nature of international politics and conflict; (b) the extent to which historical developments can be shaped by intelligent or misguided action; and (c) axioms regarding strategy and tactics for dealing with friendly and unfriendly actors in domestic and world political arenas" (George, p. 45). "Operational code" is the individual's perception and diagnosis, as filtered through the belief system, that "provides norms and standards to guide and channel his choices in specific situations" (ibid.).

Prime Minister and Minister of Foreign Affairs Sharett

Sharett was a highly frustrated prime minister. Though ostensibly the leader of his country, he could not exercise control over the most crucial component of Israel's foreign policy, her military posture, since actual (though unofficial) authority in this area rested not with him but with Ben-Gurion. Highly intelligent and gifted with sharp political instincts, Sharett fully understood the tension between his formal and actual capabilities. This tension was the main source of the frustration so well documented in his personal diary. This diary is also the best means of understanding Sharett's beliefs about the nature and prospects of Israel's relations with her Arab neighbors and the rest of the world and about the Israeli political arena during his tenure as prime minister.

On issues of foreign policy and defense Sharett held "dovish" views and headed Israel's "political activism" school of thought. Yet, if he considered the conclusion of peace agreements with the Arab states as Israel's primary foreign policy goal, he believed that this was a mission that could only be achieved in the long run, when the Arab world had recovered from the shock caused by the sudden establishment of the state of Israel. Sharett thus concluded that Israel should be patient and wait until conditions for peacemaking were ripe. Under these circumstances and given the complexity of Israel's borders and of the refugee problem, military disputes were unavoidable until a political solution could be concluded. So, to compensate for her inferiority in territorial, demographic, and natural resources, Israel should seek support from the Jewish people abroad as well as from the Western democracies where she enjoyed basic sympathy (Sharett diary, pp. 81–82).

One of the logical implications of these beliefs was the need to decrease, or at least not increase, Arab hostility towards, the Jewish state. We can thus understand Sharett's reaction to a lecture Ben-Gurion gave in a government meeting on the eve of his resignation. In a sort of "political will" Ben-Gurion foresaw 1956 as the year of maximal danger for Israel's security since by then Arab armies would be ready for a second round of battles. In order to forestall this danger the outgoing leader emphasized the need to upgrade the quality of the Israeli army. Sharett had other means in mind:

> While listening to Ben-Gurion's explanation I was again thinking that we should find an answer to the danger by nonmilitary means:

activating a solution to the refugee problem by submitting a daring and feasible indication of our willingness to pay compensation; improving relations with the great powers; [and] making every effort to reach an understanding with Egypt. (Ibid., pp. 54–55)

Sharett believed, indeed, that Egypt was the key to peace and war in the Middle East. Through this filter he perceived the coming agreement between Cairo and London on the evacuation of British forces from the Suez Zone:

The whole question is, how will the Suez agreement influence [Egypt's President] Naguib? In any event and according to any point of view, this will constitute a brilliant victory for him, but where will he go then? Because of this victory will he perceive himself as strong enough to compromise with Israel, or will the victory intoxicate him into preparing for a war with us? (Ibid., p. 115)

Sharett's views on the arena of Israeli domestic politics where he performed as prime minister are also well documented. Upon entering office he was well aware of the implications of Ben-Gurion's lack of support for his appointment as prime minister.[99] He hoped to solve this problem—not to mention that of trying to fill Ben-Gurion's shoes—through maximal cooperation and coordination at the governmental level between the ministers and at the bureaucratic level between the ministries (ibid., pp. 190, 196). Unlike Ben-Gurion, who had never bothered to intervene directly in the daily management of his government, Sharett opted for a different managerial style and intended to form a direct connection with each of the government's offices (ibid., p. 208). All too soon he found out that none of this mission was within his reach.

For our purposes the most important and relevant factor here is Sharett's belief, based on numerous experiences,[100] that his policy was not being

---

99. One of Sharett's apprehensions was that Ben-Gurion might regret his retirement to the desert and return, earlier than expected, to the decisionmaking center in Tel Aviv (Sharett diary, pp. 205, 329, 333). Certainly this could have undermined Sharett's political status even further.

100. A few examples will suffice. In October 1953, when serving as acting prime minister (Ben-Gurion was on vacation), Sharett conferred privately with acting Defense Minister Lavon to find out whether the IDF intended to conduct a retaliatory act. Lavon admitted that an operation was planned and dismissed Sharett's objections. Within a few hours the IDF carried out the Qibia reprisal in which close to seventy Jordanians, mostly civilians, were killed (ibid., pp. 36–37; Bar-Zohar, pp. 976, 979). Less than two weeks later Sharett suspected that the IDF intended to divert part of the Jordan river water to Israeli territory, a project that constituted a major source of Israel's

implemented by the defense establishment and that the reports he received from the army and the defense ministry were false. As we have already seen, and as Sharett realized, this was true. It is important to note, however, that although the dominance of the defense establishment in the conduct of Israel's foreign and defense policy was a given under Ben-Gurion, Sharett at first hoped to change this situation (ibid., pp. 340, 345–46, 373). His failure to do so only added to his growing frustration.

It is difficult to define Sharett's attitude towards the army. On the one hand, like any other Israeli he was proud of the creation of an effective Jewish military force that had proved its ability in the 1948 war and of his personal contribution to the making of the Israeli military machine. In addition, he perceived the IDF as the main (though not sole) guarantee of Israel's existence, and in this sense he was far from being pacifist or antimilitary. His main concern, though, was with what he regarded as the adventurous, hazardous, aggressive, and unrestrained tendencies that dominated the IDF's modus operandi, especially under the leadership of Lavon and Dayan. Again and again when considering military initiatives (whenever, that is, they were brought to his knowledge) he saw their cons rather than their pros. Some plans he considered politically naive and militarily counterproductive; others were simply "stupidly insane" (ibid., pp. 331–33, 357, 374, 376–79, 435). No wonder, then, that Lavon and Dayan attempted to conceal their military plans from him. As time passed, Sharett started believing that lack of discipline within the military so permeated the ranks that even Lavon and Dayan themselves could scarcely control it (ibid., pp. 524, 526, 686).

On the personal level Sharett viewed Lavon's and Dayan's behavior as the main source of his inability to control Israel's defense policy. While he no doubt appreciated Lavon's intelligence, the more he worked with him the more he became convinced that his Defense Minister suffered from time to time from mental deficiency and even sheer madness. In October 1953,

---

tense relations with Syria at the time and was a subject for discussion in the U.N. Security Council (Sharett diary, p. 85). Sharett learned ex post facto, and even then not always accurately, about such military acts as an ambush within Jordanian territory and the killing of a Jordanian army doctor (ibid., p. 244), the hijacking of Egyptian soldiers on the Gaza border (ibid., p. 431), and various aggressive acts initiated by the IDF on the Jordanian border (ibid., p. 514, 520, 523).

Ironically, as a result of these incidents Sharett had to use intelligence sources of his own in order to find out what the army was doing behind his back. Thus, for example, he was warned by the head of Mossad, Harel, on 10 January 1954 that the IDF was planning a daring operation for the same night (ibid., p. 278; for a similar incident, see p. 122). Obviously, the Arabs were not the only ones to be surprised by Israel's military operations.

when replacing Ben-Gurion, Sharett was shocked by the radical change in Lavon's stands on issues of foreign and defense policy:

> Very interesting and instructive is the revolutionary change in the thinking and spiritual tendencies of this clever and qualified person [Lavon], who at the same time can regulate so well his control mechanisms—he can remove or silence them whenever he needs— after learning the taste of command over the most powerful state machine, the IDF; how his adaption to the dominating spirit among the officers corp has changed his previous political principles and the fundamental concepts in which he believed. (Ibid., p. 50)

About fifteen months later, after having additional experiences, including that of the "unfortunate business," Sharett summarized his opinion of his Defense Minister as follows:

> Lavon proved that diabolical elements exist in his character and intellect. He plotted atrocities that were prevented only by objec-tions of the chiefs of staff—with all their readiness to conduct any adventurous operation. . . . Lavon is responsible for the creation of a regime [in the army] of false reporting, the throwing off of all governmental political restraint, and the defamation of the government among the officer corp. (Ibid., p. 683)

Between October 1953 and February 1955 Sharett struggled with the problem of controlling his Defense Minister. As he revealed later, until he found out about the "unfortunate business" he had hoped to contain Lavon through a special, unofficial party committee combined of Mapai's senior ministers. In this secret forum, whose members were Sharett and Lavon themselves as well as Finance Minister Levi Eshkol, Labor Minister Golda Meir, and Education Minister Zalman Aranne, Sharett always enjoyed the majority. The committee was designed to make decisions on all important issues of foreign and defense policy but most of all to serve as a means of controlling Lavon and preventing the embarrassing confrontations between him and Sharett, who were both from the same party, in government meetings where ministers from other parties participated as well. Despite some initial success,[101] this forum failed to contain the Defense Minister,

---

101. For example, on 11 April 1954 the committee met and rejected (four to one) the Defense Minister's request to take active retaliatory measures against Egyptian military activities in the Gaza Strip (Sharett diary, p. 451).

who succeeded in bypassing not only his Prime Minister but also the senior members of his party.

From early 1954 on Sharett believed that he had the moral right, perhaps even the obligation, to remove Lavon from office. But he felt that the party was not yet ripe for such a move because its key members were not aware of the gravity of the situation. Revealing the truth would have meant washing dirty linen in public, which Sharett wanted to avoid since it would have further undermined his personal status as premier as well as Mapai's dominance in Israel's politics. He opted instead for preparing the ground within Mapai for the discharge of Lavon. The "unfortunate business" caught him in the middle of this process (ibid., p. 623).

Ironically, the failure of the Egyptian operation prevented Sharett from immediately dismissing his Defense Minister. As long as there was any hope of saving the lives of the network members who were facing a trial and possible death penalties, Israel had to deny that she was behind their activities, something that would have been clearly indicated if Lavon were discharged (ibid.). Hence he was dismissed only in February 1955, when the trial was over and two of the network members had already been executed.

Chief of Staff Dayan constituted Sharett's second problem. As with Lavon, Sharett knew Dayan quite well before entering office. As the military commander of Jerusalem, Dayan was an active participant in the Israeli-Transjordanian armistice talks at the end of the 1948 war. He also used to take part, implicitly as Ben-Gurion's unofficial representative, in various Foreign Office meetings.[102] Simply put, Sharett was afraid of Dayan. On the one hand, he appreciated his bright and creative mind. On the other, he was worried by his stubbornness and twisted way of thinking and by what he regarded as Dayan's "very flexible integrity" (ibid., p. 194). For these reasons, but also under the influence of Makleff, whom Dayan was to replace as the IDF's chief of staff, Sharett objected to his nomination. In a private meeting with Ben-Gurion he expressed his opinion that Dayan was a soldier only during wartime but in peacetime was a man of politics. His appointment to the position of chief of staff meant the politicizing of the IDF GHQ (ibid., p. 29). In the government meeting that discussed Dayan's appointment, Sharett said: "Moshe Dayan is not a military man and is not a man of discipline. He is a daring partisan-fighter in time of war and a

102. For example, in July 1950 Dayan participated in a special meeting of senior officials of the Foreign Office, a forum in which he presented very hawkish views (Bar-Joseph, p. 161).

talented adventurous statesman in time of peace. He has no interest in running the army's economy and has no idea how to do it" (ibid., p. 202).

Throughout Sharett's tenure as prime minister his relationship with Dayan was tense. In contrast to his dealing with Lavon, however, Sharett never seriously considered the possibility of dismissing Dayan. One reason for this was formal: the responsibility for the IDF chief of staff's behavior lay with the defense minister rather than with the premier. The second and more decisive factor was that, unlike Lavon, Dayan had the strong backing of Ben-Gurion and the General Staff and his removal could have meant an undesired confrontation with both. And, in any event, Sharett considered Lavon's behavior more destructive than Dayan's.

Sharett was also dissatisfied with the performance of the DMI. One reason was the poor performance of Military Intelligence, which resulted in the false alarm following the Qibia raid (October 1953). Another was the Syrian crisis (in early February 1954), during which Sharett noted in his diary that "it became clear that we actually do not know what happens in 'the Mountain' [Jabel Druze—the Druze region in Syria] and in Syria in general. *At a time of need, a serious deficiency was found in our intelligence*" (ibid., p. 333, emphasis added). Personally, Sharett had a good working relationship with Harkabi but not with Givli, who constituted another source of concern. Following a meeting with him upon his return from studies abroad, Sharett outlined his unease in his diary: "Givli—his studies, frightening ignorance of the Middle East, a malignant one-sidedness, beastly" (ibid., pp. 484–85).

On the whole Sharett's behavior up until the dimensions of the DMI's failure in Egypt were fully revealed was characterized by a cognitive dissonance between what he strongly believed should be done and what he estimated he could do. This tension involved all aspects of policy making, from grand decisions in foreign and defense affairs to resolving the personal distrust he felt for his subordinates, especially Lavon and Dayan. Had Sharett been more decisive at an earlier stage, he could have partially resolved this conflict by dismissing Lavon. Such a move would not only have removed a major obstacle to his efforts to control Israel's foreign and defense policy but could also have served as a clear sign that unauthorized actions would not be tolerated. Since Sharett had little belief in his ability to dismiss Lavon without suffering a major political setback, however, he avoided such a move. But the more he waited, the more distorted became the Israeli line of command, for those who knew about Sharett's true relations with Lavon probably concluded that there was little or no cost at all to be paid for transgressing the norms of discipline. This could only lead to a growing inclination in the lower-ranking officers to do as their superior did, a deteriorating situation that reached its peak in the spring and summer of 1954. In this sense Sharett's personal contribution to the conditions that facilitated the "unfortunate business" was not any action he took but rather his inability to make what he knew was the necessary move: the removal of Defense Minister Lavon from his office at the earliest possible moment.

Defense Minister Lavon

The motivation behind Lavon's behavior during his tenure as Israel's defense minister remains an enigma. As we have already seen, even people like Sharett who knew him quite well could not understand the psychological roots of the revolutionary transformation in his political credo when he became defense minister and his utter disregard for the norms of proper governmental procedure. To some extent, though, the change in Lavon can be explained by his need to gain support from the military. Certainly he regarded the Defense Ministry as a springboard to the prime minister's office, and given his relatively young age (he was only forty-nine in 1954) and the seniority of the position he already held (the Defense Ministry was the most important and influential office in the Israeli government), the leadership of Israel was well within his grasp. To succeed, he knew, he must gain the support of the General Staff.

But although his radical transformation can be rationally explained, if only in part, any attempt to understand his relations with his superiors and subordinates by a similar logic is doomed to fail. For, as we have already seen, by ignoring Sharett and bypassing Dayan he undermined his own position and succeeded in building a coalition of enemies whose hatred and fear of him was their only common denominator. In this sense the Defense Minister's behavior was worse than counterproductive; it was downright self-destructive. A psychological explanation for such behavior is beyond the scope of this work, but it can be assumed that aspects of Lavon's personality not always apparent earlier in his career—arrogance, bitter sarcasm, extreme individualism, and contempt for teamwork and for the opinion of others—came into full expression once he gained the powerful position of Defense Minister (see, for example, Bar-Zohar, p. 1020).

For our purposes, however, two components of Lavon's belief system are highly relevant: his views on Israel's situation in the global and political arena and the policy she should follow in order to strengthen her position; and how he saw his relationship with his superior and his subordinates in the defense establishment.

Some of Lavon's views on the international and regional environment were illustrated in a speech he gave in late 1953. Considering the United States a hostile force, Lavon insisted on rejecting any American proposals aimed at moderating the intense Arab-Israeli conflict even at the cost of increasing Israel's isolation in the international arena. Convinced that the prime Arab goal was the destruction of Israel, he regarded the 1949 cease-fire agreements as an evil plot aimed at destroying the Jewish state. The only reliable source of help in withstanding these dire and ever-increasing threats, maintained Lavon, was the support and assistance of the Jewish people abroad. Since time was working against Israel, the logical (if only implicit) conclusion was that Israel should seek the resumption of hostilities with the Arabs as soon as possible. By thus giving military activism its purest and most extreme expression, Lavon transformed the immediate use of force into a panacea for Israel's growing external problems (Sharett diary, p. 101).

These elements of Lavon's belief system translated into an operational code that supported the wholesale use of power not only in theory but in practice. Moreover, Lavon's operational code had one specific, dangerous, highly relevant characteristic: apart from adhering to the use of traditional military force, he had a special enthusiasm for the exercise of unorthodox means. As we have already seen, upon entering office he showed great interest in DMI's Unit 131, Israel's main arm of unorthodox warfare. Small wonder, then, that in February 1954 he unilaterally cancelled the combined supervision of this unit, deciding that from now on he would personally supervise its activities (Eshed 1979, pp. 38–41; Harel 1982b, pp. 17–18).

No less relevant were Lavon's views on how to use these means, as repeatedly expressed on various occasions. For example, he proposed to Makleff, then chief of staff, that Israel should stir up strife between the United States and Jordan by sabotaging the American embassy in Amman (Bar-Zohar, p. 1022). On other occasions he recommended that Israel should conduct acts of sabotage in various Arab capitals in order to create regional chaos (Sharett diary, p. 562). He told Sharett in one of their regular meetings that Israel "should become crazy" to demonstrate to the Western powers that she was capable of anything and that therefore her interests could not be ignored (ibid., p. 767). According to Dayan's testimony before the Olshan-Dory investigation committee, during a discussion of Unit 131 Lavon proclaimed that Israel should act against the British in order to demonstrate that she was a power to be reckoned with in regional affairs (Eshed 1979, p. 40). This feature of Lavon's operational code was not limited to external affairs. In April 1954 when the government was concerned that anti-Israeli elements might gain control in the coming municipal elections in Nazareth, he suggested stirring up quarrels among the local Arabs and using the turmoil that would be created as a justification for calling off the elections (Sharett diary, pp. 431–32).

The second relevant component in Lavon's operational code was a contradiction of the norms of governmental procedures: Lavon insisted on relating to Sharett only as Minister of Foreign Affairs, ignoring his authority as Prime Minister. He made no secret of this approach, moreover, in his dealing with his subordinates (Eshed 1979, p. 44). This raises two questions. First, how did Lavon succeed in maintaining such an artificial and unilateral distinction? The answer can be found in the variables already discussed at the state level and in Sharett's personality. Second, why did Lavon behave so blatantly, expressing his contempt for Sharett throughout the defense bureaucracy? The answer to this question lies in his personal psychology, a subject beyond the scope of this work.

Lavon's unique approach to hierarchical norms was also evident in his relations with Dayan. It is known that he objected to Dayan's appointment as chief of staff and that he avoided supporting it when the subject was discussed in government meetings (Sharett diary, p. 202). We have already referred to their stormy relations, the main source of which was the independent access to lower-ranking officers that Lavon demanded and Dayan objected to. The relevant factor here is the direct link Lavon succeeded in creating between himself and the heads of the DMI despite Dayan's objections. Lavon took advantage of this link to hatch many adventurous plans, including, in May or June 1954, the option of the Egyptian operation. In so doing he created an operational environment in which the "unfortunate business" could have been initiated even without his orders.

Overall Lavon's personal behavior contributed to the making of the intelligence mishap in two principal ways. First, by initiating various plans whose logic was the same as that behind the Egyptian operation, he helped in creating Givli's assumption that the DMI's independent initiative in Egypt complemented the policies of his own defense minister. Second, by breaking down the norms of hierarchical relationship within the government and the defense establishment, and by doing it so blatantly, Lavon contributed significantly to the creation of an anarchic decisionmaking environment, thus enabling the DMI to behave even more wildly than before.

Chief of Staff Dayan

On 6 December 1954, at the end of the ceremony in which Dayan became the IDF chief of staff, government secretary Sharef advised him that from now on he would have to change his "partisan character" to one more suitable for the leader of the army. Dayan's reply was simple: "It is not I who will change; the image of the Chief of Staff will change" (Dayan 1976b, p. 116). Symbolic as it was, this answer illustrates Dayan's approach to the army now under his command, an army whose construction and esprit de corps were more his doing than anybody else's.

Dayan's opinions on the correct way to use Israel's army were firm and clear. In June 1954 when Ben-Gurion asked him whether he wanted to initiate a war he answered:

> I am against the initiation of war, but I am also against unilateral concessions on our part on any issue, and if the Arabs would like to fight over it—I do not object. Threats should not prevent our actions. For example, on the issue of the Jordan water project. We should complete it. And if the Syrians open fire and attempt to prevent our work by force—we should answer them with force. The same is true with regard to free navigation in the Eilat Straits. We should use the Straits. And if the Egyptians forcibly object—we should not be deterred from war. The approach of Sharett's government nowadays is that on any issue the preliminary question is whether or not "we are in favor of war?" When the answer is negative, the conclusion is—that we should forego any action that might cause war because the Arabs object to it. (Ibid., p. 122)

Noting further that most military reprisals and border clashes with Arab forces ended in failure for the IDF and believing that the source of the problem was negligence on the part of his predecessors, Dayan was convinced that upgrading the army's combat effectiveness was his first-priority goal. He located three specific weak points: "[T]he degree of the soldier's readiness to risk his life in fulfillment of his mission; the place and duties of the officer in battle; and the basic approach of the General Staff to casualty rates in a period of restricted hostilities" (Dayan 1976a, p. 172).

To change all this Dayan used an unorthodox approach. He made it clear throughout the army that in the future any operational failure that did not involve at least 50 percent of casualties would not be acceptable; he encouraged the use and advocated the example of Unit 101, an all-volunteer unit under Major Ariel (Arik) Sharon that was built for special operations across the border; and he short-circuited channels of military hierarchy by personally conducting surprise checkups in various units and visiting soldiers in the field to discuss operational questions with them directly.

These means proved highly effective, and within a short time the IDF's combat standards were upgraded significantly. But they also had a price. First, as Dayan himself admitted, his bypassing of the proper chain of command occasionally set a bad example, serving as an excuse for lower-ranking officers to follow suit (ibid., p. 175).[103] Second, if in the past IDF units failed to reach their operational goals, the paratroopers (who had been integrated with Unit 101) were now leading the army to new operational standards—measured mainly by enemy casualties and targets destroyed—that often exceeded the goals set for them by the political and military authorities. Dayan himself viewed this as his greatest success. Others, like Prime Minister Sharett, were shocked by the destructive results of military operations under Dayan and worried that under his leadership the army had become overly aggressive and underdisciplined.

Although Dayan's relations with Sharett were tense, they did not involve the direct confrontations each had with Lavon. While objecting to Sharett's policy, Dayan still preferred to challenge it indirectly using Lavon as a political shield. The Defense Minister, however, presented just the opposite problem. Although Dayan initially supported Lavon's appointment, he soon found out that he "not only wanted to run the army, he wanted to do so independently of the General Staff. He was making decisions on purely military matters based on the advice of outsiders and against the recommendations of my senior colleagues and myself" (ibid., p. 177).

---

103. Dayan made a distinction between: (a) situations in which independent decisions were made by the local commander in the field, which he considered legitimate; and (b) situations in which a lower-ranking officer changed the original nature of the operation beforehand without the knowledge of his superiors, which Dayan considered illegitimate and unacceptable. His main problem in this regard was with Sharon and his paratroopers' operations, and when he brought it up, Sharon promised (for what it was worth) to avoid such behavior in the future (Dayan 1976b, p. 132).

In June 1954, following six months of intensified conflict, Dayan used one such incident as a pretext for submitting his resignation. He expected that by upgrading their already tense relations into an open crisis, he would be able to compel Lavon to change his ways. But Lavon preferred to back down, and Dayan realized that his was only a tactical victory: "The crisis was over—but its ingredients remained" (ibid.).

A principal source of conflict between the two was Unit 131 of the DMI. As Dayan recalled in his testimony before the Olshan-Dory investigation committee, he was especially worried about Lavon's direct involvement in 131's affairs:

> All this time there was a conflict between the Defense Minister and me and between myself and the chief of the DMI with regard to the activation of the operational units of the DMI [of which Unit 131 was one]. Phati [Harkabi] thought that the units could and should be activated. I thought that for technical feasibility and political considerations their activation would be useless and would only cause trouble. . . . Lavon had been arguing for a long time that we should act against the British to demonstrate to them that we were a power. Phati supported these ideas, and in order to fight such a war, such units were needed. I have no doubt that the DMI lived under the impression that Pinhas Lavon might well make use of them.[104] (Eshed 1979, p. 40).

While Dayan objected to Lavon's involvement in Unit 131's affairs, and even warned Harkabi and later Givli about it (ibid., pp. 38–40), he cooperated with Lavon in order to prevent Isser Harel from getting involved in the unit's management. One reason he gave for this stand was that activation of 131 was not on the agenda at the time, but more important was his belief that Prime Minister Sharett should be kept away from the unit's affairs (ibid., p. 40). It should be emphasized that this had nothing to do with the need to supply Sharett with a plausible denial of knowledge in

---

104. Contradicting this testimony, Harkabi maintained that there was no conflict between himself and Dayan over the activation of Unit 131 while he served as the acting chief of the DMI. Moreover, at least in one case when Lavon authorized an operation by one of the DMI's operational units—the explosion of a Jordanian bridge by the KATAM unit—Harkabi had second thoughts and asked Dayan to get permission from Lavon to call off the operation. Dayan spoke with Lavon, explained Harkabi's compunctions, and the operation was called off (Harkabi interview).

case of failure but was simply an integral component of Dayan's policy of preventing Sharett's involvement in military matters (ibid., pp. 40–41).

Dayan's personal role in the decision to activate the Egyptian network remains enigmatic even today. He himself used his visit to the United States and France (12 July–19 August 1954) as a means of proving his lack of involvement in the operation (Dayan 1976a, p. 177). But, as we know, the operation started not on 16 July, the date on which Lavon allegedly ordered Givli to activate the network, but on 2 July. Dayan had also read Givli's memorandum of 16 June in which the DMI's chief suggested special activities in Egypt in order to forestall the conclusion of the Anglo-Egyptian agreement.[105] In addition, it is hard to believe that Givli kept his direct superior totally uninformed of the operation. Yet neither of them has ever hinted that Dayan knew of the operation.[106]

What is clear, however, is that Dayan used the "unfortunate business" in order to get rid of Lavon. What is not clear is whether he truly believed that Lavon had ordered Givli to activate the network at their 16 July meeting. But although Dayan knew that the operation had started earlier, in fact while he himself was still in Israel, he supported Givli's version according to which the operation only started following Lavon's order. Certainly this enabled him to wash his hands of any involvement in an embarrassing

105. Before the Olshan-Dory investigation committee Dayan testified that:

> When the evacuation of the Suez Canal began to materialize . . . there was an initiative from the chief of the DMI, who brought to our attention a memorandum and steps which he suggested be taken in order to disrupt the evacuation process. . . . I had my reservations about this memorandum. (Eshed 1979, p. 108)

The memorandum to which Dayan referred in his testimony was probably Givli's report of 16 June. It is known that Dayan rejected Givli's suggestion to send a "test ship" to the canal without an Israeli commitment to react militarily if the ship was stopped by the Egyptians. We do not know, however, if Dayan rejected the memorandum's other recommendations, which included activities by the DMI's operational units in Egypt.

106. A common belief among Israelis who knew of the "unfortunate business" when it was still a state secret was that, "if Ben-Gurion had found out who really gave the order, he would have put out his second eye." This, however, was mere speculation, although Sharett himself was aware of the possibility. In a private letter to Ben-Gurion at the height of the Lavon affair, he noted:

> Theoretically we can think of two other explanations for the affair. First, that an elite group, which included Givli and officers senior to him, was formed in the army in order to make a "defense policy" of its own and initiated a *fait accompli* in this direction.
>
> Second, that the hostility Lavon created within the military elite brought about a conspiracy against him which gave rise to an operation allegedly according to his instructions, or in his spirit in order to discredit him. . . .
>
> I could never believe these options possible but others who are investigating the affair might regard them as theoretically feasible—even without the hard facts. (Sharett's letter to Ben-Gurion, 30 October 1960, Sharett diary, p. 765)

failure. But it was also the best way to make Lavon the architect of the operation. Thus in late October, upon Colonel Givli's return to Israel from a few weeks' stay in Europe, Dayan ordered him to submit a written report of his version of the 16 July meeting. As Dayan must have known, the report Givli submitted on 1 November was false. Yet he accepted it for political reasons since it constituted sufficient evidence of Lavon's responsibility for the operation.

This, however, involved other complications. By the end of October 1954 two other reports by the commander of Unit 131 (Benzoor's 1 August and 5 October reports) were in Dayan's possession. They described how the operation had already started by the end of May and how the first acts of sabotage took place on 2 and 14 July. They proved that the DMI initiated the operation without Lavon's orders and thus contradicted Givli's version. In order to get rid of this testimony Dayan and Givli decided to dismiss Benzoor from the command of Unit 131 and ignore his reports (Eshed 1979, pp. 99–104).[107] Following the submission of his report and under pressure from Dayan, Givli briefed his colleagues on his version of the events of the 1 November meeting (ibid., p. 108). This enabled Dayan to create a military united front against Lavon, thus pounding the last nail into the Defense Minister's coffin.

Dayan's direct involvement in the "unfortunate business" is proof that the "Teflon" effect is not limited to certain American presidents. Yet we can still trace his personal contribution to the conditions that made the Egyptian operation possible. First, there was his lack of support of Sharett's policy, a policy he was obligated to follow regardless of his political preferences. One dire result of this behavior was the barring of Harel from Unit 131's affairs. Moreover, Dayan made no secret in the military or among politicians that he objected to Sharett's policy, thus increasing the IDF's reluctance to follow the Prime Minister's orders. Second and even more important, Dayan's IDF esprit de corps, which emphasized the need to achieve operational goals even at the cost of disrupting the regular chain of command, created a milieu in which unauthorized initiatives by low-ranking officers were acceptable so long as they were successful. Operations such as the "unfortunate business" were not included in Dayan's original intentions, certainly, but the result was the same.

---

107. Had Dayan and Givli really believed that Benzoor's reports were false, they could have subjected the commander of Unit 131 to a military trial. The fact that they preferred to get rid of him without any legal procedure constitutes good evidence that they knew the reports were genuine.

Chief of Military Intelligence Givli

After the Egyptian fiasco everybody who knew the true story of what had happened argued that the operation's basic concept was stupid and naive, that it was doomed to fail from the start. But the concept behind the Egyptian operation had some justification. As we know today—and part of this information was probably in the possession of the DMI in the first half of 1954—the British actually considered using military means (Operation RODEO) if the situation in the Canal Zone deteriorated further. It is not clear what might have triggered a British military action, but it is known that in early May 1954 they warned Egyptian leaders that "if, for instance, a bomb exploded in a cinema, killing a large number of troops, including women and children, the likelihood of the British public accepting any agreement was nil."[108] Even at the beginning of June when preparations for the Egyptian operation were already underway, the British were still considering the use of force against the Egyptian military in order to solve local problems in the Canal Zone.

In this sense, Machiavellian as it was, the fundamental concept behind the DMI's operation had a rationale of its own. From the professional point of view, however, it was characterized by three shortcomings. First, it was implemented too late. In July 1954 relations between London and Cairo had already improved and both sides were ready to renew the negotiations. The evacuation of some British combat forces from the Canal Zone—a move that was noted in the British press—was a clear indication that the military option had become obsolete. Second, the targets of Israeli provocations as indicated in the instructions Benzoor gave El-Ad in their Paris meetings (at the end of May and early June 1954) could hardly have prevented the renewal of the talks. Their goal was to create internal turmoil as a means of undermining Western trust in the ability of the Egyptian regime to maintain law and order, and there is no indication that the British government would have broken off negotiations for any reasons short of direct attacks against British targets. Third, because of its lack of material and proper training, the DMI's network in Egypt could hardly have achieved what it was meant to.

These considerations by themselves should have obstructed the implementation of the operation. Yet Givli decided to carry it out despite the odds

---

108. From the British Embassy in Cairo to the African Department in the Foreign Office: "Record of Conversation between Major C. Mott-Radclyffe, M.P., and Doctor Fawzi," 4 May 1954, PRO, FO 371/453.

against it and, even more important, without proper authorization from the higher military and political echelons. The major question of this section is what might have motivated Givli to make this professionally and politically grave decision?

Before turning to concrete explanations, however, we need to emphasize a principal argument: chiefs of intelligence organizations in democratic states are never a simple cog in a large bureaucratic machine. They have the ability to follow orders or not, to initiate action or to avoid it. If they use their discretion and refuse to follow orders for professional, political, or moral reasons, the worst that can happen is dismissal, retirement, a new career. This is a serious price to pay, except when we consider that their colleagues in nondemocratic regimes might well pay for similar behavior with their freedom or their lives. In open societies, moreover, such discretion is usually considered a highly valuable asset, a necessary condition for the proper functioning of an intelligence agency and one of the main criteria for selecting a person to head one.

I emphasize this point here because Colonel Givli as the head of Israeli Military Intelligence in 1954 enjoyed wide latitude for maneuverability in suggesting and selecting a response to the approaching conclusion of the Anglo-Egyptian negotiations. By selecting, without authority, the option of the "unfortunate business," he became directly responsible for Israel's worst intelligence mishap in the first decade of her existence. Even if he thought that his selection corresponded to his Defense Minister's policies, he must have known that it contradicted Sharett's policy and stood in clear opposition to the Prime Minister's efforts to settle the problem by political means. If the "unfortunate business" was a powder keg, therefore, Colonel Givli not only provided the fuse but also lit it. True, all the individuals whose action or inaction brought about a malfunctioning chain of command in Israel in 1954 assisted in creating an explosive situation. But it was Givli who used these circumstances to initiate the idea of disrupting the British evacuation plan by crude provocations, thus providing the fuse, and it was he who gave the order to launch the operation, thus detonating a moral, political, and professional explosion.

Very little has been published on Givli's personality, beliefs, and behavior during his tenure as chief of the DMI in 1954. Most of the attention in Israel was devoted to Defense Minister Lavon, who as a prime candidate for the prime minister's office in the mid-1950s, on the one hand, and a highly controversial political figure, on the other, almost inevitably led to the attachment of his name to the Lavon affair of the early 1960s. Givli drew much less attention and since his dismissal from the DMI in February 1955 has preferred to remain silent. Explaining his behavior thus is a difficult task that involves the use of speculation and circumstantial evidence no less than hard facts.

When appointed in April 1950 to head the army's Intelligence Department, Givli was thirty-one years old and had considerable experience in intelligence work. In the 1940s he served as an officer in the Hagana's Information Service (Shai) and during the 1948 war was the intelligence officer for the besieged Jerusalem district. Following a major reorganization of Military Intelligence in March 1949, he became the head of the Combat Intelligence Unit (IS-1), the largest and most senior branch in the newly organized agency. Shortly afterwards he was appointed as the deputy chief of Military Intelligence and then as its head.

In July 1952 when Shiloah left the newly established Mossad, he suggested three potential successors to Ben-Gurion, one of whom was Givli (Harel 1989, p. 222). In April 1953 the IDF sent Givli to study for a year in England and the United States. Since at that time Israeli officers were rarely sent to study abroad and the chosen few were usually the best and the brightest,[109] this in itself indicates Givli's strong position and the high expectations his superiors in the military had for him. In April 1954 he returned to Israel to head the DMI, now an independent department in the GHQ.

On the surface, then, Givli's career was quite promising. Yet his appointment as chief of Military Intelligence in 1950 aroused controversy, mainly because of his involvement in the Tobianski affair. The court that found Isser Be'eri, the then chief of Military Intelligence, guilty of misconducting the trial of Tobianski, concluded inter alia that the most the accused Hagana officer had admitted at his trial was that he might have unknowingly given information that assisted the enemy. Yet, although this admission was given under extreme pressure, it was used by the improvised court to find Tobianski guilty of treason, to sentence him to death, and to command his immediate execution. More relevant for our subject, the court emphasized Givli's role in this mockery of the judicial process, pointing out that he served not only as Tobianski's investigator but at the same time also as a witness for the prosecution and as a judge. Despite these misgivings, Givli himself was not court-martialed, though only because of technicalities (ibid., p. 126, 172; Teveth 1992a, pp. 109–134).

---

109. Among the officers sent for studies abroad in the first half of the 1950s were Makleff, Dayan, Laskov, Zur, Rabin, and Bar-Lev. They all later became IDF chiefs of staff.

Yet the affair had a long-range impact on his career. When Chief of Staff Yadin wanted to appoint him to head Military Intelligence in 1950, Ben-Gurion objected to the nomination, probably on the basis of Givli's role in the Tobianski affair. Only under pressure from Yadin did Ben-Gurion agree in the end to give Givli the title of chief rather than acting chief of Military Intelligence (Hareven interview). Yet, as long as Ben-Gurion headed the government, Givli was kept on a short tether. Harkabi, for example, became his deputy not only to improve the research capabilities of Military Intelligence but also, possibly, to ensure that no mistakes like the Tobianski affair ever happened again.

Upon returning from his studies in 1954, Givli found a far different political-military environment. Ben-Gurion's replacement as defense minister, Lavon, had no reservations about Givli's past and expressed special interest in intelligence operations as an effective means of conducting Israel's defense and foreign policy. The new Chief of Staff, Dayan, was friendly towards him, and Givli's deputy, Harkabi, left for studies in France. Finally, Military Intelligence became an independent department in the IDF GHQ, thus giving Givli direct access to the Chief of Staff and the Defense Minister. This wider room for maneuverability was complemented by the new distorted norms that as we have seen, characterized the Israeli policymaking milieu throughout this period.

Givli's career prior to his return to Israel, his dubious role in the Tobianski affair, and the new, distorted face of Israel's foreign and defense policymaking environment all help us to understand the background of his decisions about the Egyptian operation. But in analyzing why Givli chose to implement this project without authority and despite the odds against it, we should also take into account some of the personal characteristics that typified him throughout his career, as well as certain components of his way of thinking.

To begin with, Givli was ambitious. Ambition per se is not necessarily negative, but in his case it was accompanied by a lower than average moral restraint. For Givli was a true Machiavellian both personally and professionally, believing that the ends justify the means. His behavior during the Tobianski affair and in the aftermath of the "unfortunate business" is clear evidence that this trait dominated his belief system as far as his personal fate was concerned. The planning of the Egyptian operation and the logic behind it indicate that this way of thinking was not limited to the personal sphere alone but tainted his professional life as well. Also, Givli was no intellectual. He could hardly perceive reality in all its complexity, was fully committed to operational success above all else, and throughout his career never dwelt on the abstract or ethical aspects of the intelligence profession.

To these components of Givli's character and way of thinking two additional factors should be added. First, as was evident in his 16 June memorandum and the briefing he gave the Foreign Office in early August 1954, Givli believed that Israel was in perilous straits, that the evacuation of British forces from the Canal Zone endangered her very existence, and that therefore the evacuation had to be stopped at all costs. Second, in May–June 1954 Givli discussed with Lavon and Dayan various plans for preventing the British evacuation, of which the Egyptian operation was only one option among several. There is no indication that either Lavon or Dayan ever specifically warned him against implementing this plan. Indeed, there are some indications that Lavon supported the plan, although it is clear that he actually never gave it the green light before 16 July (Teveth 1992b, pp. 96–98). Considering Givli's penchant for intrigue, it is probable that he assumed his Defense Minister wanted to avoid authorizing the plan directly but would gladly adopt it if it were initiated successfully at a lower level of command.[110]

If we take these factors into account, we can make some sense of why Givli initiated the idea of the Egyptian operation and of his decision to implement it without proper authority despite its very slim chance of success.

First, Givli probably never realized that launching the operation without authority might constitute a serious crime. In the operational milieu of the first half of 1954 unauthorized operations were almost a matter of daily routine. Sharon and his Unit 101, after all, conducted most of their operations without Sharett's proper authorization and in some cases even without the authorization of Dayan himself. Yet Sharon and his unit were regarded within the military and by Dayan and Lavon themselves as splendid examples of how an officer and his men should act. In such an atmosphere Givli could have readily concluded that the conduct of an unauthorized operation, so long as it succeeded, was an act that deserved reward rather than punishment.

Second, as an operational-oriented person Givli probably believed that

---

110. This way of thinking was reflected in Givli's remark before the Olshan-Dory investigation committee that instructions such as the one Lavon allegedly gave him on 16 July are never given in writing (Teveth 1992b, p. 113; Olshan, p. 265).

nothing besides direct action could forestall the conclusion of the Anglo-Egyptian negotiations. As we have seen, the plan to send a "test ship" through the Suez Canal as a means of suspending the conclusion of the agreement was tabled by Sharett and was unacceptable to Dayan so long as the Israeli government rejected the use of military force if the ship were stopped. So Givli could do nothing to implement that particular plan. But he had an alternative option, that of using the DMI's network in Egypt to achieve similar goals. Even better, the network was a unit of the organization under his command and he had the ability to activate it directly without involving his superiors. For an operational-oriented person like Givli the mere availability of such an option constituted a major source of its appeal.

The temptation became even greater given the atmosphere in the army. All around him officers such as Sharon were making meteoric careers out of their ability to deliver combat success. Unless he made some use of the operational units under his command, Givli's only job was supplying his superiors with information and assessment, paperwork that counted for little in the military milieu surrounding him. Such limited tasks might have satisfied a more intellectually oriented person but not someone like Givli, who regarded special operations as the masterpiece of intelligence work. Add to all this the fact that in 1954 he was the only officer in the military who commanded an operational unit capable of somehow preventing, or at least delaying, a serious setback for Israel, and there is little wonder that Givli acted the way he did.

Third, Givli probably never fully grasped the unlikelihood of achieving the operation's political goals, not to mention the slim chances of operational success. True, he must have known by the end of June 1954 that, even if conducted successfully, the operation could not halt an Anglo-Egyptian agreement. But under the impetus of his ambition to present tangible achievements he probably thought of the project in terms of a "snow ball" that might ultimately bring about the desired results anyway. It seems that he never devoted much thought to the possibility that he and others might be buried under an avalanche in the eventuality of the operation's failing.

There is little doubt that wishful thinking, a typical subcomponent of the unanalytic mind, played a major role here. This mechanism influenced Givli's thinking on two issues. First, it prevented him from understanding that the improvement in Anglo-Egyptian relations in the month or so after El-Ad received his operational instructions in Paris had made the achievement of the project's political goal quite impossible. Second, it enabled him to ignore many of the operational obstacles to the successful implementation of the project. His belief that El-Ad was the best available commander for the operation in spite of serious warnings regarding his reliability, or that an untrained group of local Jews who lacked effective explosives could still conduct impressive acts of sabotage, are just two examples of the negative impact of wishful thinking on his ability to properly judge the merits of the operation.

Students of the decisionmaking process have identified certain criteria to evaluate the quality of decisions (Janis and Mann 1979, p. 11; George, p. 10). Givli's decisions during the Egyptian operation met none of these and, in fact, can serve as a model for ineffective decision making. For our purposes a comparison of Givli's behavior against some of these criteria is very illuminating. Thus, for example, Janis and Mann recommend that the policymaker carefully evaluate if indeed he knows the costs and the risks involved in each possible course of action. Givli, however, hardly considered any alternatives to the Egyptian operation and obviously avoided a careful and thorough analysis of the negative results of the option selected. Another recommendation made by Janis and Mann is that the decision maker should intensively look for new relevant information that can improve his evaluation of the alternatives. Givli not only avoided such a task but also rejected new information that could have indicated that his operation had become politically and professionally impossible. The same is true with regard to the suggestions that new information, even if it does not support the option selected, should be taken into account and that the pros and the cons of each of the alternatives should be checked again in light of this information before making final selection. Finally, Janis and Mann suggest that the decision maker should make detailed preparations for the imple- mentation of the course of action selected, while at the same time paying close attention to possible changes in the plan that may be needed in case problems arise. As we know, neither Givli nor his aides made any prepara- tions for the possibility of the operation's failure.

George (1980, p. 3) suggested six possible sources for deviation from effective decision making. Each of these contributes to an explanation of Givli's failure in making decisions in the Egyptian operation. Considerations such as the need to satisfy personal values, enhance or damage self-esteem, advance or set back career prospects, and strengthen or weaken political and bureaucratic sources supply us with a more general explanation for Givli's deviant behavior in the case under discussion.

Most of the chiefs of the DMI before and after Givli—people like Herzog,

Harkabi, Amit, Yariv, Gazit—were far more intellectual and analytic, thus being aware of the demands and difficulties of effective decision making. It is hard to believe that any of them could have gone about any political problem and its solution in the same manner as did Givli in 1954 with regard to the British evacuation and the operation that was aimed at forestalling it. But even in his case—and Givli was not without merits—the results might have been different had other capable DMI officers been directly involved in the making of the Egyptian project. In April–July 1954, however, this was not the case. It is not that such persons did not exist within the DMI but that for obvious reasons Givli preferred to keep the number of those involved in the operation to an absolute minimum. Only two officers under him, therefore, were directly involved in the project. One was Lieutenant Colonel Benzoor, the commander of Unit 131. The other was Avri El-Ad, the agent selected to command the operation. Neither of them, however, had either the professional and intellectual ability or the personal integrity to criticize Givli's plan. Thus this last potential barrier to the implementation of the operation just did not exist.

Unit 131 Commander Benzoor

Just as chiefs of intelligence organizations should use their personal discretion when evaluating the political and professional merits of a particular intelligence project, so lower-ranking intelligence officers should use their own discretion when judging a given operation's likelihood of success or failure. This principle implies that such a lower-ranking officer should have two qualities. First, he must have the right professional qualifications. In this area he is exactly like any other professional and his work is similar to that, for example, of a physician whose many years of study and practical experience have taught him how to diagnose the symptoms of a sickness and determine a suitable treatment. Second, and this is specially necessary to the intelligence profession, he must have the personal integrity and courage to offer his superiors his own opinion when it differs from theirs.

Benzoor, however, had neither of these qualifications. Serving as a Hagana agent in Iraq for less than two years, gaining some additional experience as an intelligence officer in the Harel brigade during the 1948 war, and debriefing visitors and new immigrants while serving in IS-5 after the war hardly prepared him for commanding Unit 131. When appointed to this post, moreover, Benzoor not only had to build 131 from scratch but also had to learn the art of recruiting, training, and operating agents from the ground up. This was not unusual in the amateurish Military Intelligence of the early 1950s where none of the officers had sufficient experience and training. While others, however, managed to learn the art of intelligence through trial and error and survived, ultimately becoming professionals, Benzoor failed in this task for a variety of objective and subjective reasons.

The objective obstacles to success were many: lack of qualified manpower for service in hostile Arab countries; interbureaucratic rivalry and a low level of cooperation from the Mossad; intrabureaucratic competition that made it difficult for Benzoor to receive the cooperation of other sections in the DMI needed to prepare his unit for action. Most important, however, was the fact that the acid test for success or failure came years before the network was scheduled to be ready for it.

Subjectively, Benzoor lacked many of the qualifications needed to succeed in his delicate job. Although he could have compensated for lack of professional knowledge by learning from others, there is evidence that he actively avoided seeking their advice.[111] Also, Benzoor was not notably clever or sophisticated. Supreme Court Judge Olshan, one of the two members of the committee that investigated the "unfortunate business" in early 1955, received the impression that Benzoor was a confused and unfocused person (Olshan, p. 267). Later the Cohen investigation committee of 1960 concluded that Benzoor lied both in his testimony at Avri El-Ad's trial of 1958 and before the Cohen committee itself, explaining that "his stupidity rather than this wickedness brought him to behave this way" (Eshed 1979, p. 49). It may well be that his superiors reached similar conclusions, since shortly after Dayan became the chief of staff he demanded Benzoor's replacement, a demand of which Benzoor himself was aware (ibid., p. 99). It is possible, then, that Benzoor's behavior was influenced by his knowledge of Dayan's judgment and his anxiety to demonstrate that the Chief of Staff was wrong.

Despite his professional incompetence, Benzoor was aware in April–May 1954 that the Egyptian network was not ready to conduct the operation designed for it and did not have the minimal safeguards in case of failure. He was also suspicious of El-Ad and was obviously aware of earlier warnings about his reliability and the need to keep him isolated from other DMI

111. Some Unit 131 veterans with whom I spoke believed that Benzoor maintained an unnecessarily high level of compartmentation not only for security reasons but also as a means of concealing his lack of professional knowledge and ability to command the unit.

activities. But when ordered by Givli to implement the operation he raised hardly any objections on professional grounds. Here Benzoor's second deficiency becomes apparent. For he not only failed professionally but also lacked the courage and integrity to admit failure and resist instructions that put his agents at risk without supplying them with a minimal safety net in case they were exposed. It might be that Benzoor's interest in concealing his failure to upgrade the network to a minimal operational status played an important role at this crucial juncture. But this is of course no excuse. Benzoor's main responsibility for the failure of the Egyptian operation and the collapse of the network lay in his lack of courage vis-à-vis Givli and his perhaps unintentional readiness to take exceptional risks in order to preserve his personal status.

Operation's Case Officer El-Ad

El-Ad's personality, his qualifications as an agent, and his direct responsibility for the collapse of the Egyptian network are a subject for separate research. For our purposes the most relevant question is whether or not the "unfortunate business" could have been prevented even at his level had a different agent commanded the operation. The answer to this question seems to be yes, especially if we compare El-Ad's behavior with that of Unit 131's second man in Egypt, Binnet.

As we have seen, Binnet decided, probably on his own initiative, to disconnect his mission from that of the network in Egypt. He made this decision on professional grounds, being aware that the amateurish nature of the local agents in Cairo and Alexandria severely jeopardized his own cover. Then on 21 July, two days before the operation started to collapse, Binnet received instructions from Benzoor "to do something to break off diplomatic relations between Egypt and England, in order to prevent the conclusion of the agreement on the Canal Zone. Do not wait for a confirmation. Do whatever you can" (Eshed 1979, p. 70). But Binnet ignored this urgent request, doing nothing that could have put his mission at risk.

Binnet's behavior in conditions similar to El-Ad's suggests that El-Ad too had the option of rejecting his instructions from Israel. This would be true, moreover, even if El-Ad was already a double agent at the time; the point is that, when he became aware of the shortcomings involved in the planned operation, he did nothing to call it off. Given his earlier record, it can be fairly assumed that El-Ad would have behaved exactly the same whether he was double-crossing the DMI or not, since he lacked the required qualifications, especially the professional discretion, needed to act differently. Instead, his adventurism, his need to show off, and his inability to distinguish between fantasy and reality caused him to mislead his superiors about the feasibility of the operation.

El-Ad was the last link in a long chain of incompetence stretching from Prime Minister Sharett to the network in Egypt. A more professional agent would have grasped the inability of the men under his command to carry out their mission successfully and the risks involved in trying to conduct dangerous acts of sabotage without any sort of "safety net." Yet El-Ad claimed in his memoirs that he was well aware of these problems, so it can be assumed that, if a more suitable agent had been selected to head the operation, he could have used his judgment and disobeyed orders that involved unacceptable risks, which is precisely what Binnet did. Unfortunately for those involved in this mishap, El-Ad was the least likely person to do the same.

The Personal Level of Analysis: A Summary

The preceding discussion shows that each of the individuals who composed the chain of command of the "unfortunate business" shared some responsibility for the making of this unauthorized fiasco. This does not imply, however, that the personal responsibility of the individuals involved was similar or equal. Sharett's and Lavon's responsibility, for instance, was ministerial. But whereas Sharett tried, albeit unsuccessfully, to prevent the conditions in which the operation took place, Lavon did just the opposite. Lavon, moreover, bears not only a ministerial responsibility but also a professional one, since by interfering directly in the operational aspects of the intelligence work he, intentionally or not, encouraged the DMI to implement hazardous projects like the Egyptian operation without authority and without taking the necessary precautionary measures. In this sense Lavon contributed more than anyone else to the creation of an operational environment dominated by distorted norms of behavior and a lack of separation between politics and intelligence that facilitated the "unfortunate business."

Dayan's responsibility is similar in nature to Lavon's, though not necessarily as grave. As the chief of staff of the Israeli army he was supposed to ensure the maintenance of that most fundamental norm of civil-military relations, the separation between army and politics. But since Dayan had such clear political preferences, the military under his command inevitably interfered with politics, and politicians like Lavon unavoidably intervened in professional military affairs.

Apart from his direct responsibility for the Egyptian operation and its failure, Givli as chief of Israel's Military Intelligence was also responsible for the lack of separation between politics and professional intelligence work. He lacked the integrity, and perhaps also the motivation, to prevent Lavon from interfering with intelligence operations. At the same time, he himself intervened crudely in Israel's politics by initiating and implementing without authority an operation that had clear political implications. It has been pointed out earlier, but should be emphasized again, that the "unfortunate business" demonstrates the positive correlation between a lack of separation between politics and professional intelligence work and the likelihood of making grave professional mistakes. Conversely, Givli's behavior in the case under discussion serves to confirm the argument that a high level of separation between intelligence and politics is the key not only to effective political control over intelligence activities but also to efficient intelligence performance.

Lastly, Benzoor's and El-Ad's responsibility was mostly professional, and both lacked the professional qualifications needed to give their superiors the necessary sound advice. But, considering that apart from Givli they were the only members of the DMI who were fully involved in creating the operation, their responsibility went beyond mere professionalism in that they should have had the personal integrity to object to the operation on professional grounds. It would seem, though, that even if they had recognized Givli's professional mistakes they both lacked the courage to object to his plans, thus removing the last potential obstacle to the making of the "unfortunate business."

Summary

The 1954 Egyptian operation is an example of unauthorized, crude, and fateful intervention by an intelligence organization in the conduct of a national foreign policy: unauthorized, because both the decision and its implementation were made at a very low level of the Israeli foreign and defense policymaking apparatus, probably without the knowledge, and certainly without the authorization, of higher echelons; crude, since the operation constituted an extreme interpretation of a policy that stood in clear opposition to the means and ends of the foreign policy pursued by Premier and Foreign Minister Sharett; fateful, because, intentionally or not, this initiative could have decided Israel's future for years to come.

The operation was the result of severe external pressure on a fragile decisionmaking and command-and-control system, a system that broke down under this stress since it was manned by undisciplined and incapable policymakers at all levels. Given that in over forty years of existence Israel had experienced no less severe pressures without having her decisionmaking apparatus totally collapse, we can conclude that the two factors that transformed the Egyptian operation into an "unfortunate business" were the fragility of the system and the incompetence of the persons who composed the chain of command of the Egyptian operation, stretching from Prime Minister Sharett to the agents in the field. In this sense the combination of state-level variables and the human factor gives us the best answer to the question of how such a political and professional fiasco could have happened.

8

Plotting Against the Government: British Intelligence and Politics in the 1920s

> British democracy recognizes that you need a system to protect the important things of life and keep them out of the hands of the barbarians. Things like the Opera, Radio Three, the countryside, the law, the Universities, both of them. And we are that system, gosh. We run a civilized aristocratic government machine tempered by occasional general elections. Since 1832 we have been gradually excluding the voter from government. Now we got them to a point where they just vote once every five years for which a bunch of baboons will try to interfere with our politics.—Sir Humphrey Appleby, the Secretary of the Cabinet and Head of the Home Civil Service, in the TV series *Yes Prime Minister.*

The parliamentary elections of October 1924 were unique in Britain's political history for two reasons: it was the first general election to take place while a Labour government was in power; moreover, the fate of the elections was decided, at least partially, when a secret letter from the president of the Communist International (Comintern), Gregory Zinoviev, addressed to the British Communist party, was published in the press four days prior to ballot day. The letter contained instructions to Communist sympathizers in Britain to conduct subversive activities in general, and in the armed forces in particular, in order to prepare the ground for a popular revolution. According to all indications it was leaked by intelligence officers to senior members of the Conservative party who effectively used it to help destroy the electoral chances of the Labour government by exposing what they considered to be the bankruptcy of the government's Russian policy.

The "Zinoviev letter affair" attracted much more attention than a somewhat similar episode that took place three years earlier. On 14 September 1920 intelligence reports on Bolshevik subsidies to the Labour party press organ, the *Daily Herald,* were published in the *Daily Mail* and the *Morning Post*—two of Britain's most anti-Communist papers. This unauthorized leak of highly sensitive intelligence information was only the tip of the iceberg of a larger scheme. The target in this case was not the Labour party but rather the Prime Minister, Lloyd George, who headed a Liberal-Conservative coalition and was considered by senior military and intelligence officers to be too soft in his policy towards Bolshevik Russia and its subversive activities in England.

The sole published account of this affair—Chapter 7 in the third volume of Richard Ullman's excellent history of Anglo-Soviet relations (Ullman 1972, pp. 265–314)—describes in detail some elements of the scheme. Other elements not treated by Ullman will be discussed here. This episode, which I will call the "Henry Wilson affair" after Field Marshal Sir Henry Wilson, the Chief of the Imperial General Staff in 1920 and the key figure in organizing the plot, constitutes the second case study in this chapter.

The nature of the evidence makes it particularly difficult to assess these episodes. In both cases the evidence regarding how sensitive reports were leaked to the press and by whom is incomplete and mainly circumstantial. This problem is inevitable given Whitehall's strict declassification policy towards Britain's peacetime intelligence activities. Yet, despite the lack of direct and reliable evidence, there is no doubt that British intelligence makers interfered with politics more frequently than their American and Israeli colleagues. Moreover, unlike their American and Israeli colleagues who intervened mainly in foreign policy making, British officers interfered with the domestic politics of their own country. At a lower level of intensity this interference involved indirect and direct practical aid for the Conservatives against their Labour opponents. At a higher level, in at least three cases, it amounted to an action that in some of its aspects bordered on a military coup d'état against an elected government. One case, which I will not discuss here, is the conspiracy within MI5 against Harold Wilson in the 1960s and the early 1970s. The other two are the "Henry Wilson" and the "Zinoviev letter" episodes.

These two cases have been selected in order to make and prove two arguments: first, that British intelligence services and their chiefs had during the 1920s (and, evidently, also later) a solid right-wing *Weltanschauung* and an extreme anti-Bolshevik bias; second, that under certain circumstances this bias could be translated into concrete unauthorized action against the legitimate political leadership of the nation.

As with the earlier case studies, the first part of this chapter is historical; it will trace the events surrounding these two episodes, focusing as much as possible on the action taken by senior intelligence officers against the elected government. Since the "Henry Wilson affair" has received relatively little attention in the past, it will be given more attention than the "Zinoviev letter" episode. The second and analytical part of this chapter will examine the conditions that both enabled and motivated the actions of these officers.

THE HENRY WILSON AFFAIR: AUGUST–SEPTEMBER 1920

The Background: January–August 1920

In early 1920 Anglo-Soviet relations were at a stage of no peace and no war. The Allied intervention in the Russian Civil War ended by late 1919, with the failure of the efforts of the White Russian forces to defeat the Red Army, but rapprochement between the revolutionary regime, which was committed to the destruction of the world capitalist-imperialist order, and Britain, still the cornerstone of this system, had not yet begun.

David Lloyd George, a pragmatic Prime Minister and master of compromise, regarded conciliation with Russia both as unavoidable and as the best strategy to end the Communist threat. While considering Bolshevism as a "collection of 'wild theories' " and the Bolsheviks as "barbarians," Lloyd George nevertheless believed that "like other barbarians they could be civilized, and would be if the rest of the world did not permit them to remain in their harmful isolation" (Ullman 1972, p. 467).

At the height of his political power, leading a Liberal-Conservative coalition (in which his section of the Liberal party was a minority), Lloyd George was supported in his policy by some of the most influential members of his cabinet: his political friend, Bonar Law, the leader of the Conservative party who would replace him as Prime Minister in October 1922; Austen Chamberlain, the Chancellor of the Exchequer; and Arthur Balfour, Lord President of the Council and a former Prime Minister (1902–5) and Foreign Secretary (1916–19). Although they all loathed Bolshevik theory and methods, they nevertheless favored a gradual process of rapprochement with Soviet Russia and were ready to take some risk to advance this goal.

Confronting them on this central issue were diehard anti-Bolshevik ministers, the most influential of whom was Winston Churchill, Secretary of State for War and Air since the end of 1918. Both Churchill and Walter Long, the First Lord of the Admiralty, perceived the Bolsheviks as "barbarians." Unlike their colleagues, however, they held that no compromise could be reached with Bolshevism and that in the long term only one side could survive the struggle between the "new" and the "old" order. Hence most diehards used every opportunity to deepen military intervention during the Russian Civil War, and after intervention failed they all opposed Lloyd George's rapprochement policy. Perceiving this as a futile attempt to "tame cobras" (Gilbert, p. 430), they believed that the best strategy against Bolshevism was international isolation that would, in turn, bring about the collapse of Communism in Russia. But Churchill and Long did not tend to cooperate closely on this matter. They were, moreover, a minority in the cabinet, and the Prime Minister tended to ignore them (as well as his Foreign Secretary, Lord Curzon) in shaping his Russian policy. Nevertheless, they enjoyed considerable support among parliamentary backbenchers, while the British press was also extremely anti-Bolshevik.

Communism constituted not only an external problem but an internal one as well. Since the end of the war Britain had faced continual industrial unrest and frequent threats of general strikes. Labor disturbances were not a new phenomenon in Britain,[1] but before the war strikes were merely used by workers as a means to improve their welfare. Two developments during the war—the growing power of the organized socialist movement[2] and the increased share of the government in directing the national economy—transformed any major confrontation in this domain into a critical political issue in that now "a coordinated large-scale strike posed a direct challenge to the traditional foundations of political power in Britain" (Jeffery and Hennessy, p. 7).

The domestic scene became even more complicated owing to outside influence. Widespread revolutionary sentiments and social and industrial

---

1. Miners and railwaymen conducted strikes in 1911. Some industrial disturbances—the most significant of which was the London police strike of August 1918—also took place during the war.

2. Between 1913 and 1919 the number of trade union members grew from 3,416,000 to 6,533,000 (Jeffery and Hennessy, p. 4). The 1915 establishment of the Triple Industrial Alliance—the federation of miners, railwaymen, and transport workers—with the declared purpose of coordinating industrial action on a national basis increased the power of the unions even more.

unrest in Europe further increased these feelings in Britain, and, needless to say, the success of the Bolshevik revolution in Russia could have inspired, as many in Britain feared, a similar development in England. The Russian Bolsheviks, however, were more than exemplary. Since early 1918 they had been funding and advising the efforts towards revolution of their British sympathizers. All the while the British intelligence services were accumulating plenty of evidence concerning these activities.[3]

The conflict between Lloyd George's rapprochement policy and the threat of Bolshevik subversion in Britain reached a new high during the summer of 1920. At the end of May a Russian trade delegation headed by Leonid Krasin, the Commissar for Foreign Trade, arrived in London to commence trade negotiations with Britain. Although the members of the delegation—with the exception of Krasin—committed themselves in writing not to interfere with British domestic politics while staying in England,[4] many British officials, including the intelligence chiefs, feared that subversion rather than trade was their main goal. Britain's prime expert on this subject, Sir Basil Thomson, the Director of Intelligence of the Home Office and the head of the Scotland Yard's Special Branch, had already warned in early February:

> [W]hen trade intercourse with Russia is resumed the opportunity which the Bolsheviks have been waiting for will have come. The stronghold of the Bourgeoisie, as they regard England, will be open for them, and who shall say that the steady stream of Bolshevik agitators upon the minds of immature youths will not result some day in a catastrophe. The experience of Russia and Hungary shows that it would not take much to reduce civilization to the chaos that followed the fall of the Roman Empire.[5]

3. Maxim Litvinov, the semi-official representative of the Bolshevik regime in London until September 1918, and Theodore Rothstein, a longtime member of the British Socialist party, were the main channels through which funds and instructions made their way from Moscow to London during this period (Andrew 1985, p. 236).

4. Krasin gave his word of honor that he would not indulge in subversion. The intelligence services would have been satisfied by his verbal rather than written commitment (if they were asked about this matter at all), since Krasin was considered by them to be a pragmatist and a "good Bolshevik." For a typical example of this attitude, see Report no. 0150 from the American Military Attaché in London to the DMI in Washington re "Differences Between Litvinoff and Krassin," 3 June 1920, *National Archives, Washington* (from herein *NAW*), RG 165 10058–M–2/45.

5. Directorate of Intelligence (Home Office) Special Report no. 14, 2 February 1920: "Revolutionaries and the Need for Legislation," *Public Record Office,* War Office (from herein *PRO, WO*), 32/3948.

The timing of the arrival of the delegation in London also concerned Thomson. At the end of April Poland, despite British warnings, attacked Soviet Russia and by 7 May occupied Kiev. The fate of Communist Russia, but even more so fear that Britain would send forces to aid the Poles, caused much concern in the Labour movement. By the third week of May Thomson warned the government that the "Polish offensive has revived interest in the Russian question."[6] Indeed, the "Hands Off Russia" Committee (which was established in 1919 as a Labour pressure group against British intervention in the Civil War) renewed its activities because of the offensive. But, unlike 1919, its actions were not limited now to propaganda alone. On 11 May dockers refused to load munitions for Poland on to the S.S. *Jolly George,* and four days later the ship had to leave the harbor without them. A precedent was established. For the first time workers took "direct action" not in domestic politics but in foreign policy and made their point. Yet Thomson was not terribly concerned. On the basis of his agents' reports he estimated that "most of the agitation will end in talk for there is no real support for the cause of the Russian Soviets among the working classes."[7] A week later, however, he became more alarmed:

> The agitation against the Polish offensive is undoubtedly spreading from the Labour press to the Trade Union officials and is meeting with certain response from the rank and file. It is not unlikely that the railwaymen will come into line with the dockers and refuse to handle material. This action appears to be entirely due to the agitation conducted by the "Daily Herald."[8]

The events of the following two weeks proved that Thomson's fears, as he himself had to admit, were somewhat exaggerated. The railwaymen and the transport workers declined to participate in "Direct Action for political ends," and other indicators showed that "public interest in revolution is declining."[9] June and most of July were relatively calm despite growing evidence of Bolshevik interest in fanning industrial unrest in Britain. But

6. Directorate of Intelligence (Home Office), no. 55, 20 May 1920: "Report on Revolutionary Organizations in the United Kingdom," *NAW,* RG 165 10058–M–2/5.

7. Ibid., p. 1.

8. Directorate of Intelligence (Home Office), no. 56, 27 May 1920: "Report on Revolutionary Organizations in the United Kingdom," *NAW,* RG 165, 10058–M–2/7.

9. Directorate of Intelligence (Home Office), no. 58, 10 June 1920: "Report on Revolutionary Organizations in the United Kingdom," *NAW,* RG 165 10058–M–2/9.

towards the end of July the situation was deemed to have worsened again. Thomson's weekly report of 30 July 1920 opened with a warning: "The situation has now become menacing." He learned that a miners' strike scheduled for the second half of September could develop into a general strike and a large-scale confrontation between the workers and the government. The Director of Intelligence was also alarmed by a growth of revolutionary feelings as evidenced by an "increase in sale of Bolshevik literature and in the attendance at extreme meetings in Yorkshire."[10]

The situation became even more menacing during the first weeks of August, mainly because of developments in the Russian-Polish war. By this time a resurgent Red Army was approaching the gates of Warsaw. The whole Labour movement, truly afraid of British military intervention to save Poland, organized against such action. On 9 August the Labour party leadership established the "Council of Action" with the declared intention of opposing intervention by parliamentary as well as extra-parliamentary means. Within a few days hundreds of local councils were established throughout the country. Thomson followed these developments with great concern, informing the government that the "possibility of war with Russia caused an amazing outburst of feelings." In order to demonstrate how serious the situation was, he quoted one of his agents who wrote him: "Never have we known such an excitement and antagonism to be aroused against any project as has been aroused among the workers by the possibility of war with Russia. On every hand ex-Service men are saying they will never take part in any war. The workers are dead against a war with Russia."[11]

But a direct confrontation between workers and government, so it seems, was not the main concern of the Director of Intelligence. After all, he presumably knew that, despite pressure from diehard cabinet members, Lloyd George had no intention of intervening militarily in the crisis and was seeking solely to save the Poles by securing a ceasefire between them and the Soviets. The fear that "men would be recalled to the Colours," as many in England believed, was groundless. What concerned Thomson more was the united front of "moderate" and "extreme" Labour and trade union leaders as symbolized by the establishment of the national and local Councils of Action. "It is [he warned the government] a new departure for the Labour

10. Directorate of Intelligence (Home Office), no. 65, 30 July 1920: "Report on Revolutionary Organizations in the United Kingdom," *NAW,* RG 165, 10058–M–2/23, pp. 1, 5.

11. Directorate of Intelligence (Home Office), no. 67, 12 August 1920: "Report on Revolutionary Organizations in the United Kingdom," *NAW,* RG 165, 10058–M–2/28.

Party to force the hand of the Government in a matter of foreign policy, and it is a precedent that will not be easily forgotten."[12]

During early August, moreover, Thomson was concerned by the Bolsheviks' increased ability to manipulate anti-interventionist feelings in order to suit their own purposes. Since the end of May he had warned the government that the members of the Soviet trade delegation had broken their pledge not to interfere with British domestic politics.[13] By mid-July the secret services secured detailed and reliable evidence regarding Bolshevik intentions to subsidize the *Daily Herald*;[14] by the end of the month Thomson informed the government that actual financial transactions were already under way.[15] As fears of a major crisis rose high in August, the Director of Intelligence blamed the *Daily Herald*—"the official organ of the 'Council of Action' and of Moscow"—for stirring up tensions as a "faithful service to the Soviet Government" for funds already received.[16]

Financing the *Daily Herald* was not the only means used by the Soviets to influence events in Britain. Since mid-August the code breakers of the Government Code and Cypher School (GC&CS), who were reading the diplomatic traffic between Moscow and the Soviet mission in London, secured evidence that Soviet delegates were engaged in direct propaganda. At least since the second week of August instructions in this regard were being delivered from Moscow to Kamenev, the president of the Moscow Soviet, who, together with Krasin, headed the trade mission in London from the end of July (Gilbert, p. 423).

12. Ibid., p. 1.

13. Directorate of Intelligence (Home Office), no. 56, 27 May 1920: "Report on Revolutionary Organizations in the United Kingdom," *NAW,* RG 165, 10058–M–2/7, pp. 1, 9–10. Directorate of Intelligence (Home Office), no. 0150, 3 June 1920: "Differences between Litvinoff and Krasin," *NAW,* RG 165 10058–M–2/45. Here, perhaps, Thomson was slightly alarmist. Three and a half months later he informed the government that the delegation members started their subversion activity only in mid-June (see "Weekly Report on Revolutionary Organizations in the United Kingdom," 2 September 1920, *NAW,* RG 165, 10058–M–2/34, p. 3).

14. In mid-July Thomson wrote:

> It [the *Daily Herald*] acts practically as the Soviet organ and has gone even further to the Left since Lansbury's [George Lansbury, the *Daily Herald*'s editor] visit to Russia. In Litvinoff's opinion it is doing important service to the Soviet Government and he recommends that assistance be paid in installments from the Soviet foreign office fund. . . . It is believed that Krassin [sic] will be asked to bring the funds. (Directorate of Intelligence [Home Office], no. 63, 15 July 1920: "Report on Revolutionary Organizations in the United Kingdom," *NAW,* RG 165, 10058–M–2/19, p. 6).

15. Directorate of Intelligence (Home Office), no. XX, 30 July 1920: "Report on Revolutionary Organizations in the United Kingdom," *NAW,* RG 165, 10058–M–2/23, pp. 4–5.

16. Directorate of Intelligence (Home Office), no. 68, 19 August 1920: "Report on Revolutionary Organizations in the United Kingdom," *NAW,* RG 165, 10058–M–2/23, p. 1.

Lloyd George, however, was not overly impressed by Thomson's alarmist reports nor by the new evidence that the Soviet delegates had broken their pledge. As a practical policymaker he was mainly concerned with two questions. Was the British working class ready for a revolution? And could the Bolshevik propaganda stir up such action? His answer to both queries was negative. He therefore ignored growing pressures from cabinet ministers, as well as from other officials, to expel the Bolshevik delegates from London in response to both their actions and the violation of their pledged word. As far as the Prime Minister was concerned, Thomson's warnings fell on deaf ears.

This was not the case with other politicians and high-ranking officers of the British military. For some who had objected for years to Lloyd George's Russian policy, his reluctance to expel the Bolshevik mission from London, despite this incriminating evidence, was the last straw. In the second half of August, faced with Thomson's alarmist reports and the intercepts supplied by the GC&CS, this faction started taking independent action in order to forestall what they feared might become a revolution. Military preparation for the possibility of civil war was one aspect of their action (Ullman 1972, p. 266). The other involved organized pressure on members of the cabinet and on the Prime Minister to expel the Bolshevik delegation, to explain this move by publishing the secret telegrams, to thus calm domestic unrest, and, indirectly, to end the policy of rapprochement with the Soviets as well. The driving force behind this maneuver was the Chief of the Imperial General Staff (CIGS), Field Marshal Sir Henry Wilson.

The Plot: August–September 1920

Henry Wilson

Born in 1864 to a family of Irish Protestant landlords, Henry Wilson began his army career at the age of eighteen. In February 1918, upon becoming the Chief of the Imperial General Staff (the most senior position in the British army), he had behind him thirty-six years of military service, mostly in staff work. During the last decade of his ride to the top, Wilson served as the Director of Military Operations (1910–14), Assistant to the Chief of Staff of the British Expeditionary Force to France (1914–15), Chief Liaison Officer with the French Army (1915), General Officer Commanding the

IV Army Corps in the Western Front (1916), and the British Military Representative in the Supreme War Council (1917–18) (Jeffery 1985, pp. 1–17).

Field Marshal Henry Wilson was, without doubt, one of the most political officers in modern British military history. As a junior staff officer in the Intelligence Department he had already exhibited a keen interest in "the political aspects of his work and the frequent liaison with the Foreign Office" (ibid., pp. 3–4). In the years that followed he established close contacts with Conservative politicians and, far more than other officers, was ready to use them in order to advance military and political goals. Thus he ardently supported conscription—a policy on which there was neither political nor military consensus—and in 1912 he collaborated with Unionist opposition leaders to advance it. Then in 1913, when the government decided to introduce a measure for Irish Home Rule, Wilson, who as an Ulsterman objected to this policy, favored the "very sensible" plans by the Protestants to establish a provisional government and independent armed forces of their own. During the crisis that followed he used his contacts with Unionist politicians in order to neutralize the government plan. After the crisis he declared that the army had done "what the Opposition failed to do" (ibid., pp. 6–10).

Although his reputation for right-wing political intrigue gained him some support from Conservative politicians, the Liberal Prime Minister Asquith was suspicious of him, especially because of his role in the Irish crisis. Hence Asquith rejected suggestions to promote Wilson to CIGS in early 1915, and he had to take a lesser position. Ironically, it was Lloyd George, who after becoming Secretary for War in July 1915 and Prime Minister six months later, put Wilson back on the track of rapid promotion. The two then thought highly of each other. Wilson wrote in his diary in November 1915 that only a "real fighting Government" led by Lloyd George could win the war; Lloyd George regarded Wilson as his man in the armed forces and "undoubtedly the nimblest intelligence among the soldiers of high degree" (ibid., p. 14). It was not surprising then that, when a crisis broke out in early 1918 between Wilson and the incumbent CIGS, William Robertson, Lloyd George fully supported Wilson, thus paving his road to replace Robertson as CIGS.

One of Wilson's main concerns after the war was domestic upheaval and a general strike. Government plans for coordinated action against such threats were prepared during 1919, and because of the weakness of police forces, army units played a substantial role in maintaining law and order in emergencies. Indeed, during the railway strike of September 1919 the army deployed 23,000 soldiers to protect strategic locations (Jeffery 1981, p. 379). Many high-ranking officers, however, objected to such use of the military on practical and principled grounds.[17] Even Wilson himself was hesitant to perform these duties. Yet the source of his concern was neither legal nor ethical but merely his fear that the available military manpower was overstretched. Indeed, so seriously did he take the possibility of revolution at home that in early 1920 he laid the nucleus for a military formation "capable of instant expansion and possessed of sufficient knowledge and authority to prepare plans" for such emergencies (ibid., pp. 382–83).

Connected to Wilson's growing concern for military preparations against revolution was his increasing frustration over Lloyd George's policy—or what he considered as "a lack of policy"—regarding Ireland and Russia. This was, no doubt, also the result of the Prime Minister's reluctance to seek his advice in contrast to Lloyd George's earlier practice. The CIGS expressed some of his beliefs about the government to senior officers. Thus, for example, he wrote to General Allenby in Egypt on 28 March 1920: "There is a total and absolute lack of any power to govern, whether in England against the Unions, or in Ireland against the Sinn Fein or in Egypt or in India" (Jeffery 1985, p. 154).

Wilson's fears and frustrations found their most explicit expression, however, not in letters (which could have been compromised) but in his personal diary. Already in January 1919, following an invitation by Lloyd George to Bolshevik and White Russians to the island of Prinkipo to discuss an end to the Civil War, Wilson voiced fear in his diary that the Prime Minister was a "Bolshevist," adding that his "tacit agreement to Bolshevism is a most dangerous thing." As Ullman points out, calling the Prime Minister a Bolshevist could merely mean a strong disagreement with his policy and cannot be taken literally (Ullman 1972, p. 275). Wilson's paranoia deepened, however, as time passed. In early 1920 the CIGS was already playing with the absurd idea that Lloyd George was not merely a Bolshevist but a traitor. On 15 January, following a discussion with the Prime Minister, he wrote in his diary: "We are undoubtedly coming to a

17. Typically, Adjutant-General George Macdonough, who ex officio was responsible for military aid for the civil power, wrote after the end of the railway strike: "It seems to me that we have been attempting to perform duties which appertain to the civil power, & that in doing so we have not merely greatly strained the military machine *but the British Constitution as well*" (quoted in Jeffery 1981, p. 380; emphasis added).

very, very critical time. I keep wondering if L.G. is a traitor & a Bolshevist, & I will watch him very carefully" (ibid.). In the months that followed he expressed these paranoiac fears repeatedly, especially in connection with the government's Irish policy. In May he noted: "I wonder, is L.G. allowing England to drift into Bolshevism on purpose? I always wonder this when he funks." Two months later he voiced his concerns again: "Is L.G. a traitor? I have often put this query in my Diary" (ibid., entries for 27 May and 23 July).[18]

Wilson's suspicions of the Prime Minister reached their zenith in early August. In order to manage the Russo-Polish crisis by reaching a truce, Lloyd George met with the heads of the Soviet delegation in London, Krasin and Kamenev. Wilson was present as well and loathed the friendly way the Prime Minister treated the two "cut throat" Bolsheviks. Wilson's frustration grew when, in reaction to his suggestion that orders for ceasefire be issued from the field rather than from Moscow and Warsaw since the Polish capital could have already fallen to the Red Army, the three burst into laughter. In his diary he wrote:

> It was quite clear to me that all three knew, & that LG approved of the occupation of Warsaw by the Bolsheviks. It was an amazing 5 hours meeting. It left me, as I say, with a clear sense that L.G. is in company with friends & kindred spirits when with the Bolsheviks, & it raised more acutely than ever *whether he is deliberately shepherding England into chaos & destruction.* (Entry for 6 August 1920, ibid., p. 276; emphasis in original)

The grounds for Wilson's paranoiac suspicion that Lloyd George was a Bolshevist and a traitor are uncertain. In all probability, however, they stemmed from the combination of his own approach to political intrigue, his right-wing *Weltanschauung*, and his political frustrations, together with his long acquaintance with the Prime Minister. Although Wilson knew well that Lloyd George was no fool, he nevertheless regarded the latter's policies at home and abroad as foolish. The only explanation he could find for this dissonance was that Lloyd George was acting deliberately, in the service of a foreign power.

18. Wilson's paranoiac fears were not so unique. First Sea Lord, Admiral Beatty, expressed no less absurd concerns, believing "that the army's inability to hold the Caucasus arose from some 'deep laid plot' by Churchill and Wilson, who were 'out to curry favour with some Party, Labour I suppose' " (Ferris 1989a, p. 11).

In themselves Wilson's paranoiac fears are a small (though bizarre) footnote in modern British history. But the tense atmosphere of August and September 1920 caused him to translate senseless fears into concrete actions. In the second half of August he started preparations for a military confrontation with the Council of Action. Simultaneously, in a series of meetings with high-ranking military and intelligence officers, he formulated means to compel Lloyd George to change his policy both at home and abroad in the matter of Bolshevik Russia.

The Action

On 13 August 1920 a special conference of over one thousand representatives of the Labour movement unanimously passed resolutions approving the use of strikes under the instructions of the Council of Action as a means to pressure the government to avoid intervention in the Polish-Russian war. In his weekly report of 19 August Thomson described this "surprising chapter in British industrial history" in a highly alarmist tone:

> It is being borne upon moderate men throughout the country that the "Council of Action" and its subsidiary Committees are Soviets and that the establishment of such bodies is in conflict not only with the constitution of the country but with the constitution of the Trade Unions themselves. The revolutionaries alone have no misgivings. It has been a gala week for them and some of their speakers have shown symptoms of intoxication.[19]

Notably the Director of Intelligence defined "moderate men" as being those with beliefs similar to his own. Since Lloyd George probably did not consider the Councils of Action to be "Soviets," he was not a "moderate" by Thomson's terminology. CIGS Henry Wilson, on the other hand, was a reasonable man by this criterion. Indeed, four days after the 13 August conference the CIGS started preparing military plans for what he termed "a possible war with the 'Council of Action' " (Ullman 1972, p. 266).[20] His

19. Directorate of Intelligence (Home Office): "Report on Revolutionary Organizations in the United Kingdom," no. 68, 19 August 1920: NAW, RG 165, 10058–M–2/23.

20. It is unclear whether Wilson informed the government about these plans. It is even questionable whether he informed his direct supervisor, Secretary for War Churchill, of these preparations. If Wilson did not, then he was moving towards the edge of what would be regarded as acceptable behavior. It should be noted, however, that a month later, when the miners decided to strike, the CIGS took similar measures. On this occasion it is clear that cabinet members were aware of his action (Jeffery and Hennessy, 1983, pp. 54–55).

belief that emergency action was needed grew upon reading that night a file
of recently intercepted Soviet telegrams that had been solved:

> They are [he wrote in his diary] the most scandalous productions.
> They discuss openly the best method of fomenting discord between
> France & ourselves, the best way of trapping LG & the Cabinet,
> the best way for arming the British "proletariat," the meetings
> which Kameneff had with the "Council of Action" and what "Bob"
> Williams [Transport Workers Federation leader] had promised.
> (Ibid., pp. 276–78)

Above all, Wilson stated that "the most terrifying part of it all is the fact
that L.G. & his Cabinet read all of this & *are afraid* to fling Kameneff &
Krassin [*sic*] out of England" (ibid., p. 268, emphasis in original). For the
first time Wilson recorded that he was considering independent action: "I
feel much inclined to disclose this damaging correspondence myself."[21]

Without Wilson's knowledge, however, on the same day the cabinet itself
discussed the possibility of publishing in the press the recently intercepted
telegrams. Churchill, who wanted to expel the Bolshevik delegation from
London no less than Wilson, was the driving force behind this suggestion.
The Prime Minister, however, rejected it. Instead the cabinet decided to
publish a series of radio messages between Chicherin, the Soviet Commissar
for Foreign Affairs, and Litvinov, his deputy who stayed in Copenhagen.
The subject of these messages was Bolshevik financial aid to the *Daily Herald.*

This was a prudent decision. On the one hand, it served as a warning
signal to Moscow to refrain from such activities, which might wreck the
Anglo-Soviet dialogue. On the other, it saved Lloyd George's policy of
talking with the Bolsheviks through their delegation in London. Since this
mission was not even mentioned in the telegrams, their publication would
not directly lend steam to demands for the delegation's expulsion.[22] From

21. Henry Wilson Diary, *Imperial War Museum* (from herein IWM), entry for 17 August 1920.
This entry, as well as all other entries from the Wilson diary whose source is the Imperial War
Museum, was given to me by Dr. Ferris.

22. The telegrams had to be selected quite carefully. H.A.L. Fisher, the president of the Board
of Education who participated in the meeting, noted in his diary the discussion on whether
"intercepts showing the intrigues of Russia with [the] Daily Herald should be published—[there are]
difficulties in doing so without bringing in Krassin and Kamenev who are mentioned in one crucial
quotation" (H.A.L. Fisher's diary, *Bodleian Library,* Oxford, entry for 17 August 1920. This
document was given to me by Dr. Ferris). The "crucial quotation" was not published. See also
Thomson's report to Wilson on 18 August.

the intelligence perspective, moreover, the potential damage to the ability of the GC&CS to read Bolshevik diplomatic traffic was relatively small. The cipher used by Chicherin and Litvinov ("Marta") was of a lower grade than that used in the telegrams exchanged between Moscow and the mission in London. It was hoped that the Soviets would not realize that their higher-grade ciphers were broken as well. The cabinet also attempted to conceal the fact that Britain was able to read foreign diplomatic traffic by creating the impression that the source of the telegrams was not British.[23] Yet, prudent as it was, the cabinet decision to publish only these telegrams naturally failed to satisfy the hardliners, who still demanded the expulsion of the Bolshevik delegation from London and the cancellation of the pending Anglo-Russian dialogue.

It is in this context that Wilson started on 18 August to weave the first strands of a web between high-ranking military officers, intelligence makers, and politicians, with the goal of compelling Lloyd George (who on the same day left for a long vacation in Switzerland) to change his policies. The main source for these events, Wilson's personal diary, will be used here extensively.

The CIGS's first act on the morning of 18 August was to discuss the situation with close fellow officers:

> I thought much over those "intercepts" which I read last night and this morning I discussed them with Tim [Major General Charles Harington, Deputy Chief of the Imperial General Staff] and [Lieutenant General] Bill Thwaites [Director of Military Intelligence]. It seemed to me, and they agreed, that we could not pass over them in silence thereby tacitly agreeing to the Bolsheviks plotting our destruction in our very midst, and I thought that I would write a paper.[24]

23. The form chosen to disguise the source of the telegrams was that they "were picked up by the receiving stations in several European countries" (*Daily Mail*, 19 August 1920). In order to conceal the fact that the telegrams were obtained by British intelligence, they were first released by Thomson in America and then picked up by the British dailies. *The Times*, however, called the Home Office to authenticate the messages and was told that they were indeed real as Britain and other countries had intercepted them. On the basis of this information the *Times*, unlike the rest of the British press, informed its readers that "the following wireless messages have been intercepted by the British Government" (*Times*, 19 August 1920). This angered Lloyd George mainly because it was a crude compromise of Britain's most secret source of intelligence (see Secretary of the Cabinet M. Hankey to Home Secretary E. Shortt, 21 August 1920, and Shortt's response of 23 August 1920 in *PRO*, Cabinet document 21/179). In any event, the Soviets failed to make use of the information revealed by the *Times* (Andrew 1985, p. 268).

24. Wilson diary, *IWM*, entry for 18 August 1924.

Before beginning his paper, however, Wilson called the Director of Intelligence:

> [Thomson] told me some curious things. He was publishing this morning in America and in the "Temps" this afternoon certain wireless messages which showed the connection between the Daily Herald and the Bolsheviks. One of these had an allusion to Kameneff which was cut out by the Cabinet because L.G. said that, if published, there would be an immediate call from the country for Kameneff's removal! He said that [at?] the Cabinet it was decided, in view of the "intercepts," that Curzon should write to Kameneff and say that it now appeared that he was carrying on a propaganda and asking for his reasons. After the Cabinet had gone away L.G. sent for Curzon and put so many conditions on to the letter that finally Curzon said that he could not write the letter—and did not![25]

Thomson did not limit his report to cabinet politics alone. He also revealed suspicions of Lloyd George, mainly because of his close relationship with E. F. Wise, a high-ranking official of the Food Ministry and an unofficial advisor to the Prime Minister, who was the intellectual force behind the policy of economic rapprochement with Bolshevik Russia: "Then there was the question of Wise whose name has been put out on the doors of the Admiralty and W.O. [War Office] but who still has access to 10 Downing Street. Thomson made no bones about the matter and said he was seriously beginning to think that L.G. was a traitor."[26]

Armed with this information and with confirmation from Britain's leading expert on Bolshevik subversion that his suspicion of Lloyd George was not groundless, Wilson decided to express immediately his growing concern to his political boss, the Secretary for War:

> I had two long talks with Winston [Churchill]. I told him that these intercepts had gravely disturbed me and that I found it difficult to understand the attitude of L.G. and the Cabinet, that telegrammes [sic] of this sort put a severe strain on our (soldiers) [sic] loyalty to the Cabinet as though we wished to be loyal to the Government we had a still higher loyalty to our King and to

25. Ibid.
26. Ibid.

England. Winston was much excited. He said it was quite true that L.G. was dragging the Cabinet step by step toward Bolshevism and he enumerated the different steps from Prinkipo to to-day when although pretending to uphold the integrity of Poland we did *nothing* to insure it & we prevented arms & stores passing through Danzig. He asked me to write a note and I said I would.[27]

Wilson's note to Churchill was drafted immediately. Ending his diary entry for this hectic day, the CIGS again voiced his concern regarding Lloyd George's loyalty and the danger of civil war caused by the threat of the Council of Action.[28]

Churchill, for his part, tried on the same day to reverse the cabinet decision of the day before. He assembled another file of intercepted telegrams, marked the most incriminating evidence, and sent them to Lloyd George, Bonar Law, and Balfour with a note saying: "The proofs of *mala fides* on the part of the Krassin and Kameneff mission, & of their breach of their understanding about propaganda are now becoming so serious that I feel compelled to address a memorandum to the Cabinet on the subject" (Gilbert, p. 423).

Four points should be emphasized at this stage. First, on 17 August Wilson was considering unauthorized leaks to the press of top-secret intelligence reports as a means to wreck the policy of his government. Second, Sir Basil Thomson fully cooperated with Wilson during their meeting on 18 August. Even if we do not take Thomson's words, as quoted by Wilson, that he "was seriously beginning to think L.G. was a traitor," at their face value, it is clear that the Director of Intelligence was willing to say dangerous things concerning the Prime Minister and to spread damaging information about him. It seems that he did not reject the idea of becoming a partner in a plot against the Prime Minister, although he did not become fully committed yet. Another intelligence officer, DMI Thwaites, appears to have been far more committed, although in his case his subordination and close friendship with Wilson explain his behavior. Third, although we do not know if Wilson told Churchill about his consideration of leaking the telegrams to the press or of his talks with Harington, Thwaites, and Thomson, it should nevertheless have been clear to the Secretary for War that the CIGS was preparing the ground for a collision with the Prime

27. Ibid. Quoted also in Ullman (1972), p. 278, and, partially, in Gilbert, p. 423.
28. Wilson diary, IWM, entry for 18 August 1924.

Minister. Churchill not only avoided warning Wilson in this regard but, to a certain degree, encouraged his behavior. Thus he supported action against a Prime Minister in whose cabinet he served. One should bear in mind, however, that there was nothing unconstitutional in such support as long as no intelligence documents were leaked to the press by senior officers on active duty without proper authority. Fourth, Wilson's justification for his behavior—that as a military officer he owed a higher loyalty to the King and the country than to the cabinet—reveals a dangerous way of thinking, which in similar situations in other countries had led to military coup d'états.

On 19 August the pressure against Lloyd George increased. Wilson gave Churchill the note he had prepared at the latter's request. The note summarized the situation from the CIGS's alarmist point of view. It began with a political statement that the establishment of the Council of Action rudely challenged "the authority of the Government, its right and its power to govern. . . ." Wilson then described how, while he was preparing the military machinery to face the new threat, he suddenly learned about the telegrams exchanged with the Bolshevik mission in London. After summarizing the Soviet "crimes," he made his main point:

> In view of the dispersion of our forces, in view of the dangerous weakness to which we are reduced in every theatre but more particularly in Great Britain, and in view of the insidious and disloyal propaganda to which all His Majesty's Forces are being subjected *it is a military necessity* to expose the whole of this traitorous combination, to explain to the troops what it is they may be called upon to fight and to make it clear to them by drastic action against both the "Council of Action" and the Russian delegates in England what attitude His Majesty's Government is going to adopt in this matter. Without such action I cannot say what may happen in the event of a Revolutionary attempt by the "Council of Action" in Great Britain and by affiliated societies in Ireland, Egypt, Mesopotamia, India and other theatres. (Ullman 1972, p. 279; emphasis added)

Wilson's note was not only melodramatic; it was also a distortion of reality (though this was probably unintentional) and a crude attempt to use military justifications in order to demand political action. Obviously, the CIGS wanted to crush the Council of Action, expel the Soviet delegation, and break dialogue with Russia. These needs, however, derived from what he believed to be Britain's national interest rather than from military considerations. Since he was a soldier and not a politician, however, he found it difficult to make such demands on political grounds and had to resort to military ones. Wilson's arguments were both factually erroneous and misleading: even Thomson's weekly reports said very little about subversion among and possible threat to the loyalty of the British soldiers. This, however, did not prevent the CIGS from threatening that only if his demands were met could the army be certain to stand against a popular revolt—an unlikely development in any case.

Wilson ended his note by informing the ministers that he was waiting for their decision, implicitly demanding a quick reaction. Indeed, after giving the note to Churchill, the CIGS told Harington (his deputy) and Thwaites that he would not be surprised if the note led to his resignation. Their reaction was, probably, just what he expected:

> [T]hey both said that if I went they also would go & Bill [Thwaites] said that P de B [Major General Sir Percy de Blacquiere Radcliff, Director of Military Operations, then in Warsaw with a special Anglo-French mission] would also go. This would be a severe business for the Government and indeed I don't think that they could stand it on this particular point. (Ibid., p. 279)

Thus, as Wilson perceived it, the confrontation between himself and the Prime Minister had become simply a struggle for power. Wilson's main leverage was his ability to convert the situation into an open crisis (which Lloyd George, of course, wanted to avoid) by an act of collective resignation of senior military officers. Obviously, in order to make this threat as forceful as possible, the CIGS had to enlist to his cause officers from the other services as well.

Wilson started his "mobilization campaign" with the navy where he had a natural ally in the form of Admiral Earl Beatty, the First Sea Lord, whose worldview was sometimes as odd as that of the CIGS and who had in the past been concerned about revolutionary unrest among his sailors. If he could get Beatty to join him, moreover, Wilson would not only be able to form a united front of the two dominant military services, he would also have acquired the support of a formidable figure in Whitehall. But Beatty was on vacation and Wilson had to discuss the subject with smaller fish: the Second Sea Lord, Admiral Sir Montague Browning, and the Deputy Chief of the Naval Staff, Vice Admiral Sir Osmond de B. Brook: "I showed them the intercepts in my room. They both thought my note was strong—too strong—and they did not see how they could help."[29]

This serious setback for the CIGS made the option of an open political confrontation with the Prime Minister far less attractive. He nevertheless succeeded in enlisting to his cause the Director of Naval Intelligence, Rear Admiral Hugh "Quex" Sinclair. The DNI proved to be a useful asset for Wilson's political campaign not only because he thus gained on his side two of the most important intelligence experts in Britain (Thomson and Sinclair—Thwaites was less influential) but also because the GC&CS—the department that deciphered the intercepts—was housed in the Admiralty and was under Sinclair's command.[30] As we shall see, the DNI would use this bureaucratic arrangement to support Wilson's political demands.

While the CIGS was mobilizing forces for political ends, the Director of Intelligence was doing the same. Whether consciously or not, Thomson used the 19 August weekly report to enlist his readers—all men of considerable influence—to support the publication of the intercepts and a confrontation with the Council of Action. Here, as ever, his dichotomy between "moderate" and "extremist" was quite misleading. The summary of his report—the part most likely to be read by busy decisionmakers—emphasized that the publication of the intercepts was the most fruitful strategy to overcome the danger of Bolshevik influence. One section of the summary reported that: "The publication of the wireless messages indicating that the 'Daily Herald' is subsidized from Russia has, to judge from the apologetic tone of the "Herald's" disclaimer, shaken the position of the paper. The publicity happens to have struck the exact psychological moment."[31]

Since the publications referred to by Thomson appeared in the press on 19 August—the same day that the weekly report was circulated—one might guess that these comments were written even before the first reactions to the publication were received. In any case, his remarks seem over hasty. His arguments about the striking success of the first disclosure, moreover, were presumably intended to convince cabinet members and senior civil servants

29. Ibid., entry for 19 August 1920.

30. This arrangement was the result of an interdepartmental agreement from 29 April 1919, which formulated that "whoever was director of Naval Intelligence should always be the head of both sections (constructive and destructive) of the [GC&CS] Department." See Report of Inter-Service Directorate Committee, no. D.C.23, 9 April 1923, PRO, WO 32/4897, p. 6.

31. Directorate of Intelligence (Home Office), no. 68, 19 August 1920: "Report on Revolutionary Organizations in the United Kingdom," NAW, RG 165 10058–M–2/30.

to support the publication of additional telegrams. For those who might have missed the point, Thomson put it bluntly: "Never has there been greater need for propaganda showing that the Government is not the cause of all the evils which mankind has to suffer."[32] In addition, he offered encouraging news to readers who might have feared a direct confrontation with the Council of Action. He quoted one of his "correspondents": "If the time comes for a real fight the saner men, who have been great constitutionalists when it suited themselves, will all be found to be chiefly engaged in getting revenge upon the 'Bolshevik' section." The Director of Intelligence added: "Confirmation of this report has been received from Hull and South Yorkshire and other parts of the country. The reports show that although the men would refuse response to calling up notices, they would support the Government in countering Bolshevik action."[33]

The focus of the efforts against the policy of Lloyd George during the next day was Winston Churchill. Although he left for Rugby a day earlier, he remained in touch with Thwaites to whom he had made it clear that the "more evidence you can secure to compromise Kameneff and Krassin the better. Pray keep me constantly informed" (Gilbert, p. 423). As if in answer to Churchill's prayer, on the same day Kamenev sent Lenin a detailed report describing how the Soviet delegation in London financed the *Daily Herald*. The telegram was deciphered by the GC&CS within hours and was sent to General Thwaites.[34]

In Rugby, meanwhile, Churchill was drafting a cabinet paper. It summarized the most recent intelligence reports, outlined all that was known about Bolshevik subversion, and ended with a firm warning:

> I feel bound to bring to the notice of my colleagues the perturbation which is caused to the British officers who are concerned with this intelligence work when they see what they cannot but regard as a deliberate and a dangerous conspiracy aimed at the main security of the State unfolding itself before their eyes and before the eyes of the executive Government without any steps being taken to inter-

32. Ibid., p. 2.
33. Ibid., p. 4.
34. For a text of the telegram, see Gilbert 1975, p. 424. Gilbert also notes that the message was deciphered on 20 August. For the actual day the telegram was sent, see Lord Curzon's memorandum of 2 September 1920, re "Kameneff and Krassin," in *The Public Record Office*, Foreign Office (henceforth *PRO*, FO), 371 10478, p. 202. The ability of the GC&CS to solve the Soviet messages in real time (though, probably, they did not always have this ability) demonstrates how effective and critical a means it was for the conduct of Britain's foreign policy.

fere with it. In these circumstances the Government might at any time find itself confronted with disclosures and resignations which would be deeply injurious. I therefore ask specifically, What is the service which Kameneff and Krassin are expected to render this country which justifies us in delaying their expulsion? Their presence here is a source of continued and increasing danger. It is an encouragement to every revolutionary enterprise. The miner's strike, with all its indefinite possibilities, is drawing steadily nearer. Are we really going to sit still until we see the combination of the money from Moscow, the Kameneff-Krassin propaganda, the Council of Action, and something very like a general strike all acting and reacting on one another, while at the same time our military forces are at their very weakest.[35]

Here, indeed, Churchill told his colleagues, even more bluntly than Wilson (whose note was to accompany that of Churchill), what the cabinet must do and what might happen should it refuse to do so. The cabinet must expel the Soviet mission; if it failed to do so, it could find itself in a deep crisis owing to collective resignation of the most senior officers of the military services, accompanied by the disclosure of intelligence evidence to justify this act.

Churchill's motivations at this stage, as throughout the crisis, were complex. He felt very strongly concerning the issue at hand but was not himself willing to resign over it. He wanted, so it seems, to cause the cabinet to change its Russian policy but was ready to do so only through the normal process of policy making. There is no evidence to suggest that he favored an unauthorized leak of this material even as a last resort, although one cannot be certain about that point. The Secretary for War, moreover, was affected by the danger that senior members of the fighting services would resign over this issue, an action that he, no doubt, regarded as honorable and constitutional. He presumably did not share the same views regarding the danger that these officers might disclose intelligence—an approach that would be of dubious constitutionality. Notably, however, there is no evidence that Churchill openly tried to dissuade Henry Wilson from doing the latter, although his actions over the course of the next few weeks can in part be seen as an attempt to prevent this from occurring.

35. Ullman 1972, pp. 280–81. Gilbert (1975), pp. 424–25, gives the date the note was first drafted and quotes most of it but does not quote Churchill's ultimatum.

Churchill's own attitudes were confused; hence, instead of adopting a heroic constitutional position vis-à-vis Wilson, he instead adopted a strategy of crisis management that was normal among British politicians confronted with similar dilemmas.

Even though Churchill and Wilson had different motivations, and even though Churchill was using the arguments of Wilson and others to further his own ends, the Secretary for War was nonetheless also providing some degree of support to the aims of the CIGS. If prior to receiving Churchill's and Wilson's notes the main concern of the cabinet was only the Bolshevik threat, after receiving them the fear of a direct confrontation with a group of high-ranking officers might have become at least as forceful. There is no evidence, however, to suggest that the cabinet members were seriously concerned with the possibility of Wilson's and other senior officers' resignations.

The weekend of 21–22 August was rather calm, with the exception of one telegram from Chicherin in Moscow to Kamenev in London instructing the latter "to carry on a campaign in the Press."[36] The message was probably deciphered by the GC&CS immediately and served to heighten the already tense situation. Most decision makers were, however, out of town: Lloyd George was still vacationing in Lucerne, Churchill was in Rugby, and other senior cabinet ministers were in the country. Action was resumed when the weekend concluded.

On 23 August Churchill returned to London where he met Thwaites and Wilson. The former gave him the most recent telegrams solved by the GC&CS; to the latter Churchill gave his note of 20 August. Wilson's reaction was mixed. While the Secretary for War clearly supported his demands to expel the Bolshevik mission and to act against the Council of Action, Churchill avoided any unambiguous statement that he might take drastic action if the demands were not accepted. In his diary that night Wilson noted bitterly: "He [Churchill] does not mention that *he* had thought of resigning!" (Ullman 1972, p. 281; emphasis in original).

In these circumstances Wilson regarded his main task as being to persuade Churchill to fully commit himself against Lloyd George. In a rather emotional session on 24 August,

> I told Winston it was the chance of his life to come out as an
> Englishman & that in one bound he would recover his lost position

36. The telegram was sent on 21 August. See Lord Curzon's memorandum of 2 September 1920, *PRO*, FO 371 10478, p. 203. It is possible that more than one telegram was sent.

& be hailed as saviour by all that is best in England. I think we have got him pretty well fixed. I warned him that we soldiers might have to take action if he did not & that in that case his position would be impossible. He agreed. He said he was "much worried" about LGs attitude and so am I, and it will take some explaining to ease my mind of the suspicion that LG is a traitor. (Ibid.; Gilbert, p. 425)

Wilson's own account of the talk (the only account extant) reveals that the CIGS was ready to use "sticks" not only against the Prime Minister but also, combined with "carrots," against his immediate political superior and closest ally in the cabinet. His success, though, was very limited. Churchill refused to leap to the fore; he was even hesitant to send the memorandum to senior cabinet ministers.

Information that arrived from Warsaw the same day confirmed earlier reports concerning the Polish counteroffensive that drove the Red Army in ruin far back toward the east. To a less biased mind this might have signaled the end of the crisis: now the popular perception of possible British military intervention that had originally invoked the establishment of the Council of Action and led to intensive Bolshevik propaganda efforts might be expected to alter. To Wilson, however, this turn of events merely offered a promise of complete victory over Bolshevism and the policy of Lloyd George: "As I said to Winston [he wrote in his diary], what a wonderful moment for kicking out Kameneff and Krassin" (Gilbert, p. 425).

In order to enlist maximal support for his cause, on the same day the CIGS conferred with the Chief of the Air Staff, Air Marshal Lord Hugh Trenchard. The meeting was more fruitful than the earlier one with the admirals: "Trenchard with whom I discussed this matter later and to whom I showed the 2 notes [Churchill's and his own] and the intercepts thinks like Basil Thomson, that Lloyd George *is* a traitor."[37] Although the possibility of collective resignation was not discussed in this meeting (had it been Wilson would have mentioned it), it is obvious that the CIGS had in Trenchard a valuable ally in the third military service.

At this stage of events, then, Wilson had behind him a group of military officers and intelligence experts who were either fully or half-heartedly committed to his plans: his deputy "Tim" Harington and the directors of Military and Naval Intelligence, Thwaites and Sinclair, were fully behind

37. Wilson diary, *IWM*, entry for 24 August 1920 (emphasis in original).

him; the Director of (Civil) Intelligence, Sir Basil Thomson, and the head of the air service, Sir Hugh Trenchard, were forthcoming yet not fully committed. On the basis of earlier talks he held with the First Sea Lord, Admiral Beatty, and on recent information received from DNI Sinclair, Wilson hoped to acquire support from the head of the naval service as well (Ullman 1972, p. 280). A collective resignation of this group of officers could certainly shake the cabinet severely and might even lead to its collapse.

On 25 August, and only after another "motivation talk" by Wilson, Churchill at last sent his note and that of the CIGS together with another set of recently solved telegrams to the senior members of the cabinet. He was prudent enough, though, to avoid burning any bridges regarding the Prime Minister. Thus he refrained from any reference to the possibility (which probably he never considered seriously) of joining in any collective resignation, and a day later he sent Lloyd George an additional letter of a much more conciliatory tone.

Perhaps in an effort to gain additional allies in the cabinet, Wilson met that day with Charles Hardinge, the Permanent Under-Secretary in the Foreign Office—a man with powerful and less than complimentary opinions of the Foreign Secretary, Curzon. To the inquiry how Curzon could tolerate the situation, "Hardinge said Curzon would cling to office no matter *what* happened." This ended any possibility of enlisting the Foreign Secretary, if indeed this was Wilson's intention. He voiced his cynical opinion of Lord Curzon: "What a fine type of English gentlemen."[38]

Wilson also noted a rumor that the Bolshevik delegation might soon leave London of its own will. He hoped that "this is not true. I want to force L.G. to fling them out."[39] These few words reveal an odd but illuminating order of priorities: merely seeing Britain getting rid of the delegation and the threat it constituted was now of relatively minor importance. What Wilson really wanted was a public and decisive prestige victory. He sought to rub in the dirt not only the Bolshevik noses but also the nose of his own Prime Minister, to humiliate the Bolshevik regime, to destroy the Prime Minister's Russian policy, to smash all threats of treachery and subversion, and, perhaps, to defeat Lloyd George for his own sake.

Twenty-six August was another active day. Cabinet ministers began to react to Churchill's and Wilson's notes. Churchill informed the CIGS that

38. Ibid., entry for 25 August 1920.
39. Ibid.

Balfour cabled Lloyd George in Lucerne, asking him to consider expelling the trade delegation.[40] Later that day Wilson would hear from Thomson that Home Secretary Shortt intended to send Lloyd George a similar telegram.[41] As Wilson would learn in the next few days, Chancellor of the Exchequer, Austen Chamberlain, the Secretary for Colonies, Viscount Milner, and the Foreign Secretary, Lord Curzon—all favored what he termed a "qualified action." None, however, would break with the Prime Minister over this issue (Ullman 1972, p. 283). This was, no doubt, disappointing but not surprising news for Wilson, who had a low opinion of politicians—"frocks," in his terminology, deriving from "frock coats."

In response to a request by Churchill, Wilson began 26 August by meeting with the intelligence experts in order to prepare memoranda on the nature of the Bolshevik threat and on the desirability of publishing the intercepted telegrams. The distribution of labor was natural: Thomson's paper was to show "the connection between Kameneff and our Labour etc.," that of Sinclair to demonstrate "the Bolshevik danger to the Navy, of the establishment of Soviets in the ports etc." (ibid.). Wilson found no difficulties in overcoming a "minor" problem regarding publication of the intercepts: "Sinclair gave strong reasons against it but wavered them when I told him that the object was to expose our Council of Action and stop the Extremists from stampeding the decent miners, railwaymen, etc. He will draw up a paper for me."[42]

Simultaneously, Wilson and his staff started operational preparations for a confrontation with the Council of Action. Stockpiles of arms—rifles, machine guns, and, later, also tanks—were to be prepared at infantry depots "to start up loyalists when they join up" (ibid., p. 266). It is not clear whether these preparations were reported to the political echelons.

Churchill, meanwhile, wrote another letter to the Prime Minister. Perhaps because he already appreciated the lukewarm response of other senior cabinet members to his memorandum, this note was quite concilia-tory and rested on the authority of experts rather than on political threats.

40. In fact, the information Churchill gave Wilson was not true: Balfour neither asked the Prime Minister to consider expelling the delegation nor wrote his telegram in reaction to the memoranda. Rather he suggested that Lloyd George should consider asking the Soviets to recall Kamenev (Ullman 1972, p. 283, n. 42). If Churchill indeed deceived Wilson intentionally, this is a good indication of his concern that the situation might get out of control and that the CIGS might act independently in response to the disappointing reactions by politicians.

41. Wilson diary, *IWM*, entry for 26 August 1920. For the content of this message and Lloyd George's reply, see Ullman 1972, pp. 292–93.

42. Wilson diary, *IWM*, entry for 26 August 1924.

Churchill informed Lloyd George that he had "a reason to believe that the military and naval personnel engaged in the secret telegrams, including the Directors of Military and Naval Intelligence, consider that the advantages of publishing the telegrams far exceed the disadvantages" (Gilbert, p. 425).

This argument was disingenuous, Churchill sought to give Lloyd George—in Switzerland and thus ignorant of the military-intelligence maneuver—the impression that a united front of intelligence officers supported publication on the basis of professional considerations alone. Churchill, of course, knew well that the directors of intelligence were motivated by a mixture of professional and purely political beliefs. Sinclair's change of mind proves the point. While Churchill probably was not aware of Sinclair's views, he knew those at least of Wilson.

Thomson's weekly report, which was distributed on 26 August, reemphasized the danger of revolution:

> Though the threatened strike of the miners looms so large, it is probably not really the most dangerous factor in the present situation. The real danger is the very rapid growth of revolutionary feelings that has followed the establishment of the "Council of Action." Even the steadier men appear to be interested, and, so far, no opposition has been reported. Revolutionaries are making the most of their opportunity and, in the words of one man "the spirit of revolt grows every day" especially in the engineering trades and among miners and railwaymen.[43]

On 27 August DNI Sinclair drafted, with Thomson's aid, a memorandum on the "pros and the cons" of the publication of the telegrams. On the surface it was a balanced paper, containing strong professional arguments against publication. Sinclair maintained that publication will reveal "that the British Government has a definite system whereby the messages of other Governments are decoded and read," perhaps causing other countries to upgrade their ciphers and hampering or even wrecking British success in this sphere. Furthermore, the political uproar might cripple the ability of

---

43. Directorate of Intelligence (Home Office), no. 69, 26 August 1920: "Report on Revolutionary Organizations in the United Kingdom," *NAW*, RG 165 10058–M–2/33. The report did not include any reference to the 19 August publication of the Soviet telegrams concerning subsidies to the *Daily Herald*. This is somewhat curious given Thomson's enthusiastic reference to this subject a week earlier. Perhaps it indicates that the release of this secret information had a rather limited success after all.

the government to intercept copies of the telegrams sent to and from Britain. The arguments for publication were all political and well known. In essence, Sinclair argued that publication of the telegrams would deliver a severe blow to Bolshevik influence in England, to the *Daily Herald,* and to the Labour movement and its Council of Action (Ullman 1972, p. 285).

The Director of Naval Intelligence, of course, was neither a member of the cabinet nor a political advisor. He was rather a naval officer of the second grade who, owing to a bureaucratic arrangement between the Admiralty, the War Office, and the Foreign Office, had become ex officio chief of the Government Code & Cypher School.[44] The GC&CS, further-more, was not just another intelligence organization but the jewel in the crown of British intelligence—in Curzon's words, "the most valuable source of our secret information . . . the most accurate and, withal, intrinsically the cheapest, means of obtaining secret political information that exists" (Jeffery 1986, p. 455). The DNI nevertheless was willing to use political arguments—ones clearly outside the scope of his responsibility—to support an act that, he admitted, might compromise the whole future of the GC&CS. This paper and Sinclair's behavior throughout the affair reveal his lack of professionalism as an intelligence officer and an almost hysterical overreaction to political events.

During the next days the Chief of the Imperial General Staff and his three partners from the intelligence services continued to prepare the documents needed to persuade the cabinet to change the Prime Minister's Russian policy. On the evening of 31 August they met with Churchill at his house to discuss the "publication of all these 'intercepts' which keep pouring in."[45] Churchill asked Thomson and Sinclair to prepare a cabinet paper demonstrating why the Soviet delegation should be expelled (Gilbert, p. 428). It seems that this demand was not only formal but involved ulterior political motives as well. By making it Churchill sought to compel Thomson to take a clear stand on the issue of publication. He needed Thomson, since other cabinet ministers—mainly First Lord of Admiralty Long and Foreign Secretary Curzon (though in Curzon's case Churchill might not have known it)—had great faith in the Director of Intelligence and his advice. In this sense a clear stand by Thomson could also help Churchill to decide how to pursue his own political goals.

44. Report of Inter-Service Directorate Committee, no. D.C. 23, 9 April 1923, *PRO,* WO 32/4897, p. 6. See also Denniston, p. 49.
45. Wilson diary, *IWM,* entry for 31 August 1920.

Although Wilson was satisfied that "there was some straight talking [during the meeting, and that] Winston is wholly in favor of kicking out Kameneff and Krassin," he was nevertheless discouraged by the Secretary for War's unwillingness to make an open stand. Churchill, instead, was waiting to hear from Austen Chamberlain, Curzon, and Milner. The CIGS had no illusions about how they would act, and he repeated his concerns about the Prime Minister: "Lloyd George's inaction is impossible to understand except on the understanding that he is a traitor and this is the solution of [DMI] Bill [Thwaites], [DNI] Sinclair, and [Director of Intelligence] Basil Thomson."[46]

On the morning of 1 September, Wilson, Thomson, Sinclair, and Colonel Dick of Military Intelligence who represented the DMI met to write the position paper Churchill had requested.[47] The document was submitted to the Secretary for War at noon. Its message was simple and clear:

> The presence of the Russian Trading Delegation has become in our opinion the gravest danger which this country has had to face since the armistice.
>
> This being so, we think that the publication of the de-cyphered cables has become so imperative that we must face the risks that will be entailed. (Ullman 1972, p. 287)

The paper said nothing about the risks entailed to Britain's most valuable intelligence asset. Instead, it described the best way to publish the intercepted telegrams and to avoid the political embarrassment involved in officially revealing the existence of a British code-breaking organization (ibid.).

Through this paper the chiefs of the three intelligence services violated—just as Sinclair had four days before—their professional values. That they had maneuvered in secret for over two weeks, that at least some of them seriously considered the possibility that the Prime Minister was a traitor, and that their motivations were purely political remained unknown to cabinet members. To the latter the paper represented an objective estimate of unbiased professional intelligence personnel. If the intelligence community were ready to sacrifice valuable intelligence assets, how could cabinet members—who knew that they had no understanding of the problems

46. Ibid.
47. Ibid., entry for 1 September 1920.

involved—be more royalist than the King? In this sense Britain's top intelligence personnel used their positions in order to reach political ends. In doing so, moreover, they sought to deceive their cabinet as well.[48]

Nor was this the only means by which they did so: they distorted the situation through a highly selective use of evidence. The same telegrams that supported the alarmist estimates contained more reassuring information. For example, on 25 August Kamenev told Moscow that the power of the right wingers in the Labour movement had made it difficult to ensure the endorsement of even moderate pro-Soviet resolutions. Hence "it is no use cherishing too optimistic hopes of the strength of the [Labour] movement" (Ullman 1972, pp. 269–70). Five days later he urged his bosses to allow him to return home, counting as one of his reasons for this demand the fact that "I am languishing here for lack of something to do" (ibid., p. 301). Although we do not know when these and similar telegrams were solved, given the normal speed of solution of Russian messages they probably became available during the time the alarmist memoranda were written. These types of messages were not delivered to the cabinet with such flourish; nor did they lead the intelligence makers themselves to take a less alarmist view of the situation. Indeed, knowledge of the flagging energy of the bear might well simply have spurred Wilson on to deliver the coup de grace.

Churchill's submission of the cabinet paper prepared by Wilson, Thomson, and Sinclair intensified the concerted effort of intelligence makers, military officers, and politicians against the Prime Minister's policy. Indeed, their pressure was already leading more and more ministers to support the explusion of the Bolshevik delegation. Churchill quickly exploited the situation. At one o'clock on the morning of 2 September he met two of Lloyd George's regular supporters, Sir Robert Horne, the President of the Board of Trade, and Sir Eric Geddes, the Minister of Transport. Wilson,

48. A. G. Denniston is uncertain whether Sinclair discussed the question of publication with the head of the GC&CS. Even if he did so, however, he did not circulate the advice of Britain's responsible expert on the subject, who might well have objected to any disclosures of his department's secret work. While Denniston's position on this issue in 1920 is uncertain, he clearly opposed such actions later. As he wrote in 1944:

> The only real operational intelligence came from our work on the Soviet traffic. We were able to attack their systems step by step with success from the days of Litvinov's first visit to Copenhagen, of Kamenev as their first representative in London followed by Krassin, until the famous Arcos Raid in 1927 . . . when HMG found it necessary to compromise our work beyond any question. From that time the Soviet government introduced OTP [One Time Pad] for their diplomatic and commercial traffic to all capitals where they had diplomatic representatives. (Denniston, p. 55)

present at the meeting, recorded that they decided "to get Bonar [Law] . . . to hold a Cabinet tomorrow afternoon & then if all agreed he is to write to LG & call for the expulsion of Kameneff etc' " (Gilbert, p. 428).

The decision marked the intriguers' finest hour. Wilson was satisfied to note that Horne and Geddes were "as strong as Winston & I for expulsion" (ibid.). In addition, he heard from Sinclair on 1 September that the First Sea Lord, Admiral Beatty, was going to write Lloyd George a strong letter demanding the expulsion of the Soviets.[49]

At 11:00 A.M. on 2 September Bonar Law summoned a "conference of ministers" to 10 Downing Street, attended only by Balfour, Horne, and the Director of Intelligence, Thomson. Churchill, who left that morning for a two-week holiday, was absent. Thomson circulated the latest telegrams solved by GC&CS. One of them proved to be the ace in the plotters' sleeve, as the following account reveals:

> Everyone felt that the last intercept from Lenin where he lays down propaganda as *the* business of the Russian Delegation put the lid on and that there was nothing for it but to clear them out as quickly as possible. Apart from this telegram Eric Geddes was doubtful whether an unprejudiced reader would see in the telegrams more than hostile diplomacy. He put his view to B.L. [Bonar Law] this afternoon and urged that the country knew already about the subsidy to the "Herald"; but when he read this final telegram from Lenin, he took the view of this morning's Conference. Horne took a very serious view of the undermining influence of the Russians on our Labour people.[50]

49. Wilson diary, *IWM*, entry for 2 September 1920.

50. From Thomas Jones, Deputy Secretary to the Cabinet to Sir Maurice Hankey, Secretary to the Cabinet (who stayed with the Prime Minister in Lucerne), 2 September 1920, PRO Lloyd George MSS, F/24/3/8. (I thank Dr. Ferris for giving me this document.) The telegram that angered the members of the cabinet was sent from Lenin to Kamenev on 20 August. It read:

> Use all your forces to explain this to the British workers. Write articles for them yourself, and develop this idea, teaching them the theory of Marx. Give them practical demonstrations how to make use of the vacillations of people like [the secretary of the Labour Party, Arthur] Henderson, and teach them how to agitate among the masses. *In this lies your chief task.* But of course all this must be done absolutely unofficially, and the most prudent diplomacy must be maintained. (Quoted in a memorandum by Foreign Secretary, Lord Curzon, re: "Kameneff and Krassin," 2 September 1920, PRO, FO 371–10478, p. 2; emphasis added. For a full text of the telegram see also Ullman 1972, p. 269)

This evidence led the three ministers to agree that the Soviet delegation should be expelled and that the information regarding its subversive activities should be published.[51] Most illuminating was this additional argument: "So many people now knew the facts that they would be bound to come out and the Government would then be in the position of having allowed them to remain during an industrial crisis though it was fully informed about their actions" (Ullman 1972, pp. 296–97).[52] Three years later, as we shall see, Sir Eyre Crowe chose a similar rationale to explain his decision to release the Zinoviev letter to the press.

The minutes of the meeting, a draft of a statement to announce the decision, and the latest intercepted telegrams were sent to Lloyd George in Lucerne. In another letter Bonar Law asked the Prime Minister to confirm the decision by 4 September. If he did so, Bonar Law would instruct Kamenev and the delegation to leave immediately (ibid., p. 297).

Lloyd George, meanwhile, was drafting a note describing his views. His political instincts probably warned him of growing opposition to his Russian policy at home, which he wished to preempt. The note explains the sound rationale behind the policy Wilson believed to be treason.

> I am [Lloyd George wrote] not much concerned about the propaganda conducted by these men. It is crude [and] violent and displays a complete ignorance not only of the facts but, what is more important, of British working-class psychology. It does more to discredit Bolshevism than any amount of general abuse directed against it. The more the working class get to know about its doctrines the less they will like it. It is only formidable at a distance when seen through impenetrable mists. . . . The real dangers in England do not emanate from Bolshevism. Bolshevism is almost a safeguard to society, for it infects all classes with a horror of what may happen if the present organisation of society is overthrown. (Rowland, p. 527)

51. Thomas Jones informed Hankey that the ministers preferred to publish the telegrams "*in extenso*," as a white paper rather than as a narrative with quotations. This, however, could invoke personal problems for Lloyd George: "If all the telegrams are published as is proposed, the references to Wise will come out and may indirectly affect the P.M." (Thomas Jones to Hankey, 2 September 1920, *PRO*, FO 371–10478, p. 2).

52. Thomson's weekly report of 2 September summarized in detail the activities of the Russian trade delegation since its arrival in London in May. At least part of this summary was based on solved intercepts. Since the circulation of this report was relatively wide—much wider than the circulation of the telegrams—the likelihood of unauthorized leaks of this information to the press grew significantly.

The Prime Minister had other reasons to avoid expelling the delegation: the ability to read its communications, which gave the government "a real insight into Bolshevist intentions and policy"; the embarrassment involved in admitting that His Majesty's Government was reading the letters of its Soviet guests; the damage such an admission would cause to the government abroad and, even more important, among the working class; the ability of the Bolsheviks to conduct propaganda by other means than their delegates in London; the leverage the mere threat of expulsion gave the government in restraining Soviet subversion in Britain and all over the empire; and the economic benefits derived from trading with Russia. Consequently, Lloyd George proposed to warn Kamenev and Krasin to change their ways but urged that Britain avoid considering expulsion. If the cabinet rejected his suggestion, he asked that a final decision wait until his return to London within a week (Ullman 1972, pp. 293–95; Rowland, pp. 527–28).

As we have mentioned, the events of 1 and 2 September marked success for the intriguers. Now, since even Lloyd George's supporters demanded the expulsion of the delegation, the small group of military and intelligence officers could do little save keep a weather eye on the situation in the cabinet, the main theater of contest. Since the debate within the cabinet is of secondary relevance to our subject, it will only be discussed here briefly.

Lloyd George received the dispatch from London late on 3 September, possibly on the fourth. He immediately answered, emphasizing the need to avoid acts that might alienate Liberal and even Labour opinion and asked Bonar Law to postpone any decision until 7 September. A day after his arrival he convened an informal meeting of a small group of ministers—none of whom was a diehard anti-Bolshevik—who agreed to delay the decision for a few more days (Ullman 1972, pp. 298–300; Rowland, pp. 528–29; Gilbert, pp. 428–29).

On the same day that the informal meeting was held, the Cabinet Secretary, Sir Maurice Hankey—a sober-minded and impartial civil servant who regarded Wilson's fears of imminent revolution as "absurdly alarmist"—gave the Prime Minister a memorandum titled "how far we shall lose by publishing the de-coded messages." Hankey, who learned of the intention to publish the telegrams while staying in Lucerne, was mainly concerned with the possible loss of the government's "most valuable and trustworthy source of secret information" (Roskill, pp. 226, 189; Ullman 1972, p. 290). He argued that, no matter what means were taken to conceal the source of the information, the Soviets would ultimately discover that it was their decoded messages. This could cause great damage:

This particular cypher [Hankey explained] is a very ingenious one which was discovered by great cleverness and hard work. The key of the cypher is changed daily and sometimes as often as three times in one message. Hence if it becomes known that we de-coded the messages all the Governments of the world will probably soon discover that no messages are safe. (Roskill, p. 189; Ullman 1972, p. 290)

Although it was a known secret that governments read each other's diplomatic traffic, Hankey continued, there were professional and political reasons not to reveal that Britain was doing so. Professionally, "continental nations are apt to consider us as lacking in astuteness and to underrate us in this respect. It is a pity to remove this amiable weakness of theirs." Politically, "public opinion may experience a shock if it realizes what has been going on." Moreover, the use of other sources of information would enable the government to make "a perfectly good case" against the delegation without compromising the GC&CS (Ullman 1972, p. 291).

Lloyd George apparently made immediate use of Hankey's memorandum. A day after its submission the Director of Naval Intelligence sent the Prime Minister's secretary, J. T. Davies, a note that again justified the publication of the telegrams. Since Sinclair had no reason to forward this letter to the Prime Minister's office on his own initiative, he presumably had been requested to do so following Hankey's memorandum. The note offered no new information but provided good insight into Sinclair's psychology:

From a Naval point of view [Sinclair wrote] I consider the expulsion of these persons to be absolutely essential. I am perfectly convinced that they are at the bottom of all the endeavours to promote unrest in H.M. Navy. The extent of the strenuous efforts that are being made to spread Bolshevism amongst officers and men does not appear to be realised. . . .

Apart, however, from purely Naval point of view, as Head of the Code and Cypher School, I am most strongly of opinion that publication of the telegrams offers such an opportunity of dealing a death blow to the revolutionary movement in this country as may never occur again. I will go so far as to say that *even if the publication of the telegrams was to result in not another message being decoded, then the present situation would fully justify it.* (Ibid., p. 289; emphasis in original)

In this note Sinclair not only took an extreme position regarding the possibility of losing the nation's most valuable source of secret information but also made deceptive use of his title in order to justify his political stand. Despite his nominal role as the head of the GC&CS, Sinclair was not better qualified than others, or even qualified at all, to make judgments on purely political questions. Indeed, if the note was brought to the attention of Lloyd George or Hankey, it probably proved to be counterproductive. It challenged none of Hankey's contentions; it merely demonstrated that the DNI stood on fundamentally political rather than professional grounds.

On the same day that Sinclair submitted his note, Kamenev officially informed the Prime Minister—who may have known it already, courtesy of the GC&CS—that he intended to go back to Moscow for a week "for consultations." Since his return to London would require a British visa and since granting such a visa implied a British decision to let the delegation stay, the cabinet could no longer delay a decision on the latter's future. Accordingly, it convened on 10 September, a few hours before Lloyd George was to meet Kamenev. Given that the Prime Minister was back in London, it is not so surprising that most cabinet members approached the issue now in a far more conciliatory mood. Worried about the future of Anglo-Soviet trade relations if the delegation were to be expelled, they gave the Prime Minister a free hand in the matter (ibid., pp. 300–301).

Lloyd George, presumably frustrated by the Soviet delegation's behavior and also needing to demonstrate some action in accordance with earlier cabinet decisions, used the opportunity of meeting Kamenev (Krasin, Bonar Law, and Hankey, among others, were also present) to express his anger. The Soviets, he made it plain, would have to pay for the delegation's "gross breach of faith," and the price was simple: Britain would not let Kamenev return once he left. Through this artful and artificial means Lloyd George would retain the rest of the delegation under Krasin in London and maintain the trade negotiations. The Prime Minister was less careful in concealing his sources of information. Although he did not explicitly use the intercepted telegrams, he nevertheless left little doubt about the nature of the evidence he had against Kamenev (ibid., pp. 303–7).

These events were a major setback for the intriguers. On 8 and 9 September Wilson still hoped that the delegation would be expelled. On 10 September, however, even before learning of the cabinet's decision, he was considering again the threat of collective resignation. In a talk with Harington and Thwaites he raised the possibility of "getting [First Sea Lord] Beatty and [Air Marshal] Trenchard to join me in telling Prime Minister that if he did not expel Kameneff we 3 would resign. The threat would in my opinion be sufficient and Lloyd George would grovel but of course we must be prepared to carry it out."[53] The Prime Minister's reluctance to take firm action "makes me more suspicious than ever about L.G. and I am gradually becoming certain that partly from cowardice and partly from sympathy he is siding with the Bolsheviks."[54]

A day later the Deputy Chief of Naval Staff, Admiral Brook, who earlier had refused to participate in Wilson's plans, told the CIGS that he did not think Beatty or Wilson could take so political a step. Wilson rejected the warning and maintained that the present action was less political than were the actions of July 1914.[55] Two days later, on 13 September, after receiving another "scandalous intercept," Wilson suggested to Trenchard that together with Beatty they tell the Prime Minister that

> unless the Russians were expelled and the Council of Action were shown up we would resign and then explain our reasons. Trenchard rather favored our going to Lloyd George and saying if he did not send the Russians away we would publish all the intercepts. I don't like this plan very much as we should be putting ourselves in the wrong by publishing, whereas after resignation we could publish to clear our action in resigning.[56]

There is, indeed, a difference between challenging the government while in uniform and after resignation. In this sense, by Wilson's account, Trenchard was ready to take firmer action than even the CIGS. Neither of them, however, had gone to the Prime Minister. Although the domestic situation remained tense throughout most of September, Lloyd George succeeded—by expelling Kamenev—in decreasing the intensity of Bolshevik subversion in Britain and in calming demands in his cabinet for the expulsion of the rest of the Bolshevik delegates. And with Churchill still vacationing in France the diehard military and intelligence officers had no senior ally in the cabinet to help their cause.

53. Wilson diary, *IWM*, entry for 10 September 1920.
54. Ibid., entries for 8, 9, 10 September 1920.
55. Ibid., entry for 11 September 1920. The event Wilson referred to was the March 1914 collective resignation of fifty-eight officers of the 3rd Cavalry Brigade at the Curragh Camp in Ireland in protest of the government's Irish policy. Wilson, a personal friend of the brigade commander who headed the "mutineers," supported this act and, indeed, was working against the government during this event (Jeffery 1985, pp. 9–10).
56. Wilson diary, *IWM*, entry for 13 September 1920.

But somebody, whether on his own or together with others, decided to give this cause another chance. His act proved to be the finale of the "Henry Wilson affair."

The Last Act

On 15 September 1920 two of Britain's most ardent anti-Bolshevik papers, the *Daily Mail* and the *Morning Post,* published detailed accounts of how the Soviets financed the *Daily Herald.* Under the headline "How Russian Jewels Were Sold," the *Daily Mail* described the first in a series of financial transactions that took place in early 1920. This transaction, as we recall, was partially disclosed by the 19 August release to the press of intercepted telegrams between Chicherin and Litvinov. On this subject the articles revealed new details, but none of them was of exceptional significance. The latter part of the story was far more important:

> The next transaction, as far as is at present known [the *Daily Mail* told its readers], began with the return of [one of the *Daily Herald*'s directors] Mr. Francis Meynell from his second visit to Scandinavia, and the second arrival of Messrs. Kameneff and Krassin [*sic*] in London. The latter brought with them packets of gems, some pearls, but most of them diamonds. The diamonds were stones which had been removed from their settings. Some of them were of a large size and great value. (*Daily Mail,* 15 September 1920, pp. 7–8)

The article went on to tell how the diamonds were given by the Soviet delegates to Meynell, how a third party was used to sell them, and what were the exact sums of money that became available to the *Daily Herald* through these transactions.

Even if some of the information in these revelations could have come from nonintelligence sources (for example, from city bankers who might have heard rumors of the gems sale), the accurate details regarding Kamenev's and Krasin's role in the financial transactions could have come only from government sources who enjoyed direct access to intelligence documents. This was also the conclusion of Lloyd George's cabinet, which on the same day discussed the unauthorized leak of sensitive intelligence information to the two papers. The timing of the publications was especially embarrassing for the cabinet. A day earlier, in a letter published in the press, Kamenev denied any involvement in subversion while staying in Britain. Now the cabinet was considering the release to the press of a statement, based on intelligence information, that would prove Kamenev's statement a lie. The minutes of the cabinet meeting of 15 September read:

> Attention was drawn to the fact that the "Morning Post" and the "Daily Mail" in their issues of September 15th had published detailed accounts of the financial transaction between the Russian Trade Delegation and the "Daily Herald." It was pointed out that those disclosures printed only in organs notoriously hostile to the Bolsheviks would detract from the value of the proposed statement to be published by the Government in the whole of the Press. The revelations in the "Morning Post" and the "Daily Mail" appeared to be based on official information and the premature issue of this, at the very moment when the Government were considering the expediency of issuing a statement of this definite question, was generally deplored.[57]

The disclosures in the *Daily Mail* and *Morning Post* differed on one critical point from the government's official response to Kamenev's letter. The official statement dealt only with Kamenev's activities and avoided referring to other members of the Bolshevik delegation.[58] This was in line with Lloyd George's policy of sacrificing Kamenev in order to save the continuation of the dialogue with the Soviets through the mission in London. The disclosures in the two dailies, however, revealed that it was not only Kamenev who broke his pledge not to intervene in Britain's domestic affairs but also Krasin. And since both participated in these activities, the articles could have evoked a demand for the expulsion of the whole delegation rather than Kamenev alone.

Who leaked the secret information to the two papers? Christopher Andrew, who discussed this leak in his study of the history of the British intelligence services, concluded that the most probable source of this disclosure was "an outraged intelligence officer" (Andrew 1985, p. 270). He is obviously right. Indeed, the most probable candidate for this act is the man who headed Britain's anti-Bolshevik activities, Sir Basil Thomson

---

57. Minutes of Cabinet Meeting, 51(20), 15 September 1920, *PRO*, Cabinet document 23/22.
58. For the text of the official statement see ibid., Appendix I.

himself. Although most of the evidence against him is circumstantial, as is usually the case in this type of affair, there is also a direct reference to his role in this act.

To start with the circumstantial evidence, Thomson of course had access to all of the intelligence information about Bolshevik subversion in Britain, and he had in the past practiced the technique of leaking to the press secret reports (e.g., 18–19 August 1920). Furthermore, Thomson was a member of Wilson's plot, the primary target of which was the expulsion of the whole Bolshevik delegation from London as a means of putting an end to Lloyd George's rapprochement policy with the Soviets. In his secret reports he made it clear that the presence of the delegation in England constituted an acute danger to the country.[59] In addition, on 16 September Thomson enthusiastically reported on the effect of the disclosures in the press on the Soviet subsidies to the *Daily Herald.*[60] Given that the government's official paper (which referred solely to Kamenev) appeared in the press only that morning, there is little doubt that Thomson's comments were aimed at justifying the unauthorized disclosures of 15 September.

Finally, there is direct evidence that connects the Director of Intelligence to this leak. H.A.L. Fisher, the President of the Board of Education, who in accordance with cabinet decisions prepared the official statement in response to Kamenev's letter,[61] wrote in his diary on 15 September: "LG is very angry that Scotland Yard has already given away [one word illegible] of the secret to the Morning Post and Daily Mail. The DM [Daily Mail]

---

59. For example, Thomson's weekly report of 2 September warned: "It is not too much to say that the Russian Trading Delegation has become a greater menace to the stability of this country than anything that has happened since the armistice." See Directorate of Intelligence (Home Office), no. 72, 2 September 1920: "Revolutionary Organizations in the United Kingdom," *NAW,* 10058–M–2/34, p. 3. This warning echoed the one in the memorandum to the cabinet prepared by Thomson, Sinclair, and Wilson a day earlier.

60. The summary of the 16 September weekly report included the following paragraph:

> The disclosures regarding the "Daily Herald" subsidy from Russia are reported to have shaken the position of the paper and there is evidence that a considerable body of the workers has lost confidence in it. The Labour leaders who are members of the Board realized that they have been placed in a very false position (Directorate of Intelligence [Home Office], no. 74, 16 September 1920: "Revolutionary Organizations in the United Kingdom," *NAW,* 10058–M–2/36, p. 1)

In another section of this report, under the headline "The Daily Herald," Thomson wrote: "There can be no question that the recent revelations have been a serious blow to the prestige of the 'Daily Herald.' It is reported that the mentioning of the word 'Herald' by speakers in the London area has provoked jeers and criticism" (ibid., p. 4).

61. Minutes of Cabinet Meeting, 51(20), 15 September 1920, *PRO,* Cabinet document 23/22, para. 5.

actually publishes photos of the diamonds." Fisher also recorded in the diary
the Prime Minister's saying that Basil Thomson should have found real proof
that Lansbury (the chief editor of the *Daily Herald*) had the notes (obtained
from the financial transactions with the Soviets).[62]

Thomson, needless to say, was involved in preparing Fisher's official
response to Kamenev. It is very probable that since this statement did not
refer to the whole Bolshevik delegation he decided, either on his own or
with the advice of some of his colleagues, to wreck Lloyd George's policy in
this regard by disclosing that the government's focus on Kamenev was wrong
and deceptive. Since the cabinet never conducted an investigation into this
incident, we can only assume that it was Thomson who conducted this
unauthorized act, but cannot say so conclusively.

Summary

Summarizing the revolutionary events of 1920, Sir Basil Thomson started
his annual report with a prudent observation:

> In the annual survey of the year 1919 it was remarked that there is
> no subject on which it is more unwise to base forecasts: societies
> and individuals who are a menace to the community in one month
> disappeared three months later and the whole current of working
> class thought may be turned into a new channel. In December 1919

---

62. H.A.L. Fisher diary, *Bodleian Library*, entry for 15 September 1920.

In addition to Fisher's diary there is also a letter from Austen Chamberlain to Lord Curzon dated
6 November 1921 that possibly connects Thomson to this leak. In justifying the decision to fire
Thomson, in November 1921 Chamberlain also made the points that:

> I remember that B. T. [Basil Thomson] made an awful mess at the time we ordered
> Litvinoff out of the country and refused him permission to return. You will remember
> that we wanted certain information be given to unofficial currency throughout the Press
> and B. T. so mishandled it that the Morning Post alone got it and coming from that
> source the whole affair was manque. (Curzon papers, *India Office Library and Records*,
> F.112/219 A)

This evidence is rather problematic. It is true that Litvinov was expelled from London and that
the British government refused his return as the head of the Soviet trade delegation. There is,
however, no evidence that the *Morning Post* (or any other paper) has published any leaks about
Litvinov. It is possible, then, that Chamberlain confused Litvinov with Kamenev. If this is the
case, it is possible that Thomson had a mandate from the cabinet to leak some information to the
press. It nevertheless does not explain why Krasin's name was mentioned as well and why the
cabinet condemned this act.

the air was full of discussions on nationalisation—and nationalisation is dead, or at least in a state of suspended animation. In August the Councils of Action, which threatened to become Soviets, burst into view, and the Councils of Action are dead, or at least moribund.[63]

Had the Director of Intelligence adopted this prudent approach to the August–September 1920 events, he would have probably been more reluctant to join forces with Field Marshal Henry Wilson and the others against Lloyd George. For the simple truth was, as Thomson now had to admit, that Lloyd George was right and the alarmist group of military and intelligence officers who conspired against him for fear of revolution wrong. As A.J.P. Taylor summarized the revolutionary threat of the early 1920s in his brilliant study of English history, "Most socialists talked class war, though without any serious intention of using more violent weapons than the strike and the ballot box" (Taylor, p. 192).

There is, of course, nothing unusual in making mistakes in intelligence estimates. But the three intelligence makers who were involved in the August–September 1920 episode had gone far beyond making such mistakes. Together with the military officers—and to some extent with Winston Churchill—Thomson, Sinclair, and Thwaites conspired in order to compel the Prime Minister to change his policies regarding the most crucial national issues. Their immediate goal was the expulsion of the whole Soviet trade delegation from Britain—an act to which the Prime Minister firmly and successfully objected. But they had even more far-reaching goals: crushing the Council of Action (an act that, according to Wilson, could lead to a civil war); putting an end to the rapprochement policy vis-à-vis Bolshevik Russia; and, possibly, though indirectly and as a means to reach their political goals, forcing the Prime Minister out of office by openly challenging—through collective resignation and the use of secret information—his domestic and foreign policies.

In order to attain these goals, the three chiefs of intelligence were ready to violate extensively their professional and ethical codes in at least three, and probably four, respects. First, they estimated the situation, verbally and in written reports, on the basis of political beliefs rather than exclusively on intelligence information. Second, they misled the cabinet by emphasizing

---

63. Directorate of Intelligence (Home Office): "A Survey of Revolutionary Movements in Great Britain in the Year 1920," January 1921, PRO, Cabinet document 24/118, p. 1.

alarmist messages and concealing others of a more reassuring tone. Third, they were ready to sacrifice the GC&CS, Britain's most valuable intelligence asset in the conduct of foreign policy (even when a plausible alternative to the public disclosure of the Soviet telegrams was suggested by Hankey) simply in order to ensure that their political goals were fully achieved. Fourth, if we accept the evidence that it was Thomson who leaked the intelligence information to the *Daily Mail* and *Morning Post* on 14 September, then we have an additional violation: the unauthorized disclosure to the press of sensitive intelligence reports in order to refute the government's policy.

The conditions that fostered this kind of behavior, and the motivation behind it, will be analyzed later, following the second British case study. At this stage, however, a few words about the fate of the principal characters in our story is in order.

Henry Wilson ended his four years as the Chief of the Imperial General Staff in early 1922 and entered politics. In February 1922 he became a member of the Parliament for the Conservative party. Four months later he was murdered on the doorstep of his London home by two Irish terrorists.

Sir Basil Thomson continued to function as the Director of Intelligence until he formally resigned, but in actuality was fired by Lloyd George, in November 1921.[64] He started a new career as a writer of fiction and nonfiction about police work and intelligence. In December 1925 he was arrested with a woman and was charged and found guilty in court for "committing an act in violation of public decency" (Andrew 1985, p. 283). The intelligence virus and fear of Communist subversion never left Thomson. In 1930 he lived in Paris and was engaged in "making reports on the activities of the Russian bolshevicks [sic] in this neighborhood."[65] One can only hope that he avoided mixing his fiction writing with intelligence reporting.

Rear Admiral Hugh "Quex" Sinclair continued to be the Director of Naval Intelligence for some time and then became the Chief of the

64. According to Thomson, the cause for the dispute was "his anti-Bolshevik and communist intelligence work [which] was interfering with Lloyd George's . . . purpose of recognizing the Soviet Government." The Prime Minister's pretext for firing Thomson was that he "was not giving him sufficient information on the situation in Ireland." See from Major Solbert (the American Military Attaché in London) to Major Churchill (G–2, War Department, Washington), re: Sir Basil Thomson, 9 May 1922, *NAW,* RG 165, 11013–9/5.

65. From Brigadier-General Harts (the Military Attaché in Paris) to the Assistant Chief of Staff (G–2, War Department, Washington), 27 January 1930, *NAW,* RG 165 2090–238/2.

Submarine Service. In June 1923, when the head of the Secret Intelligence Service, Captain Sir Mansfield Cumming, died, and in accordance with the tradition that a naval person head the SIS, Sinclair became the chief of this service. Ironically, in 1922 the GC&CS was transferred from the Admiralty to the Foreign Office and thus, upon becoming the head of SIS, Sinclair became responsible, again, for Britain's most valuable intelligence asset. He learned his lesson, however, and would never again support the use of intercepted telegrams for publication. But Sinclair did not draw the other important lesson from the August–September 1920 affair, namely, that intelligence makers (like all other civil servants) should be politically impartial. In October 1924 he had the option of deciding the fate of the elections by leaking the Zinoviev letter to the press. As we shall see, of all possible candidates he was the most likely person to have conducted this unconstitutional act.

THE ZINOVIEV LETTER: OCTOBER 1924

The Background: January–October 1924

The coming to power of a Labour government in January 1924 stirred up a wave of hysterical fears among many Englishmen for the fate of the empire, the civil and the military services, private savings, and even marriage, or, in short, the basic foundations of the traditional English society and way of life. While the bulk of the civil service retained doubts about the Labour government, however, by and large they chose to play according to the accepted rules. Labour did nothing to cause the establishment to regret its decision. From the start Ramsay MacDonald and his cabinet members "recognized that they could make no fundamental changes, even if they knew what to make: they were in 'office, but not in power.' Their object was to show that Labour could govern, maybe also that it could administer in a more warm-hearted way" (Taylor, p. 270).

Indeed, with the exception of new initiatives in housing and education, Labour's domestic policy reflected more continuity than change. Most telling was the government's way of dealing with industrial unrest. As with their Liberal and Conservative predecessors, Labour ministers were ready shortly after entering office to use the Emergency Powers Act—which was so harshly criticized by them while in opposition—in order to curtail strikes by dockers and London tram workers (ibid., pp. 271–75).

Prime Minister MacDonald, who served also as the Foreign Secretary, was more daring in his foreign policy, where he achieved some major successes. His Russian policy, though, was rather prudent. He officially recognized the Soviet government less than two weeks after entering office but nevertheless insisted on Soviet payment of prerevolutionary debts as a condition for a new trade agreement between the two states. For Soviet Russia, now in the midst of a severe economic crisis, improved trade relations with Britain were of crucial importance, but MacDonald's demand could hardly be met owing to lack of sufficient financial resources. Thus Moscow asked for a British loan as a precondition for payment of old debts, and negotiations to reach a comprehensive agreement between the two states began in April 1924.

Paradoxically, from the Soviets' point of view a Labour government was more a curse than a blessing. In ideological terms, it proved that socialists could come to power by democratic means and not only through a revolution as maintained by Bolshevik doctrine. In practical terms, the Labour government could hardly deliver its promised goods—in this case the financial loan—because of bitter criticism in Parliament, because of divisions within the Labour cabinet itself, and because of lack of leverage on the city businessmen.[66] These, indeed, were the main obstacles that led to the breakdown of the Anglo-Soviet trade negotiations in early August 1924. In a last-minute effort and under pressure from the left wing of the Labour party an agreement was reached, but the main questions—Soviet debts and a British loan—were still to be ratified in the Parliament. During the election campaign of October 1924 the Zinoviev letter added much fuel to the Conservative claims against the government for its readiness to grant a loan to the Soviets.

Relations between Labour and the intelligence services were somewhat strained in the beginning but improved later. The intelligence branches of the fighting services and the Special Branch adopted an entirely constitutionally correct attitude towards the government. No evidence at all suggests that GC&CS and MI5 did anything else. One may suspect, however, that the establishment of the Labour government came as a nightmare to some

66. This paradox had led to assertions that the Soviets had an interest in getting Labour out of office and perhaps did so successfully through the Zinoviev letter (Grant, pp. 264–77).

members of SIS. Conversely, many leaders of the Labour party had been subjects of secret surveillance: for years their letters were read, and their personal files were routinely updated. From Labour's point of view, some of the intelligence services represented a form of political police used by right-wing governments for surveillance against a legitimate and law-abiding opposition. Altogether relations between the government and the intelligence services during the first months of Labour in office were cool and were dominated by some degree of mutual distrust.

The intelligence community during this period adopted the stance of being economical with the truth: the services did not lie but did not necessarily tell the whole truth either. The most curious aspect of this issue was GC&CS's stance. Sir Eyre Crowe, the Permanent Under-Secretary of the Foreign Office—the department officially responsible for GC&CS since 1922—seemed to have taken advantage of the establishment of an entirely new cabinet to reduce to a minimum the number of cabinet ministers who either knew of the existence of GC&CS or regularly received its reports on solved messages. Crowe therefore informed only MacDonald that Britain possessed a code-breaking department, and MacDonald, for his own reasons, did not inform any of his colleagues of this fact until the last period of the Labour government (Andrew 1985, pp. 298–300). Labour policymakers, for their part, were not too eager to receive intelligence reports and, in the event they did receive them, tended to suspect them as biased. For example, upon receiving his first weekly report on revolutionary organizations in the United Kingdom, the Prime Minister expressed dissatisfaction not only with the professional quality of the document but also with the fact that only extremists on the left but not on the right were subject to investigation (ibid.; Marquand, pp. 314–15).

As time passed, however, the two antagonists learned to live with each other. Cabinet members, especially Home Secretary Arthur Henderson, discovered the value of intelligence in dealing with industrial unrest, and intelligence makers' earlier fears of a "revolutionary" government lessened in light of Labour's performance. In mid-April 1924 the cabinet appointed a special committee to investigate Communist involvement in industrial unrest. On the basis of intelligence from the Special Branch, the SIS, and MI5, the committee agreed with the services that the Comintern was financing the Communist party of Great Britain (CPGB) as well as Communist members of the trade unions. Furthermore, it recommended to the cabinet that "the Home Secretary should be authorized to disclose informally and in strict confidence, to responsible Trade Union Leaders such information in his possession as to Communistic activities as he may think fit."[67]

Government-intelligence relations went through two additional tests during April and May, when two secret letters from Gregory Zinoviev, the President of the Comintern, to British Communists were intercepted by the services. The first Zinoviev letter, dated 7 April, which was seized during the second half of April by SIS,[68] demanded massive demonstrations on the upcoming 1 May as a means "of exerting a certain amount of pressure upon the [British] Government" towards, the opening of Anglo-Soviet economic negotiations. If negotiations collapsed, Zinoviev instructed, the CPGB was to take all measures to "call wide working masses to the street" for the same purpose. In conclusion the letter informed the local Communists that M. Tomski of the Soviet mission in London would be their contact man in all questions, including financial ones.[69]

Home Secretary Henderson, who learned of the letter from the weekly report, suggested to MacDonald that he consider asking Rakovsky, the head of the Soviet delegation in London, for explanations regarding Tomski's role. Henderson made it clear that such a move could be done only if the authenticity of the letter was proven and if its use would not compromise intelligence sources.[70] The Foreign Office experts who analyzed the problem were of the opinion that additional evidence of Soviet subversion in England was required in order to build a more solid case for diplomatic action.[71] MacDonald accepted their opinion, and the Foreign Office informed the Home Office that no protest could be made at this stage. Nevertheless, the department made it clear that if the Home Office (that is, the Special Branch) could produce "unquestionable evidence of definite acts in this

67. Minutes of Cabinet Meeting on Industrial Unrest Committee, Interim Report C.P. 273 (24), 30 April 1924, PRO, Cabinet document 24/166, p. 4. For discussion of this report and the government reaction, see also Andrew 1985, pp. 300–301; Barnes, pp. 945–46.

68. The fact that the source of this Zinoviev letter was SIS is apparent from a note sent from the Home Office to the Foreign Office asking to consult "the Foreign Office department which furnished the copy to the Metropolitan Police" in ensuring the authenticity of the letter. See Under Secretary of State, Home Office, to Under Secretary of State, Foreign Office, 3 May 1924, PRO, FO 371–10478.

69. Special Branch, New Scotland Yard: "Report on Revolutionary Organizations in the United Kingdom," no. 253, 1 May 1924, PRO, FO 371–10478, pp. 12–14.

70. Under-Secretary of State, Home Office, to Under-Secretary of State, Foreign Office, 3 May 1924, PRO, FO 371–10478.

71. See minutes by H.F.B. Maxse, C. A. Mounsey, N. Bland, and Sir Eyre Crowe to the above-mentioned letter, in ibid.

country by Mr. Tomski or other members of the Soviet Delegation Mr. Ramsay MacDonald will be glad to consider such evidence with a view to taking the matter up with Mr. Rakovsky."[72]

At approximately the same time another letter from Zinoviev to the CPGB was brought to the attention of MacDonald. Dated 17 March 1924, the letter described the composition of the Soviet delegation that was soon to arrive in England for the opening of the Anglo-Soviet talks and informed the local Communists that:

> Of the comrades afore-mentioned, comrade Tomski is provided with full powers by the IKKI [Executive Committee, Third International] and the Executive Bureau of the Profintern [Red Trade Unions International] and the members of the Central Committee of the British Communist Party are requested to refer to him in all questions which may arise during the sojourn in Great Britain of the delegation.[73]

The British Communists were asked to preempt the expected anti-Soviet propaganda campaign and to conduct a campaign of their own in favor of both the coming delegation and friendly relations between the two states. Specifically the letter suggested that young members of the CPGB should participate in the protection of the Soviet delegates, an assignment they could do "better than the official police."[74]

On 19 May Henderson sent a copy of this letter to MacDonald in connection with a parliamentary question about subversion by Soviet delegates in England.[75] He also enclosed minutes by W.T.F. Horwood, the Commissioner of the Metropolitan Police (to which the Special Branch belonged), as well as the correspondence with the Foreign Office regarding the first Zinoviev letter that was described above.

The Police Commissioner admitted that he had in his possession recent instructions from the Soviet leadership forbidding any direct relations between Soviet delegates abroad and local Communists and that he had no

---

72. From the Under-Secretary of the Foreign Office to the Under-Secretary of the Home Office, N 3944/G, 12 May 1924, in ibid.

73. From the President of the IKKI, G. Zinoviev, and the General Secretary of the IKKI, Kolarov, to the Central Committee, British Communist party, 17 March 1924, *PRO*, Prem 1/49.

74. Ibid.

75. Arthur Henderson to the Prime Minister, 19 May 1924, in ibid.

definite evidence of such contact in England, but he explained this lack of evidence by the fact that:

> I have carried out no form of espionage on the activities of the present delegation for reasons I think will be obvious, i.e., an accusation of espionage made with justification would in my judgement jeopardize the negotiations and make the position of the Government difficult if not impossible.[76]

Horwood nevertheless added that he was certain that the Soviet delegates "will seize every opportunity presented by their visit here of seeking to undermine and destroy the Constitutional Government of this country as indeed of any other country which they visit." He enclosed the Zinoviev letter of 17 March and an article signed by Zinoviev that appeared in the Communist International official organ on 24 February as proofs of these intentions.[77]

In line with the Foreign Office position, the Police Commissioner's minutes, and the Home Office advice, MacDonald informed the Parliament on 19 May that "the Soviet delegates are here on a friendly mission, and, unless and until definite evidence to the contrary is forthcoming, it is to be presumed that they will abstain from actions which could only stultify the negotiations now pending."[78]

With these letters and additional intelligence information on Soviet subversion in mind, the cabinet decided when approving on May 15 the Industrial Unrest Committee interim report that the committee should, among other actions,

> make exploration of the question of the best method of making use of the information at the disposal of the Home Secretary in regard to Communist activities, and, in doing so, should take into consideration the general view of the Cabinet in favor of some

76. W.T.F. Horwood: "Minutes by Commissioner of Police," 16.5.24, in ibid.

77. Ibid.

78. "Propaganda by Soviet Delegation," PRO, FO 371–10478 N/4342/108/38. About a month later Lord Curzon referred in a parliamentary question to preparations by the Comintern in Moscow to send one hundred agitators with forged passports to England. MacDonald answered that he did not know how well founded this information was but assured the Parliament that the authorities were aware of the problem in general and would take appropriate action if the need arose. See Parliamentary Question, 23 June 1924, ibid., N/5323.

form of publicity, whether by the method of Parliamentary debate or otherwise.[79]

The two Zinoviev letters and the cabinet decision are highly relevant for our subject for three reasons. First, they make clear that the famous letter of September 1924 was not an isolated case. In this sense the mere existence of the previous letters helps to explain the relatively calm reaction of the Foreign Office and Prime Minister when receiving the third Zinoviev letter in October. Second, they show that the Foreign Office experts analyzed the problem and recommended against making diplomatic use of the letters on the basis of professional considerations, a process that constitutes a precedent for their behavior during the events of October. The police (in fact, the Special Branch) displayed similar prudence. Third, they demonstrate that key Labour policymakers supported the use of such evidence as long as its authenticity was beyond doubt. Behaving this way, MacDonald, Henderson, and their cabinet colleagues ignored partisan considerations, mainly the potential damage to the prestige of the government and the party because of revelation of intelligence documents that would have justified the opposition's attacks on the government. In fact, the position they took on publication was firmer than that of Lloyd George and other Liberal and Conservative ministers when facing a similar dilemma in August–September 1920.

Subversion continued to be on the cabinet agenda and was the immediate cause for the government's fall. By early autumn 1924 the Labour government was very vulnerable. MacDonald's political strategy throughout 1924 had hinged on the need simultaneously to seem both a responsible party of government and also a party of political and social reform. He had increasingly found it difficult, however, to balance these needs, and by late September 1924 he entirely lost his ability to do so. The Campbell case, an incident in which the attorney general declined recommendations to put to trial a well-known Communist for publishing an inciting article in the *Worker's Weekly*, was used by the Conservatives to move a parliamentary vote of censure on the grounds that the government was interfering politically with the course of justice. Liberal support to the Labour government had eroded already during the summer, and most Liberal M.P.s joined the Conservatives in defeating the government, which fell on 8 October. A day later SIS circulated a copy of the Zinoviev letter to Whitehall.

79. Cabinet 32 (24), 15 May 1924, *PRO*, Cabinet document 23/48.

The Official Story: The Letter, the Foreign Office, and MacDonald

Copies of the Zinoviev letter were sent on 9 October to the Foreign Office Permanent Under-Secretary, Sir Eyre Crowe, through his private secretary, Nevile Bland (who was also the liaison officer of the department with SIS), and to J. D. Gregory, the head of the Foreign Office's Northern Department, which was in charge of diplomatic relations with Soviet Russia. Additional copies were sent simultaneously to the Admiralty, the War Office, the Air Ministry, Scotland Yard, and MI5. Enclosed with the letter was a cover note from Hugh Sinclair, the head of SIS, emphasizing that the letter constituted a "flagrant violation" of the Anglo-Russian treaty of August 1924. The note added that "the authenticity of the document is un-doubted."[80]

The document was dated 15 September 1924 and was, from a British perspective, far more provocative than the earlier Zinoviev letters. Although the need for popular pressure to achieve the ratification of the Anglo-Soviet treaty was the main theme of its first part, the second part instructed the CPGB to carry out an all-out propaganda campaign against the government's domestic and foreign policy. Most worrisome, however, was the letter's third part in which the British Communists were instructed to create "cells in all the units of the troops . . . and also among factories working on munitions and at military store depots" in order to paralyze military preparations for war if the need arose. The letter, moreover, presented practical suggestions for laying the groundwork for a British Red Army.[81]

Crowe and Gregory received the letter on 10 October. Despite SIS assurances, Crowe was aware that the document could be a forgery and so waited for additional evidence regarding its authenticity before sending it to Prime Minister and Foreign Secretary MacDonald. Corroborative proof of the letter's authenticity was obtained on Saturday, 11 October, and was communicated to Crowe on 13 October. On the same day MacDonald left London for an election campaign that would carry him all over the country.

---

80. Untitled note, 9.10.24, *PRO*, FO 371–10478 N7838/G. Crowe (1975), p. 417, identifies Sinclair as the one who signed the letter, but she probably used her father's (Sir Eyre Crowe's) private papers. The signature on the copy of the letter that was sent to Gregory is clearly not that of Sinclair, who used to sign as "C" in green ink.

81. *PRO*, FO 371–10478 N 7838/G.

He would return to London only on 30 October, a day after ballot day and five days after the letter was published in the press.[82]

On 14 October the letter was registered in the Foreign Office. The experts of the Northern Department were rather skeptical about the effectiveness of any use of the letter as a means to put an end to Bolshevik subversion. William Strang, the second secretary in the Department, argued that publication or official protest would play into the hands of the Third International and only embarrass the Soviet government and the pragmatists in the Soviet leadership. In any event, Strang wrote, the Soviet government would deny any responsibility for the Comintern activities. He nevertheless concluded that publication would do no harm in the long run given the assurances that the letter was authentic. Gregory, the head of the Northern Department, expressed a short but firm objection to publication or protest, maintaining that the Soviets would immediately deny the document's authenticity (as they had done in the past) and that such an act would compromise intelligence sources.[83] The Permanent Under-Secretary had a different position. Even if protest and publication would bear no immediate fruit, such actions should nevertheless be taken on grounds of principle. It would be unfair, Crowe argued, to conceal such information from the public, and it would be unwise not to protest such blatant violations of the Anglo-Soviet accord.[84]

A copy of the letter together with the Foreign Office minutes were sent on 15 October to MacDonald, who received them either late the same day or the morning after, thus learning for the first time of the letter's existence. Perhaps motivated by the need to take a firm stand on the issue, he immediately informed the Foreign Office that he favored publication by way of an official protest to Rakovsky, as long as the authenticity of the document was ensured. He also instructed Crowe to prepare a draft of protest. His note, which was written on 16 October, arrived in the Foreign Office a day later. The head of the Northern Department started drafting a

82. "History of the Zinoviev Incident," in *The Public Record Office*, Home Office (henceforth *PRO*, HO) 45–13795–52100; Marquand, pp. 379–87.

83. Gregory was very consistent in this stand. In 1921 he objected constantly to the use of intelligence documents for diplomatic protests, maintaining on at least four different occasions that such acts had no chance of success. See Foreign Office Confidential Print no. 11861, "Violations of the Russian Trade Agreement, 1921," *Cambridge University Library*, pp. 12, 14, 16, 76.

84. Minutes by Strang, Gregory, and Crowe on the Zinoviev letter, *PRO*, FO 371–10478 N 7838/G.

formal protest at once, but because of the weekend it was finished and submitted to Crowe only on Monday, the twentieth. Crowe himself toughened the tone of the note extensively and sent it for MacDonald's confirmation on 21 October. He also informed the Prime Minister that the Foreign Office intended to release the letter and the protest to the press as soon as it was handed to Rakovsky. Since the Prime Minister was traveling in the country, Crowe's draft reached him only on 23 October. MacDonald amended the note significantly, toughening the tone even more, and returned it to the Foreign Office.[85]

MacDonald's draft arrived on the morning of Friday, 24 October. Although the Prime Minister would argue later that he expected a revised version to be returned to him for final approval, and that therefore he did not initial his draft, Crowe took it as a final endorsement and passed it to the Northern Department for action. Accordingly, a formal note of protest to Rakovsky was typed and signed—as was the practice when the Foreign Secretary was away—by the head of the Northern Department, J. D. Gregory.[86]

On the afternoon of the same day the Foreign Office learned that the *Daily Mail* had in its possession a copy of the letter, which it had distributed to other newspapers for publication on Saturday morning. According to the official report on the incident, "this fact . . . was one of the reasons which made it desirable to the Department that publication, which was considered to have been approved by the Prime Minister in any event, should take place on Saturday rather than on the following Sunday or Monday."[87]

The Permanent Under-Secretary of the Foreign Office, who made the decision to release the communication to the press, elaborated in a private note to MacDonald on the considerations that led him to take this course of action:

> What would have been the impression if—as would inevitably happen—it was discovered that the Foreign Office had been in possession of the incriminating document for some time but had concealed this fact and refrained from all action? Would it not have been said that information vitally concerning the security of the Empire had been deliberately suppressed during the elections which

85. "History of the Zinoviev Letter," *PRO*, HO 45-13795-521000, pp. 1–2. For a content analysis of the changes in the drafts, see Crowe, pp. 419–24.

86. "History of the Zinoviev Letter," *PRO*, 40 45-13795-521000, p. 2.

87. Ibid.

were meanwhile to be affected by propaganda? I thought it would be wrong to allow my government and my Prime Minister personally to be exposed to such a calumnious charge if it could be avoided. This was one of my motives in so strongly urging a public and instant protest.[88]

Crowe's arguments are indeed very convincing. Even from the Prime Minister's point of view hardly any other course of action was possible once the Foreign Office learned that the letter was to be published on the following morning. In this sense it is obvious (though the official report does not say so) that the whole political scandal could have been avoided if not for the fact that copies of the letter were leaked at the most critical time to the *Daily Mail*.

The official investigation of the incident did not at all consider the crucial question of how the Zinoviev letter became available to Britain's anti-Bolshevik press. This was partially the result of a traditional approach to unauthorized leaks and of the difficulties involved in tracing the truth in this type of event. Freedom of the press and the right of journalists to protect their sources was, of course, another principal argument against such investigation. But the real reason for avoiding such an inquiry was neither practical nor principled but political. As some members of the Conservative party already knew, an extensive investigation would have revealed a conspiracy of active and retired intelligence makers, senior Conservative politicians, and anti-Labour journalists that had led to the leak. Such a revelation would have harmed the Conservative party (now in power) and, naturally, had to be avoided.

The Hidden Layer: Intelligence Officers, Conservative Politicians, and the Anti-Labour Press

There is hardly any doubt that intelligence officers, by direct or indirect action, made the Zinoviev letter available to the press. As MacDonald told the Parliament during the March 1928 debate over the incident: "The circulation [of the letter] that took place was not a circulation between Political Departments, but circulation between the Intelligence Sub-Depart-

88. A private note from Crowe to MacDonald, 25 October 1924, PRO, FO 371–10478.

ments of the various big offices concerned with the subject." These offices, as he later added, were the Foreign Office, the Home Office, the Admiralty, and the War Office.[89] Since we do not have any reason to doubt MacDonald's statement,[90] our point of departure in this discussion is that the leak came from at least one of the intelligence services to which the letter was sent on 9 October. Who precisely leaked it is a more complicated problem.

In the 1920 episode Henry Wilson's diary served as a means to penetrate the "black box" of the conspiracy, which otherwise was not recorded in any official documents or personal memoirs. The evidence in the "Zinoviev letter affair" is more sketchy and circumstantial. But even here we have three pieces of information that shed much light on the way the letter became available to the press. The first is the public account of Thomas Marlowe, the Mail's editor in 1924, who four years later revealed some details on how the Zinoviev letter had come into his possession. The second is a private letter Marlowe wrote to the editor of the Times, Geoffrey Dawson, in which he reveals some other aspects of the affair. The third is a short account of events that was recorded by Donald im Thurn—the man who, according to the Conservatives, made the letter available for publication.

Marlowe's statement was published in the press in March 1928 in the form of a letter to the editor of the Observer. He testified that the first time he had heard of the letter was on the morning of Thursday, 23 October, upon coming to his office. On his desk he found a message from "an old and trusted friend." The note was delivered the night before and it said: "There is a document in London which you ought to have. It shows the relations between the Bolsheviks and the Labour Leaders. The Prime Minister knows all about it, but is trying to avoid publication. It has been circulated today to Foreign Office, Home Office, Admiralty and War Office."[91]

Even according to Marlowe's statement, his obtaining the document was a rather simple matter. Upon receiving the note he immediately called another friend who was at first somewhat reluctant to help but then, after consulting a third person, gave him a copy of the Zinoviev letter on early

89. House of Commons: Parliamentary Debates (London: His Majesty's Stationery Office), vol. 215, no. 30, Monday, 19 March 1928, pp. 50–51, 56.

90. Obviously, MacDonald did not refer to the Foreign Office diplomats, whose knowledge of the letter was a well-known fact. However, given the information we have on Gregory's and Maxse's objection to publication, and Crowe's sincere frustration on learning of the leak, it is very unlikely that any of them was the source of the leak.

91. Sunday Observer, 4 March 1928. As we know, the message was wrong in asserting that the letter was circulated "today" (i.e., 22 October 1924); in fact, it was circulated to the same departments almost two weeks earlier.

Friday afternoon. An additional copy of the letter became available to him through another source, even without a prior request.[92] Altogether, according to Marlowe's statement, at least four persons were involved in leaking the letter, through three different channels. Although he refrained from naming them, their identity becomes somewhat more clear from an examination of im Thurn's diary and notes.

Donald im Thurn became widely known as the source for Marlowe's information through his statement, read by Conservative Prime Minister Stanley Baldwin, in the parliamentary debate of March 1928. A few hours before the debate started im Thurn met with the Prime Minister and gave him the statement in which he argued that he had already learned of the existence of the letter on 8 October. He claimed to have received its complete text a day later from a business acquaintance of his who was "in close touch with Communist circles" in Britain. As a concerned citizen, im Thurn took action to ensure that "the Government Department mainly concerned" with the issue would know of the letter's existence and that the editor of the *Daily Mail* would receive, through a third party, a copy of the letter for publication. On the basis of this statement Baldwin denied any involvement of the intelligence services in the affair.[93]

Whether Baldwin knew it or not, im Thurn's statement was in part a severe case of the adage "economical with the truth" and, given its reference to lack of involvement by the intelligence services and Conservative politicians, a blatant lie.

Donald im Thurn, an upper-class businessman with close connections to anti-Bolshevik exile circles in London, had served as intelligence officer in MI5 during the war and maintained contacts with the service afterward. During October 1924, when he became involved in the "Zinoviev letter affair," he kept a secret diary in which he recorded his and others' roles in the scheme to leak the letter to the press. This diary as well as later notes taken by im Thurn on the incident tell a different story from the one proclaimed by Baldwin in Parliament.[94]

92. Ibid.
93. *House of Commons: Parliamentary Debates*, vol. 215, no. 30, Monday, 19 March 1928, pp. 69–72.
94. For the full text of im Thurn's diary, see Chester, Fay, and Young, Appendix I, pp. 197–200. Chester, Fay, and Young, British reporters who investigated the incident in 1966–67 as a team of the *Sunday Times*, are the main source for this aspect of the story. Although they make mistakes in other details of the affair, especially the description of how the letter was forged (it was probably genuine), their account of how it became available to the *Daily Mail* is nevertheless solid and very detailed.

The diary reveals that im Thurn did learn of the letter on 8 October. It contains no evidence, however, to support his 1928 statement that the source of the knowledge was an individual close to British Communists. This part of the statement was possibly added, perhaps by intelligence officers, in order to disguise the real identity of the source and to smear the CPGB as a group of unreliable Communists. It is quite logical, though we have no evidence to prove it, that the original source was one of im Thurn's acquaintances from the intelligence community. The falseness of im Thurn's 1928 statement is evident in another, even more important, respect: im Thurn did not get the full text of the letter on 9 October, nor on any later date. As his diary shows, he never had the letter in his hands. On this point, however, we have even more convincing evidence in the form of Thomas Marlowe's private letter to the editor of the *Times*. While Marlowe avoided stating who gave him the letter, he categorically ruled out im Thurn as a possible source: "All that I could have said was that I had never seen or heard of im Thurn, that I had never had any communication with him and that I did not receive the letter from him either directly or indirectly."[95] Thus falls the argument that im Thurn was the *Daily Mail*'s source of the document.

But if im Thurn had no direct role in giving the letter to the *Mail*, he nevertheless played a crucial role in generating the triangular relationship between intelligence officers, Conservative politicians, and anti-Labour journalists that made the leak inevitable. Since 14 October (which, as we recall, was the date when the Foreign Office had started its analysis of the document) im Thurn was in contact with senior officers of four different intelligence services, first in an effort to validate the existence of the letter and then to ensure its publication. The list of officers with whom he was in touch during the following week reads like a "Who's Who" of Britain's intelligence community. It included Major General Wyndham Childs, the head of the Special Branch of the Metropolitan Police; Rear Admiral Hotham, the Director of Naval Intelligence; Rear Admiral Hugh "Quex" Sinclair, the head of the SIS; and Colonel Vernon Kell, the head of MI5 (with whom im Thurn had indirect contact through a friend named "Alexander" who worked with Kell). Some of the intelligence chiefs were less cooperative than others. Childs denied that he had seen the letter, and

---

95. Thomas Marlowe to Geoffrey Dawson, 18 March 1930, Geoffrey Dawson Papers, *The Bodleian Library*, vol. 75. I received this document from Dr. John Ferris.

the DNI became angry when im Thurn succeeded in forcing him to admit that the letter existed. Kell, at least according to "Alexander," supported wide distribution of the document but refused to see im Thurn. Sinclair, whose service obtained the first copy of the letter, called im Thurn on 21 October to inform him that the letter would receive wide distribution among government departments.[96]

Two aspects of im Thurn's dialogue with the services' chiefs are striking. The first is the ease with which the chiefs agreed to discuss crucial and sensitive national secrets with a private citizen. The second is that none of them informed nonintelligence authorities of the fact that somebody outside the system knew about the letter and was trying to get hold of it for publication. Sinclair's behavior in this regard is most remarkable. Other chiefs would have found it hard to inform officials or politicians outside their departments of im Thurn's activities because the distribution of the letter was limited only to the intelligence community. Sinclair, on the other hand, could have at least informed the Permanent Under-Secretary of the Foreign Office to whom the letter was already circulated and under whose authority the SIS operated. There is no indication, however, that he had ever done so, and Crowe's reaction on learning that the *Daily Mail* had the letter is a clear indication that he was not informed of im Thurn (and other activities known to the head of the SIS) before Friday afternoon.

Simultaneously with his investigation in the services, im Thurn also approached Conservative politicians. His link to the Tories was Major Guy Kindersley, a personal friend and a Conservative MP. Through him im Thurn met Lord Younger, the ex-chairman of the party, and Stanley Jackson, the present chairman, and informed them of the letter's existence. According to the deal that was cut on 15 October, im Thurn was to find out who in the intelligence community had the letter, for which the Tories were to pay him 10,000 pounds, allegedly for the anonymous source who informed him of the letter in the first place. They all agreed that the best strategy would be to let the *Times* publish the document at a moment that would guarantee maximal political impact. Following this agreement, im Thurn continued his investigation to locate the whereabouts of the letter. At the same time, he also made contact with Fleet Street. Here his personal contribution was rather negligible, for all he did was to meet with the

96. Ibid., pp. 76–90.

Times's political correspondent and encourage him to use his own sources to get a copy of the letter.[97]

But im Thurn, as we noticed before, was not the link between the intelligence services and the *Daily Mail*. In fact, after informing the Tories of the existence of the letter, his role in the events that led to the publication diminished. The focus of activity now became the Central Office of the Conservative party, a political machine possessing excellent access to Whitehall in general and the intelligence community in particular.

The record of the concrete course of action taken within this organ is very sketchy. Yet circumstantial evidence suggests that the Tories acted in two complementary directions. One course of action was to prepare the ground for publication of the letter by alerting the public that a political bombshell was to explode before ballot day. Thus, on 21 October, journalists were briefed by "a high official of the Unionist Party" to watch Zinoviev and were told that "[b]efore another week has elapsed his name will be the storm centre of the General Election."[98] Following this or another briefing, the *Daily Mail* published on 22 October a short, and at the time also enigmatic, article about a Russian who escaped from his country "after being sentenced to death by Zinovieff . . . who in a recent speech wished Mr. MacDonald success in the election." Zinoviev was described in the article as a personal friend to senior Labour leaders and also as the man responsible for the death of "thousands of men, women and youths" in Bolshevik Russia.[99]

The second course of action taken by the Tories was to guarantee that the press would get hold of the letter. Thus, after ensuring, through im Thurn and possibly other channels, that the letter had been sent to all intelligence services, it was decided, probably by Lord Younger and Jackson, to inform the editor of the *Daily Mail* of the letter's existence and of the possibility that the government was trying to suppress its publication until ballot day. This was done, as we have seen, on 22 October, and Marlowe found the message on his desk on the following morning.

The editor of the *Daily Mail* publicly referred to the man who delivered him this message as "an old and trusted friend." Had he revealed his

97. Chester, Fay, and Young, pp. 79–80, 92. An additional source for im Thurn's contacts with the Tories is Kindersly's account of the story that he prepared shortly before his death in 1956 and which was used by Chester, Fay, and Young.

98. Extract from the *Star*, Saturday, 25 October 1924, in *PRO*, 30/69 1260.

99. *Daily Mail*, 22 October 1924, *PRO*, 30/69 1260.

full identity, the connection between the Conservatives, the intelligence services, and the right-wing press would have become far more apparent.

Earlier accounts of the episode identified Marlowe's "friend" as Vice Admiral Sir Reginald "Blinker" Hall,[100] the legendary wartime Director of Naval Intelligence and a man of high influence and excellent past and present connections in the British intelligence community. Since 1923 he served as a principal agent in the Conservative party's Central Office. During the war Hall had proved to be an outstanding intelligence maker. By the end of the war his reputation was so high that he was considered by some as a most suitable candidate to become the Foreign Secretary (James, p. 175). This is not surprising given the fact that much of Hall's work as DNI was political rather than professional. His most impressive wartime coup, the handling of the Zimmermann telegram, is a fine example of his expertise, for the whole operation to bring the United States into the war was conducted and controlled by Hall personally with no intervention by the Foreign Office or by other persons outside the Admiralty. Here, with the cabinet's approval, Hall acted as a foreign secretary no less than as an intelligence maker. But he also had a tendency to take action without political authority. In 1915, for example, he initiated, without the knowledge of the cabinet, contacts with Turkish representatives and suggested that they sell, in exchange for four million pounds, free passage to the British fleet through the Dardanelles. Winston Churchill, the First Lord of Admiralty, was shocked on learning of Hall's independent initiative.[101]

At the end of the war Hall retired from the navy and became a Conservative politician but did not give up his old contacts. In Parliament he expressed extreme anti-Labour sentiments and acted (for example, when Thomson was fired in 1921) as the champion of the intelligence services, blaming Labour for pressuring Lloyd George to get rid of "the one man our enemies had cause to fear" (Andrew 1985, p. 307). Hall was also active in other types of political work that gained him far less publicity. In 1919 he was the president of an organization titled "National Propaganda," a private organ for special political action. During the railway strike of October 1919

---

100. The first to identify Hall in this role was im Thurn, who used to annotate newspaper clips about the affair. In 1928 he wrote of Marlowe's "old and trusted friend"—R. Hall (Chester, Fay, and Young, p. 98). On the basis of this evidence this was also the conclusion of the investigation team of the *Sunday Times*. For an analysis of the value of im Thurn's evidence in the affair, see Ferris and Bar-Joseph, pp. 102–6.

101. For this incident as well as others, including unauthorized leaks to the press, see Andrew 1985, pp. 306–7.

the members of National Propaganda worked in concert with government agencies against the strikers. The exact nature of this action is not clear, but it included "dangerous duties, which had been declined by our paid agents."[102] The project was financed by the "Whips Fund," an emergency fund raised "for the purpose of defraying propaganda expenses during the difficult period in which the railway strike occurred." Notably, immediately after the end of the strike, the fund was dispersed for "political reasons."[103]

These sketchy details suggest that "Hall's Organization," as it was known by Whitehall officials, was a "private army" of right-wing vigilantes operating in the dim light between legal and illegal activity. Although it was a private organ that was financed by private or special party funds, it was used by the government for roles that government agencies were unable to carry out, either because they were illegal or because they were considered to be too political, or both. Although National Propaganda was still active in 1922, it is not known if and how it was ever activated after the railway strike.

Given his well-known modus operandi in handling politically sensitive intelligence reports, his close connections within the intelligence community, his special position in the Unionist party machine, and his longtime personal friendship with Marlowe, Hall certainly had all the necessary qualities to become a key figure in the conspiracy. Indeed, he probably was. A strong circumstantial argument can be made for his being Marlowe's other "friend"—the one the *Mail's* editor called on Thursday after learning of the existence of the letter a day earlier (Ferris and Bar-Joseph, pp. 109–10). But Hall's role was not the one traditionally attributed to him— that of Marlowe's "old and trusted friend." This becomes clear in light of another piece of evidence.

A few hours before the parliamentary debate of March 1928 Lieutenant Colonel Frederick Browning—a veteran intelligence officer and a personal friend of Marlowe and Hall—met with Robert Vansittart, the then head of the American Department in the Foreign Office (and later the Foreign Office Permanent Under-Secretary), and J.C.C. Davidson, a key figure in the Conservative party machine. The two told him what Prime Minister Baldwin was about to say (that it was im Thurn who gave Marlowe the letter) and asked him to support this statement. Browning refused, telling

102. From Sir Vincent Caillard, the President of National Propaganda, to the Ministry of Labour, 25 March 1920, *PRO*, Treasury report 164/21/15.

103. Captain H. Mason (a volunteer in Hall's organization), to D. Ferguson, the Treasury, 26 June 1922 (ibid.). I thank Dr. Ferris for calling my attention to the existence of the documents that refer to "National Propaganda."

them: "I cannot [support the statement] because it is not true. It is true that im Thurn first told me about the letter, and that I telephoned to Marlowe but it is not true that he gave me a copy of the letter or that I gave a copy to Marlowe."[104]

Browning, who by this evidence was almost certainly Marlowe's "old and trusted friend," was indeed a typical participant in the conspiracy. In 1924 he was a private businessman, but during the war he had served in various intelligence agencies. Quite typically, one of his first roles was to head a semi-official, quasi-illegal censorship organization established by DNI Hall when the latter found out that correspondence between England and neutral countries was going on without, what he considered, proper censorship. Browning's censors were not government employees but volunteers from the National Service League, an organization he had helped to run in the prewar years. At least some of the letters opened were those of politicians suspected by Hall and Browning to be passing information to the enemy through neutral countries (Andrew 1985, pp. 176–77). Browning moved later to the Ministry of Munitions and then joined MI1c, the predecessor and later the military section of SIS. By the end of the war he was the deputy to the head of MI1c, Sir Mansfield Cumming.

Browning's work with Hall in 1914 and his telephone conversation with Marlowe in October 1924 were not the start but merely the zenith of a longtime friendship and cooperative relationship. Hall and Browning were friends from boyhood, and Marlowe was a frequent visitor to Browning's home for quite some time. Needless to say, they all shared similar political beliefs and regarded the ousting of the Labour government from office as a legitimate end that justified all necessary means. In this sense the investigation team of the *Sunday Times*, which erred in identifying Hall's and Browning's roles in the conspiracy, was nevertheless right in concluding that the informal relationship between the three "provided the ideal network on which to base a plot to distribute the Zinoviev letter" (Chester, Fay, and Young, p. 105).

Much of the mystery, however, remains. Although we now have a good knowledge of who first informed Marlowe about the existence of the letter, we lack any direct evidence concerning the identity of the other conspirators

104. Thomas Marlowe to Geoffrey Dawson, 18 March 1930, Geoffrey Dawson Papers, *The Bodleian Library*, vol. 75. Browning met with Marlowe a few days after this talk in order to deliver him a request from Vansittart (whose personal involvement in this incident is rather peculiar) and Davidson that he would not publish a correction to Baldwin's parliamentary statement.

who gave him the two copies. Yet even here some of the thick fog that surrounded the episode has recently been cleared.

Although the evidence in this case is only circumstantial, it is quite possible that the chief culprit in the second chain through which the Zinoviev letter was leaked to Marlowe was Joseph Ball. In 1924 Ball held the rank of General Staff Officer Two (GSO 2) in MI5, heading, most likely, the service's "B" branch that was charged with secret investigations of espionage and subversion against military forces in Britain (Ferris and Bar-Joseph, pp. 125–26). Given his rank and role, Ball was certainly concerned with the Zinoviev letter. So, however, were other MI5 officers. Soviet subversion was, after all, their main problem, and in this sense they all shared an interest in making the letter public. Unlike his colleagues, however, Ball can also be linked to two vital indicators for involvement in the affair: press leaks and partisan commitments. In 1920, for example, while investigating allegations against George Lansbury, the editor of the *Daily Herald*, Ball suggested that it be arranged for the more incriminating evidence against the Labour leader to reach the anti-Labour press (ibid., pp. 126–27). More important, in the mid-1920s—possibly even while still serving in MI5[105]—Ball joined the Unionist Central Office, organizing within this party machine a "Special Information Section to keep us informed of the enemy [that is, the Labour party] and his plans." There is no doubt that in this role Ball was using the same techniques, perhaps even the informants, he had used during his MI5 service (ibid., pp. 127–28).

On the basis of mostly circumstantial evidence, Chester, Fay, and Young concluded that the "third person" mentioned in Marlowe's published statement, the one who was consulted before the leak, was the head of SIS, Sir Hugh "Quex" Sinclair. Sinclair served as Hall's deputy in the Naval Intelligence Department (NID) (Beesly 1982, p. 304), and he must have known Browning, who served in a similar capacity in MI1c. There is, moreover, evidence that connections between Browning and Sinclair and, possibly, Hall were not terminated after the war ended (Chester, Fay, and Young, pp. 106–7). To this we can add that, as we already know from his

---

105. On this point British historians disagree. Most of them date 1927 as the year in which Ball joined the Central Office (Rhodes, pp. 271–72; Dilks, p. 486; Andrew 1985, p. 339; Cockett, pp. 131–32; Blake, p. 68). In contrast, John Ramsden, one of Britain's leading authorities on the Central Office, maintains (but without providing a source reference) that Ball was already hired by the Central Office in early 1924 (Ramsden, pp. 197, 205). Needless to say, if Ramsden's claim could be proved, then Ball's participation in the conspiracy would have become far more obvious. For a discussion of this issue, see also Ferris and Bar-Joseph, pp. 129–30.

role in the August–September 1920 affair, Sinclair was certainly capable of taking unauthorized action, including the leak of secret documents, to promote political goals.

It should nevertheless be emphasized that there is no conclusive evidence that either Ball or Sinclair were involved in the conspiracy, nor, of course, that they leaked the letter. Given that SIS in London consisted of, perhaps, forty people who functioned in a clublike atmosphere in which the "need-to-know" principle was virtually unknown, and that about sixty more officials, mostly from the various intelligence branches, knew of the letter, we can assume that any of them could have leaked it to the press. In this sense the identity of the persons who supplied the *Daily Mail*'s editor, directly and indirectly, with two copies of the letter remains uncertain. Our historical curiosity in this regard will probably remain unsatisfied at least for the time being.

Summary

The "Zinoviev letter affair" is a telling story of how politically frustrated intelligence makers cooperated with opposition leaders against a legitimate government in power. Many aspects of this affair—for instance, the way MacDonald handled (or mishandled) it, or the effect the incident had on the results of the elections and its impact on developments within the Labour party—were not discussed here since they are irrelevant to our main interest. The same is true with regard to the never-ending debate over whether the letter was genuine or not.[106] This latter question, however, has some bearing on this study if it could be proved that Britain's intelligence makers believed that the letter was forged but nevertheless convinced the administration that it was genuine because of their political goals. I did not find any good evidence that this was the case, and hence I tend to regard the intelligence officers involved as inculpable in this respect.

There is, however, no doubt that they were guilty in other respects. All

---

106. The political debate about the letter's authenticity is a classical example of "where you sit is where you stand." Conservatives believed automatically that the document was genuine whereas Labour furiously regarded it as a forgery. Academicians were less biased. Andrew (1985) makes a very good and convincing case for the letter's authenticity (pp. 309–13), but as even he had to admit elsewhere, the question will remain open until "the far distant day when the Soviet government and the British secret service open their archives" (Andrew 1977, p. 675). At present this day seems to be rather near.

of them avoided informing their superiors of im Thurn's private investigation into the matter. They were aware that an important piece of intelligence, one whose distribution was limited almost entirely to the intelligence services, was in danger of slipping into the public domain. They were aware that a general election was occurring and what the potential political consequences of such a leak could be. They took no step to prevent this from occurring and thus, willingly or not, made themselves passive participants in the events that followed. Some in the intelligence community, moreover, participated actively in a conspiracy that was intended to affect the results of the British general elections.

When comparing the 1920 episode with the 1924 case, we find some similarities and differences. They differ on two essential points. First, in the 1920 case the initiative for the plot came from the military, and the intelligence officers played only a secondary role, though of major importance. In the 1924 case no military participation took place, and if our assumption that im Thurn's first informer was a member of the services is correct, then it was intelligence personnel who initiated the whole plot. Second, the scheme in 1920 was borne out of a background of high domestic tension and real fear for the fate of Britain. In this sense, as groundless as Wilson's hysteric fears were, he and the others plotted in order to save the country from what they believed to be an immediate and concrete threat. In 1924 the domestic situation was less tense and fear of successful Soviet subversion had declined. Moreover, in contrast to Lloyd George, Labour policymakers supported the publication of intelligence evidence of Soviet subversion as long as their authenticity was beyond doubt. Since the quality of the intelligence documents in 1924 was not as good as in 1920 (when there were no doubts about authenticity because evidence was obtained through GC&CS), there was no specific reason for the intelligence officers involved to behave as they did. They acted so simply because they loathed the Labour party and had the opportunity to cripple its chances in the elections.

The similarities between the 1920 case and the "Zinoviev letter affair" are rather striking. In both cases intelligence officers cooperated with outsiders in order to reach certain political goals. In both cases the intelligence modus operandi was ultimately the same: a leak to the press of secret documents highly embarrassing to the government. There is also a third similarity: in both cases we do not know who was ultimately responsible for the leaks, partially because the repertoire of candidates includes almost every chief of the intelligence services.

This by itself hints at our most important conclusion at this stage. It shows that in Britain during the 1920s intelligence officers were exceptionally willing to take a direct part in the politics of their country and directly affect the results of the democratic elections. In 1920 intelligence chiefs were actively participating in an attempt to change an important element of government policy and were doing so on clear political grounds. The instance of 1924 in this regard is more complex. Given the uncertainty of the evidence, one cannot identify a culprit; one can, however, identify the realm in which the culprit can be found. At one end of the spectrum stand individuals such as Joseph Ball and Admiral Sinclair. If such men were involved, this would virtually be an instance bordering on a coup d'état. On the other hand is the possibility that Marlowe's sources were a handful of junior members of an intelligence organization, probably MI5 or SIS. In such an instance the secret services as institutions would be innocent of any active involvement in unconstitutional behavior, but the mere fact that this could occur—that a handful of junior civil servants could have both the desire and the opportunity to so dramatically manipulate the political process—reveals the danger to the British state posed by the ramshackle structure and amateur ethos of some of the British intelligence services.

PLOTTING AGAINST THE GOVERNMENT: HOW COULD IT HAVE HAPPENED?

The vast sources of information that were available in the American and Israeli case studies enabled us to focus on the personal traits and operational milieus of individual intelligence makers as a major source for explaining the "Bay of Pigs" and the "unfortunate business" episodes. The use of such sources is not possible in the British cases. Fortunately, however, they are also not essential. Such a focus is not possible because we do not have enough information about the character of the intelligence officers involved in the 1920 and 1924 episodes and the environment in which they operated. With the exception of Admiral Hall, none of our leading actors—Thomson, Sinclair, Thwaites, Ball, Kell, or Childs—has ever been the subject of an in-depth study. Even in the case of Hall the available accounts (mainly James 1955 and Beesly 1982) are filled with admiration for his outstanding qualification as the DNI during wartime but shed very little light (or none at all) on his performance and behavior in the aftermath of the war. Nor do we have thorough studies of the formal and informal interaction between the intelligence makers and their operational environment, which in previous cases facilitated our understanding of situational causes for the deviant behavior of intelligence makers (such as Richard Bissell and Colonel Givli).

To a large extent, however, this kind of information is also not vital for analyzing the present cases. As I have already argued, the mass participation of the chief intelligence makers in the 1920 and 1924 plots constitutes by itself evidence that typical collective traits rather than a singular personality trait can give us a better explanation of the British cases. Despite differences in character or belief systems between Thomson, Sinclair, and Thwaites, they all shared enough in common to facilitate their participation in Henry Wilson's plot. The same is true with regard to the chiefs of the SIS (Sinclair), MI5 (Kell), the Special Branch (Childs), and the NID (Hotham)—all of whom knew of im Thurn's investigation into the Zinoviev letter and yet avoided alerting their civilian superiors to this action. This common denominator, which I will discuss later, is the main factor that distinguishes the British from the American and Israeli cases and explains, to a large extent, the motivation behind the crude interference of the intelligence makers in British politics in 1920 and 1924.

Important as these collective traits are, the British intelligence community of the 1920s could act the way it did only in a certain setting. The context for its operation included two major factors: first, a perception of threat that served as a catalyst for action; and second, a government and bureaucratic system that, owing to certain defective features, had left the services with insufficient political supervision, thus generating the environment in which the intelligence makers could act against their own elected government. Only after analyzing this context can we turn to the issue of motivation.

The Catalyst

It is clear that the October Revolution and the foreign policy of Bolshevik Russia constituted a predominant threat to Britain as well as to other nations in the interwar period. The mere success of the Bolsheviks in Russia was by itself vivid evidence of the vitality of their ideas and methods. Their ability to remain in power despite the civil war and the Allied military intervention added another impetus in this direction. Then there was Bolshevik foreign policy, which declared world revolution as its principal goal and coupled words with deeds by establishing the Third International (Comintern) in 1919 and by practicing massive subversive activities of which Britain and the British Empire were prime targets. Lastly, in addition to the foreign threat, serious domestic unrest in Britain was another major source for concern. Indeed, there is no doubt that the combination of outside subversion with industrial unrest at home had created a serious and tense situation.

Under these circumstances the fear of revolution in England, which was voiced by a formidable group of politicians, businessmen, journalists, and military officers as well as other high-ranking officials in 1920, had ample foundation. To a certain extent the intelligence makers' fears of revolution were even more justified, because they were more familiar than others with the practice of Bolshevik subversion and because they had a duty to obstruct it. But the fundamental task of a professional intelligence officer is to distinguish between real and imaginary threats, and as we know the likelihood of a revolution in Britain was far smaller than what the intelligence makers estimated it to be. Lloyd George understood this, and so did other less-biased and more sophisticated policymakers.

Foreign threat, though still in existence, played a lesser role in 1924. The catalyst for the intelligence action in this case was the function of two situational factors: the timing of the elections; and the availability of the Zinoviev letter, which offered the opportunity to translate political frustrations into concrete action aimed at wrecking Labour's chances to win the elections.

In 1920 the intelligence makers' threat perception derived more from their political beliefs than from professional considerations. In 1924 professional considerations hardly played any role in the decision to leak the letter to the press. Here, even more than in 1920, action was motivated by simple political preferences that had very little (if anything at all) to do with the intelligence profession.

We shall return to the question of motivation later in this section. At this stage we can point to the lack of basic norms of public behavior that should have prevented the intelligence officers from interfering with their own country's politics despite menacing or undesired situations. The fact that they were not deterred from doing so constitutes evidence, then, that British society and its governmental system were not strong enough to prevent such behavior.

The Environment

Beliefs: Secrecy, Gentlemanly Ethos, Liberalism, and Patriotism

Certain beliefs and norms typical of English tradition and culture have made it more difficult for cabinet members and especially prime ministers to supervise the work of the services. Four of these norms are highly relevant to our subject. The first is the belief in the need for utmost secrecy regarding every aspect of intelligence work. Austen Chamberlain gave this belief vivid expression when arguing in 1924 that it was "of the essence of a Secret Service that it must be secret" (Porter, p. 169). Whitehall's traditional objection to declassification of intelligence documents is a clear indication that this norm remains dominant even today.

The second is the belief that there is an inherent contradiction between the gentlemanly ethic and the "dirty" nature of intelligence work. The British, of course, had never adopted in practice the normative approach of Henry Stimson, the American Secretary of State who maintained in 1929 that "Gentlemen do not read each other's mail." They were always willing to read the diplomatic traffic of friends and foes, the obstacles in reaching this goal being technical rather than ethical. But they nevertheless believed (with the exception of Winston Churchill) that the national leadership should not get too involved in intelligence work since such involvement was highly incompatible with its gentlemanly caste and the norms of "fair play."

Third, British politicians followed the Whig tradition regarding the relationship between state and society. They did not wish to raise the power of the state too far for fear that power would corrupt the British constitution. As a concomitant of that attitude they wished to maintain firm boundaries between the realms of politics and of intelligence. Should politicians become too involved with intelligence, they could easily use intelligence as a means to distort the shape of domestic politics—something that the British believed was fairly common among certain states in continental Europe. They did not wish to expose British politicians to the continual temptation of being able to use the intelligence services as a means to blacken the reputation of their political enemies. This was an admirable doctrine. Paradoxically, however, their desire to keep politicians out of intelligence made it much easier for individuals in the intelligence community to affect the course of politics.

The fourth belief is the unfounded yet popular notion that investigating and blaming the intelligence community for certain acts is unpatriotic and unfair. The root of this belief comes not only from the fact that the community's work is aimed at protecting the nation against foreign threats but also from the notion that its work has to be done under a thick veil of secrecy, which prevents its members from defending themselves adequately against public accusations.

These beliefs have led to two devastating results. First, succeeding prime ministers (Winston Churchill was, again, the exception)[107] avoided giving the necessary attention to the intelligence services, thus leaving the community with too much freedom of action. A vivid expression of this tendency was the relative lack of uninterrupted interaction between prime ministers and central intelligence makers. Although Thomson, as Director of Intelligence, had direct access to the cabinet, none of his successors enjoyed such a privilege. This was also the case with the directors of SIS, MI5, and the army and naval intelligence services. The opposite was also true. Prime ministers rarely met with the chiefs of intelligence services and thus had insufficient first-hand cognizance of what they really did or thought. Typically, the intelligence services and their directors are hardly mentioned in the memoirs of British prime ministers (and this is not simply the result of the need to conceal the services' activities). This situation remained the same in the years to come: Harold Wilson admitted that he "saw so little of the heads of MI5 and MI6 that I used to confuse their names" (Andrew 1985, p. 502).[108]

The second defective result of these beliefs was the government's reluctance to conduct investigations into cases where intelligence services were suspected of having abused their power. It is not clear how much was known to Lloyd George about the plot against him in 1920, and therefore this case

107. Churchill's passion for intelligence—especially for the "cloak and dagger" aspects of the profession—involved other problems in government-intelligence relations, especially that of too much involvement in professional intelligence work by a dedicated but amateur prime minister. On this subject, see Andrew 1989, pp. 181–93.

108. It is important to note in this connection that both Lloyd George and MacDonald were not present in London when the plots against them took place. Incidental as this might be, it is very possible that events would have gone otherwise had it not been for this fact. There is, however, a noteworthy difference between these two events. In 1920 the content of the leak was the key issue. In 1924 the timing of the leak was the key issue. In the first case the intention was to change government policy; hence the presence of Lloyd George alone might not have been enough to change the course of events. In 1924 the intent was to affect the outcome of the general elections—indeed, the leak was only important because it coincided with the elections; therefore, had MacDonald been in London, it seems quite possible that he could and would have recognized the political danger that loomed before him and avoided it.

constitutes insufficient evidence here. But MacDonald was highly suspicious of the way the services handled the Zinoviev letter and had ample evidence to demand a thorough official investigation into their role in this case. The investigation committee that was established by the government following the October 1924 elections focused nevertheless on the Foreign Office's conduct in the affair and avoided any inquiries into the more critical question of how the letter became available to the press. Even MacDonald himself, when defining the episode in the parliamentary debate of 1928 as "a case of a successful conspiracy," refrained from linking the intelligence community directly to the leak, putting the responsibility for this act instead on "foreigners, including the controllers of our own newspapers."[109] Behaving in this way MacDonald was obviously also influenced by the belief that blaming the services publicly would be widely perceived as an unpatriotic and unfair act.

As a result, plotting against the government did not necessarily entail significant cost to individuals or institutions in the intelligence community. This by itself only intensified similar behavior under comparable conditions in the future.[110] Here lies a considerable difference between the American and the Israeli approach to the problem and that of the British. Although investigations—public ones such as those conducted in the United States following "Watergate" and the "Iran-contra affair," or secret ones as was the case with Israel subsequent to the 1954 "unfortunate business"—have not always revealed the whole truth and, to some extent, involved parochial political interests, they nevertheless had a considerable impact on the future behavior of the intelligence community by serving as a warning signal against further abuse of power. Such signals were not transmitted in Britain, and this failure constituted another impetus for the services to interfere so crudely in the politics of their own country.

The Civil Service System: Subordination, Amateurism, and the "Old Boys Net"

A national civil service is essential for the proper running of the modern state, but the nature and the power of such bureaucracies vary from one

---

109. *House of Commons: Parliamentary Debates*, vol. 215, no. 30, Monday, 19 March 1928, p. 53.
110. Not much has changed in this regard even fifty years later. Despite allegations that MI5 officers plotted against Harold Wilson, no official investigation into this case has ever taken place, and the only sources of information regarding this episode are biased personal memoirs and unreliable journalistic accounts that still leave too many questions unanswered.

country to another. Certain characteristics of the British civil service have made it more powerful and less dependent on the political leadership than in most other modern democratic regimes. These features found their most profound expression in the intelligence services and in their modus operandi, contributing significantly to their tendency and ability to act against the government.

The first of these features involves the principal question of who formally employs the civil servants and to which entity they owe their supreme loyalty. In nonmonarchical regimes it is either the "state" or the "constitution," which are both rather abstract entities. In Britain it is the Crown—embodied by a man or a woman who is, by far, much less abstract.

The British civil servant is formally defined as "a servant of the Crown employed in a civil capacity who is paid wholly and directly from money voted by the Parliament" (Punnett, p. 306). Although this definition excludes military officers since they are not employed in civil capacities, this is only a formal distinction. Practically, the armed forces perceive themselves and are perceived as servants of the Crown but in military rather than civilian roles. The result has been that Britain's intelligence makers—all members of the civil service, whether they were civilians like Thomson and Ball or military officers such as Sinclair and Thwaites—believed that they owed their highest loyalty not to the government in power nor to prime ministers who come and go but to the King. In 1920 and 1924, when they perceived a conflict between cabinet policy and what they considered as the proper course of action, this type of formal subordination supplied them with ample justification to act against the government.

Field Marshal Wilson gave this approach clear expression when he told Winston Churchill in mid-August 1920 that the Bolshevik intercepts and Lloyd George's reaction to them "put a severe strain on our (Soldiers) [sic] loyalty to the Cabinet as[,] though we wished to be loyal to the Government[,] we had a higher loyalty still to our King & England" (Ullman 1972, p. 278). Whether Wilson used this distinction merely as a justification for his plot or whether he really believed in it (I tend to believe the latter) is less relevant. What is important here is that the system gave him a formal outlet to act the way he did (and he was keen to use it). Given, furthermore, that King George V was himself an ardent anti-Bolshevik who wanted to see the Soviet delegation expelled from London (ibid., p. 303), this could only add to Wilson's and his coconspirators' motivations to pursue their goals. Although we do not have sufficient empirical evidence to support this notion, it is quite probable that the conspirators of 1924 used a similar excuse when leaking the Zinoviev letter. After all, the King's dislike of the Labour government was quite well known to them.

A second characteristic of the British civil service system that is relevant to our subject involves the preference for the educated amateur over the professional to lead the nation's administration. This tendency, which is perhaps less evident today but was clearly dominant in the period under discussion, took administration to be an art rather than a profession and regarded classical education in a good university (that is, Cambridge or Oxford) as better preparation for senior administrators than narrow specialization for specific roles. It led to a policy, evident even today, in which "senior mandarins are switched overnight from running prisons to encouraging exports" (Sampson, p. 259).

The impact of this factor on other branches of the civil service is irrelevant to our subject. But it had a devastating effect on the way in which the heads of the intelligence services were selected for their roles. Applying this approach meant that officers could reach the demanding positions of the intelligence services with little or no experience at all in intelligence work, being expected to compensate for this lack of experience by personal qualities and general managerial skills.

The "highly educated amateur" approach found its most vivid expression in the armed services, which believed, so it seems, that leading a division or commanding a battleship was ample preparation for heading an intelligence service. This was clearly the case with Hall, Sinclair, and Thwaites. Hall became DNI in October 1914 not because of personal choice or prior experience (except for a suitable background—his father was the Director of the Naval Intelligence Division in the late nineteenth century) but because his health broke down and he could not continue his combat service at sea. Sinclair, with over thirty years of naval experience and a lifelong interest in torpedoes (rather than intelligence), replaced Hall at the end of the war, after a short period in which he served as his deputy. Typically, serving as DNI was only one station—not necessarily the most important one—in Sinclair's career. After three years he left the NID to return to sea duty until Cumming's sudden death in 1923 brought him unexpectedly back to the intelligence ranks as the new head of SIS. Thwaites had no prior experience in intelligence work before becoming DMI in September 1918 either, and after leaving the Military Intelligence Department (MID) in 1922 he returned to a traditional military career.

Their civilian colleagues followed a similar path, though they arrived at their roles somewhat better prepared. Thomson became the head of the

Special Branch after a colorful career that included posts in the colonial service in Fiji, Tonga, and New Guinea as well as a post educating the sons of the king of Siam. He then served as deputy governor and later governor in the Prison Service of the Home Office—positions that gave him at least some experience in police work. When becoming the Director of Intelligence in 1919 he already had six years' experience in domestic surveillance as the chief of the Special Branch.

The policy of selecting amateurs rather than professionals to head senior positions in the civil service has probably been fairly successful in most departments but not in the intelligence services, which are more demanding. An administrator can successfully run a large hospital but will not operate on patients if he is not a physician. The chiefs of services, on the other hand, were automatically considered (and usually also considered themselves) to be intelligence experts capable of performing complicated work, such as the conduct of national intelligence estimates, shortly or even immediately upon entering office. As we have seen in the 1920 episode, officers such as Sinclair and Thwaites made ample use of their nominal positions as intelligence experts, demanding a certain course of action because they were allegedly the ones who knew best what should be done. In actuality, however, since they were inexperienced, they were not professional intelligence makers in the true sense of the word but only amateurs who served in professional roles. A critical result of this state of affairs was that their actions were based more on political preferences than on empirical evidence and professional skills. Sinclair's behavior illustrates this point. In 1920, as we have seen, he favored the publication of the Soviet telegrams even if it "was to result in not another message being decoded" (Ullman 1972, p. 289). But he learned his lesson, and while later serving as the head of the SIS he firmly objected to any use of solved telegrams for publication.

This British preference for the educated amateur over the professional was not always the norm. Although Vernon Kell, the director of MI5, and Mansfield Cumming, the chief of SIS, came to head these agencies with little prior experience in intelligence work, by 1920 each of them had more than ten years of practical experience, by far more than the rest of their colleagues in the army and the navy. It might be incidental, but it is possible that their personal expertise contributed to their absence from Henry Wilson's plot.[111]

111. Certain other factors enter the equation. Kell was quite right wing while Cumming was an

The third feature of the civil service that is highly relevant to our subject involves the traditional recruitment policy of the "old boys net." In other departments of the civil service some formal requirements and examinations already were part of the recruitment process in the 1920s. This, however, was not the case with the intelligence community. The thick veil of secrecy under which the services were shrouded enabled their members to enlist personnel solely on the basis of personal acquaintance, with no formal examinations and, not less important, with no significant vetting. Typically, the fact that one member of the services knew personally the nominee (or his father or his uncle) was considered as a sufficient guarantee for a successful recruitment process and served as the main—and in most cases the only—tool of getting new blood into the community.

The result of the "old boys net" enlisting system was that the services became closed clubs of members linked by similar backgrounds—upper-class families and elitist public school education[112]—and identical political beliefs. Outsiders, who might have had better qualifications for intelligence work, could not join the "club" because they did not have the necessary access to the services or because they did not enjoy the proper background. Furthermore, given that the chief enemy of the services in the 1920s was Bolshevism and that those who were already in were diehard anti-Bolsheviks, a highly important qualification for entering the intelligence community was a solid right-wing, anti-Communist stand.[113]

More than any other factor, the "old boys net" recruitment system determined the character of the British services and the patterns of their behavior. How the nature of these organs contributed to their behavior in the 1920 and 1924 cases will be discussed next.

---

extreme reactionary and, moreover, an intelligence "buccaneer." In institutional terms, however, both MI5 and SIS were peripheral to the issues at hand.

112. The only exception to this rule was the Special Branch, which, as part of the Metropolitan Police, recruited its members mainly among the working and lower-middle classes (Porter, p. 168). As for the heads of the intelligence services, the first outsider to enter this "club" was Sir Percy Sillitoe, the head of MI5 between 1946 and 1953. Relations between Sillitoe and his "upper-class" colleagues were tense, among other reasons, because he lacked the elite family background and Oxbridge education that they had (Andrew 1985, pp. 489–91).

113. Quite typically, an intelligence club was established in the aftermath of the great war, probably by Vernon Kell, the chief of MI5. Named "IB Club," or sometimes "IP Club" (IP for "Important Persons," "Intelligence Persons," and/or "Intelligent Persons"), this association functioned at least until 1939, and its members—several hundred—were officers from all the intelligence services. What makes the IB/IP Club so relevant for our subject is the fact that senior Unionist politicians, such as Baldwin (who was an honorary member) or Davidson, were also members of the club (Ferris and Bar-Joseph, pp. 111–14; Rhodes, p. 381; West 1981, p. 48; Cave Brown 1987, p. 124).

The Motivation: The Nature of the "Intelligence Club"

Certain types of work attract certain types of people. One does not become a politician if one hates power, nor a Catholic priest if one is a womanizer. It appears that in Britain following the October Revolution one could not have become a high-ranking intelligence officer unless one was an arch-conservative and a rabid anti-Bolshevik. This tendency of the heads of the services towards the extreme right has been referred to occasionally before. But since it is so essential for understanding the motivation behind the 1920 and 1924 plots, the tendency deserves a closer look.

In some cases the evidence is only circumstantial. DMI Thwaites, for example, has left us with no clear indication about his political beliefs. Yet the fact that he accepted CIGS Wilson's suspicions that Lloyd George was a Bolshevik and a traitor leaves us doubtless that he did not vote for the Labour party on ballot day. The Director of MI5, Vernon Kell, left a more artistic expression of his political stands. The New Year's card prepared by the Security Service in 1920 shows the main threat to Britain in the form of subverters, the most dominant of which are Bolshevik revolutionaries (with a typical Jewish nose),[114] digging under the statue of liberty and security (Andrew 1985, p. 243, and picture between p. 270 and p. 271). Kell together with Sinclair—of whose political beliefs we have circumstantial evidence also through his behavior in the 1920 and 1924 plots—had reputations for being "terrific anti-Bolsheviks" (ibid., p. 337).

In other cases the evidence is more direct. Rear Admiral Hall was very clear when he told his staff in a farewell speech upon leaving the service that:

> Above all we must thank God for our victory over the German nation; and now I want to give you all a word of warning. Hard and

---

114. Anti-Semitism was a common trait within the British upper class in general. Henry Wilson's letters afford a good illustration of the phenomenon. In early 1920, for example, he wrote DMI Thwaites about a meeting he was to hold with representatives from Georgia and Azerbaijan, adding that:

> I hear that three out of four Georgian and Azerbaijani Delegates who are coming to see me are Jews. Do you think just by chance that it would suit the international view of German origin if we scattered our forces over the world and left England undefended? You might ask the first Jew boy you meet in Whitehall on your way to lunch. (Jeffery 1985, pp. 148–49)

Whereas the bulk of the English establishment merely evinced social anti-Semitism, members of the intelligence community seemed to hold much deeper fears of "international Judaism," mainly because so many of the Bolshevik leaders were of Jewish origin.

bitter as the battle had been, we have now to face a far, far more ruthless foe, a foe that is hydra-headed, and whose evil power will spread over the whole world, and that foe is [Bolshevik] Russia. (James, p. 177)

The head of the Special Branch since 1921, Sir Wyndham Childs, took a similar stand. In his memoirs he noted that he "always took the view . . . that the Communist organization was and is a seditious organization." His principal fear of British Communists "centered around their methods of contaminating our youth." Little wonder, then, that he found the aims of the British Fascists to be "laudable," though their methods were "damnable and illegal" (Childs, pp. 209, 221, 223). His predecessor, Sir Basil Thomson, went even further:

> . . . people who live under the Bolshevik regime describe it as a sort of infectious disease, spreading rapidly, but insidiously, until like a cancer it eats away the fabric of society, and the patient ceases even to wish for his own recovery. A nation attacked by it may, if we may judge from the state of Russia, be reduced to a political and social morass, which may last perhaps for a generation or more, with no hope of reaction; whilst civilisation crumbles away and the country returns to its original barbarism. (Andrew 1985, pp. 228–29).

These ideological attributes—more suitable for *Der Steurmer* and "The Protocols of the Elders of Zion" than for professional intelligence officers—could hardly facilitate the cool-headed designs needed to deal with the Bolshevik menace. Even more important for our subject, holding such perceptions put the heads of the services on the extreme right of the British political map. From such a vantage point, other organs or individuals who held more moderate views could easily be mistaken to be less patriotic and, in severe cases and in times of crisis, even as traitors or Bolsheviks themselves. Lloyd George almost fell victim to this perception, and so did other moderate politicians.

Yet, important as this feature is, it is not sufficient to give a full explanation of the services' behavior. Additional components of the intelligence makers' collective belief system are needed here. The first of these features was their belief that, merely by serving as the nation's *cordon sanitaire* in its struggle against the Bolsheviks, they had also become the best national experts on the subject. They presumed to understand not only the nature of the enemy but also the best strategy and tactics on how to win the war against it. How valid was this belief is difficult to answer. But it is clear that its former part was relatively more valid than the latter. After all, these men had read the Bolsheviks' secret communications and had agents in the enemy's camp; all information about Communist Russia and her activities was channeled precisely to them. Having the raw information, however, ensured neither a correct comprehension of the problem nor, of course, an accurate discovery of the optimal means to solve it. The fact that intelligence information had to go through the extreme anti-Bolshevik prism of the intelligence makers' minds was by itself a major obstacle to their ability to understand and consider reality in an unbiased form.[115] Neither were they more capable than others of determining the national strategy to win the anti-Bolshevik conflict. This strategy involved many components other than knowledge of the enemy itself, components that the intelligence makers had no better knowledge or experience of than other policymakers. Lloyd George's sophisticated estimation of the situation in 1920 was by far closer to reality than the simplistic estimations of the services. Being unaware, however, of their own shortcomings, people like Hall, Sinclair, or Thomson simply thought that they knew the problem and its solution best and acted according to this belief.

Closely related to this "we know best" attitude were disrespectful feelings expressed by some intelligence makers towards central policymakers, who were assumed to be attentive to parochial political concerns rather than to the national interest. Henry Wilson—though a military officer and not an intelligence expert—voiced this attitude best in his personal diary and letters when routinely naming politicians as "frocks" and expressing low opinions of their qualities. It is clear from certain entries of his diary that this belief was not only his own but was shared by large segments of the military and the intelligence communities as well. Needless to say, this perception had some impact on determining a certain course of action, as was the case in 1920, when narrow political interests were perceived by intelligence and military officers to determine the national policy. And

---

115. Lacking good evidence of how intelligence makers reacted to new situations, we have to resort, again, to Wilson's actions, which are better documented. For example, as we recall, in early August 1920 he demanded the expulsion of the Soviet delegation from London because of fear that Warsaw might fall to Communist hands. The change of the situation due to a successful Polish counteroffensive had no influence on his approach to the problem, for he regarded this new reality as an excellent opportunity to expel the Bolsheviks.

since, as we have already seen, they practically regarded themselves as the servants of the Crown—or as "royalists," in contrast to politicians who were either Liberals, Conservatives, or Labourites—they found a convenient outlet to channel their frustrations in the form of unauthorized action that, in their opinion, was in the best interest of the King and the country.

The destructive role of these beliefs was further intensified by a defective decisionmaking process that dominated action in the 1920 case. Partly because the participants in Wilson's plot were extremists with a mind for intrigue, and partly because they indulged in unauthorized secret activity rather than in a formal and more open decisionmaking process, they were highly exposed to groupthinking symptoms, mainly a high level of group cohesiveness, solidarity, and conformity. This was evidenced, for example, by several circumstances: the automatic rejection by Wilson of the opinion of the high-ranking naval officers who had reservations about the validity of his estimates as well as about the course of action he wanted to take; the condoning by Harington, Thwaites, Thomson, Sinclair, and Trenchard of Wilson's absurd notion that Lloyd George was a "Bolshevik" and a "traitor"; the ease by which Sinclair changed his opinion about the necessity to publish the intercepted telegrams despite the damage this would cause to the GC&CS; or the way various memoranda to defend the plotters' political stand were drawn, without their writers even considering the possibility that their perceptions might be wrong.

Defects in the decisionmaking process played a lesser role in the 1924 case. Although we do not have any evidence of how the decision to leak the Zinoviev letter was made, it seems that there was no orderly decisionmaking process here. If there were any doubts among the plotters in this case, they must have involved only tactical issues such as the best way to make the document available to the press or the optimal timing for taking the action. The principal decision to leak the letter appears to have been taken individually and intuitively as a result of the political opportunities suggested by publication of the letter in the context of the elections. After all, in 1924 concern for the fate of the nation as a result of a popular upheaval was relatively minor compared to the situation in 1920 since the Bolshevik threat and labor unrest were not as menacing as they had been four years earlier. Moreover, from the intelligence makers' point of view, the record of MacDonald's cabinet in dealing with this problem should have been just as good (or bad) as that of earlier governments. We can conclude then, though without the support of any empirical evidence, that the decision to leak the Zinoviev letter was motivated mainly by political biases and preferences of some of Britain's intelligence makers.

The decision could also have been influenced, as some have suggested, by parochial considerations—namely, the fear that the Labour government might abolish the services for ideological reasons (Chester, Fay, and Young, p. 108; Andrew 1985, p. 308). This argument makes sense from the bureaucratic point of view, but we do not have evidence on the topic. At least Special Branch and MI5, however, must have realized that Labour was surprisingly receptive to their arguments, and the same is true with regard to MID and NID. Although there were calls in the past, mainly between 1919 and 1921, to abolish the services—especially what Labour politicians used to label "political police"—and although such calls were repeated following the Zinoviev letter episode, there are no indications that significant Labour policymakers were thinking of or speaking of taking this step at the time when they were in power. As equally important could have been the concern that the Labour return to power might ultimately put an end to the doctrine of "continuity" that had dominated British foreign policy since the 1880s. Moreover, it could threaten the dominance of the small group of professionals (including the heads of the services) that managed the foreign affairs of the empire no matter what party was in power. After all, during the early 1920s issues of foreign policy became a topic of partisan politics and public debate precisely because of the rise of the Labour movement.

All in all, then, although the rationale for intelligence interference in politics in 1920 and 1924 derives from the same sources, there is some variance between the two cases regarding the situational causes for action. In 1920 the cause was a combination of misperceptions and hysteric fears for the immediate fate of the nation. The minds of the plotters created a rather imaginary crisis, and their initiative to save the nation from a nonexistent threat was amplified by a highly defective decisionmaking process. In 1924 the decision to interfere was more calculated and was based on longer-range calculations. It came as a reaction to the political opportunities suggested by the coincidence of the discovery of the Zinoviev letter and the timing of the elections, and was probably taken intuitively without involving any serious discussion.

Can we single out some variables that best explain the extreme behavior that occurred under the British system of intelligence? Here, of course, we are on shaky ground, but two main variables appear to be more important than others. First, the British civil service had greater influence in the formulation of policy than was the case in the United States and Israel. In Britain, Parliament was usually subordinate to the dictates of the cabinet, while the civil service had unusual freedom in shaping the formulation (as opposed to the execution) of policy. This power could, in principle, be used for good or ill; the important point here is that it existed. Hence a rogue elephant in the civil service or the intelligence community had a greater ability to manipulate the policy process and perceived himself to have wider room to maneuver in doing so. This variable explains the ability; when it comes to the desire to do so, the "old boys net" has greater explanatory power. This system had the most devastating effect on the nature of the services and on their behavior, for it created the phenomenon of a closed club shrouded by a thick veil of secrecy. This made the agencies free from government control and thus free to pursue their own political ends. When such organs were headed by extremists and inexperienced managers, their tendency to interfere with the politics of their own country intensified; under certain situations—at times of crisis or when a prime opportunity occurred—this interference became virtually inevitable.

Summary

When compared to the American and Israeli cases, the British case studies are different in two respects, similar in one. The first difference involves the realm of intervention. In contrast to the "Bay of Pigs" and the "unfortunate business" incidents, where unauthorized action by the intelligence services was taken in the field of foreign policy, in the British cases intervention was taken in the domain of domestic politics. This was somewhat more subtle in the 1920 case. Although the plotters' immediate goal was to compel Lloyd George to expel the Bolshevik delegation from London, these actions would patently affect domestic politics in Britain as well. The 1924 episode constitutes a far more clear-cut case of domestic intervention since the immediate goal of the intelligence action was to get Labour out of office.

The second difference involves the intensity of the intelligence services' interference with politics and the lessons learned. In the United States and Israel the executive branches and the intelligence communities learned very carefully from the lessons of their fiascoes. It was far more difficult for the CIA to mislead the president when conducting a venture similar to the "Bay of Pigs" after 1961, and the readiness of the agency's officers to take a similar initiative declined significantly as well. The same is true with regard to the inclination and the ability of Israel's intelligence makers to conduct unauthorized operations after 1954. In Britain, in contrast, we had one case of crude intelligence-military intervention in politics in 1920 and less than four years later another venture of the same type. The plot against Harold Wilson fifty years later suggests, moreover, that the same inclination and ability on behalf of some intelligence personnel remained in effect.

The intensity and severity of the British services' intervention in politics suggest that there is a fundamental problem in government-intelligence relations in this country. We have already discussed the conditions that enabled the services to abuse their power and the motivation behind this abuse. One can only wonder about the rationality that has prevented British governments, until the beginning of the 1990s, from taking drastic measures to change this state of affairs. A possible answer is that governments (mainly of the Conservatives) were often not concerned with the loyalty of the services whereas those that were (mainly Labour) either did not have enough power to change the situation or were not willing to face the political problems that would confront any attempt to do so. We can conclude, then, that under such conditions the likelihood of intelligence intervention in politics remained higher in Britain than in the United States and Israel.

Lastly, there is one similarity between our previous cases and the British ones. In the "Bay of Pigs" and the "unfortunate business" episodes we found a direct and positive correlation between the tendency to make ethical mistakes (that is, intervention in politics) and the inclination to err professionally. In the American and the Israeli cases this correlation was highly evident because the intelligence action ended in a humiliating fiasco. Although in Britain the intelligence action did not end in the same way (mainly because it did not involve risky covert operations), it nevertheless revealed a low level of intelligence professionalism. This was more clearly evident in the 1920 case when senior intelligence officers erred fundamentally in estimating the likelihood of a revolution in Britain and when they campaigned for publication of intelligence documents despite the very high cost involved in losing the nation's most valuable source of secret information. No such cost was to be paid in the 1924 case, a fact that by itself eased the decision to leak the Zinoviev letter to the press.

Yet the most devastating result of the right-wing elitist orientation of the British intelligence community became clear only decades later. Being the extreme anti-Bolshevik and anti-Socialist organizations that they were, the services focused solely on the British left as a source of potential danger to the nation's security. But the real danger, as became known only in the 1950s with the exposure of the Oxbridge moles, came not from the Communists or the Labourites but from the elite of the Foreign Office and the intelligence community itself. Had the services been less politically biased, they could have prevented, or at least minimized, the damage caused by Philby, Burgess, Maclean, and Blunt. Yet their hubristic belief that no traitor could be "one of us" led them in the long run to suffer a defeat far more humiliating and traumatic than the "Bay of Pigs" and "unfortunate business" incidents. Unlike their American and Israeli colleagues, British intelligence makers seem to have never fully recovered from this devastating professional failure, which took place under their own noses and in their own backyards.

Part III

Conclusions

Introduction

The first part of this book introduced a theoretical framework for the analysis of intelligence-state relations. Its second part focused—through the detailed construction and analysis for four case studies—on a major pathology of this relationship: intelligence intervention in politics. As presented in the summary of the theoretical part, this empirical evidence had two tasks. The first was to give specific answers to three general questions: (1) By what means do intelligence organizations intervene in politics? (2) Why do they do it? (3) What conditions, at all levels of analysis, make it possible for them to behave this way? The second task was to provide a partial empirical test of three interrelated propositions:

1. That unauthorized attempts by intelligence to alter government policies are the culmination of a process in which the political and intelligence systems fail to properly isolate intelligence from politics.
2. That there is a high correlation between these attempts and a low level of intelligence professionalism, as expressed in the way the intelligence officers involved performed their operational duties.
3. That the unilateral-constitutional control system is not sufficient to prevent intelligence from interfering with politics and that a multilateral-constitutional control system is more likely to attain this goal.

The specific case studies have already stated many conclusions regarding the three questions and the specific propositions. Part III will first review the answers to the three questions and then summarize the conclusions regarding the propositions.

9

Intelligence Intervention: Means, Ends, and Conditions

THE MEANS

The three types of means used by intelligence organizations to intervene in politics include: manipulation, including concealment, of information over which intelligence has a monopoly; unauthorized action, mainly through the use of covert operations instruments; and a conspiracy against the government, made feasible by the veil of secrecy that clouds intelligence work. The intelligence action in each of the case studies (the two British episodes are analyzed here together) was governed by the use of one of these means.

In the Bay of Pigs affair the CIA's drive to obtain political authorization for the Cuban invasion, especially as the decision about implementation of the operation drew closer, was characterized by manipulation of information. In briefing their prime targets—the President and his advisors—CIA planners deliberately exaggerated the ability of the Cuban Exile Force to reach its operational goals (or at least to avoid a total failure), and understated the power of the Castro regime to defend itself. Secondary targets were the Joint Chiefs, whose professional approval of the operation was a necessary condition for political authorization, and the CEF itself, which was led to believe that the American military would intervene if the need arose.

Unauthorized action and conspiracy were far less prominent than manipulation of information in the CIA's political action. On the one hand, the way the agency altered the concept of the Cuban project and implemented this change in November 1960 involved a dimension of unauthorized action. Yet, owing to some confusion between President Eisenhower and his intelligence officers, it remains unclear whether the CIA really had no authority to make this decision. In any event, it received political approval, though only ex post facto. Apart from this incident the CIA did not take any other significant unauthorized actions. Similarly, the planners of the Bay of Pigs did not indulge in a conspiracy against their political bosses, although some of them were aware that the assumptions they made when planning the operation involved principal political considerations beyond their sphere of responsibility. These, however, remained tacit. As Allen Dulles put it: "We *felt* that when the chips were down . . . any action required for success would be authorized rather than permit the enterprise to fail (Vandenbroucke, p. 369; emphasis added).

The Israeli "unfortunate business affair" of July 1954 was clearly an unauthorized action. The order by the Director of Military Intelligence, Colonel Givli, to implement the Egyptian operation received neither political nor military approval. As though Givli himself later argued that Defense Minister Lavon had authorized the operation, the sequence of events of this episode proves that, even if this were true, such approval could have been given only two weeks after the operation had started and had no effect on the way it ended.

The elements of manipulation of information and conspiracy were less dominant in this case. Obviously, Colonel Givli concealed information from his superiors with regard to both the unit that carried out the operation (Unit 131 over which Givli had gained a monopoly since early 1954) and to his own instructions to launch the Egyptian operation. In this sense concealment, as is always the case in the conduct of unauthorized action, was only instrumental in reaching a more important goal. Conspiracy was not involved in this case because the operation was the creation of a single man who did not let others participate in his venture. After all, only Colonel Givli knew that the order to launch the operation was given and that it was not authorized by any of his political or military superiors.

The dominant feature in the two British cases was conspiracy. Both in the 1920 "Henry Wilson affair" and in the 1924 "Zinoviev letter" episode the action against the government was collective, and in both cases the participants were well aware of the political implications of their actions. The unconstitutional dimensions of these actions must have been very clear in the 1924 case, though somewhat more vague to the participants of the Henry Wilson conspiracy. In the latter case, however, this dimension was raised in discussions with other military officers who declined to participate in the plot. The conspiracy of 1920 was more intense in the sense that it lasted longer (close to a month) and involved a number of occasions during which the participants met to discuss their course of action.

Although there is no conclusive evidence to suggest that the Zinoviev letter was forged, there is enough documentary evidence to show that the Secret Intelligence Service believed that the letter was genuine. Hence it was concluded that the leak of the letter to Conservative politicians and the press constituted the use of an opportunity rather than the creation of one. Nevertheless, the conspiratorial dimensions of this case are the clearest available, for all participants in this venture aimed precisely at damaging Labour's ability to win the elections.

Manipulation of information and unauthorized action played only an instrumental role in the British episodes. The first type of action was rather clear in the Henry Wilson case of 1920, when alarming reports of Bolshevik subversion were delivered to policymakers while others of a more reassuring tone were not. Since there was no interaction with policymakers in the 1924 leak of the Zinoviev letter, this element was hardly present in this case. In both cases unauthorized action was present in the form of leaks of secret intelligence documents to the press. These were instrumental to the efforts of the plotters in compelling the Prime Minister to alter his policy in 1920 and in damaging the chances of the Prime Minister to remain in office in 1924.

THE ENDS

As is clear from the detailed analysis of each of the case studies, the intelligence officers involved were motivated by various considerations and intentions, some of which were less salient than others. This section will focus only on the dominant goal of each action.

The ultimate goal of the CIA in the Bay of Pigs was to bring about the downfall of Castro's regime in Cuba. This goal received the bipartisan backing of two presidents and was aimed at changing a situation in the domain of foreign politics. There are no indications that the CIA had any ulterior motives in domestic politics, except for demonstrating to the new administration its value in solving foreign policy problems, a bureaucratic desire that cannot be considered unconstitutional.

Colonel Givli's direct goal in ordering the Egyptian operation was to wreck the Anglo-Egyptian agreement on the evacuation of the Suez Canal Zone. Although it was intended to change a situation in foreign affairs, the Egyptian operation also had potential bearing on Israel's domestic politics, for it reflected an extreme variant of a policy line diametrically opposed to the foreign policy of the Prime Minister and Minister of Foreign Affairs, Sharett. In this sense, unlike the case of the Bay of Pigs, the Israeli unauthorized operation involved a deliberate attempt to divert Israel's foreign policy from the direction given it by the Prime Minister and many of his cabinet members. Colonel Givli must have been aware of this dimension of his venture, but there is no indication that he ever considered the effect that the operation might have on the political status of Sharett or Israel's political elite. Hence this episode is considered here as a case of an unauthorized action in the domain of foreign policy alone.

The immediate goal of the plotters in the Henry Wilson affair of 1920 was the expulsion from London of the Soviet trade delegation. All of them, however, were aware that this was only one component (though a major one) in a power struggle with Prime Minister Lloyd George over Britain's Russian policy and over what the plotters considered to be the possibility of a revolution at home. From their perspective, then, the struggle was over major foreign and domestic policies. Moreover, they intended, through the unauthorized publication of secret intelligence in the press and possible collective resignation, to directly confront Lloyd George and most of his cabinet members unless they accepted their demands. Some of the plotters believed that taking such measures would bring down the government. Hence, although the immediate goal of the plot was in the domain of foreign policy, it also involved considerations and goals in domestic politics.

Given that MacDonald's Labour government was as firm on the issue of Bolshevik subversion as its predecessors, security considerations could not be used even as an excuse for the leak of the Zinoviev letter. This act was motivated purely by political considerations. The intelligence officers who participated in it were merely "voting" this unorthodox way for the Conservative opposition and against the government in office. In this sense, as far as ends are concerned, even if intelligence action in this case did not precisely constitute a coup d'état, it certainly bordered on such.

Altogether the evidence presented in this book includes a wide range of considerations and goals that may motivate intelligence to intervene in politics: from an attempt to change a presidential decision regarding the means to be used in a large-scale covert operation, through challenging the foreign policy of the government, to compelling a prime minister to change his foreign and domestic policies, and ending with an act aimed at changing the government as a whole. With the exception of the Bay of Pigs, where the source of the friction with the political echelon involved professional no less than political considerations, in all other cases the root of the conflict was political. Professional considerations served merely as an excuse for political action by intelligence officers. In this sense the empirical evidence shows that, just as some policymakers prefer to be their own intelligence officers, some intelligence officers prefer to be their own political policymakers.

THE CONDITIONS

This study grouped the conditions that made intelligence intervention in politics possible according to four levels of analysis: the international system, the state, the bureaucratic, and the personal level. Each of the cases yielded different explanations.

In the American case the most important factor that explained the behavior of the CIA in the Bay of Pigs episode was the personality of the agency's Deputy Director for Plans, Richard Bissell, who as the chief architect of the project played a decisive role in the policymaking process that led to the invasion. In the Israeli case the critical factors were found at two levels: weak political control of intelligence at the state level, and specific features in the behavior of Director of Military Intelligence Givli, Prime Minister Sharett, Defense Minister Lavon, and Chief of Staff Dayan at the personal level. In the British cases the critical variables derived from the state and the bureaucratic levels: a political culture that made it difficult to control the intelligence agencies, combined with a recruitment system that led to the construction of unprofessional intelligence "clubs" that were not subjected to very much political control at all.

On the basis of these findings it is appropriate to develop some general hypotheses regarding the critical factors that make intelligence intervention in politics more or less likely to occur.

The International System

The critical factor at this level of analysis is the presence of *crisis*, a development in the international system that is perceived as a threat to important national values. When other aspects of crisis—namely, surprise and a limited reaction time—are also present, they add to the sense of urgency and to the need for action in order to neutralize the threat.

In each of the four cases the contribution of external pressure to the intelligence intervention was clear. The Castro regime posed a threat to American hegemony in the Western Hemisphere at the height of the Cold War; the British decision to withdraw from the Suez Canal Zone posed a major threat to Israel's security; and the rising Bolshevik power provoked real fears in Britain as to the possibility of revolution both at home and throughout the empire.

Significant as they are, in order to have an impact on intelligence behavior such structural developments must be perceived as serious threats by some members of the intelligence community and the government. After all, external "objective" threats are channeled through individual perceptions (which in turn are influenced by political culture, social status, education, previous experience, etc.), and the variance in threat perceptions makes up the basis for conflict of opinion and unauthorized intelligence action. Hence, at the structural level, crisis constitutes a *catalyst*, stimulating situations in which intelligence agencies and individuals may be tempted to intervene in politics.

The State Level

Variables at the state level shape the type and the quality of political control systems placed over intelligence activities. Most influential in this respect are the state political system and the value placed on national security in relation to other dominant values of the country's political culture. The impact of the political system (presidential or parliamentary) on the control system has been partly discussed already. Hence this section will put more emphasis on the impact of values from the political culture.

In the four case studies a unilateral-constitutional system was operative. Yet the ability of the political echelon to monitor intelligence activities differed in each country. The White House monopoly of control over the CIA (since the agency's establishment and until the mid-1970s) derived mainly from a lack of real interest on the part of the Congress, the media, and the public to join the process. Their attitude was motivated not only by the belief that such a role fell within the responsibilities of the executive branch and that this branch could be trusted to live up to this responsibility but also by the conviction that winning the Cold War was the ultimate goal of American foreign policy and justified extreme means.[1] In the case of the Bay of Pigs this belief was vividly expressed in the national consensus that Castro should be removed from power. This commitment weakened the control system over the CIA, for it made all participants in the planning of the operation believe that political limitations were less important than achieving the main goal. Thus, for example, although President Kennedy demanded that the Joint Chiefs review the feasibility of the invasion plan, they did so in a perfunctory manner, in part because they believed that if the CIA failed in its mission the American military would be called in to intervene.

In the parliamentary systems of Britain and Israel a powerful political linkage exists between the executive and the legislative branches. As a result, in both states the tendency of the Parliament to challenge the daily management of state affairs is less than in the United States. In addition, in both states national security values are deemed superior to other national values. This priority has always been used effectively by British and Israeli governments to reject suggestions to open the system to nonexecutive control on the basis of the argument that intelligence affairs must be kept secret and are too important to become politicized.

Although the values they share are similar, Britain and Israel employ the system of unilateral-constitutional control differently. At least until recent years the British civil service, an organ far more powerful than in Israel (or the United States), played a major role in limiting the ability of politicians to control the intelligence community. Since the prime bureaucratic interest of this service has always been to prevent outsiders from gaining control over its activities, it served as a powerful and effective buffer not only between the intelligence community—itself part of the civil service—and the Parliament or the press but also between this community and the

1. A typical example of this attitude is the "Report of the Special Study Group [Doolittle Committee] on the Covert Activities of the Central Intelligence Agency," 30 September 1954. The report stated inter alia that:

> As it remains national policy, another important requirement is an aggressive covert psychological, political and paramilitary organization more effective, more unique and, if necessary, more ruthless than that employed by the enemy. No one should be permitted to stand in the way of the prompt, efficient and secure accomplishment of this mission. . . . There are no rules in such a game. Hitherto accepted norms of human conduct do not apply. If the United States is to survive, long-standing American concepts of "fair play" must be reconsidered. (Quoted in Leary 1984, pp. 143–44)

government in power. In this sense, whereas other countries have institutionalized means to control intelligence activities, the British political system has institutionalized a system to prevent such control. However, since the end of the Cold War this system has started to go through some significant changes. By mid-1993 arrangements had been made to bring MI5 and MI6 (but not the GCHQ, at least for the time being) under the scrutiny of Parliament.

A second difference between the British and Israeli systems of unilateral-constitutional control is that, unlike Britain, two of Israel's three intelligence agencies—the domestic Security Service (Shabak) and the foreign Intelligence Service (Mossad)—are directly subordinate to the prime minister and belong to his office. The third agency, Military Intelligence, belongs to the army, but its chief is considered in practical terms as the government's intelligence officer, and the prime minister usually has direct access to this agency as well. The result is that the chain of command between the state leader and his intelligence community is far shorter and tighter in Israel than in Britain.

The differences between the Israeli and British methods of control manifest themselves most clearly in terms of the postmortem of intelligence intervention in politics. It is quite rare in Britain for a complete investigation of any intelligence abuse of power to take place, just as it is quite uncommon for heads of the intelligence agencies to be removed from their positions for such behavior. The cases of Sir Basil Thomson, the Director of Intelligence, who was fired in 1921 because of his anti-Bolshevik activities that interfered with Lloyd George's Russian policy and his incompetence over Irish matters, or of MI6 (SIS) head Sir John "Sinbad" Sinclair, who was fired following the "Crabb affair" in 1956,[2] are exceptions. The more normal practice is that which took place after the Zinoviev letter incident, at which time no thorough investigation took place into the responsibility of the services for the leak of the letter. In Israel, in contrast, there is at least a tradition of investigating intelligence, as is evidenced by statistics

2. In 1956, during the visit of Khrushchev and Bulganin to Britain, MI6 with the cooperation of MI5 and Naval Intelligence, arranged for Lionel Crabb, Britain's gallant frogman, to inspect the warships that brought the Soviet leaders to Britain. This was done despite a direct order by Prime Minister Eden to avoid any intelligence operations during this visit. Crabb was caught underwater and later probably died on board the very ship that he was supposed to inspect. The Soviets used this incident to embarrass their British hosts, and a furious Eden replaced the Director-General of MI6, Sir John Sinclair (not to be confused with his predecessor, Vice Admiral Hugh "Quex" Sinclair, who headed SIS between 1923 and 1939), with the chief of MI5, Sir Dick White. For further details of this incident, see Pincher 1984, pp. 232–37, and Rusbridger 1989, pp. 63–71.

showing that about 50 percent of the directors of Military Intelligence have been fired because of professional and political wrongdoing. This fact by itself serves as a practical, though insufficient, means to deter the directors of the Israeli intelligence community from interfering with politics.

Altogether, then, state-level factors in the United States, Israel, and Britain shaped three variations of the unilateral-constitutional control system. The American political system gives the president effective means to control intelligence but also opens the way for Congress and other actors to participate in this task. In the case of the Bay of Pigs the system failed because of the urgent need, perceived by the White House, the Congress, the military, and the CIA, to topple Castro. The Israeli system gives the prime minister effective means of control over two intelligence agencies but less institutionalized access to Military Intelligence. In 1954 the link between the prime minister and this agency was very weak, owing to lack of authority on the part of Sharett in military affairs. The British control system is the weakest of all three. It is hampered by the buffer set up by the civil service, by the long chain of command between the prime minister's office and the specific intelligence agencies, and by a national belief system that objects to tight control of the services in the name of national security and "patriotism." These were the main causes at the state level for the failure of the system in 1920 and 1924.

The Bureaucratic Level

Analysis of the individual case studies led to the identification of a number of factors at the bureaucratic level that are typical of intelligence work and that have made intelligence misconduct more feasible. Most important among these variables are secrecy and its byproduct, compartmentation— both of which have made it far easier for intelligence officers such as DDP Richard Bissell of the CIA or Colonel Givli of the DMI to act in the way they did. Other factors at this level, mainly interbureaucratic competition, embodied in the desire to show policymakers the ability of a certain service to solve policy problems, contributed to the motivation for the action.

Unlike in the United States and Israel where bureaucratic-level variables have only made intelligence intervention in politics more feasible, in Britain a variable at this level has played the decisive role in the tendency of intelligence to abuse its power. Here the "old boys net" recruitment system has determined the collective features of the intelligence community and has made it far more politically active than those of the United States and Israel. The most important feature of the British intelligence "club" has been its right-wing *Weltanschauung*. The impact of this feature was amplified by a number of other characteristics typical of this community: a "we-know-best" approach; a high level of group cohesiveness on the basis of similar social background, education, and ideology; and a tendency to engage in "worst-case analyses" that bordered, at times, on simple hysteria.

The British example is striking, especially when compared to the political and professional profiles of the American and Israeli intelligence communities, in which a far more open recruitment system has always been employed. Obviously, these latter communities include individuals who share the British characteristics, just as some individual British officers are an exception in their own intelligence communities. But in general the collective beliefs and patterns of behavior of the American and the Israeli intelligence communities reflect the national consensus—or at least the mainstream beliefs—of their countries. Thus, if in the United States and Israel the services constitute a "people's intelligence," in Britain the intelligence community constitutes a "conservative–upper-class intelligence."

It should be noted, however, that this characterization of the British intelligence community is valid only for peacetime. In both World War I and World War II a large number of "amateurs" joined the services and rapidly changed their collective characters. Once the war ended, the "amateurs" left the intelligence community, which quickly regained its old peacetime patterns. Notably, British intelligence performance in both wars is generally credited with being far more successful than its peacetime performance.[3] This contrast by itself supports the argument that the per-

---

3. The record of British intelligence in World War I and World War II is indeed impressive. In counterintelligence MI5 was highly efficient in tracking all German agents during World War I (see e.g. Andrew 1985, p. 182). It was even more successful in World War II, where it not only tracked all German agents but also turned most of them into double agents (Masterman 1972). British code breakers, mostly amateurs, were highly successful in breaking German and other nations' military and diplomatic codes in World War I (Beesly 1982; Andrew 1985, pp. 86–126) and developed this ability even further in World War II. The story of Ultra, the cryptanalysis coup that enabled the Allies to read the German Enigma cipher throughout most of the war and the way it was used by the generals, has received much attention since Winterbotham (1974) first revealed the "Ultra secret." For the most concise and authoritative account on how this coup was achieved, see Hinsley et al., vol. 1, app. 1 (pp. 487–95), and vol. 3, pt. 2, app. 30 (pp. 945–59). For other accounts, mainly by veterans of Bletchley Park, where schoolmasters, university professors, chess players, mathematicians, businessmen, and other amateurs broke German high-grade ciphers, see Calvocoressi 1980, Welchman 1982, and Hodges 1983. For some important studies describing the

formance of the British intelligence community at times of peace has been rather amateurish.

The relationship between the professional and political profiles of intelligence organizations and their tendency to intervene in politics will be discussed in more detail below. Here it suffices to emphasize that, although bureaucratic-level variables are usually regarded as factors that only make it possible for intelligence to intervene in politics, this book shows that under certain circumstances, as in Britain, they can also determine the strength of the tendency to intervene.

The Personal Level

Crisis at the international level serves as a catalyst to provoke intelligence to intervene in politics; variables at the state level make up the type and the quality of the political control system; and factors at the bureaucratic level determine the ability—sometimes also the strength of the tendency—of intelligence to abuse its power. But, in the final analysis, the personalities of the men who inhabit both the political and intelligence institutions determine the nature, the scope, and the result of intelligence interference with politics—hence the need to identify the qualities that make some leaders more capable than others of controlling intelligence and the features that doom some intelligence officers more than others to intervene in politics.

The Political Leadership

Two qualities enable political leaders to control their intelligence communities: personal authority and awareness of the need to be constantly vigilant

---

impact of their work on the war effort, see Hinsley et al. 1979–88, Jones 1978 (scientific intelligence), Beesly 1978 (naval intelligence), Levin 1978, and Bennett 1979 and 1989. Although deception (except for Allenby's operations in the Middle East theater) played only a minor role in British strategy in World War I, it was far more important in World War II, where the "double-cross" system and "Ultra" facilitated highly successful strategic deception. On this subject, see Montagu 1954 and 1978, Mure 1977 and 1980, and Handel 1987. Cave Brown (1975) is more popular, yet also less accurate.

Typically, whereas studies on British intelligence during wars are about successes, the literature on the services during peacetime, especially the Cold War era, is about flops, mostly the failure of British counterintelligence services to track the "Oxbridge moles" and other Soviet spies in Britain after 1945. Clearly this difference reflects the dissimilar realities of British intelligence performance in times of war and peace.

over these communities. Eisenhower, Churchill, and Ben-Gurion, for example, had both of these qualities, although they differed in the way they employed them. Eisenhower preferred a loose system of control over the CIA, even at the height of the Cold War when the agency played a major role in U.S. foreign policy. He could act this way precisely because he knew that his personal record and prestige would prevent the agency from challenging his authority and because sources of conflict between him and the CIA were minimal owing to the fact that they both shared the same Cold War ideology. Indeed, although towards the end of his administration Eisenhower lost some control of the CIA (as evidenced by the unauthorized implementation of a new concept for the Cuban operation), his method of loose control proved, in general, to be sufficient to prevent the CIA from resorting to any significant unconstitutional acts.

Churchill, a charismatic and authoritative leader, had an enthusiastic interest in intelligence and maintained a special relationship with Britain's intelligence community long before he became prime minister. Indeed, his appetite for intelligence action, mainly of the cloak-and-dagger type, led him occasionally to intervene in professional intelligence work. The respect of his intelligence makers for his leadership, combined with his personal interest in the subject, were sufficient to prevent (as far as is known) intelligence from resorting to unauthorized actions throughout his premiership.[4]

Similar to Eisenhower and Churchill, Ben-Gurion enjoyed much respect and authority in Israel's military and intelligence communities of the 1950s. Despite the absence of proper norms of public behavior in general, and of professional conduct in intelligence-government relations in particular, Ben-Gurion's personal authority enabled him to maintain a very tight control over the intelligence services. Perhaps the most vivid evidence of the quality of this control is the fact that, out of the five heads of military and civilian agencies who served under him, only one was not forced to resign. Yet at the same time, unlike Churchill, Ben-Gurion avoided interfering with professional intelligence work. By combining tight control without such interference, he established the foundation for a rather healthy government-intelligence relationship in Israel.

Lack of control over intelligence, and even more so lack of sufficient authority, lead to the opposite results. For example, upon entering office President Kennedy administered tighter control over intelligence than his

---

4. For an interesting discussion of Churchill's relationship with the British intelligence community, see Andrew 1989, pp. 181–93.

predecessor, as evidenced by the intense interaction between himself and the chiefs of the CIA in preparation for the Cuban operation. He nevertheless lacked the experience and authority of Eisenhower. MacDonald in Britain and Sharett in Israel are examples of leaders who were weak from the beginning in their relationship with the intelligence community. Their intelligence services did not share their ideologies, had little, or no faith at all, in their policies, and had no respect for their right to control intelligence activities. Moreover, neither MacDonald nor Sharett paid enough attention to their services. The results were the political fiascoes of 1924 in Britain and 1954 in Israel.

Intelligence: The Operational and the Analytical Modes

An analysis of the behavior of some intelligence officers (such as DDP Richard Bissell, DMI Colonel Givli, or Rear Admiral Sir Hugh "Quex" Sinclair) brings to light common features that distinguish them from more professional intelligence makers (for example, DCI Richard Helms or Colonel Harkabi of Israel's Military Intelligence). The former represent the action-oriented operational mode;[5] the latter, the analytical mode. The differences between these two modes provide us with a final explanation for the tendency of intelligence to intervene in politics.

The mind of the operational-type officer is action-oriented. He sees political problems as difficulties that can be solved by action and refuses to accept conditions in which little can be done to change an undesired situation. Richard Bissell's perception of the problems that Communist Cuba posed to American foreign policy is typical in this regard: despite growing evidence that Castro could not be toppled by means of covert action, Bissell continued to be committed to his operation, never realizing that perhaps the best way to get rid of Castro was through political and economic pressures alone. Similarly, Colonel Givli refused to accept that no action could delay or prevent the conclusion of the Anglo-Egyptian accord in 1954 and believed that only a successful covert operation could attain this goal.

The orientation towards action leads the operational-type officer to

5. The term "mode" should not be confused here with the professional ethic of the operational officer nor, obviously, with the ethic of the planner of operations. As will be shown below, professional planning of operations, which is a staff function, requires precisely the same qualifications demanded from the intelligence "analytic" officer.

perceive the general situation through the prism of his operation, thus confusing tactics with strategy and means with ends. Rather than forcing the operation to serve political ends, he subordinates political ends to serve his operation. Hence he is also likely to develop a conception of reality that will fit with operational demands. The belief of Bissell and Dulles that President Kennedy would revise his decision to avoid direct American intervention in the Cuba operation despite Kennedy's commitment to this principle is a fine example of the way the operational mode works to solve inconsistency between reality and planning: the operational officer simply resorts to wishful thinking.

The obsession of the action-oriented officer to carry out his operation makes him a risk-taker. This can be partly explained by his tendency to combine a tactical "Pollyanna" syndrome with a strategic "Cassandra" syndrome. In other words, he is likely to engage in a best-case analysis when estimating the feasibility and the necessity of his operations. At the same time, he estimates the long-range situation (especially if the operation is not implemented) in terms of a worst-case analysis. This duality explains his tendency to learn more from successful operations than from those that failed. This, of course, leads him to overestimate the importance of covert action for national security and to reject any criticism that doubts the logic behind his action. After all, he "knows best."

These features were described in three of the case studies. The intelligence officers who participated in the Henry Wilson plot shared the apocalyptic view of a coming revolution in Britain unless they took immediate measures to prevent such a development. Givli perceived a dramatic decrease in Israel's ability to survive following the Anglo-Egyptian accord and failed to understand the poor chances of his operation to forestall this threat. Similarly, the architects of the Cuban operation ignored many weaknesses in their planning simply because they regarded the possibility of Castro remaining in power as too dangerous from an American perspective.

The analytic intelligence officer is just the opposite. He is a realist who is aware of the limits of his power. He is prudent, avoids both best-case and worst-case analyses, and estimates the merits of action solely on the basis of its net contribution to the state's national interest (as Helms did, for example, in the case of the Cuban operation). He changes the operation according to the constraints of reality; is eager to learn from failures; is open to criticism; and is risk-averse, although in critical situations he is ready to take a calculated risk. Most important, he perceives the primary goal of his profession as supplying policymakers with relevant, timely, and accurate information and analysis, regarding covert operations as a secondary priority of his profession, and accepts the subordination of his profession to the state, embodied in the elected leadership.

In sum, the operational-mode officer places a premium on action; the analytical-mode less so. When the political echelon objects to a certain type of action favored by the operational type, he will look for ways to bypass this objection. His analytical colleague will be more inclined to accept the political judgment. Therefore, the operational-mode officer is far more likely than his analytical colleague to intervene in politics. Intelligence agencies headed by operational mode officers are less likely to be professional than agencies headed by analytical-mode officers.

Summary

This discussion presented six variables from four levels of analysis that were found to be most critical in shaping the likelihood of intelligence interference with politics. The emphasis here is on the concept of "likelihood," for there is no certainty, even when all conditions that favor intervention are present, that such action will indeed take place. In turn, there can be no certainty that intervention will *not* occur in the cases where all these conditions are absent. In this sense none of the six variables constitutes either a necessary or sufficient condition for causing or preventing intelligence intervention in politics. Table 6 summarizes these variables.

Table 6. Intelligence intervention in politics: The critical conditions

Level	Variable	High Likelihood of Intervention	Low Likelihood of Intervention
International	Crisis (catalyst)	Present	Not present
State	Type of political control	Loose unilateral	Tight unilateral or multilateral
	National security value	Above other values	Equal to other values
Bureaucratic	Recruitment system	Old boys net (politically biased)	Open and equal (politically unbiased)
Personal	Intelligence leadership	Operational mode	Analytical mode
	Political leadership	No authority; no interest in intelligence	Authoritative; interested in intelligence

10

The Hypotheses

The previous section summarized the empirical evidence on the general questions of this study: how and why intelligence intervenes in politics, and what conditions make this intervention possible. This section summarizes the empirical evidence in relation to the three hypotheses of this study: (1) that there is a direct link between insufficient isolation of intelligence from politics and intelligence attempts to alter policies, as described in the four case studies; (2) that there is a high correlation between an insufficient level of intelligence professionalism and this type of behavior; and (3) that unilateral-constitutional control methods are often insufficient to prevent such behavior and that the multilateral-constitutional system can control intelligence better.

PROPOSITION I: "REALISTS," "PROFESSIONALS," AND INTERVENTION

The debate between supporters of maximal isolation of intelligence from politics (the "professionals") and their antagonists (the "realists"), who claim that intelligence should not be completely separated from politics, was reviewed earlier. In summarizing the debate I proposed that there might be a causal link between insufficient separation of intelligence from politics (at a level acceptable for the "realists") and cases in which intelligence breaks out of political control in an attempt to conduct policies of its own. Certainly, neither the "realists" nor, of course, the "professionals" consider intelligence abuse of power as described in our case studies as desirable or even excusable. They nevertheless fail to take this consideration into account when making their arguments. The existence of this link is clearly illustrated by the empirical evidence.

The political limitations placed on CIA operations were not clearly enough defined during the years of the Eisenhower administration. Given this background, a number of earlier experiences encouraged CIA planners to behave as they did when preparing the Bay of Pigs operation. Most illuminating in this respect was "Operation Success," the CIA's 1954 venture to overthrow President Arbenz from power in Guatemala. Although President Eisenhower made it clear prior to the implementation of that operation that no direct American intervention would be permitted, once the operation was under way he removed this limitation under pressure from DCI Dulles and despite the State Department's objections (Etheridge 1985; Higgins 1987). The director of the U-2 program, Richard Bissell, occasionally undertook initiatives beyond his responsibility as an intelligence officer. Yet neither he nor Dulles was ever called upon to account for these unauthorized initiatives, even when they were revealed, mainly because the project was so successful. And in preparing the Cuban venture the CIA planners changed the strategic concept of the operation and implemented this change without receiving any political authorization. Political approval was received only weeks later.

As a number of examples in the "unfortunate business" case study showed, the boundaries between intelligence and politics were even more obscured in Israel in 1954. The military in general and Military Intelligence in particular were hardly accountable to Prime Minister Sharett. Under Defense Minister Lavon and Chief of Staff Dayan the army conducted acts of retaliation against Arab states without receiving proper governmental authorization, initiated border incidents in order to justify the use of force, and planned risky covert operations having significant political implications without consulting anybody outside the armed forces. In many incidents, as was the case with the "unfortunate business" affair, the Prime Minister learned about his army's actions from press and radio reports. Even by these standards Colonel Givli's initiative to launch the Egyptian operation was unusual, but not rare.

The role model for the British intelligence officers of the 1920s was Sir Reginald "Blinker" Hall, the wartime director of Naval Intelligence. Brilliant as he was as an intelligence officer, Hall was also involved in politics more than any other intelligence officer of his time. On some occasions, as was the case with his handling of the "Zimmerman telegram," where he acted as Britain's de facto foreign secretary, bypassing the Foreign Office, this was done with political approval. On other occasions, such as his wartime negotiations with the Turkish government or leaks to the press of secret information, Hall acted with no political authority. Nevertheless, "by the end of the war his reputation stood so high that he was spoken of as a future Foreign Secretary" (James, p. 175).

This lack of sufficient separation between intelligence and politics in the United States, Israel, and Britain was a critical factor in the socialization of the intelligence officers involved in the case studies. DCI Dulles and DDP Bissell assumed that President Kennedy would alter his earlier objection to the use of American force if the need arose precisely because President Eisenhower did the same six years earlier. Colonel Givli could hardly grasp the ethical wrongdoing in launching the Egyptian operation because such behavior was the norm rather the exception in Israel in 1954. And the British intelligence makers who participated in the Henry Wilson plot of 1920 and the leak of the Zinoviev letter of 1924 merely followed the examples set earlier by Hall, who never paid for interfering so bluntly in politics.

If an open door tempts a saint, then surely insufficient isolation of intelligence from politics can lead to escalating abuse of the political system by ambitious intelligence officers. In this sense manipulation of information, unauthorized action, and conspiracy by intelligence officers against politicians were all merely functions of this lack of separation. Hence this study strongly objects to the "realist" approach. "Political virginity," the term used by the "realists" to define the goal of the "professionals," may be impossible. But it should still be maintained as much as possible, since the alternative may ultimately lead to the prostitution of intelligence work. By accepting the impossibility of "political virginity" as a fact of life, and not necessarily as an evil one, the protagonists of the "realist" approach open the door to an ever-increasing process that will compromise the integrity and the value of intelligence work. Ultimately this process may lead to severe political and intelligence fiascoes, as evidenced by our case studies. Certainly, this is not the "realists' " intention, but the result is just the same.

In this context a few additional remarks are appropriate. The onus for separating intelligence from politics lies first and foremost with politicians who need good intelligence. Some politicians, however, are less aware of this responsibility than others. For this reason the intelligence maker, who is usually more aware of the problem, should serve as the gatekeeper, ensuring that the door for political interference with intelligence and vice versa remains always closed. Certainly, this means that he should be highly professional in terms of both expertise and ethics, and such a combination of qualities is, sometimes, not so easy to come by. Indeed, selecting the right person to head a national intelligence agency is not an easy or simple job. But decision making is neither easy nor simple, and the policymaker who has to make the selection should regard these qualities as the most important criteria when making his choice.

It is also important to note here that, while politicians may come and go, intelligence making is usually a long-term career. Some policymakers may believe (as Ben-Gurion did in 1950 when accepting Givli as chief of the DMI) that they can control their intelligence makers and ensure that they will not intervene in politics. For this reason they might regard professional ethics and personal integrity as less relevant when making their selection. This is a mistake, however, since once they are out of office it is another person, perhaps less qualified, who has to keep a watchful eye on their appointee. Thus the combination of Ben-Gurion and Givli could work; the combination of Sharett, Lavon, and Givli could not.

Finally, we need to make a distinction between the short-term and long-term consequences of failing to separate intelligence from politics. In the short run such behavior can be rewarded by political goods for both the intelligence maker and the policymaker. This is precisely why it is so tempting and why the problem of separating intelligence from politics is so complex. But in the long run there is usually a high price to be paid. From Lavon and Givli in the "unfortunate business" through Bissell and Dulles in the Bay of Pigs, to the 1980s saga of the Iran-contra affair and Robert Gates's hearings of the early 1990s, politicians and intelligence makers learned this lesson. Hence in the long run it is in the self-interest of politicians and their intelligence experts to maintain clear separation between these two domains.

PROPOSITION II: PROFESSIONALISM AND THE TENDENCY TO INTERVENE

The second proposition suggested that there is a high correlation between the tendency of intelligence to intervene in politics and a low level of intelligence professionalism. The empirical evidence of the case studies fully supports this assumption. It also supports the argument that insufficient knowledge of various aspects of intelligence work enhances the tendency to intervene in politics.

Neither Dulles, nor Bissell, nor any other CIA officer of the Cuban task force (with the possible exception of Colonel Hawkins) had sufficient knowledge and experience in planning complicated amphibious operations. True, such an assignment hardly constitutes classic intelligence work, yet for more than a year in 1960–61 this was their main task. Their inability to grasp the complexity of this venture led them to underestimate the difficulties involved and to indulge in operational wishful thinking. The result was amateurish staff work, producing an operation with hardly any chance of success given the political limitations as set by the President. The only way out of this dissonance, which was partly recognized by the architects of the project, was an overly optimistic assumption that once the operation was under way President Kennedy would permit the use of American force. Ironically, in making this assumption they were not only wrong ethically but also professionally: ethically, by infusing political considerations, which were clearly beyond their sphere of responsibility, into operational planning; and professionally, by failing to foresee their own president's reaction to a possible operational failure.

The Israeli intelligence officers who participated in the making of the "unfortunate business" showed a similar lack of professional qualities. We have already discussed in detail the deficient qualifications of the director of Military Intelligence (Givli), the commander of Unit 131 (Benzoor), and the case officer of the Egyptian network (El-Ad), as well as the impact of their amateurishness on the way the operation was planned and conducted. Indeed, one can understand their failure to grasp the poor likelihood of operational (not to mention political) success only by taking into account their low level of professionalism as intelligence officers and planners of covert operations. The Israeli case also brought to light the other side of this coin. It showed that, when an intelligence operation is pursued so eagerly that it has to be concealed not only from foes but also from friends, the ability to judge its merits on purely professional grounds decreases significantly.

The analysis of the British case studies produced a similar correlation. Most striking in this regard was the enthusiastic readiness of Director of Naval Intelligence Sinclair to sacrifice Britain's most valuable means of intelligence collection—the Government Code and Cypher School—in order to obtain the expulsion of the Soviet trade delegation from London.

Such unprofessional thinking can be understood only by taking into account Sinclair's lack of experience in intelligence work. Indeed, after gaining more experience as an intelligence officer, he and his colleagues ruled out any diplomatic use of this sensitive source.

Given that the American and the Israeli case studies deal with covert operations, it might be argued that these cases are less relevant to the theory presented in the first part of this book, which discussed mainly the analytic aspects of intelligence work. This argument is wrong for two reasons. First, the intelligence officers who performed so poorly in both their professional and ethical conduct were not covert operations officers but general managers of intelligence agencies. After all, Dulles, Givli, Thomson, Sinclair, and Thwaites all headed intelligence agencies whose main task was the collection, analysis, and distribution of information. Even Bissell, who ex officio was in charge of covert operations, was considered by President Kennedy as a professional intelligence maker and the main candidate to replace Dulles. In this sense the political and professional failures of these officers did not derive from their poor qualities as covert operation officers but from two other sources: unprofessional qualifications as general managers of intelligence and insufficient knowledge and experiences needed for success in the specific task they were doing.

The second reason for the relevance of these cases to my theory is that the *planning* of covert operations demands precisely the same professional qualifications as the analysis of intelligence information and, in fact, to draw on critical intelligence inputs and estimates in order to assess the viability of a covert plan. I emphasize "planning" here to distinguish this task from that of the operations officer. The task of the general manager of intelligence is staff work, the task of the operations officer is field work, and each task demands, of course, different qualifications.

The prime enemies of the professional planning of covert (or any other) operations include wishful thinking, indulgence in best- and worst-case scenarios, and overcommitment to the operation, which produces confusion between means and ends. These are also the enemies of professional analysis work. Hence the architects of the American and Israeli operations performed poorly as both operations planners and analysts: one cannot be a professional planner without acquiring the qualification of the professional analyst. In this sense, although the senior intelligence officers involved in the planning of the American and Israeli operations were required to act as professional planners, in reality their behavior was closer to the mode of field officers.

In sum, then, empirical evidence confirms that a low level of intelligence expertise and ethic goes hand in hand with the tendency to intervene in politics. In the conflict between the professional "superego" and the political drive, insufficient professionalism is not strong enough to contain the drive of political ambitions. Hence a low level of intelligence professionalism facilitates intervention in politics.

PROPOSITION III: INTERVENTION AND POLITICAL CONTROL

This study postulated that the unilateral-constitutional control method—the system that existed in all the cases under investigation—is not sufficient to prevent intelligence from intervening in politics. Consequently, it was argued, the system of multilateral-constitutional control will maintain better supervision over the services.

The first part of this proposition was fully confirmed by the empirical evidence of this study. After all, the control systems in the United States (until the mid-1970s), Israel, and Britain were all of the same type, and they all failed in similar ways. Nevertheless, as shown by the discussion of the way in which the systems were employed in the three countries, significant variations among them established their different abilities to control intelligence. In this sense the American control system, even in its unilateral form, may be regarded as preferable to the Israeli method. In turn, the British version may be considered as the least desirable.

It is more difficult, however, to categorically conclude that the multilateral-constitutional control system is preferable to the unilateral system because it is only one variable that affects the likelihood of intervention and because there is not yet enough empirical evidence to prove its efficiency. However, the way in which this system has functioned in the United States since the mid-1970s seems to support this assumption. After all, the system has not produced a politicization of the American intelligence community, and at the same time it seems to provide a rather effective means of control, simply because it is not dependent upon the executive branch alone. However, the acid test of any control system is its ability to prevent intelligence intervention in politics precisely when there is a strong drive in this direction on the part intelligence specialists. Now more professional than it was in the late 1950s, the present American intelligence community does not present this control system with the same kind of tests it had to weather thirty years ago. Hence, until such tests come, its quality as a system can only be estimated.

Summary

To some extent this study has bitten off more than it has chewed. This is especially true with regard to the argument that intelligence professionalism and multilateral-constitutional political control systems are the optimal barriers against intelligence abuse of power. Here additional research can be highly useful, especially by showing how these two means can prevent intelligence from intervening in politics. After all, the case studies of this book only showed that lack of sufficient professionalism and the use of unilateral-institutional control systems can lead to such intervention.

The case that can be used to positively support this argument is the Iran-contra affair. For our purposes the aim in examining the Iran-contra episode should be to show that, despite the long tradition of the CIA and the Mossad being in charge of this type of covert operations, the actual role of these agencies in this scandal was minimal. Such a study will show that the CIA was reluctant—despite being headed by Casey, a chief architect of Iran-contra—to participate in this venture precisely because the agency was professional enough to estimate the low likelihood of keeping it secret and prudent enough not to get into a controversial policy and a possible political conflict between the executive and legislative branches. The Mossad was professional enough to estimate correctly that the operation's likelihood of success was low and that a failure could provoke allegations against Israel in Congress and the American public.

The reluctance of experienced intelligence officers to participate in this venture compelled policymakers to use nonintelligence channels: the White House National Security Council staff and private American, Israeli, and Iranian businessmen. They were all eager to take action. Yet their behavior was influenced by parochial political and personal interests and by a lack of sufficient professional experience that prevented them from estimating correctly the low chances of the operation to remain secret and ultimately to succeed.

But although it is clear that there is still work to be done, this study nevertheless covered some ground. Its conclusions summarized the empirical evidence with regard to the main elements of intelligence intervention in politics. Specifically, they pointed out various weaknesses in the political and intelligence systems that make such behavior possible. It would border on truism to offer ways to improve the situation, for such suggestions derive directly from the conclusions of this discussion. Thus, for example, it is obvious that, as far as the problem of intelligence intervention in politics is concerned, prudent separation between the two domains should be main-tained while permitting and encouraging the necessary interaction between them. Similarly, it would be trite, though nonetheless important, to suggest an upgrading of the professional level of intelligence, or maintenance of a multilateral-constitutional control system rather than the unilateral method.

Specific ways to limit the possibility of intelligence interference with politics may be somewhat more practical. Among the more relevant sugges-tions: the replacement of the "old boys net" recruitment systems (where they still exist) with open, equal, and nonpolitical recruitment methods; the use of various means to teach intelligence officers the main lessons from previous cases of intelligence intervention in politics, emphasizing that such behavior is typical of the amateur rather than of the professional officer; the adoption of a promotion policy that gives preference to analytic-mode rather than to operational-mode officers; and the establishment of institutionalized and independent bodies to investigate any possibility of intelligence abuse of power or political interference with professional intelligence affairs.

Will such means help to improve intelligence-state relations? Probably they will. Will they make the system failsafe? Obviously not. After all, intelligence and politics have worked together since the dawn of human history and no single means, or combination of them, will be able to fully uproot unprofessional and unethical behavior from this domain.

A Note on Sources for the Israeli Case Study

The 1954 Israeli "unfortunate business" constitutes one of the most interesting and challenging cases in the history of modern intelligence. Yet, despite the many lessons to be learned from this affair, it sparked relatively little academic and nonacademic interest outside of Israel. The result has been a very limited number of professional and semi-professional studies of this episode available in English. Of these some are fairly good; others are very poor, hindering rather than assisting in understanding this complex venture. None of the studies available in English gives a solid comprehensive description of the affair and a good analytical explanation of its sources.

Probably the best account of the "unfortunate business" in English is Golan's *Operation Sussanah*. This book describes the affair from the perspective of the network members (as told to Golan) after their release from Egypt. Although their account is detailed, honest, and unbiased, the book's scope is nevertheless limited and it hardly touches on the intelligence and political aspects of the operation beyond the knowledge of these persons. It must be noted, moreover, that none of the persons I interviewed was familiar with "Susannah" as the operation's code name. Stewart (1980, pp. 59–99) is a study of the history of Israel's intelligence community until the late 1970s and includes a relatively good summary of the affair. What it lacks most is a thorough analytical discussion of the deeper roots of the DMI's behavior. A good short analysis of the background to the Egyptian operation and a comparison between this mishap and the DMI's failure of October 1973 is available in Hareven (1978). Cohen (1988) is a good study of the operational environment and performance of Israel's Military Intelligence in the first half of the 1950s.

Unlike the basically sound works mentioned above, there are less successful accounts such as Deacon (1978), which, owing to many factual errors and a lack of even a minimal understanding of Israeli and Middle Eastern politics in the mid-1950s, constitutes a serious danger for any reader who is really interested in knowing what the affair was all about. To a more limited extent the same is true with regard to El-Ad (1976a). As it is far more detailed and avoids many of Deacon's crude errors, this book could have been an excellent primary source for studying the subject except for El-Ad's predilection for fantasy. Given that El-Ad (who died in 1993) was defined by Israelis who knew him well as a pathological liar who could not distinguish between reality and fantasy, any use of his book must be very careful and should be double-checked by the use of other, more reliable sources such as Golan (1978).

Israeli published studies give a far better factual description of the affair. Early authors from the first half of the 1960s, such as Hassin and Horowitz (1961), Ben-Gurion (1965), and Arieli (1966), were not permitted, for security reasons, to reveal what the "unfortunate business" was all about and instead used euphemisms such as "the senior officer" (Givli), "the reserve officer" (Benzoor), or "the third man" (El-Ad). Neither the nature of the operation nor its targets were ever mentioned. In this sense these early accounts are relatively useless given the modern and detailed studies now available. These include mainly Eshed (1979), Teveth (1992b), Harel (1980 and 1982b), and Sharett (1978).

Eshed's book is an updated version of a special inquiry he made in 1961–64 (with Ben-Gurion's blessing) to find out "who gave the order" Eshed, an Israeli journalist, received access to most of the classified documentation on the episode between 1954 and 1961, and in this sense his study is an excellent source of evidence. His analysis, however, is rather disappointing. It seems that he either was used by or cooperated with some of Ben-Gurion's close aides to prove that Lavon was responsible directly for the Egyptian operation. Probably because of his commitment to this thesis, Eshed ignores many facts and simple common-sense explanations that cast doubt on his main argument.

Teveth, one of Ben-Gurion's most talented biographers, used much of the material he collected in connection with his writing on Ben-Gurion in order to complete a well-documented and updated study of the Lavon affair (Teveth 1992b). Unlike Eshed, Teveth seems to be unbiased, and he concludes that the chief culprit in the affair was Colonel Givli and not Lavon. His study, however, focuses more on the political consequences of the "unfortunate business" than on the operational and intelligence aspects of the 1954 episode. Nevertheless, Teveth (1992b) is probably the best study on this subject.

Harel's works (1980 and 1982b) are two polemical studies. The first was written in response to El-Ad (1976) and attempts to prove, quite convincingly, that El-Ad was a double agent who betrayed the DMI and exposed the members of the network under his command to the Egyptians. The book contains some serious and credible accusations against Unit 131's recruitment policy in the early 1950s and demonstrates how unprofessionally El-Ad was handled by the DMI before, during, and after the "unfortunate business." Harel (1982b) is a response to Eshed (1979). Using similar documentation to Eshed's, Harel makes a very convincing argument that the DMI rather than Lavon was directly responsible for the mishap of 1954. Although there is little doubt that Harel had some motivated biases in conducting these studies—after all, a bitter rivalry existed between the Mossad under his command and the DMI in the 1950s—his conclusions are nevertheless logical and convincing.

The best source for understanding the true nature of the Israeli political system under which the "unfortunate business" could have happened is Sharett's personal diary, covering the period between October 1953 and November 1957. This rare document describes not only the events as they were seen from Sharett's vantage point as Prime Minister (January 1954–November 1955) and Minister of Foreign Affairs (until June 1956) but also his personal feelings, beliefs, hopes, and frustrations. Unluckily, between mid-June 1954 and early January 1955—the most crucial time period for our subject—Sharett, owing to severe time pressures, outlined in his diary only the daily main events.

Olshan, a Supreme Court judge who was one of the two members of the committee that investigated the "unfortunate business" in early 1955, devoted one chapter of his memoirs (Olshan 1978, pp. 262–99) to the affair. This constitutes a good analysis of his and his colleague's perceptions of the question "who gave the order?" Dayan's memoirs shed some light on the complex relationship within Israel's political and military decisionmaking environment in 1954. It is important to note that there are significant differences between the Hebrew (Dayan 1976b) and the English (Dayan 1976a) versions. The Hebrew one is more detailed, and for this reason I used this version rather than the English one in some cases.

Nonpublished sources include archived documents and interviews. The British, perhaps being more aware than the Israelis of the importance of recording history, opened most of the files of the 1954 Anglo-Egyptian negotiations on the evacuation of their forces from the Canal Zone. The Israelis, either because of their well-known sensitivity about military and intelligence affairs or for political reasons, prefer to keep a large part of the relevant documentation classified even now. The rather absurd result of this policy is that, although some parts of these documents were published—sometimes in a biased form—more than ten years ago, some of the documents themselves are still classified for the student of the affair today.

The last available sources of information are the persons who were directly and indirectly involved in the making of the "unfortunate business." Most of them agreed to be interviewed; some asked not to be mentioned by name, and I respected this request. Colonel (ret.) Benyamin Givli as well as Lavon's personal assistant (later the Israeli ambassador to the United States), Ephraim Evron, refused my requests for interviews. Being aware of the limitation of the human mind to recall events that took place almost forty years ago, I treated the information received in these interviews quite carefully.

List of References

ARCHIVES

Bodleian Library, Oxford University, England.
Cambridge University Library, Cambridge University, England.
Declassified Documents Reference Service (DDRS), United States.
Imperial War Museum (IWM), London.
India Office Library and Records, London.
Israel State Archives (ISA), Jerusalem.
National Archives (NAW), Washington, D.C.
Public Record Office (PRO), London.

DOCUMENTS

Alleged Assassination Plots Involving Foreign Leaders (Am Interim Report of the Select Committee to Study Governmental Operations with Respect to Intelligence Activities). Senate Report 94/1 No. 94-465, November 20, 1975.

Hearings before the Select Committee on Intelligence of the United States Senate. "On the Nomination of Robert M. Gates to be Director of Central Intelligence, 16 September–18 October 1991." U.S. Senate, 102d Cong., 1st sess. Washington, D.C.: 1992.

House of Commons: Parliamentary Debates. London: His Majesty's Stationery Office.

W. G. Jackson, 1973. *Allen Welsh Dulles as Director of Central Intelligence: 26 February 1953–29 November 1961.* Historical staff, CIA (released through the Historical Review Program of the CIA, 26 April 1994, HRP 91–2).

Operation Zapata: The "Ultrasensitive" Report and Testimony of the Board of Inquiry on the Bay of Pigs. Frederick, Md.: Aletheia Books, 1981.

Report of the Congressional Committees Investigating the Iran-Contra Affair with Supplement, Minority, and Additional Views. 100th Cong., 1st sess. Washington, D.C.: 1987.

The Tower Commission Report: The Full Text of the President's Special Review Board. New York: Times Books, 1987.

U.S. Intelligence Agencies and Activities: Risks and Control of Foreign Intelligence. Hearings before the Select Committee on Intelligence, U.S. House of Representatives, 94th Cong., 1st sess., pt. 5, November–December 1975.

NEWSPAPERS AND JOURNALS

al-Ahram (Egypt)
Daily Herald (England)
Daily Mail (England)
Economist (England)
Ha'Aretz (Israel)
Hadashot (Israel)
Ma'ariv (Israel)
Manchester Guardian (England)
Morning Post (England)
New York Times (US)
Star (England)
Sunday Observer (England)

PUBLISHED SOURCES

Allison, G. T. 1971. *Essence of Decision: Explaining the Cuban Missile Crisis*. Boston: Little, Brown & Co..

Ambrose, S. E. 1981. *Ike's Spies: Eisenhower and the Espionage Establishment*. Garden City: Doubleday.

Andrew, C. 1977. "The British Secret Service and Anglo-Soviet Relations in the 1920s, Part I: From the Trade Negotiations to the Zinoviev Letter." *The Historical Journal* 20, no. 3, pp. 673–706.

———. 1984. "Codebreakers and Foreign Offices: The French, British, and American Experience." In *The Missing Dimension: Government and Intelligence Communities in the Twentieth Century*, ed. C. Andrew and D. Dilks, pp. 33–53. Urbana and Chicago: University of Illinois Press.

———. 1985. *Her Majesty's Secret Service: The Making of the British Intelligence Community*. New York: Viking.

———. 1989. "Churchill and Intelligence." In *Leaders and Intelligence*, ed. M. I. Handel, pp. 181–93. London: Frank Cass.

———, and Dilks, D. 1984. "Introduction." In *The Missing Dimension: Governments and Intelligence Communities in the Twentieth Century*, pp. 1–16. Urbana and Chicago: University of Illinois Press.

Arieli, Y. 1966. *Haknunia* (The Conspiracy). Tel Aviv: Kadima. (Hebrew).

Bar-Joseph, U. 1987. *The Best of Enemies: Israel and Transjordan in the War of 1948*. London: Frank Cass.

Barnes, T. 1979. "Special Branch and the First Labour Government." *The Historical Journal* 22, no. 4, pp. 941–51.

Bar-Zohar, M. 1977. *Ben-Gurion*. Vol. 2. Tel Aviv: Am Oved. (Hebrew).

Beesly, P. 1978. *Very Special Intelligence*. New York: Doubleday.

———. 1982. *Room 40: British Naval Intelligence, 1914–1918*. New York: Harcourt Brace Jovanovich.

Ben-Gurion, D. 1965. *Dvarim Kehawayatam* (Things as They Are). Tel Aviv: Am Hassefer. (Hebrew).

Benjamin, B. 1984. *The CBS Benjamin Report*. Washington, D.C.: The Media Institute.

Ben-Meir, Y. 1987. *Kabalat Hachlatot Besugiat Habitahon Hale'umi: Hahebet Hayisraeli*

(National Security Decision Making: The Israeli Case). Tel Aviv: Hakibbutz Hameuchad. (Hebrew).

Bennett, R. 1979. *Ultra in the West: The Normandy Campaign 1944–1945.* New York: Charles Scribner's Sons.

———. 1989. *Ultra and the Mediterranean Strategy, 1941–1945.* New York: William Morrow & Co.

Beschloss, M. R. 1986. *Mayday: Eisenhower, Khrushchev, and the U-2 Affair.* New York: Harper & Row.

Betts, R. K. 1979. *Soldiers, Statesmen, and Cold War Crises.* Cambridge, Mass.: Harvard University Press.

———. 1980. "Intelligence for Policymaking." *The Washington Quarterly* 3, no. 3, pp. 118–29.

———. 1988. "Policy-makers and Intelligence Analysts: Love, Hate, or Indifference?" *Intelligence and National Security* 3, no. 1, pp. 184–89.

Bissell, R. M. 1984. "Response to Lucien S. Vandenbroucke, 'The "Confessions" of Allen Dulles: New Evidence on the Bay of Pigs.'" *Diplomatic History* 8, no. 4, pp. 377–80.

Black, I., and Morris, B. 1991. *Israel's Secret Wars: A History of Israel's Intelligence Services.* New York: Grove Weidenfeld.

Blake, Lord. 1981. "Ball, Sir (George) Joseph." In *The Dictionary of National Biography, 1961–1970,* ed. William T. and C. S. Nicholls. London: Oxford University Press.

Blitzer, W. 1989. *Territory of Lies: The Exclusive Story of Jonathan Jay Pollard: The American Who Betrayed His Country for Israel and How He Was Betrayed.* New York: Harper & Row.

Bunyan, T. 1976. *The Political Police in Britain.* London: Julian Friedman.

Callwell, C. E. 1927. *Field Marshal Sir Henry Wilson: His Life and Diaries.* London: Cassell.

Calvocoressi, P. 1980. *Top Secret Ultra.* New York: Pantheon.

Carr, E. H. 1979. "Communications: The Zinoviev Letter." *Historical Journal* 22, no. 1, pp. 209–10.

Cave Brown, A. 1975. *Bodyguard of Lies.* New York: Harper & Row.

———. 1987. *C: The Secret Life of Sir Stewart Menzies.* New York: Macmillan Co.

CBS Television Network. *The Uncounted Enemy: A Vietnam Deception.* Broadcast of January 23, 1982.

Chester, L.; Fay, S.; and Young, H. 1967. *The Zinoviev Letter.* London: Heineman.

Childs, W. 1930. *Episodes and Reflections.* N.p.: London.

Cockett, R. B. 1990. "Ball, Chamberlain, and Truth." *Historical Journal* 33, no. 1, pp. 131–42.

Cohen, R. 1988. "Israeli Military Intelligence before the 1956 Campaign." *Intelligence and National Security* 3, no. 1, pp. 100–40.

Colby, W., and Forbath, P. 1978. *Honorable Men: My Life in the CIA.* New York: Simon & Schuster.

Cooper, C. L. 1972. "The CIA and Decision-Making." *Foreign Affairs,* January, pp. 223–36.

Crowe, S. 1975. "The Zinoviev Letter: A Reappraisal." *Journal of Contemporary History* 10, no. 3, pp. 407–32.

Cubbage, T. L. 1989. "Westmoreland vs. CBS: Was Intelligence Corrupted by Policy Demands." In *Leaders and Intelligence,* ed. M. I. Handel. London: Frank Cass.

Dayan, M. (1976a). *Moshe Dayan: The Story of My Life.* New York: William Morrow.

——. (1976b). *Avnei Derech: Autobiographia* (Mile-Stones: An Autobiography). Jerusalem: Edanim. (Hebrew).

Deacon, R. 1978. *The Israeli Secret Service*. London: Hamish Hamilton.

Dekel, E. 1959. *Shai: The Exploits of the Hagana Intelligence*. New York and London: Thomas Yoseloff.

Denniston, A. G. 1986. "The Government Code and Cypher School between the Wars." *Intelligence and National Security* 1, no. 1, pp. 48–70.

Dilks, D. 1984. *Neville Chamberlain*, vol. 1, *Pioneering and Reform, 1869–1929*. London: Cambridge University Press.

Dorril, S., and Ramsay, R. 1991. *SMEAR: Wilson and the Secret State*. London: Fourth Estate.

Dror, Y. 1984. *Hamistarevim Shel Hapalmach* (The Arabists of the *Palmach*). Tel Aviv: Hakibbutz Hameuchad. (Hebrew).

Dulles, A. 1965. *The Craft of Intelligence*. New York: Signet Books.

El-Ad, A., with Creech, J. 1976a. *Ha'Adam HaShlishi* (The Third Man). Tel Aviv: Special Edition. (Hebrew).

——. 1976b. *Decline of Honor*. Chicago: Henry Regnery.

Elon, A. 1971. *The Israelis: Founders and Sons*. New York: Holt, Rinehart & Winston.

Eshed, H. 1979. *Mi Natan et Ha'Hora'a?* (Who Gave the Order?). Jerusalem: Edanim. (Hebrew).

——. 1988. *Mossad Shel I'sh Ehad* (One Man "Mossad"—Reuven Shiloah: Father of Israeli Intelligence). Jerusalem: Edanim. (Hebrew).

Etheredge, L. S. 1985. *Can Governments Learn? American Foreign Policy and Central American Revolutions*. New York: Pergamon Press.

Ferris, J. R. 1987. "Whitehall's Black Chamber: British Cryptology and the Government Code and Cypher School, 1919–1929." *Intelligence and National Security* 2, no. 1, pp. 54–91.

——. 1989a. *The Evolution of British Strategic Policy, 1919–1926*. London: Macmillan Co.

——. 1989b. "From Broadway House to Bletchley Park: The Diary of Captain Malcolm Kennedy, 1934–1946." *Intelligence and National Security* 4, no. 3, pp. 421–50.

——, and Bar-Joseph, U. 1993. "Getting Marlowe to Hold His Tongue: The Conservative Party, the Intelligence Services, and the Zinoviev Letter." *Intelligence and National Security* 8, no. 4, pp. 100–37.

Finer, S. E. 1988. *The Man on Horseback: The Role of the Military in Politics*. Boulder, Colo.: Westview Press.

Gates, R. M. 1987/1988. "The CIA and American Foreign Policy." *Foreign Affairs* 66, no. 2, pp. 215–30.

——. 1989. "An Opportunity Unfulfilled: The Use and Perceptions of Intelligence at the White House." *The Washington Quarterly*, Winter, pp. 35–44.

Gelber, Y. 1986. *Gari'in LeTzava Ivri Sadir* (The Emergence of a Jewish Army). Jerusalem: Ben-Zvi. (Hebrew).

George, A. L. 1980. *Presidential Decisionmaking in Foreign Policy: The Effective Use of Information and Advice*. Boulder, Colo.: Westview Press.

——, and Keohane, R. O. 1980. "The Concept of National Interests: Uses and Limitations." In *Presidential Decisionmaking in Foreign Policy: The Effective Use of Information and Advice*, A. L. George, pp. 217–37. Boulder, Colo.: Westview Press.

Gilbert, M. 1975. *Winston S. Churchill*, vol. 4, *1916–1922: The Stricken World*. Boston: Houghton Mifflin.

Golan, A. 1976. *Mivtza Sussanah* (Operation Sussanah). Jerusalem: Edanim. (Hebrew).

———. 1978. *Operation Sussanah*. New York: Harper & Row.

Gorodetsky, G. 1977. *The Precarious Truce: Anglo-Soviet Relations, 1924–1927.* Cambridge: Cambridge University Press.

Granot, O. 1981. *Chail HaModi'in* (The Military Intelligence Corps). Tel Aviv: Revivim. (Hebrew).

Grant, N. 1966/1967. "The Zinoviev Letter Case." *Soviet Studies* 19: 264–77.

Guthman, E. O., and Shulman, J., eds. 1988. *Robert Kennedy in His Own Words: The Unpublished Recollections of the Kennedy Years.* Toronto: Bantam Books.

Handel, M. I. 1987. "The Politics of Intelligence." *Intelligence and National Security* 2, no. 4, pp. 5–46.

———, ed. 1987. *Strategic and Operational Deception in the Second World War.* London: Frank Cass.

Harel, I. 1980. *Anatomya Shel Bgida* (Anatomy of Treason: The "Third Man" and the Collapse of the Israeli Spy Network in Egypt, 1954). Jerusalem: Edanim. (Hebrew).

———. 1982a. *The German Scientists Crisis: 1962–1963.* Tel Aviv: Ma'ariv. (Hebrew).

———. 1982b. *Kam I'sh al Ahiv* (When Man Rose against Man: A Reevaluation of the "Lavon Affair"). Jerusalem: Keter. (Hebrew).

———. 1989. *Bitahon VeDemocratya* (Security and Democracy). Tel Aviv: Edanim (Hebrew).

Hareven, A. 1978. "Disturbed Hierarchy: Israeli Intelligence in 1954 and 1973." *The Jerusalem Quarterly* no. 9, pp. 3–19.

Harkabi, Y. 1984. "The Intelligence-Policymaker Tangle." *The Jerusalem Quarterly*, Winter, pp. 125–31.

Hassin, E., and Horowitz, D. 1961. *HaParasha* (The Affair). Tel Aviv: Am Hassefer. (Hebrew).

Hastedt, G. P. 1987. "The New Context of Intelligence Estimating: Politicization or Publicizing?" In *Intelligence and Intelligence Policy in a Democratic Society*, ed. S. J. Cimbala, pp. 47–67. New York: Transnational Publishers.

Higgins, T. 1987. *The Perfect Failure: Kennedy, Eisenhower, and the CIA at the Bay of Pigs.* New York: Norton.

Hilel, S. 1985. *Ruah Kadim: Bishlichut Machtartit Learzot Arav.* (Eastern Wind: An Underground Mission to Arab Countries). Jerusalem: Edanim. (Hebrew).

Hilsman, R. 1956. *Strategic Intelligence and National Decisions.* Glenco, Ill.: The Free Press.

———. 1967. *To Move a Nation: The Politics of Foreign Policy in the Administration of John F. Kennedy.* New York: Delta.

Hinsley, F. H.; Thomas, E. E.; Ransom, C. F.; and Knight, R. C. 1979–1988, *British Intelligence in the Second World War.* London: Her Majesty's Stationery Office.

Hodges, A. 1983. *Alan Turing: The Enigma.* New York: Simon & Schuster.

Hughes, T. L. 1976. *The Fate of Facts in a World of Men: Foreign Policy and Intelligence Making.* New York: Foreign Policy Association, no. 233.

Hulnick, A. S. 1986. "The Intelligence Producer-Policy Consumer Linkage: A Theoretical Approach." *Intelligence and National Security* 1, no. 2, pp. 212–33.

———. 1987. "Relations between Intelligence Producers and Policy Consumers: A New Way of Looking at an Old Problem." In *Intelligence and Intelligence Policy in a Democratic Society*, ed. S. J. Cimbala, pp. 129–44. New York: Transnational Publishers.

———. 1991. "Controlling Intelligence Estimates." In *Controlling Intelligence*, ed. G. P. Hastedt, pp. 81–96. London: Frank Cass.

Hunt, H. 1973. *Give Us This Day*. New Rochelle: Arlington House.

Huntington, S. P. 1959. *The Soldier and the State: The Theory and Politics of Civil-Military Relations*. Cambridge, Mass.: Harvard University Press.

James, W. 1955. *The Eyes of the Navy: A Biographical Study of Admiral Sir Reginald Hall*. London: Methuen.

Janis, I. L. 1972. *Victims of Groupthink: A Psychological Study of Foreign Policy Decisions and Fiascoes*. Boston: Houghton Miffin Co.

———, and Mann, L. 1979. *Decision Making: A Psychological Analysis of Conflict*. New York: The Free Press.

Janowitz, M. 1957. "Military Elites and the Study of War." *Journal of Conflict Resolution*, no. 1, pp. 9–18.

———. 1964. *The Military in the Political Development of New Nations: An Essay in Comparative Analysis*. Chicago: University of Chicago Press.

———. 1971. *The Professional Soldier: A Social and Political Portrait*. New York: The Free Press.

Jeffery, K. 1981. "The British Army and Internal Security, 1919–1939." *The Historical Journal* 24, no. 2, pp. 377–97.

———, ed. 1985. *The Military Correspondence of Field Marshal Sir Henry Wilson: 1918–1922*. London: Bodley Head.

———. 1986. "The Government Code and Cypher School; A Memorandum by Lord Curzon." *Intelligence and National Security* 1, no. 3, pp. 454–58.

———, and Hennessy, P. 1983. *State of Emergency*. London: Routledge & Kegan Paul.

Jeffreys-Jones, R. 1989. *The CIA and American Democracy*. New Haven: Yale University Press.

Jervis, R. 1976. *Perception and Misperception in International Politics*. Princeton: Princeton University Press.

———. 1986. "What's Wrong with the Intelligence Process?" *International Journal of Intelligence and Counterintelligence* 1, no. 1, pp. 28–41.

Johnson, H. 1964. *The Bay of Pigs: The Leader's Story of Brigade 2506*. New York: Norton & Co.

Jones, R. V. 1978. *The Wizard War: British Scientific Intelligence, 1939–1945*. London: Hamish Hamilton.

———. 1989. *Reflections on Intelligence*. London: Heinemann.

———. 1990. "Intelligence and Command." In *Leaders and Intelligence*, ed. M. I. Handel, pp. 288–98. London: Frank Cass.

Kam, E. 1988. *Surprise Attack: The Victim's Perspective*. Cambridge, Mass.: Harvard University Press.

Kent, S. 1949. *Strategic Intelligence for American World Policy*. Princeton: Princeton University Press.

———. 1969. "Estimates and Influence." *Foreign Service Journal*, April.

Kirkpatrick, L. B. 1968. *The Real CIA*. New York: Macmillan Co.

———. 1972. "Paramilitary Case Study: The Bay of Pigs." *Naval War College Review* 25, no. 2, pp. 32–42.

Knightly, P. 1986. *The Second Oldest Profession: The Spy as a Bureaucrat, Patriot, Fantasist, and Whore*. London: Andre Deutsch.

Laqueur, W. 1985. *A World of Secrets: The Uses and Limits of Intelligence*. New York: Basic Books.

Leary, W. M., ed. 1984. *The Central Intelligence Agency: History and Documents*. Alabama: University of Alabama Press.

Leigh, D. 1988. *The Wilson Plot: How the Spycatchers and Their American Allies Tried to Overthrow the British Government*. New York: Pantheon Books.

Levin, R. 1978. *Ultra Goes to War*. New York: McGraw Hill.

Luckham, A. R. 1971. "A Comparative Typology of Civil-Military Relations." *Government and Opposition*, no. 6, pp. 5–35.

McLachlan, D. 1968. *Room 39: A Study in Naval Intelligence*. New York: Atheneum.

Marchetti, V., and Marks, J. D. 1984. *The CIA and the Cult of Intelligence*. New York: Dell.

Marquand, D. 1977. *Ramsay MacDonald*. London: Jonathan Cape.

Masterman, J. C. 1972. *The Double Cross System in the War of 1939 to 1945*. New Haven: Yale University Press.

Masters, A. 1986. *The Man Who Was M: The Life of Maxwell Knight*. London: Grafton.

Melman, Y., and Raviv, D. 1989. *The Imperfect Spies: The History of Israeli Intelligence*. London: Sidgwick & Jackson.

Montagu, E. 1954. *The Man Who Never Was*. Philadelphia: J. B. Lippincott.

———. 1978. *Beyond Top Secret Ultra*. New York: Coward, McCann & Geoghegan.

Mure, D. 1977. *Practice to Deceive*. London: William Kimber.

———. 1980. *Master of Deception: Tangled Webs in London and the Middle East*. London: William Kimber.

Naor, A. 1986. *Memshala BeMilhama* (Cabinet at War: The Functioning of the Israeli Cabinet during the Lebanon War, 1982). Jerusalem: Lahav. (Hebrew).

Olshan, I. 1978. *Deen U'Dvarim* (Law and Controversy). Jerusalem: Shoken. (Hebrew).

Palmer, A. 1984. "The History of the D-Notice Committee." In *The Missing Dimension: Governments and Intelligence Communities in the Twentieth Century*, ed. C. Andrew and D. Dilks, pp. 227–49. Urbana and Chicago: University of Illinois Press.

Parsons, T. 1968. "Professions," in *Encyclopedia of the Social Sciences*. Vol. 12. New York: Macmillan Co. & The Free Press.

Phillips, D. A. 1977. *The Night Watch*. New York: Ballantine Books.

Pincher, C. 1981. *Their Trade is Treachery*. London: Sidgwick & Jackson.

———. 1984. *Too Secret Too Long*. New York: St. Martin's Press.

———. 1988. *The Spycatcher Affair*. New York: St. Martin's Press.

Popper, K. R. 1957. *The Poverty of Historicism*. New York: Harper & Row.

Porter, B. 1989. *Plots and Paranoia: A History of Political Espionage in Britain, 1790–1988*. London: Unwin Hyman.

Powers, T. 1979. *The Man Who Kept the Secrets: Richard Helms and the CIA*. New York: Alfred A. Knopf.

Prados, J. 1986. *President's Secret Wars: CIA and Pentagon Covert Operation since World War II*. New York: William Morrow.

Punnett, R. M. 1968. *British Government and Politics*. New York: Norton.

Pye, L. W. 1968. "Political Culture." In *International Encyclopedia of the Social Sciences*, ed. D. L. Sills, vol. 12, pp. 218–25. New York: Macmillan Co. and The Free Press.

Ramsden, J. 1987. *The Age of Balfour and Baldwin, 1902–1940*. London: Longman.

Ranelagh, J. 1987. *The Agency: The Rise and Decline of the CIA*. New York: Simon & Schuster.

Ransom, H. H. 1987. "The Politicization of Intelligence." In *Intelligence and Intelligence Policy in a Democratic Society*, ed. S. J. Cimbala, pp. 25–46. New York: Transnational Publishers.

Rapoport, R. C. 1962. "A Comparative Theory of Military and Political Types." In *Changing Patterns of Military Politics*, ed. S. P. Huntington. New York: The Free Press.

Rhodes, James R., ed. 1969. *Memoirs of a Conservative: J.C.C. Davidson's Memoirs and Papers, 1910–1937*. London: Weidenfeld and Nicholson.

Roskill, S. 1972. *Hankey: Man of Secrets*, vol. 2, *1919–1931*. London: Collins.

Rowland, P. 1976. *David Lloyd George: A Biography*. New York: Macmillan Co.

Rusbridger, J. 1989. *The Intelligence Game*. London: The Bodley Head.

Sampson, A. 1965. *Anatomy of Britain Today*. New York: Harper & Row.

Schiff, Z., and Ya'ari, E. 1984. *Israel's Lebanon War*. New York: Simon & Schuster.

Schlesinger, A. M. 1965. *A Thousand Days: John F. Kennedy in the White House*. Boston: Houghton Mifflin Co.

———. 1978. *Robert Kennedy and His Times*. Boston: Houghton Mifflin Co.

Sharett, M. 1978. *Yoman I'shi* (A Personal Diary). Vols. 1–4. Tel Aviv: Ma'ariv. (Hebrew).

Smith, J. B. 1976. *Portrait of a Cold Warrior*. New York: G.P. Putman's Sons.

Sorenson, T. S. 1965. *Kennedy*. New York: Harper & Row.

Stewart, S. 1980. *The Spymasters of Israel*. New York: Ballantine Books.

Taylor, A.J.P. 1975. *English History, 1914–1945*. London: Penguin Books.

Teveth, S. 1992a. *Shearing Time: Firing Squad at Beth-Jiz*. Tel Aviv: Ish-Dor.

———. 1992b. *Shearing Time: Calaban*. Tel Aviv: Ish-Dor.

Ullman, R. H. 1961. *Intervention and the War*. In *Anglo-Soviet Relations, 1917–1921*. Vol. 1. Princeton: Princeton University Press.

———. 1972. *The Anglo-Soviet Accord*. In *Anglo-Soviet Relations, 1917–1921*. Vol. 2. Princeton: Princeton University Press.

Vandenbroucke, L. S. 1984. "The 'Confessions' of Allen Dulles: New Evidence on the Bay of Pigs." *Diplomatic History* 8, no. 4, pp. 365–75.

Welchman, G. 1982. *The Hut Six Story: Breaking the Enigma Codes*. New York: McGraw Hill.

West N. [Allason Rupert]. 1981. *MI5*. New York: Military Heritage Press.

———. 1986. *GCHQ: The Secret Wireless War, 1900–1986*. London: Weidenfeld & Nicolson.

Whaley, B. 1973. *Codeword Barbarossa*. Cambridge: MIT Press.

Winterbotham, F. W. 1974. *The Ultra Secret*. New York: Harper & Row.

Woodward, B. 1987. *Veil: The Secret Wars of the CIA, 1981–1987*. New York: Simon & Schuster.

Wright, P., with Greengrass, P. 1987. *Spycatcher: The Candid Autobiography of a Senior Intelligence Officer*. New York: Viking.

Wyden, P. 1979. *Bay of Pigs: The Untold Story*. New York: Simon & Schuster.

Ya'ari, E. 1975. *Mitsraim VeHaFedayin* (Egypt and the Fedayin). Givat Haviva: Center for Arabic and Afro-Asian Studies. (Hebrew).

INTERVIEWS

Allen George. Veteran CIA officer. Arlington, Virginia, February 22, 1990.

Amit Meir. Major General (Ret.). Director of Military Intelligence (Israel) 1961–63; Director of Mossad, 1963–68. Ramat Gan, Israel, January 18, 1989.

Benzoor Mordechai. Commander of Unit 131 between late 1951 and late 1954. Haifa, Israel, November 24, 1988.

Biberman Shlomo. Defense Military Intelligence (DMI) officer, in charge of radio communications of Unit 131 in 1953–54. Tel Aviv: Israel, January 13, 1989.

Dar Avraham. An officer in Unit 131, recruited the Egyptian network in 1951. Haifa, Israel, January 3, 1989.

Gazit Sholomo. Major General (Ret.). Director of Military Intelligence (Israel), 1974–79. Washington, D.C., January 1990.

Hareven Alouph. Military assistant to Colonel Givli. Jerusalem, Israel, October 31, 1988.

Harkabi Yhoshafat. Major General (Ret.). Acting chief of Military Intelligence, April 1953–April 1954; Director of Military Intelligence (Israel), 1955–59. Jerusalem, Israel, October 13, 1988.

Segre Avni Dan. Israel's press secretary at the embassy in Paris and a participant in the Israeli-Egyptian dialogue of the early and mid-1950s. Stanford, March 1989.

Whipple David. Veteran CIA officer. Arlington, Virginia, February 21, 1990.

Index